NEW ESSAYS ON

F. SCOTT FITZGERALD'S

NEGLECTED

STORIES

NEW ESSAYS ON

F. SCOTT FITZGERALD'S

NEGLECTED

STORIES

Edited with an Introduction by

JACKSON R. BRYER

University of Missouri Press   Columbia and London

Copyright © 1996 by
The Curators of the University of Missouri
University of Missouri Press, Columbia, Missouri 65201
Printed and bound in the United States of America
All rights reserved
5 4 3 2 1   00 99 98 97 96

Library of Congress Cataloging-in-Publication Data

New essays on F. Scott Fitzgerald's neglected stories / edited with an introduction by
    Jackson R. Bryer.
        p.   cm.
    Includes bibliographical references (p.   ) and index.
    ISBN 0-8262-1039-2 (alk. paper)
    1. Fitzgerald, F. Scott (Francis Scott), 1896–1940—Criticism and interpretation.
I. Bryer, Jackson R.
    PS3511.I9Z75   1996
    813'.52—dc20   95-26157
                                                                                 CIP

Designer: Kristie Lee
Typesetter: BOOKCOMP
Printer and Binder: Thomson-Shore, Inc.
Typefaces: Minion and Gill Sans

For John Kuehl, my friend for a quarter-century, my collaborator, and a trailblazer to whom all Fitzgerald scholars, teachers, and readers owe a debt of gratitude.

CONTENTS

ACKNOWLEDGMENTS

For a variety of often unglamorous tasks always cheerfully performed in the preparation of this volume, I thank Drew Eisenhauer and Robin Evans. Beverly Jarrett of the University of Missouri Press had faith in this project from the very beginning and patiently awaited its emergence as a finished manuscript; Managing Editor Jane Lago and editor Annette Wenda carefully shepherded it through the publication process. Catherine Burroughs and Lawrence Broer read the manuscript and made a number of helpful and encouraging comments; I have shamelessly borrowed from Broer's observations in composing the Introduction, as he said many things better than I could have. As always, Mary C. Hartig improved my writing and saved me from total embarrassment.

NEW ESSAYS ON

F. SCOTT FITZGERALD'S

NEGLECTED

STORIES

INTRODUCTION

JACKSON R. BRYER

As I was preparing this introduction, I ran across a copy of Milton Crane's anthology, *50 Great American Short Stories*. First published in 1965, it had gone through twenty-one printings by 1983 (the date on the copy I own)—eloquent testimony to its popularity and to its probable adoption as a text in numerous high school and college courses. What I found worthy of note—though really not that surprising— about Crane's volume is that, while it includes many predictable choices (Hawthorne's "Young Goodman Brown," Poe's "Ms. Found in a Bottle," London's "To Build a Fire," Harte's "The Outcasts of Poker Flats," Crane's "The Bride Comes to Yellow Sky"), as well as some more unexpected ones (Melville's "The Fiddler," Twain's "Luck," Faulkner's "The Old People," Hemingway's "A Man of the World"), and some obscure inclusions (Fitz-James O'Brien, John McNulty, Robert M. Coates, John Collier, James Reid Parker, Seymour Freedgood), it does not contain a story by F. Scott Fitzgerald. Crane's decision to exclude Fitzgerald from his anthology seems an apt indication of the generally low regard in which the short fiction of one of America's greatest modern writers is held.

Despite the fact that Fitzgerald wrote 178 short stories, all but a very few of which are now easily found, they tend to be overlooked in favor of his novels. To be sure, Milton Crane to the contrary notwithstanding, they are quite often anthologized, alongside stories by Hemingway, Faulkner, Steinbeck, and other modernists; and, in the last three decades, many of Fitzgerald's most obscure stories have been exhumed from the pages of the periodicals in which they originally appeared and have been collected in such readily accessible volumes as *The Pat Hobby Stories, The Basil and Josephine Stories, Bits of Paradise: 21 Uncollected Stories by F. Scott and Zelda Fitzgerald,* and *The Price Was High: The Last Uncollected Stories of F. Scott Fitzgerald.* Given this availability of virtually all of Fitzgerald's short stories, one might expect that critics and scholars would have, in the last fifteen years, begun to turn their attention to that aspect of his art. But, for the most part, this has not happened. In an attempt to redirect attention to Fitzgerald's stories, in 1982 I edited *The Short Stories of F. Scott Fitzgerald: New Approaches in Criticism,* which included twenty-two original essays; and in the last five years there have been three full-length books on the stories (Alice Hall Petry's *Fitzgerald's Craft of Short Fiction: The Collected Stories—1920–1935,* John Kuehl's *F. Scott Fitzgerald: A Study of the Short Fiction,* and Bryant Mangum's *A Fortune Yet: Money in the Art of F. Scott Fitzgerald's Short Stories).* Nevertheless, relatively speaking, scholarly neglect of Fitzgerald's short fiction has continued unabated.

This can be documented most graphically and simply by looking at the annual *MLA Bibliography.* In the Introduction to *The Short Stories of F. Scott Fitzgerald,* I noted that, through 1979, there had been just seventy-five articles and book chapters devoted to Fitzgerald's stories. Since 1979, again using the *MLA Bibliography* as a source (while undoubtedly not exhaustive, it certainly is representative), there have been fifty-eight articles and book chapters on Fitzgerald's stories listed (twenty-two of these are the essays in my 1982 collection, which means that, other than that volume, there have been just thirty-six pieces on Fitzgerald's stories in the last thirteen years).

Beyond these statistics is another continuing trend, which I also alluded to in 1982 and which is in many ways the impetus behind this present collection. Such criticism as there has been on Fitzgerald's short fiction has tended to focus almost exclusively on his most popular (or most frequently anthologized) stories, principally "Babylon Revisited" (the subject of twenty-six essays), "Absolution" (eleven essays), "The Rich Boy" (ten essays), "The Ice Palace" (seven essays), "May Day" (seven essays), and "Winter Dreams" (six essays). Most of Fitzgerald's stories have been the subjects of little more than passing mention, if they have been discussed at all. My 1982 collection tried to address that situation, offering the first full-length considerations of "Rags Martin-Jones and the Pr-nce of W-les," "The Adjuster," "The Bridal Party," and "Financing Finnegan"; but the majority of the essays in that volume and since have dealt with eight Fitzgerald stories (the six mentioned earlier as well as "The Diamond as Big as the Ritz" and "Crazy Sunday"). Again, a glance at the *MLA Bibliography* provides verification: Since 1979, besides the essays in my 1982 collection, only twelve essays have dealt with Fitzgerald stories other than the "big eight."

Most critics, readers, and students seem to continue to accept the popular conception that all but a very few of the stories are worthless potboilers, written hastily in order to raise money to support their author while he wrote his novels. This myth is given added credibility by Fitzgerald's own disparaging comments (he referred to his stories as "trash" and, in an oft-cited letter to Hemingway, remarked on the high price they commanded from the *Saturday Evening Post*, "Here's a last flicker of the old cheap pride: the *Post* now pays the old whore $4000 a screw. But now it's because she's mastered the 40 positions— in her youth one was enough."[1] I suspect that, accepting Fitzgerald's own assessment (or one part of it; on other occasions, he spoke more positively of his stories) combined with the fact that much of his shorter fiction *was* published originally in the *Post*—a middle-class low-brow periodical that demanded artistic compromises of its authors—students and critics have simply not read most of Fitzgerald's short stories. In much the same way, they seem ignorant of *This Side of Paradise, The Beautiful and Damned,* and *The Last Tycoon,* concentrating instead on *The Great Gatsby* and *Tender Is the Night.*

This volume, as was my 1982 collection, is based on the conviction that Fitzgerald's achievement as a writer of short fiction is worthy of our attention. Unlike that earlier book, this one focuses exclusively on stories that hitherto have received little or no serious comment. I was to some extent prompted by Susan F. Beegel's exemplary 1989 collection, *Hemingway's Neglected Short Fiction: New Perspectives.* If one could put together an entire book of studies of critically ignored Hemingway stories when there have been well over four times as many studies of

1. Andrew Turnbull, ed., *The Letters of F. Scott Fitzgerald*, 307.

Hemingway's short fiction as there have been of Fitzgerald's (Hemingway wrote 109 stories; Fitzgerald wrote 178), surely an equally worthwhile volume could be devoted to the latter's *truly* neglected stories. I began by writing a letter of inquiry to several Fitzgerald scholars, asking them each to select a favorite unstudied story and write an essay about it. I was surprised by the response: Everyone wrote back in the affirmative and each selected a different story. There were no turf wars, with most expressing enthusiasm for the story they had selected and welcoming the opportunity to rescue it from obscurity.

The roster of contributors includes many veteran Fitzgerald scholars (Scott Donaldson, Alan Margolies, John Kuehl, Bryant Mangum, Robert Roulston, Barry Gross, Ruth Prigozy, James L. W. West III, and Milton R. Stern), as well as younger academics who represent the future of Fitzgerald studies (Gerald Pike, Edward Gillin, Susan F. Beegel, Heidi Kunz Bullock, and Alice Hall Petry). But there are also distinguished critics of American literature whose primary focus has not usually been Fitzgerald (Robert Merrill, Alan Cheuse, James J. Martine, Victor A. Doyno, Bruce L. Grenberg, George Monteiro, Arthur Waldhorn, Peter L. Hays, and James Nagel). As with my 1982 collection, which drew upon the talents of a similarly diverse group of essayists, the aim was to produce a variety of critical perspectives rather than adhere to any particular viewpoint. Accordingly, here each contributor was given total latitude as to how he or she would design his or her essay; I asked only that each begin by briefly indicating the circumstances of the story's composition and its publication history and by summarizing whatever previous critical notice it had received. Plot summaries were encouraged, due to the obscurity of many of the stories selected, but they were not required.

The collection is divided into two principal sections. The first contains studies of individual stories and is arranged chronologically using the date of the story's first publication. The second includes essays on Fitzgerald's three story groups—the Basil and Josephine stories, the Count of Darkness stories, and the Pat Hobby stories—all of which have been as neglected by critics as have the stories dealt with in the first section. The reader will find that these essays make no extravagant claims for the excellence of the stories studied; in fact, if anything, the contributors more often go out of their way to point out the defects of these stories as well as their virtues. In doing so, they show through detailed exegesis just how Fitzgerald frequently compromised his art to satisfy popular tastes, employing sentimental or surprise endings, contrived plots, and unsatisfactory prose. By looking clear-sightedly at these often not totally successful stories, we are afforded the opportunity to observe their author, in James L. W. West III's words, "taking dangerous chances as he walks the tightrope between artistic respectability and popular appeal." But we also can see that, even on that tightrope, Fitzgerald's artistry consistently functioned at quite a high level. Given the close readings they receive here, these stories emerge as far more artistically worthy than their previous relegation to footnotes and passing comments would suggest.

Every one of these stories, to varying degrees, is what Ruth Prigozy calls a "quintessential Fitzgerald" piece of fiction, if not his best then still valuable for the light shed on his primary literary concerns. A number of the essays show how a story captures a particular moment in Fitzgerald's life, offering further testimony regarding the intensely autobiographical nature of his fiction and affording insights as well into his mode of composition and his artistic and human aims. Whether they focus on the hero's hedonism, on the worship of youth and glamour, or on the desire for money at the cost of one's artistic integrity, many of these stories demonstrate anew Fitzgerald's remarkable capacity for self-criticism, for composing what James J. Martine refers to as "laments," for creating beauty from his own unhappiness or ambivalence.

These essays also make plain that Fitzgerald did not just write about poor boys in love with rich girls who ultimately lose the rich girls to rich boys, which is another popular misconception and oversimplification. Other Fitzgerald themes such as the confusion of the material and the spiritual, the longing for lost youth, the need for adulation, self-indulgence versus self-denial, the fraudulence of the American dream, parvenu vulgarity, the preciousness of fading beauty, emotional bank-ruptcy, and the conflict between the world of reality and imagination are struggled with in the stories, just as they are in the novels. Fitzgerald's lifelong fascination with and aspiration to a life of wealth has too often blinded critics and casual readers to the complexity and multifaceted insights of his fiction. By focusing on the numerous thematic strands in the shorter fiction, these essays convincingly suggest how the stories both reflect back to previous novels or stories and look forward to novels in progress or stories not yet written. This helps us to see the richness of the tight-knit fabric of Fitzgerald's work as a whole.

This fabric is revealed most clearly in the many connections made between the neglected stories and the more well-known novels and stories. Bryant Mangum demonstrates how Daisy Cary of "The Bowl" becomes the prototype for Rosemary Hoyt in *Tender Is the Night;* Bruce L. Grenberg connects the themes of "Outside the Cabinet Maker's" to both *The Great Gatsby* and *Tender Is the Night;* Gerald Pike's careful study of "The Spire and the Gargoyle" relates the style of that very early story to stylistic patterns and voices throughout Fitzgerald's work; Alan Margolies links "Jacob's Ladder" to both "Winter Dreams" and "The Rich Boy"; Robert Roulston sees "The Swimmer" looking back to *The Great Gatsby* and forward to *Tender Is the Night;* Scott Donaldson and John Kuehl view "Two Wrongs" and "One Trip Abroad," respectively, as preliminary studies for *Tender Is the Night;* and Alice Hall Petry looks at "The Lost Decade" alongside "The Crack-Up" essays.

Ultimately, though, these essays should not be read merely or even primarily for what they can tell us about Fitzgerald's life or about his novels and better-known stories. While we do learn a great deal from them that enhances our understanding and appreciation of all his fiction and of how he used his own life in that fiction, we find much convincing evidence as well that these overlooked stories are in and of themselves deserving of our scrutiny. None of these essays is designed to be the definitive study of a particular story. They are not the "last word"; rather, they are designed as suggestive "first words" of what we hope will be a continuing discovery of the pleasures of the full range of Fitzgerald's short fiction.

PART I

STUDIES OF INDIVIDUAL STORIES

A STYLE IS BORN: THE RHETORIC OF LOSS IN "THE SPIRE AND THE GARGOYLE"

GERALD PIKE

"The Spire and the Gargoyle" has been reprinted only once (in John Kuehl's *The Apprentice Fiction of F. Scott Fitzgerald*) since its original publication in February of 1917 in the *Nassau Literary Magazine*. Critical commentary has been fairly sparse and for the most part, as in John Higgins's *F. Scott Fitzgerald: A Study of the Stories,* has focused on the autobiographical nature of the work. In *F. Scott Fitzgerald: A Study of the Short Fiction,* John Kuehl extends this line of criticism by pointing out that the story offers an early instance of Fitzgerald's essentially moral fictive vision. Bryant Mangum in *A Fortune Yet* sees the story as the first of Fitzgerald's "lost Eden" stories, initiated by Fitzgerald's flunking out of Princeton and being thrown over by Ginevra King. Otherwise, critical discussion has centered on the story's inclusion in *The Romantic Egoist* and *This Side of Paradise,* which is most fully and effectively covered in James L. W. West III's *The Making of "This Side of Paradise."*[1]

"The Spire and the Gargoyle" does offer an intriguing portrait of Fitzgerald's checkered career at Princeton. It was published not long

---

1. John Kuehl, ed., *The Apprentice Fiction of F. Scott Fitzgerald: 1909–1917,* 102–14; John A. Higgins, *F. Scott Fitzgerald: A Study of the Stories,* 7–12; John Kuehl, *F. Scott Fitzgerald: A Study of the Short Fiction,* 150; Bryant Mangum, *A Fortune Yet: Money in the Art of F. Scott Fitzgerald's Short Stories,* 16–18; James L. W. West III, *The Making of "This Side of Paradise,"* 33–34.

after his return to the university in September 1916, following his premature departure in December 1915 when he was forced to drop out, not only because of poor health but also because of the weak academic performance that had described his school work since entering Princeton in September 1913. Although he excelled in extracurricular literary ventures such as the Triangle Club and was published regularly in the *Nassau Literary Magazine,* he constantly had to make up courses, and most often his marks were barely passing. He was frequently on academic restriction and unable to participate in the school productions he had helped to create. Fitzgerald left Princeton without a degree in 1917 to join the army, and not having graduated was always a source of personal anxiety, comparable in fact to his sense of incompletion for never having fought in World War I. He did not return to Princeton, and the war ended before he could "make it over," forever cutting him off from a glory central to his youthful dreams, to self-fulfillment.

"The Spire and the Gargoyle," written in the very thick of what had become a carnivalization of Fitzgerald's academic intentions, forecasts a long-standing theme visible in his letters and in his nonfiction: the superior mind's struggle with irreconcilable and simultaneous desires for rational stasis and artistic flux. The story, like Princeton itself, presents a partial blueprint for Fitzgerald's ambivalent self-image as a writer, a thinker, and a moral being. As in much of Fitzgerald's fiction, the autobiographical elements tend to overshadow the stylistic ones, and while studies linking the experiences of the creator with his creation can be illuminating, they tend to obscure the craft behind genius. As much as "The Spire and the Gargoyle" offers a look into some of its author's personal dilemmas and establishes themes developed in subsequent work, it also offers a vivid glimpse into the stylistic leverage central to his success as a writer: the tools that allowed for the expression of his particular artistic vision. But before looking into these matters, a brief plot summary is in order, particularly given the rather remote presence of this early work (even "neglected" seems too generous for this story).

"The Spire and the Gargoyle" is the story of a boy who, seduced by New York's romantic magnetism, spends too much time answering the call of his heart while ignoring the call of his mind. As a result, he flunks out of the university. The story opens on "the boy," who is lying on the night-drenched lawn beneath the spires of the university. He has just failed an exam and tries to win the sympathy of the preceptor who is leaving the exam. The boy likens the preceptor to a "gargoyle," like those that wreathe the spires of the university.

Five years later he meets the gargoyle in an art museum in New York. The preceptor has forgotten him, thus deflating the protagonist's sense of personal injury. He also learns that the gargoyle has had to leave the university himself, stepping down to a job at a Brooklyn high school to support his large family. They spend an afternoon in a restaurant "knit together by the toast and the sense of exile."[2] The story closes with a return to the university the next week. The still-nameless hero (having graduated from "the boy" to "the man") sees his old preceptor on the train but avoids him, preferring to "draw to himself every impression he could from this ride" (112). But in the fog of the train station, the preceptor bumps into him. They exchange greetings. The elder asks, "Are you—ah—pretending to be a student again?" and then explains that he is visiting his younger brother who teaches there now. The hero wishes that he too had someone who would invite him to be "put up for a space" (113). They part company, and as the gargoyle advances into the fog ("the little figure walking off, propelled jerkily by his ridiculous legs"), the protagonist realizes that he is "alone face to face with the spirit that should have dominated his life" and that the university is "a stream where he had once thrown a stone but the faint ripple had long since vanished" (113). He stands for a minute, adding his "hot tears of anger and helplessness" to the rain, and then turns to reclaim his seat on the train: "Wearily he sank into a red plush seat, and pressed his hot forehead against the damp window pane" (114).

---

2. Kuehl, ed., *Apprentice Fiction*, 111. All subsequent page references to "The Spire and the Gargoyle" are to this edition and will appear parenthetically in the text. Also, true to Kuehl's text, passages are transcribed according to their original publication form, including occasional typographical errors. Kuehl explains his rationale: "The apprentice fiction appears here exactly the way these magazines printed it—typographical errors and all—for essentially two reasons: to obviate the necessity on the reader's part of examining nearly inaccessible documents in order to determine precisely the original texts of Fitzgerald's prep-school and college stories; to obviate the necessity on the editor's part of entering that treacherous world of emendations where so many arbitrary decisions must be made" (vii).

"The Spire and the Gargoyle" is certainly one of Fitzgerald's best apprentice stories, and it has particular appeal as an early indicator of voices that Fitzgerald uses throughout his career. Not only are the voices present, but Fitzgerald's manipulation of them, one with another, is prefigurative as well. But before looking at voice in this story, other more general stylistic matters deserve attention.

Typical of many of Fitzgerald's more ambitious stories, "The Spire and the Gargoyle" is balanced by its three-part structure that in this case places the main character at the university, moves five years forward to New York, and then, a few days later, returns him to the university for a brief and somber reunion. But the real symmetry derives from the repetition of images that come at the beginning and end of the story. Prominent among these is the face of the protagonist, hot with a sense of failure, being soothed by Nature, by her cool dampness. A typically romantic confluence of opposites, this image embodies both his alienation from the cloistered spires of the university as well as the tenacity of Nature as a healing force, a cool hand on his forehead. In a single brush stroke the image conveys both his suffering and his comfort.

But the fabric of the story most germane to its "deep structure," as Roger Fowler calls it, begins not with the arrangement of thematic details such as the complementary movements of the gargoyle and the protagonist between the university and New York, but in the voices representing conflicting forces within the lives of these two principal characters.[3] Fitzgerald's extreme ambivalence toward Princeton beats at the heart of "The Spire and the Gargoyle," and to develop the complex framework of figures and emotions on which the tale depends he uses several voices.

3. Roger Fowler, *Linguistics and the Novel*, 10. Fowler defines the distinction between surface and deep structures: "More important than these quasi-physical impressions are the influences of surface structure on the reader's apprehension of *rhetorical* facets of the text. What this means is that the manner of expression, as much as the content expressed, allows the reader to construct an image, not of the author himself, but of the posture he has created for that particular work. In terms of the linguistic theory employed here, features of tone and style are controlled by the relationship between the surface structure and the deep structure of sentences. I think it will be realized that the distinction between these two levels of structure is a version of the established belief that in linguistic communication there are available 'different ways' (surface structures) 'of saying the same thing' (deep structure)."

First is a *clipped declarative voice,* which is a subset of the more general *flat objective* one that runs throughout his short fiction. The next is the voice of *style indirect libre* as the French call it or the German *erlebte Rede.* For want of a standard term suitable to English, I have followed Ann Banfield's lead by adopting Jespersen's *represented speech* to describe this particular form (though Banfield uses the more accurate but also more cumbersome "represented speech act").[4] Simply stated, in Fitzgerald's work represented speech depicts the consciousness of a particular character, without using direct or indirect dialogue. The last is a voice most commonly associated with Fitzgerald's technique, which I have chosen to call the *self-conscious poetic*—"self-conscious" because it always seems conscious of itself as a departure from the dominant narrative voice, and also self-conscious in that it often carries a degree of self-directed sardonic humor. Rather than inspecting the features of these voices here, in a vacuum, we will examine them within the context of the story, so that our definitions of these terms might be as descriptive (and least prescriptive) as possible.

The opening line of "The Spire and the Gargoyle" uses the clipped declarative voice that Fitzgerald develops throughout his career. This voice has the authority of brevity, drawing attention to itself for what it omits and for its short and therefore unusual appearance on the page. The opening line is followed by an animistic description of a Princeton-like nightscape:

> The night mist fell. From beyond the moon it rolled, clustered about the spires and towers, and then settled below them so that the dreaming peaks seemed still in lofty aspiration toward the stars. Figures that dotted the daytime like ants now brushed along as ghosts in and out of the night. Even the buildings seemed infinitely more mysterious as they loomed suddenly out of the darkness, outlined each by a hundred faint squares of yellow light. (105)

The anomalous look and character of the lead sentence draws attention and invites speculation. Short sentences have a particular authority, like

---

4. Ann Banfield, *Unspeakable Sentences: Narration and Representation in the Language of Fiction,* 12.

those of the intelligent speaker who chooses to speak little and whose few words therefore acquire weight. Pared down to essential information, the sentence is imagistic in its brevity and austere, an effect enhanced by the rhythmic stresses falling on the last three of its four words. What then happens when this technique is repeated throughout the story? We are conscious of the form, of its authority, but also conscious of its repetition, so that one short emphatic sentence invites comparison with others. But before looking at the "metatext" established by the network of short sentences within the story, we should first see how this particular sentence, prominent in its placement at the beginning of the story, functions.

"The night mist fell" speaks with the somber finality of funereal drums, describing a falling mist that collapses terrain, buildings, and people into a common visual dimension. Animism lends texture to the description and to the integrative force of this mist that humanizes objects as it objectifies humans. The moon, the stars, and the buildings all become transmogrified under the common blanket of mist. The human figures that are reduced to ant status in daylight are "now brushed along as ghosts." The buildings' "dreaming peaks seemed still in lofty aspiration toward the stars." And "even the buildings seemed infinitely more mysterious as they loomed suddenly out of the darkness." The details expand upon the understated density of the clipped declarative like deferential annotators, elaborating the theme of people and place being synonymous under certain natural forces such as the mist, the figure that opens and closes the story.

A few sentences later, the central character is portrayed not as a person but as a blotting out of "a square of light." Indeed, the boy is first referred to as an "it": "It [this 'blotting'] paused and resolved itself into a boy who stretched his arms wearily, and advancing threw himself full length on the damp grass by the sun-dial" (105). Even when the character assumes a human dimension, he is still limited to the nonspecific. He is "the boy," a designation typical of naturalist literature and one that reemphasizes the condition in which the failed scholar finds himself, one as fixed and final as Nature herself and as absolute. He is a part of the landscape; that is all. This opening paragraph establishes the dominant voices of the story. The first is clipped and declarative and speaks with the authority of omission. The second, fraught with modifiers, is far from economical and paints with self-consciously poetic language the boy's dream vision of the university. Stretched between the extremes of these two voices, the boy's conflict acquires an additional tension.

The third paragraph reenacts the basic structure of the first and further emphasizes the role of the two dominant voices in the story. The paragraph opens with another clipped declarative sentence that is followed by the flat objective voice appropriate to quantifiable matters, the mundane details that have decided the boy's fate:

> In his case it all depended on this examination. If he passed it he would become a sophomore the following fall; if he failed, it meant that his college days faded out with the last splendors of June. Fifty cut recitations in his first wild term had made necessary the extra course of which he had just taken the examination. (106)

Within this passage, "the last splendors of June" stands apart, a poetic insertion briefly intruding upon the flat objective and just at that point in the sentence where the boy's point of view colors perception. The phrase, then, is a brief instance of represented speech. The last word of this sentence ("examination") marks a pivotal shift in voice. As the content turns from the disastrous examination to the romantic distractions that led the boy into his present jeopardy, the language reflects this change, becoming adjectival and poetic. The paragraph continues:

> Winter muses, unacademic and cloistered by Forty-second Street and Broadway, had stolen hours from the dreary stretches of February and March. Later, time had crept insidiously through the lazy April afternoons and seemed so intangible in the long Spring twilights. So June found him unprepared. Evening after evening the senior singing, drifting over the campus and up to his window, drew his mind for an instant to the unconscious poetry of it and he, goading on his spoiled and over-indulged faculties, bent to the revengeful books again. Through the careless shell that covered his undergraduate consciousness had broken a deep and almost reverent liking for the gray walls and gothic peaks and all they symbolized in the store of the ages of antiquity. (106)

I include this entire paragraph for two reasons. First, as indicated, I wish to point out the shift from the flat objective to the self-conscious poetic voice, an adjustment that complements and enacts the shift in content. Second, another short, emphatic sentence appears in the middle of this long passage of ornate description: "So June found him unprepared." This insertion, in the midst of subjective and purple prose, provides a perfect counterpoint to the paragraph's lead sentence ("In his case it all depended on this examination.") by echoing that initial voice of reality. The short sentences display, in form and content, the cold eye of the natural world reflected in the sure, steady obligations of the academic world. So the process of our reading, if we can summarize it, begins with a short declaration, rendered in the most clinical terms, of the boy's "case" with all attendant legal overtones of the "sentence" that might be enforced should he fail. Then, after two more sentences in an objective tone, the voice shifts to the self-conscious poetic, which articulates the boy's predicament in romantic terms appropriate to his fall from academic grace.

In the midst of this reverie, the brief emphatic voice of reason reenters the discussion, like the knocking at the gate in *Macbeth*. After this momentary intrusion, the paragraph resumes in a language as freighted with modifiers as the short sentences are free of them. In short, the language of rationality has no qualifiers (adjectives and adverbs) because its message is unqualified, whereas the language of youth's exposure to urban grandeur is laden with the qualified language of dense modification. Barely a single noun in the second voice stands unaided by an adjective, and in this we hear the tone of the young visionary, but always in counterpoint to the refrain of tenacious reality rendered in simple, direct tones. The short, emphatic sentence is replicated in the dialogue of the story as well. The first instance of speech is the boy's: " 'Well, it's over,' he whispered aloud to himself, wetting his hands in the damp, and running them through his hair. 'All over' " (107).

At first this speech seems to be cumulative, with the "All over" tagged on for emphasis. We should notice, however, that by using a period after "hair" instead of a comma, Fitzgerald represents this speech as two discrete statements separated by some vivid tactile imagery. And while the first statement ("Well, it's over") is elemental, the "All over" is even more so. The first, though very brief, allows the second to be even briefer, and sentence brevity, as in the instances of description cited earlier, acquires resonance. In fact, by formal definition, the second statement is not a complete statement at all. It is a fragment with no subject, not even the indefinite "it" of the first bit of dialogue. Yet the antecedent, the thing that is "over," is even more resonant in the second instance than in the first. The language of reality, this time coming from the boy, seeks out the most efficient linguistic expression. The boy's words, by virtue of their brevity, recall the clipped declarative descriptions cited earlier. It is as if the voice of reality has infiltrated the voice of the boy, and his first words appropriately carry the weight of the unadorned world with its unadorned speech, the same voice that earlier intruded upon his romantic attractions in the retrospective paragraph.

A quick look at the self-conscious poetic language of the paragraph preceding the above dialogue will suffice for us to appreciate more fully the distinctive nature of these short declarations: "In view of his window a tower sprang upward, grew into a spire, yearning higher till its uppermost end was half invisible against the morning skies" (106). Later in this paragraph the narrative voice remarks that "there was something terribly pure in the slope of the chaste stone, something which led and directed and called." This voice dominates the first section's descriptive passages and is appropriate to the boy's romantic observations, providing in its ornamentation a pronounced backdrop and contrast to the voice of the shorter sentences.

When the boy manages to corner the gargoyle on his way home, their exchange is reminiscent of the boy's initial monologue:

> "Awful night," said the boy.
> The gargoyle only grunted. (107)

Two points stand out in this exchange. First, the boy speaks as before, in fragments that manage to capture the sweep of the moment. It is an awful night, full of awe, full of dread, full of promise wasted. The gargoyle's response is even more minimal than the boy's entreaty. The gargoyle offers no words at all, yet he conveys meaning succinctly. Second, Fitzgerald takes care to represent these snippets in separate paragraphs. As a result they stand out on the page and set up a pattern repeated throughout the story: the extremely short paragraph composed of dialogue unadorned by any description. This arrangement depicts an obvious *exchange* of dialogue that would have been effaced had

Fitzgerald chosen to write it as a single paragraph such as " 'Awful night,' said the boy. The gargoyle only grunted." As a result of these two points—attention to sentence brevity and to the explicit depiction of dialogue exchange—the two characters are joined under a common voice. And their commonality, in spite of obvious differences of character and circumstance, is central to the thematic development of the story.

Although very different, the two characters are united in a common conflict—the discrepancy between their aspirations and the contingencies of reality. The boy suffers from the pleasures of New York pulling against the practical demands of college; the gargoyle must balance his own desire for higher scholarship against the demands of a family. Both characters are marginalized when obligations override desire. They both lose at the same juncture, though they come at it from opposite directions. And this association is represented not only by their sharing physical proximity in all three phases of the story but also at a linguistic level, through the voice of omission.

While the description in the first section of the story is rendered primarily in the self-conscious poetic voice cited earlier, the second section's description falls more under the category of the flat objective appropriate to the mood of an older protagonist who has, to a large extent, cut himself off from his hyperbolic youth. The following is the first portion of the opening paragraph of the second section, typical of the voice controlling the descriptive passages in this section:

> Regularly every two weeks he had been drifting out Fifth Avenue. On crisp autumn afternoons the tops of the shining auto busses were particularly alluring. From the roofs of other passing busses a face barely seen, an interested glance, a flash of color assumed the proportion of an intrigue. He had left college five years before and the busses and the art gallery and a few books were his intellectual relaxation. (108)

In section 2 the first overt instance of the clipped declarative comes at the beginning of the third paragraph. As in section 1, the voice is conspicuous in its brevity. Unlike those in section 1, however, here the brief sentence carries a more optimistic message: "Yet he was happy this afternoon" (109). He is happy in spite of the ubiquitous sense that "his whole range [of reading] was pitifully narrow" and that "he was still and now [because of his flunking out] always would be in the stage where every work and very [sic] author had to be introduced and sometimes interpreted to him" (108). Just as the protagonist has matured, so has the voice describing his circumstances grown more sober. In common with section 1, though, is the use of the clipped declarative to state, in summary fashion, the imperfect circumstances of this central character.

In section 2, the gargoyle and the protagonist meet by chance in a museum and spend a long afternoon reminiscing over the school that has exiled them both. Here Fitzgerald offers another "apprentice" instance of represented speech, penetrating the surface of consciousness as it surreptitiously conveys indirect discourse. In this instance, it is also rendered in the clipped declarative: "When six o'clock pushed itself into the crowded hours it was with real regret that they shook hands, and the little man, manipulating his short legs in mad expostulation, raced after a Brooklyn car. Yes, it had been distinctly exhilarating" (111). The protagonist's represented speech in the closing sentence above is echoed at the bottom of the paragraph, this time to convey the indirect dialogue of the gargoyle: " . . . but through all his [the gargoyle's] hopeful talk there was a kind of inevitability that he would teach in a Brooklyn high school till the last bell called him to his last class. Yes, he went back [to the university] occasionally" (111).

The repetition of "yes" and the general voice, the represented speech first of the protagonist and second of the gargoyle, links these two sentences and reinforces the idea that the characters are similarly linked by circumstances best rendered in the clipped declarative. Again, real circumstances, the impositions of reality, establish the domain of this voice. To emphasize this point, we need only return to the earlier instance of represented speech (the protagonist's) and the description that immediately follows it: "Yes, it had been distinctly exhilarating. They had talked of academic atmospheres, of hopes that lay in the ivied walls, of little things that could only have counted after the mystic hand of the separation had made them akin" (111).

The metaphorical nature of this description, particularly such phrases as "the mystic hand of the separation," recalls the poetic voice of section 1 more than the flat objectivity of section 2. Given that the conversation has returned to a former time, this shift is appropriate. The efficacy of Fitzgerald's returning here to the voice of youth anticipates a chief source of technical leverage in his later short stories. He uses voices to manipulate the texture of circumstances and to set up a network of associations, so that we hear the voice, though it may not register consciously, and connect it with the other portions of the text in which that voice occurs. In this way we are drawn into the conversation; rather than merely observing it, we participate in it by sharing even subliminal comprehension of tonalities associated with the clipped objectivity of current circumstances as opposed to memory's poetry. In short, we hear the past just as the characters do; and we are reminded of the common ground, the common sympathies, shared by these two seemingly disparate sorts.

The first of three closing paragraphs illustrates Fitzgerald's manipulation of voice very nicely. Again, in order to appreciate the full configuration of voices, the paragraph should be read in total:

> Minutes passed. The train was silent. The several blurs on the station platform became impersonal and melted into the background. He was alone face to face with the spirit that should have dominated his life, the mother that he had renounced. It was a stream where he had once thrown a stone but the faint ripple had long since vanished. Here he had taken nothing, he had given nothing; nothing?—his eyes wandered slowly upward—up—up—until by straining them he could see where the spire began—and with his eyes went his soul. But the mist was upon both. He could not climb with the spire. (113)

The opening sentences are in the clipped declarative voice and function as they have throughout the story: to depict the authority of a largely predatory reality. The sentences grow incrementally longer as the paragraph develops. Parallel to this increase, a complementary shift in tone occurs—starting with the clipped declarative and building to a kind of verbal crescendo past the metaphor at the geographic center of the paragraph ("It was a stream where he had once thrown a stone but the faint ripple had long since vanished.") to the climax of "—and with his eyes went his soul." What follows the period after "soul" is a grace note before the closing two sentences, which again take up the clipped voice of insurmountable circumstance that opened the paragraph.

Like the earlier paragraph that describes the protagonist's meeting with the gargoyle in New York, the paragraph above also contains a brief instance of represented speech: "Here he had taken nothing, he had given nothing; nothing?—his eyes wandered slowly upward—up—up. . . ." This unusual sentence with its peculiar punctuation poses the rhetorical question "nothing?" in the represented speech of the protagonist. Curiously, though rhetorical in tone, the question implies no clear answer. The issue of the man's accomplishment remains open, like the message of the story. This is no polemic against the inequities of an Ivy League education. Represented speech, as in the New York sequence, draws the audience into the consciousness of the character so that we share that question with him as it resonates to the end of the story.

John A. Higgins finds fault with the conclusion of "The Spire and the Gargoyle":

> The style of the ending unfortunately anticipates the "rhetorical blanket" conclusions of "Winter Dreams" and " 'The Sensible Thing,' " where Fitzgerald tries to make the reader share the hero's self-pity without sufficient cause. The protagonist in this story does not deserve pity, for he has admittedly failed through indolence. The central weakness of "The Spire and the Gargoyle," then, is that Fitzgerald is too close to his protagonist to see him objectively.[5]

Higgins's comment demonstrates another instance of biography intruding on our reading of Fitzgerald's work and so reveals more about Higgins's biases than about the shortcomings of Fitzgerald's technique. Because the story is an obvious product of Fitzgerald's academic failure at Princeton, Higgins misreads the story as mere fictively rendered autobiography. Higgins reveals this reductive reading in such phrases as

---

5. Higgins, *Fitzgerald: Study of the Stories,* 8. Kuehl echoes this sentiment in *Apprentice Fiction,* 115, stating that " 'The Spire and the Gargoyle' had suffered from personal involvement" so that rather than showing or implying, Fitzgerald "had 'told' [and] made everything explicit." I should add here that my response to Higgins's analysis is in no way a condemnation of his book, a generally strong work that was, until fairly recently, the only book-length study of Fitzgerald's short fiction available in the United States. Higgins's remains a definitive commentary on "The Spire and the Gargoyle," and because I believe it errs in a way that typifies the shortcomings of much Fitzgerald criticism, my response may seem disproportionately vehement and negative.

"sufficient cause" and "failed through indolence." Surely the protagonist's ruined life is "sufficient cause" for the story's emotional conclusion; and clearly the cause of this fall is far too complex to be simply attributed to his "indolence." Higgins overlooks the interlocking of characters and place in the story. The university and New York are as much characters in the narrative as are the gargoyle and the boy, and all share equally in building the complex network of voices and images that constitutes the story's depiction of frustrated hopes, of fate that falls like a final curtain before the self-realized character is allowed to speak his opening lines.

The story is not simply about the boy; it is about the relationship between the spire and the gargoyle, between the boy and the preceptor, between heaven and earth. Mostly it is about the measureless equation that can preclude even the most ardent desire and whims of fate that can thwart even the best of intentions. In this, all are locked; and the fate of the preceptor's "little figure walking off, propelled by his ridiculous legs," is no less tragic than the protagonist's as he reboards the train.

Turnbull states that Fitzgerald regarded "The Spire and the Gargoyle" as his first mature writing, and considering the sophistication of voice in the piece, particularly the extent to which the interplay of voices anticipates his later short fiction, this seems an acceptable assessment. Higgins finds the symbolism "too obvious": "That the spire symbolizes aspiration and success is stated directly three times on one page, and the preceptor is explicitly identified as the gargoyle."[6] This is true, but it overlooks the complexity these symbols assume once multiple voices begin to suggest a connection between the "gargoyle" and his student. Had Fitzgerald been inclined toward a symbolic tale, he certainly would not have called the preceptor a "gargoyle," nor would he have allowed himself the indulgence of equating spires with aspiration. The story's "message," if it has one, is that "aspiration" is a fickle and illusive thing, that spires can be misleading, and that assigning blame for failure in the modern world is just as difficult as sticking to one's aspirations. Critics,

---

6. Andrew Turnbull, *Scott Fitzgerald*, 70. Higgins cites this assessment in *Fitzgerald: Study of the Stories*, 8, as does Matthew J. Bruccoli in *Some Sort of Epic Grandeur: The Life of F. Scott Fitzgerald*, 71, and Mangum in *Fortune Yet*, 58, though no source is offered by either Higgins, Bruccoli, or Mangum. This leads me to suspect that all have borrowed, either directly or indirectly, from Turnbull, who fails to provide a source in his biography.

thus far, have undervalued the preceptor's victimization. This oversight is probably due to both a conditioned sensitivity to point of view and the assumption that because the action focuses on the student then it is entirely his story. The use of voice indicates otherwise. Furthermore, both characters share every major scene in all three sections of the story; and this equality is further enhanced by their common lack of names, their shared objectification in the naturalistic tradition. It is *their* story, not just the youth's.

"The Spire and the Gargoyle" is not one of Fitzgerald's short story masterpieces, but it is "neglected"—like most of his apprentice work. It is, like Picasso's student sketches, indicative of remarkable technical skill in a remarkably young artist, a skill that underpins all subsequent work, regardless of how experimental or sophisticated it may become. By examining the interplay of Fitzgerald's trademark poetic voice with the more objective voice in this early story, we see a technique central to his mastery of this form. We begin to establish flexible categories that allow for a more generous testing of his nearly 180 short stories, to appreciate neglected stories such as those studied in this volume. Mostly, however, looking into Fitzgerald's technique in some sense saves his work from the tyranny of biographical speculation, and returns us to the real beauty of his achievement, his remarkable aesthetic sense of craft, so much admired by his contemporary writers, that can create such vivid fictive moments as palpable as any we may encounter in our own lives.

"DALYRIMPLE GOES WRONG": THE BEST
OF THE NEGLECTED EARLY STORIES

ROBERT MERRILL

F. Scott Fitzgerald's references to himself as a "whore" are often cited as evidence of his melodramatic exaggeration, even self-posturing, when writing about his own short fiction.[1] Critics who quote these remarks usually proceed to praise Fitzgerald as a short story writer, citing Fitzgerald's dozen or so best stories as among the best by any American. In reviewing the 178 stories Fitzgerald wrote, however, these obviously sympathetic readers almost always seem to agree with Brian Way that Fitzgerald "tended to publish his mistakes instead of destroying them." They tend to be especially dismissive about early stories such as those in *Flappers and Philosophers,* Fitzgerald's first published collection. Richard Lehan speaks of these stories as "slight"; John Kuehl suggests that among the stories in this collection "only 'The Ice Palace' transcends entertainment"; and Sergio Perosa characterizes one piece, "Dalyrimple Goes Wrong," as "undoubtedly one of the worst" stories Fitzgerald ever wrote.[2] It seems to me that "Dalyrimple Goes Wrong" is in fact one of

1. For Fitzgerald's comments, see Andrew Turnbull, ed., *The Letters of F. Scott Fitzgerald,* 195, 307, 481. For the critical maneuver I remark, see John Kuehl, *F. Scott Fitzgerald: A Study of the Short Fiction,* 7, and Brian Way, *F. Scott Fitzgerald and the Art of Social Fiction,* 72.
2. Way, *Social Fiction,* 49; Richard D. Lehan, "The Romantic Self and the Uses of Place in the Stories of F. Scott Fitzgerald," 5; Kuehl, *Fitzgerald: Study of the Short Fiction,* 33; Sergio Perosa, *The Art of F. Scott Fitzgerald,* 34.

Fitzgerald's more interesting early stories and an especially good example of how little understood Fitzgerald's short fiction remains today despite the vast amount of critical attention bestowed on Fitzgerald since his death in 1941.[3] Brief as it is, the discussion to follow will be longer than all the criticism previously devoted to this story. I hope that it will also illustrate the critical riches yet to be explored (or even discovered) in Fitzgerald's canon.

I should add that it is not my intention to elevate "Dalyrimple Goes Wrong" to the level of such Fitzgerald stories as "Babylon Revisited," "Absolution," and "Crazy Sunday." As I will acknowledge, this early story is often uneven or worse, and comparison with an early Hemingway story, "Soldier's Home," is hardly to Fitzgerald's advantage. I will nonetheless pursue this comparison because I think Fitzgerald's story is sufficiently interesting to bear the critical burden of such study. I also want to challenge Alice Hall Petry's claim that "Dalyrimple Goes Wrong" is "quite atypical of Fitzgerald's work." To the contrary, I believe that "Dalyrimple Goes Wrong" anticipates several of Fitzgerald's later (and admittedly greater) studies of the social order that came into fabulous but fragile being in the aftermath of World War I. Neither Fitzgerald's worst nor best work, "Dalyrimple Goes Wrong" reveals much that is most typical of Fitzgerald as a writer early and late. Indeed, it seems to me the best of Fitzgerald's neglected early stories.[4]

I.

Arthur Mizener tells us that in August 1919 Edmund Wilson wrote to Fitzgerald to ask him to contribute to a volume of "realistic war stories." "Come now!" Wilson exhorted, "clear your mind of cant! . . .

---

3. "Dalyrimple Goes Wrong" is not always dismissed. For brief but earnest comments, see Kenneth Eble, *F. Scott Fitzgerald*, 66; Arthur Mizener, *The Far Side of Paradise: A Biography of F. Scott Fitzgerald*, 161; Robert Sklar, *F. Scott Fitzgerald: The Last Laocoön*, 64–65. The story has been anthologized at least once; see Ensaf Thune and Ruth Prigozy, eds., *Short Stories: A Critical Anthology*, 294–307. Even these sympathetic critics make modest claims for the story, however.

4. Alice Hall Petry, *Fitzgerald's Craft of Short Fiction: The Collected Stories—1920–1935*, 14. The nonneglected (and superior) stories would be "The Ice Palace," "The Diamond as Big as the Ritz," and "May Day." I think that "Dalyrimple Goes Wrong" is the best story (after "The Ice Palace") in *Flappers and Philosophers*.

Concentrate in one short story a world of tragedy, comedy, irony and beauty!!!" This request was not as odd as it may seem to us today, for Fitzgerald had recently served a stint in the army and was probably thought to know something about the military if not the world war he did not actually experience firsthand. Fitzgerald did not send Wilson such a story. At the time he was fully engaged with transforming *The Romantic Egotist* into *This Side of Paradise,* and once finished with his first published novel he spent the fall of 1919 producing eight new short stories designed for eastern magazines such as *The Smart Set* and the *Saturday Evening Post.* Nonetheless, the first of these new stories, "Dalyrimple Goes Wrong," can plausibly be seen as the closest Fitzgerald ever came to responding to Wilson's request. Written in September 1919, first published in *The Smart Set* in February 1920, and republished shortly thereafter in *Flappers and Philosophers,* "Dalyrimple Goes Wrong" does not concentrate in one story a world of tragedy, comedy, irony, and beauty, but it does deal with the problem of the returning war veteran—much as Hemingway's "Soldier's Home" was to do a few years later.[5]

Ruth Prigozy has already noticed the basic similarities between "Dalyrimple Goes Wrong" and "Soldier's Home": "Both deal with the postwar sensibility, the community's fickle adulation of the war hero, and the effects of youthful disillusionment with American values on the lives of returned soldiers." If Hemingway seems the more authoritative guide to these subjects, it is no doubt because he had actual combat experience on which to draw. In "Soldier's Home," Hemingway wrote about the postwar sensibility, as Prigozy puts it, but he was able to contrast this sensibility with a convincing (indeed, haunting) portrait of his protagonist's combat experiences in World War I. One thinks especially of Krebs's discovery that he was capable of responding to the worst pressures of combat with surprising resolve and success. After the war, in talking with those who know nothing of such things, Krebs is forced to lie about what he did and felt in combat, and the result is that

5. Mizener, *Far Side,* 91. For information about the composition and publication of "Dalyrimple Goes Wrong," see ibid., 98–99, and Jackson R. Bryer, ed., *The Short Stories of F. Scott Fitzgerald: New Approaches in Criticism,* 355.

he must deny the truth of his experience: "All of the times that had been able to make him feel cool and clear inside himself when he thought of them; the times so long back when he had done the one thing, the only thing for a man to do, easily and naturally, when he might have done something else, now lost their cool, valuable quality and then were lost themselves."[6]

Krebs finds that even other veterans feel obliged to remember the war as it is supposed to have been rather than as they actually experienced it: " . . . when he occasionally met another man who had really been a soldier and they talked a few minutes in the dressing room at a dance he fell into the easy pose of the old soldier among other soldiers: that he had been badly, sickeningly frightened all the time. In this way he lost everything." Hemingway may not have needed his observation of combat to disparage the most flagrant atrocity stories, "detailed accounts of German women found chained to machine guns in the Argonne forest," but his experience comes through clearly in his memorable depiction of a naïve midwesterner who finds that he is really rather good at dealing with the terrible necessities of combat but who cannot relate these experiences to a postwar environment in which no one cares what he has discovered about himself in a distant world far beyond their own experience.[7]

Like Hemingway, Fitzgerald notes the American public's extremely superficial adulation of its war heroes. Fitzgerald's twenty-three-year-old protagonist, Bryan Dalyrimple, returns from the war a more honored figure than Hemingway's Krebs; indeed, Dalyrimple is told "that he was second in importance only to General Pershing and Sergeant York."[8] Whereas Krebs comes home a little later than the men with whom he served and encounters the first reaction against such adulation of the returning veterans, Dalyrimple returns at the height of patriotic fervor. The mayor of his hometown puts him up in his own house, reporters and photographers seek him out, and girls who hardly remember him make

6. Thune and Prigozy, eds., *Short Stories,* 63; Ernest Hemingway, *The Short Stories of Ernest Hemingway,* 145–46.

7. Hemingway, *Short Stories of Ernest Hemingway,* 146.

8. F. Scott Fitzgerald, *Flappers and Philosophers,* 219. All subsequent page references to "Dalyrimple Goes Wrong" are to this 1920 edition and will appear parenthetically in the text.

much of his return. Within a month, however, it dawns on Dalyrimple that the celebration is over—the mayor's wife wants him to go elsewhere, the reporters have other concerns, and the young girls are nowhere to be seen (220–21). Like Hemingway, Fitzgerald makes it clear that celebrating war heroes is a ritualistic gesture with virtually no real meaning to an American public that has no conception of what war is like, how it changes people like Krebs forever.

Fitzgerald's treatment of the returning veteran is interesting because it confirms his opposition to what he once termed the war "hysteria" of his time and because it balances Fitzgerald's well-known romanticism concerning the combat experience he was denied when World War I ended before he was sent overseas.[9] Nonetheless, it must be noted that Fitzgerald's treatment of combat experience is much less convincing than Hemingway's and rather less crucial to "Dalyrimple Goes Wrong" than Hemingway's experience was to "Soldier's Home." Understandably, Fitzgerald has little to say about memories of war and in fact focuses on his protagonist's attempts to succeed in the postwar economy. And what Fitzgerald does offer us concerning Dalyrimple in Europe is vague and unpersuasive. We are told that "Bryan played the star in an affair which included a Lewis gun and a nine-day romp behind the retreating German lines, so luck triumphant or sentiment rampant awarded him a row of medals" (219), as if such an experience can be adequately captured in the term "romp" and otherwise left to the reader's imagination. Later we are told that Dalyrimple's "machine-gun episode" had taught him to rely on his intuition and to eschew elaborate planning (235).

As it happens, Dalyrimple seems to have had something like Krebs's experience in war, discovering his own intuitive skills and capacity for "lightning decision" (235). As Dalyrimple continues to image his experiences as a "romp," however, we must wonder whether the positive side to his war experiences can be taken seriously. Indeed, we must wonder whether Fitzgerald meant us to take Dalyrimple seriously on this subject or whether Dalyrimple is presented as a young man who passed through one of the world's worst wars essentially untouched by the experience. As a war story, "Dalyrimple Goes Wrong" fails to answer

9. Mizener, *Far Side*, 69.

this question and perhaps never really addresses it. As the comparison with a story such as "Soldier's Home" suggests, we must look elsewhere for the appeal of this early Fitzgerald story.

II.

Oddly enough, we cannot look for Fitzgerald's characteristic treatment of "young love," the subject of virtually all the other 1919–1920 stories. "Dalyrimple Goes Wrong" is one of the few Fitzgerald stories, early or late, in which the protagonist neither kisses nor is kissed. Indeed, Petry thinks the tale "untypical" because it is "a Dreiseresque study of free will, politics, and economics."[10] I agree that the story's interest lies in its treatment of philosophical, political, and economic factors impinging on Fitzgerald's protagonist ("hero" would be misleading), though I cannot see the story as untypical of the author of early stories such as "May Day" (1920) and "The Diamond as Big as the Ritz" (1922), let alone *The Great Gatsby* and *Tender Is the Night.*

"Dalyrimple Goes Wrong" refutes Way's contention that the early Fitzgerald was an uncritical critic of his time, for the story in fact hints at Fitzgerald's lifelong sympathies for socialism.[11] Bryan Dalyrimple is presented as a twenty-three-year-old who has never worked (220), for whom "the ways and means of economy were a closed book" (225). Once he realizes that he cannot rest in the role of returned war hero, Dalyrimple secures work from a wholesale grocer named Theron G. Macy who assures him that after a brief period in which he learns the stock he will be "on the road" as one of Macy's trusted salesmen. Dalyrimple's experiences with the company are such that we are invited to share Fitzgerald's highly critical, even jaundiced, views on American commercial life.

It soon becomes apparent even to the naïve Dalyrimple that his short stint learning the stock may be a very long one. One of Dalyrimple's colleagues, Charley Moore, tells of working in the same position for

10. Scott Donaldson, "Money and Marriage in Fitzgerald's Stories," 78; Petry, *Fitzgerald's Craft*, 14.

11. Way, *Social Fiction*, 62. On Fitzgerald's political sympathies, see James W. Tuttleton, *The Novel of Manners in America*, 188–89.

four years despite Macy's assurances about moving on "soon" to the life of a salesman (224), and Dalyrimple inadvertently discovers that Macy's "weak-chinned nephew" has started at twenty dollars a month more than Dalyrimple and has ascended to a private office and new responsibilities within three weeks (226–27). By contrast, Charley Moore has moved from thirty-five dollars a month to sixty dollars a month during his four years "learning" the stock (224). Macy's willingness to manipulate the Bryan Dalyrimples of the world is all too obvious. Nor is Dalyrimple the most exploited of Macy's employees. Dalyrimple comes to learn about "cave-dwellers" who labor in the basement of Macy's company. These men (if there are women in Macy's business we never see them) have worked for ten or even fifteen years at sixty dollars a month, "rolling barrels and carrying boxes through damp, cement-walled corridors, lost in that echoing half-darkness between seven and five-thirty and, like himself, compelled several times a month to work until nine at night" (225). These cave-dwellers represent the worst of capitalism's excesses and serve as a compelling illustration of Dalyrimple's own fate if he does not intervene in the scenario drafted by men such as Theron Macy.

Fitzgerald's indictment of the business world is not a crude one, however. Dalyrimple himself is hardly an innocent victim, as we soon see in his criminal rebellion against his perceived "fate." And Charley Moore is an especially interesting qualification of Fitzgerald's apparent portrait of economic exploitation. Charley, we are told, has "that faint musk of weakness hanging about him that is often mistaken for the scent of evil." He has "drifted into indulgence and laziness as casually as he had drifted into life, and was to drift out" (223), an observation that makes it clear that Charley responds to Macy's exploitation with the "lazy" compliance of an all-too-willing victim. As Fitzgerald bluntly notes, "The Charley Moores are always going to change jobs next month. They do, once or twice in their careers, after which they sit around comparing their last job with the present one, to the infinite disparagement of the latter" (224).

Thus Fitzgerald can say that "Charley was listlessly struggling that losing struggle against mental, moral, and physical anaemia that takes place ceaselessly on the lower fringe of the middle classes" (224), which is indeed a Dreiseresque note in a story consistently marked by Dreiser's— and Fitzgerald's—concern for capturing the economic realities of exploitation *and* mindless complicity. Dalyrimple hardly identifies with the Charley Moores against the Theron Macys. Indeed, it is Fitzgerald's point that Dalyrimple's primary response to his new situation is not to attack Macy's unjust power but to avoid becoming another Charley Moore. Later, as we look at the story's conclusion, we can return to the question of whether Fitzgerald identifies with Bryan's response to economic exploitation.

As in more famous works such as *Tender Is the Night*, Fitzgerald's focus is not on the economic system per se but its effects on a young American rather like himself. "Dalyrimple Goes Wrong" is therefore a psychological study, but a *comic* psychological study. Dalyrimple turns to Macy because the businessman offers "a chance to get ahead," and for Dalyrimple to "get on" is nothing less than "the rule of life" (227). Whereas Dalyrimple's effortless successes in combat leave him fundamentally untouched by the experience of World War I, his frustrations at Macy's compel him to reconsider "old childhood principles" (229), even the assumption that one should cling to a moral perspective on life (229–30). He decides that to succeed "You had to cut corners, that was all. Pull—relationship—wealthy marriages" (229). And if you don't inherit these advantages, as Macy's nephew has done, you have to do whatever is necessary to achieve the leverage (as in money) they make possible. Reasoning thus, Dalyrimple embarks on a series of robberies intended to provide the funds hard work promises never to offer. The first of these stick-ups, described in section 3, might be attributed to Dalyrimple's outrage at discovering his fate at Macy's. As he goes on to commit several other robberies, however, it soon becomes apparent that Dalyrimple is consciously acting as a philosophical "rebel" (his own term [233]) who wants to make his own way in life.

Dalyrimple's crimes are treated with wry humor. Although Kuehl objects to sections 4, 6, and 7 as "extraneous" to Fitzgerald's purposes, it is in these sections that Fitzgerald captures both Dalyrimple's ludicrous conduct in pursuing his career in crime and his equally ludicrous self-justifications. In section 4, after his first impulsive hold-up, Dalyrimple comes to feel "morally lonely" (232) and puffs himself up as a new kind of criminal, "not the spiritual rebel, Don Juan; not the philosophical rebel, Faust; but a new psychological rebel of his own century—defying the sentimental a priori forms of his own mind—" (233). Later, in section 6, he returns a set of false teeth he has inadvertently taken during one of his heists, wrapping the teeth in brown paper and printing FALSE TEETH on the package in "clumsy pencil letters" (238). By throwing this package on the lawn of the house he burgled, Dalyrimple stands convicted of a sentimentality remarkably at odds with his rebellious, amoral self-image. And in section 7 Dalyrimple continues to glorify "his emancipation from petty scruples and remorses," but finds that it is a little difficult to sustain the image of himself as a philosophical or psychological rebel. "It was more consoling," he thinks, "to think of every one else as a fool" (239). Dalyrimple's comic rationalizations reach their height here, and it is in this section entirely given over to Dalyrimple's confused thoughts that Fitzgerald most obviously "gently mocks" his young protagonist.[12]

Fitzgerald has often been accused of "agreeing" all too frequently with his shallow characters, but his ironic stance toward Bryan Dalyrimple should not be cited in this connection.[13] When Dalyrimple thinks that "Happiness was what he wanted—a slowly rising scale of gratifications of the normal appetites" (233), we are no doubt intended to sympathize with him. But when he goes on to suppose that "the materials, if not the inspiration of happiness, could be bought with money" (233), we should feel toward Dalyrimple roughly as we will later feel toward James Gatz. That is, we should understand why he feels as he does but note as well the disastrous simplicity of the equation worked out here. That Fitzgerald himself remarks the irony is implicit throughout the story, but especially in the allusion to Shakespeare that follows Dalyrimple's reflections by one page. Here Dalyrimple prepares for one of his robberies, while "in the air lay a faint suggestion of acerbity, inspirational rather than chilling" (233). Dalyrimple finds himself thinking of a line "which an early memory had endowed with a hushed, awesome beauty": "The moon is down—I have not heard the clock!" (234). Unbeknownst to Dalyrimple, the reference is to *Macbeth*, 1.7.2, where Banquo and his son Fleance (who speaks the line) move through the night with a torch and are encountered by their "friend," the noble Macbeth. The allusion relates Dalyrimple to the

12. Kuehl, *Fitzgerald: Study of the Short Fiction*, 28; Ruth Prigozy, " 'Dalyrimple Goes Wrong,' " 24.
13. Mizener, *Far Side*, 117.

greatest of all philosophical rebels and rationalizers, the Macbeth who comes to find that not all the "reasons" for his crimes can do away with his own inner sense of guilt. Dalyrimple succeeds in his own effort to excuse his actions because he is shallower than Macbeth. Indeed, the implicit comparison is so incongruous as to cast a thickly ironic, even comic light on the whole story.

Bryan Dalyrimple's Zarathustrian rationalizations may be the stuff of comedy, but Fitzgerald's handling of the other characters—Macy, Charley Moore, the cave-dwellers—compels us to sympathize with Dalyrimple even as we note his adolescent response to the all-too-normal frustrations of daily life (so intractable to the instinctive solutions Dalyrimple found at hand during combat). Our sympathy is surely tested, however, by what Kuehl calls "the O. Henry surprise ending." Here, as Prigozy notes, Dalyrimple is rewarded for abandoning morality, as Macy and one of his business/political friends, Alfred J. Fraser, decide to put Dalyrimple into the state senate.[14] The ironies are numerous here, for Fraser and Macy have mistaken Dalyrimple's cover as a compliant employee (his role by day) as acceptance of the system they represent— exactly what Dalyrimple's robberies are meant to reject. Dalyrimple is praised for "sticking" to his onerous first job when in fact he has rebelled absolutely against the job and everything connected with it. Now he is offered what he wants—money, security, a touch of power—if he will agree to do the older men's bidding. It is essential that he cannot have too many ideas of his own about how things ought to be run (243). In the end all Dalyrimple must do to achieve his goals is give up any pretense to independence.

Dalyrimple supposes that this handsome offer validates his philosophical "position": " . . . so life was this after all—cutting corners— cutting corners—common sense, that was the rule. No more foolish risks now unless necessity called—but it was being hard that counted— Never to let remorse or self-reproach lose him a night's sleep" (243). The reference—unintended on Dalyrimple's part—is again to Macbeth, who found that he could not stifle remorse and lost the ability to sleep

14. Kuehl, *Fitzgerald: Study of the Short Fiction,* 30; Thune and Prigozy, eds., *Short Stories,* 64.

altogether. The immensely more superficial Bryan Dalyrimple takes his good fortune to confirm his views on life when in fact it points up the terrible gap between our merits and our rewards, our attempts to shape life and what life gives us in return. Dalyrimple is not being rewarded for what he has done, but for what he appears to have done (an irony altogether lost unless we reject Petry's view that the older men know about Dalyrimple's robberies).[15] Next time the wheel may well turn, and Dalyrimple will discover that those who depend on the value of appearances are defenseless against the logic of randomness embodied in their acknowledged or unacknowledged "philosophy."

"Dalyrimple Goes Wrong" is Fitzgerald's earliest ironic treatment of the Horatio Alger success story, as Matthew J. Bruccoli has remarked, and it seems to me a treatment that very much confirms Petry's view that *Flappers and Philosophers* is "a serious and even disturbing book" beneath its froth and comedy. Fitzgerald himself seems to have agreed, for "Dalyrimple Goes Wrong" is one of the four stories from *Flappers and Philosophers* he recommended to H. L. Mencken as "worth reading." (The others were "The Ice Palace," "The Cut-Glass Bowl," and "Benediction."[16]) The moral confusion we see in the story's protagonist does not really bear comparison with that of Gatsby or of Dick Diver, but it is the occasion for an amusing and somewhat disturbing story we would do well to retain in the active Fitzgerald canon.

15. Petry, *Fitzgerald's Craft*, 42.

16. Matthew J. Bruccoli, *Some Sort of Epic Grandeur: The Life of F. Scott Fitzgerald*, 106; Petry, *Fitzgerald's Craft*, 51. Bruccoli somewhat dismisses Fitzgerald's praise for "Dalyrimple Goes Wrong" and "Benediction" because Fitzgerald was writing to Mencken, the first publisher of these two stories (147–48). Bruccoli may be right, of course, but I would like to think Fitzgerald did value this story beyond the many stories he dismissed as "trash" and worse.

THE GRACE OF "BENEDICTION"

EDWARD GILLIN

When F. Scott Fitzgerald mailed a copy of *Flappers and Philosophers* to H. L. Mencken, the young author inscribed his first short story collection with a warning. Deprecating the bulk of the selections as "trash" or merely "amusing," Fitzgerald acknowledged just four to be "worth reading": "The Ice Palace," "The Cut-Glass Bowl," "Benediction," and "Dalyrimple Goes Wrong." Matthew J. Bruccoli judges that the latter two stories were so designated simply to flatter Mencken's critical judgment, since his *Smart Set* had previously published both ("Benediction" made its first appearance in the magazine's February 1920 issue). Another distinguished critic, Robert Sklar, contends with equal skepticism that the cynical endings of these pieces are all that recommend them. Bruccoli in 1989, like Malcolm Cowley in 1951 and the *Bodley Head* editors in the 1960s, chose to leave "Benediction" out of volumes meant to collect Fitzgerald's finest short story work.[1]

1. Matthew J. Bruccoli and Margaret M. Duggan, eds., *Correspondence of F. Scott Fitzgerald*, 68; Matthew J. Bruccoli, *Some Sort of Epic Grandeur: The Life of F. Scott Fitzgerald*, 147; Robert Sklar, *F. Scott Fitzgerald: The Last Laocoön*, 64. Both "Benediction" and its earlier version, "The Ordeal," have been omitted from Matthew J. Bruccoli, ed., *The Short Stories of F. Scott Fitzgerald: A New Collection*, from F. Scott Fitzgerald, *The Stories of F. Scott Fitzgerald: A Selection of 28 Stories*, and from the *Bodley Head* editions of Fitzgerald's short fiction, vols. 5 and 6. "Benediction" was reprinted in several minor anthologies published before 1962; the most notable of these, *"The Smart Set" Anthology*, ed. Burton

Yet in 1935 when Fitzgerald, obviously intent on preserving his literary reputation, lobbied the English firm of Chatto and Windus to
publish an anthology of his best short fiction, he urged the inclusion
of "Benediction."[2] Fitzgerald could be an acute self-critic. In fact, he
designated among his twenty-one selections virtually every piece that
has found critical acclaim over time, from "May Day" (1920) and
"The Diamond as Big as the Ritz" (1922) to "Crazy Sunday" (1932)
and "Babylon Revisited" (1931). Thus his inclusion of "Benediction"
among the stories he placed highest value upon offers an interesting
challenge to scholarly readers who have generally resisted the author's
own estimation.

Most contemporary reviewers of *Flappers and Philosophers* who mentioned "Benediction" favored it with bland comments. On this level there
was significant disagreement only about the degree of sentimentality
in the story: Whereas the *San Francisco Chronicle* of January 23, 1921,
praised the piece's avoidance of sentimentality and moralism, *The Nation*
on September 18, 1920, implied that it was "falsely effective" by precisely
such standards. At least three 1920 reviews—the September 26 *New
York Times Book Review and Magazine,* the November 6 *Boston Evening
Transcript,* and December's *The Smart Set*—labeled "Benediction" the
best piece in the collection. Of these, the *Transcript* review, generally
negative about the archness of *Flappers and Philosophers,* complained
that the "masterly" workmanship of "Benediction" was spoiled by an
unfortunate ending. Mencken, who reviewed for *The Smart Set,* was
also unimpressed by the collection as a whole but praised "Benediction"
as a well-written exception. Making the characteristic, if undocumented,
charge that "Benediction" had brought down the "maledictions of the
Jesuits" when it first appeared in his own magazine, he still saw "no
reason why any intelligent Catholic should object to it in the slightest."

Rascoe and Groff Conklin, appended a note describing the piece as a "delicately beautiful
story" written when Fitzgerald "first became master of his brilliant gifts" (68). None of the
anthologies featuring "Benediction" is still in print; for further information on these titles
consult Matthew J. Bruccoli's *F. Scott Fitzgerald: A Descriptive Bibliography* and its two
supplements, *Supplement to "F. Scott Fitzgerald: A Descriptive Bibliography,"* and *F. Scott
Fitzgerald: A Descriptive Bibliography,* rev. ed.
    2. Bruccoli and Duggan, eds., *Correspondence,* 401.

Like Mencken, the *New York Times Book Review* correspondent found a degree of "real feeling" in "Benediction": "Here, it seems, Mr. Fitzgerald has most finely fused the best of the Russian school which he irradiates, with the O. Henry tinge which may be observed in almost all his stories."[3]

This remark by an anonymous reviewer possibly represents the high point of the story's critical reputation over the years. Relatively ignored by the anthologists, "Benediction" has been largely neglected by Fitzgerald scholars as well. Perhaps this has been a kindness after all, since several references to the piece are less than fortunate. Sergio Perosa praises the "sense of traditional value" when the story's heroine in the end refuses a hasty marriage—a clear misinterpretation of fictional events. Sklar mentions the piece in his critical study of the author in order to proclaim the uncanny coincidence of Fitzgerald's naming its flapper heroine "Lois Moran," because that was the name of the young actress the author met and became romantically linked with seven years after the publication of "Benediction." Since Fitzgerald does *not* in fact assign a surname to the "Lois" of his story, Sklar's insistence on this point is baffling.

Even unintentional references to "Benediction" can cause confusion. Henry Dan Piper dismisses the weak cleverness of Fitzgerald's undergraduate writing with a mention of the "tricky surprise ending" that spoils "The Ordeal," which appeared in the *Nassau Literary Magazine* in June 1915. Yet this tale of a young seminarian's struggle to overcome the allure of the world before taking his first vows features a straightforward enough ending. Years after writing "The Ordeal," however, Fitzgerald substantially rewrote this undergraduate piece into the story published in 1920 as "Benediction." In revising his *Nassau Literary Magazine* version Fitzgerald changed the unnamed protagonist facing preliminary vows in "The Ordeal" to "Kieth" [*sic*], a 36-year-old seminarian who has completed seventeen of the eighteen years' rigorous preparation toward ordination as a Jesuit priest. In "Benediction," Kieth's situation becomes dramatically subordinate to a frame story involving his nineteen-year-old

---

3. The reviews mentioned in this paragraph have been compiled in Jackson R. Bryer, ed., *F. Scott Fitzgerald: The Critical Reception,* 34–58.

sister, Lois, who is involved in a troubled relationship with a man named
Howard. Lois makes a key decision—arguably "tricky" or "surprising"—
at the end of "Benediction" when she decides to go ahead with her love
affair. Surely this development in the conclusion of the story written five
years *later* is what Piper had in mind when he criticized an immature
cleverness in the ending of "The Ordeal."[4]

Both John Kuehl and Kenneth Eble stress the revisions from "The Ordeal" to "Benediction" in concluding that Fitzgerald's religious sensibility
had radically fallen off between 1915 and 1919. This same aspect draws
the attention of Joan M. Allen, who offers a carefully weighed criticism of
"The Ordeal" and the portion of "Benediction" that bears most strongly
on the earlier story. Allen finds that the seminarian's situation mirrors
Fitzgerald's own sense of an important conflict: between a material world
that satisfied great emotional needs and a world of spirit that beckoned
to the instinct toward transcendence. Accepting Kieth as a thinly fictionalized version of Thomas Delihant, the Jesuit cousin Fitzgerald greatly
admired, Allen simply views the frame story as contrast—Lois's worldly
affairs establish her rejection of "palpable values of the pious Catholic
life at the monastery."[5]

Other critics who carefully examine "Benediction" include their readings in book-length studies of Fitzgerald's short fiction. John A. Higgins
remarks that "Benediction" may have weakened effects achieved earlier
in "The Ordeal." But considering his statement that "Benediction" was
its author's "best story so far," Higgins's vaguely contradictory points
lack substance or clarity. Like Allen, Higgins views the fiction almost
entirely in terms of the inner narrative concerning Kieth's experiences.
Alice Hall Petry is far less willing to relegate Lois's role in the fiction
to mere background. Petry brings the first full attention to "Benediction"'s frame, analyzing it as part of a sophisticated and fully unified
plot structure. This analysis is sympathetic to Lois, who is viewed as a
young woman in need of spiritual guidance. Petry is correspondingly

4. Sergio Perosa, *The Art of F. Scott Fitzgerald,* 30–31; Sklar, *Fitzgerald: Last Laocoön,* 65,
228; Henry Dan Piper, *F. Scott Fitzgerald: A Critical Portrait,* 28.
5. John Kuehl, ed., *The Apprentice Fiction of F. Scott Fitzgerald: 1909–1917,* 78–81;
Kenneth Eble, *F. Scott Fitzgerald,* 58; Joan M. Allen, *Candles and Carnival Lights: The
Catholic Sensibility of F. Scott Fitzgerald,* 43–45.

harsh toward Kieth, who is regarded as an ineffectual counselor and an ineffectual human being who has escaped the real world by hiding behind the cloistered walls of a spiritually sterile church. This perspective is not entirely new; in a 1984 biography of F. Scott and Zelda Fitzgerald, James Mellow fleetingly describes "Benediction" as a story where a male protagonist clings to his faith while a "more venturesome woman opts for life and the uncertainties of the future." More recently, Bryant Mangum, who praises "Benediction" as "both serious and good," has described the story's conflict as a tension between Christian living and worldly life; Mangum sees Lois's ultimate repudiation of her brother's monastic piety as the ironic triumph of material values in a story thematically suited to its *Smart Set* audience.[6] But because Petry's analysis is an elaborate and thoughtful treatment on this theme and features what may be considered a typical reading of the story's frame, her criticism will be cited as a point of reference in subsequent remarks.

At the opening of "Benediction," in the sticky heat of a Baltimore train station, young Lois studies a message from her lover:

"Darling": *it began*—"I understand and I'm happier than life ever meant me to be. If I could give you the things you've always been in tune with—but I can't, Lois; we can't marry and we can't lose each other and let all this glorious love end in nothing.

"Until your letter came, dear, I'd been sitting here in the half dark thinking and thinking where I could go and ever forget you; abroad, perhaps, to drift through Italy or Spain and dream away the pain of having lost you where the crumbling ruins of older, mellower civilizations would mirror only the desolation of my heart—and then your letter came.

"Sweetest, bravest girl, if you'll wire me I'll meet you in Wilmington— till then I'll be here just waiting and hoping for every long dream of you to come true.

"Howard"[7]

---

6. John A. Higgins, *F. Scott Fitzgerald: A Study of the Stories,* 17–18; Alice Hall Petry, *Fitzgerald's Craft of Short Fiction: The Collected Stories—1920–1935,* 29–39; James R. Mellow, *Invented Lives: F. Scott and Zelda Fitzgerald,* 38; Bryant Mangum, *A Fortune Yet: Money in the Art of F. Scott Fitzgerald's Short Stories,* 26, 35.

7. F. Scott Fitzgerald, *Flappers and Philosophers,* 141. All subsequent page references to "Benediction" are to the 1959 edition and will appear parenthetically in the text.

In this letter, memorized after so many readings, Lois finds reflections of its author: "the mingled sweetness and sadness in his dark eyes, the furtive, restless excitement she felt sometimes when he talked to her, his dreamy sensuousness . . ." (141). The fond recollections are enough momentarily to break down the "cowardice" that's been holding Lois back. She will "never be sorry," she vows, if she simply allows fate to take its course. So she sends off a telegraphed reply:

> "Arrived Baltimore today spend day with my brother meet me Wilmington three P.M. Wednesday Love
>
> "Lois."

But her internal refrain "And never be sorry . . . and never be sorry" (142) suggests the unease haunting her impulsive decision.

Since the earliest reviews of *Flappers and Philosophers,* critics have insinuated that this exchange is not merely about a rendezvous but also about sexual sin. The presumption undoubtedly arises from the effort to juxtapose the frame narrative with the moralism apparent in the Kieth material. While this inclination makes sense in terms of a writer who freely professed to being a "moralist at heart," one difficulty lies in the assumption that Fitzgerald's morality was of an entirely conventional sort. Furthermore, the Catholic subject matter of "Benediction" requires a sensitivity to Fitzgerald's religious tradition. Petry's reading of a rather liberated Lois demands less a Catholic than a downright puritanical explication of certain events in the story. Her analysis suggests Lois must be read as a virgin who "has in effect decided to exchange her virtue for fifty-four cents," the money being the cost of her telegraphed reply. To sustain this point Petry indulges a Puritan's penchant for reading signs: She interprets the statement that "Lois was nineteen and very romantic and curious and courageous" (141) as "the story's euphemism for agreeing to sleep with Howard."[8] Indeed, almost every critic describing the ending of "Benediction" (including Allen, Mangum, and Higgins) has believed with Petry that, for better or worse, Lois's final decision to keep

---

8. Andrew Turnbull, ed., *The Letters of F. Scott Fitzgerald,* 63; Petry, *Fitzgerald's Craft,* 31, 39.

her tryst with Howard constitutes her willful repudiation of conventional religious proscriptions against extramarital sex.

Several factors militate against such a reading. Young men rendezvous with young women in several of the stories in *Flappers and Philosophers,* of course, without unsavory suggestions; the exuberant celebration of youthful love seems the whole point of a piece such as "The Offshore Pirate." Howard's "we can't marry" may, at first glance, appear to be a willful declaration. This positions him as a debonair playboy or a married man (the logical development of a "sin" plot in which he would represent the temptation to evil). But the actual plot belies such suggestions. At a critical moment of the story, with no edge of irony implied, Lois likens Kieth's much admired "sweetness"—an inner strength—to Howard's similar qualities. Howard's romantic melancholy tempts him to wander foreign lands to "dream away the pain" if he loses Lois. Hardly the reaction of a rake—or something a married man might easily manage—the pathetic journey envisioned accords with the response that other Fitzgerald heroes (such as Jay Gatsby) will consider apt when faced with losing their golden girls.

Petry sentimentalizes Lois as a child left alone since age two with a sickly mother while, for seventeen long years, older brother Kieth has been "hiding out in the priesthood."[9] Again, the text resists such a reading. The fourteen years since Lois last saw her brother have been spent traveling back and forth to Europe in company with her apparently healthy and wealthy mother, and Lois enjoys the social status that ensures that her exploits as a brilliant debutante appear regularly in the papers. "I know what a gay time you've been having," Kieth says (145), and this matter-of-fact remark is certainly not challenged by his sister. Indeed, when the seminarian credits Lois with having endured hardship lately on account of their mother's most recent "nervous" troubles, the nineteen-year-old privately reflects on how little she has actually done; she can offer only the lame protest, "Youth shouldn't be sacrificed to age" (146).

This self-centered observation, which Kieth neatly turns aside by a sympathetic remark, stands near the thematic center of "Benediction."

9. Petry, *Fitzgerald's Craft,* 33.

The contrasting truth of Kieth's situation is clear to his sister and ought to be clear to the reader. It is Kieth, of course, who has given up great prospects of worldly success. In "The Ordeal," Fitzgerald melodramatized this kind of decision. The young seminarian hero of that tale—seemingly destined for careers in law or diplomacy, for a lifetime of travel and pleasure—devastated father, mother, and relatives with news of his intention to become a Jesuit: "They told him he was ruining a promising young life because of a sentimental notion of self sacrifice, a boyish dream."[10] In "Benediction," Fitzgerald details no such flashback; instead the family disturbances of "The Ordeal" are now skillfully implied by a Hemingway-like concentration of selected detail. The long sojourns in Europe, the dim snapshot memory Lois retains of Kieth, the stark fact that sister has not bothered to visit brother for fourteen years, even though mother "comes down" at rare intervals—all imply a proud family's abandonment of their willful and materially unsuccessful son. Such abandonment is quietly yet unmistakably conveyed through Lois's wary aversion to the *"common"* element of life—the element Kieth has chosen (146; emphasis Fitzgerald's).

But though Kieth is, in so many ways, Lois's counterpart ("we're rather sensitive, you and I, to things like this," he says [146]), the seminarian has somehow managed to rise above a fear of life's all-too-human coarseness. Shyly he describes the call to a religious life that stunned himself not least of all one ordinary day on a crowded Pullman car (147). Petry misjudges the mundane quality of this experience, together with a reference to the sweating bodies of ball-playing seminarians, as evidence of a kind of worldly contamination that has infected life at the "holy and cloistered" monastery.[11] But Fitzgerald, like the more orthodox Flannery O'Connor, simply demonstrates an awareness of the dual nature of humanity stressed in the Roman Catholic tradition. In youth, both writers doubtlessly received instruction from catechisms that defined man as a creature of body and soul, made in the image of God. Their church condemned Gnosticism because that heresy denied the significance of physical nature; the Gnostics were thereby charged with

10. Kuehl, ed., *Apprentice Fiction*, 82.
11. Petry, *Fitzgerald's Craft*, 32–33.

misrepresenting the truth about humanity as well as the true nature of Christianity's founder.

One legacy from this tradition for the Catholic writer is an almost unavoidable irony that arises from detecting the distance between human potential and the imperfections of mortality. O'Connor played this irony in a major key. (Ruefully she was to discover among her fiercest critics many fellow Christians, disturbed by the "ugliness" of her fictional vision, who construed her anti-Gnosticism as spiritually degrading.) Fitzgerald plays the same irony in a minor key in "Benediction," where, from the outset, descriptions of the setting lurch from spiritualized natural beauty to material vulgarity ("Trees like tall, languid ladies with feather fans coquetting airily over the ugly roof of the monastery" [142]). The result may not be the perfect "holy" atmosphere for an uncompromising idealist; then again, the story's narrator reminds us quite early that the Society of Jesus had been founded "by a tough-minded soldier who trained men to hold a breach or a salon, preach a sermon or write a treaty, and do it and not argue" (143). This pronouncement on Ignatius Loyola's Jesuits again reveals no hint of disdain. In fact it accords neatly with the spirit of Amory Blaine, protagonist of Fitzgerald's soon-to-be-published first novel, whose growing skepticism about the Church of Rome remains edged with respect for this "traditionary bulwark against the decay of morals."[12] Perhaps not coincidentally, Amory's story climaxes with a "supercilious sacrifice," a gesture of self-surrender that he knows will go unappreciated by the oblivious souls around him. Failing to find love when ambitious Rosalind Connage throws him over for better financial security with a wealthier suitor, Amory learns a crucial ingredient to the greatest love—the ability to surrender oneself completely for another's sake.

This particular form of negative capability marks Fitzgerald's two seminary stories as well. They are studies of self-effacement and utter renunciation of worldly interests in the face of an irresistible calling. It is probably not irrelevant that one of the author's closest Princeton friends vividly recalled Fitzgerald bursting into his room one day in the spring of 1915 aglow with enthusiasm about Francis Thompson's "The Hound

12. F. Scott Fitzgerald, *This Side of Paradise*, 281.

of Heaven," since the composition of "The Ordeal" coincides with this period of excitement over the Catholic poet's famed work. Strikingly, the disagreeable self-denials necessitated by the call to religious vocation in "The Ordeal" and in "Benediction" correspond to circumstances of the persona in the Thompson poem who resists the relentless pursuit of a loving God: "Yet was I sore adread / Lest, having Him, I must have naught beside."[13]

Realizing that cooperating with the call of such divine love—which the world easily takes as a retreat or surrender—has cost Kieth many "fine chances" in life, Lois can only exclaim at the paradox she has uncovered. "Sweetness is hard," she notes suddenly (148). Furthermore, she is able to connect this kind of unselfish devotion with her sweet-hard sweetheart Howard, a man who has surrendered to her in a manner she cannot yet reciprocate. And to determine just where the spiritual and the sacrificial love exemplified in Kieth overlap with the more worldly romantic love of Howard, we must pause to consider more closely the biographical circumstances of F. Scott Fitzgerald at the time he was composing "Benediction." These circumstances represent, as we shall see, the most obvious challenge to a "sin" interpretation of the theme.

The story was written during the early autumn of 1919. Since late spring that year the author's glittering love affair with Zelda Sayre had fallen into shambles. Uncertain of Fitzgerald's financial ability to support a lifestyle suited to her needs, Zelda (with prodding from a "nervous" Mrs. Sayre, who considered young Scott Fitzgerald a poor candidate for her daughter's hand) had broken off their brief engagement. A despondent Fitzgerald retreated to St. Paul to work on the manuscript of his first book, which he undoubtedly viewed at least in part as a means of resecuring the wayward affection and esteem of his ex-fiancée. When *This Side of Paradise* was accepted for publication, the possibility became more substantial. "Benediction" was written around September–October 1919, precisely during the delicate period of reestablishing ties with Zelda, who might yet be convinced to overcome the doubts that had led to her earlier rebuff.

13. Andrew Turnbull, *Scott Fitzgerald,* 58; Francis Thompson, *Complete Poems of Francis Thompson,* 88.

Circumstantial evidence strengthens the connection between the story and autobiography, at any rate. Aside from the straitened finances linking the author to his fictional counterpart Howard, the story's geography is reminiscent of the Fitzgerald courtship. Lois presumably lives south of the Mason-Dixon line, stopping off in Baltimore as she does en route to Wilmington, Delaware. Meanwhile, Ivy League–educated Howard may be heading down to Wilmington from New York City; this was where Scott Fitzgerald resided in the frantic period of attempting to make money before his engagement was broken off. Zelda characteristically chose the adjective "nervous" to describe the qualms she and Mrs. Sayre felt about the engagement to Scott; this is also the word used to describe the disorder Lois's tiresome mother suffers from in the story.

The formula of Howard's telegram, with its salutatory endearment "Darling," is identical to the formula of several existent telegrams from Fitzgerald during the crisis period of his premarital relationship with Zelda. Interestingly, one of these telegrams (dated February 22, 1919) contains fifty-one words, the other (dated one month later) contains forty-nine. Did some teasing exchange about its author's heedless disregard for Western Union's strict fifty-word rate schedule get written into the opening line of "Benediction," where a scrupulous clerk scans a woman's message "to determine whether it contained the innocuous forty-nine words or the fatal fifty-one" (141)? Even if not, there are certainly enough parallels of situation to return to Howard's fictional telegram suspecting that his three words "we can't marry" are *not* a declaration of intent so much as an admission of defeat. "If I could give you the things you've always been in tune with . . . ," Howard mourns, almost as if in response to the Zelda Sayre who had admonished her struggling real-life admirer, "I'd just hate to live a sordid, colorless existence because you'd soon love me less—and less."[14]

Certainly the arduous task of winning Zelda's hand and the mixed emotional legacy of this love affair would be the central experience inspiring Fitzgerald's literary career. In many ways the need to become perfectly committed to a value outside oneself—to an institution or a concept or, most often, a person—is a theme sustaining his fiction from

14. Bruccoli and Duggan, eds., *Correspondence*, 38; Turnbull, *Scott Fitzgerald*, 92–93.

This Side of Paradise to *The Last Tycoon*. It isn't difficult in retrospect
to view "Benediction"—reworked from the undergraduate piece about
seminarian life largely through the superimposition of a plot involving
the dilemma of young lovers—as one of the earliest of these works. With
such a view in mind, readers may even see how the short story anticipates
Tender Is the Night. In "Benediction" the middle-aged protagonist's
devotion to a higher professional calling is simply juxtaposed against
a plot about the demands of love; in the novel the dual commitments
and the theme of sacrifice will be blended to great effect in Dick
Diver's dilemma. Aptly enough, the protagonist of *Tender Is the Night* is
conceived in Fitzgerald's working notes as a "spoiled priest," and complex
religious symbolism pervades Dick Diver's story.[15]

In any event—as no previous critic has sufficiently noted—the threatened romance in the frame story of "Benediction" has an absolute bearing on the climactic chapel scene of the inner narrative. Lois is slightly
uneasy about attending benediction services at the seminary; "Mass is
the limit of my religious exertions," she says (153). This confession has
two qualities, as Fitzgerald undoubtedly realized. On the one hand, it
presents Lois as a self-conscious if not altogether ardent Catholic. She
is suitably familiar with the *minimum* liturgical obligation of her faith:
attendance at weekly mass. The ritual she is "not much used to" (153),
on the other hand, is voluntary rather than mandatory. Benediction is a
service of worship in the sheerest theological sense. During the ritual the
consecrated host is exposed in a monstrance for the direct adoration of
the congregation. The hymns of the service ("O Salutaris Hostia") and
the compelling litany of the Divine Praises ("Blessed Be God; Blessed
Be His Holy Name . . .") function to evoke the utter transcendence
of God, the complete abnegation of worshippers before the body of
Christ.

It is abnegation of any sort, religious or otherwise, that self-reliant
Lois is "not much used to," of course. Not surprisingly, the praying
seminarians around her of a sudden seem cold, "unnatural," even dead
(151). In a gesture befitting her desperate effort to preserve the hard
borders of a cherished individualism, Lois "drew her arms in close to

---

15. Arthur Mizener, *The Far Side of Paradise: A Biography of F. Scott Fitzgerald*, 307.

her side, away from Kieth and Jarvis" (152). Only at a climatic moment of mystical dread—significantly just as she is about to lose consciousness— does she cry out for her brother. When she does, she finds some release from the iron prison of self: "But though a warm peace was filling her mind and heart she felt oddly broken and chastened, as if some one had held her stripped soul up and laughed" (153). This sensation, with all its humbling side effects, represents what Flannery O'Connor would surely have recognized as a moment of grace.

From the first moment of consideration in Lois's mind, Kieth the seminarian has represented a person who "had already made a momentous decision about his life" (143). Moments before the chapel visit this startlingly impressive brother had discussed the nature of his choice, with its element of "giving up fine chances outside": " 'Here in this old monkery, Lois' he continued with a smile, 'they try to get all that self-pity and pride in our own wills out of us right at the first. They put us to scrubbing floors—and other things. It's like that idea of saving your life by losing it' " (149).

If one can save one's life by losing it, Zelda Sayre had recently strengthened F. Scott Fitzgerald's conviction that one could lose one's life by saving it. In "Benediction" the author reified some of the issues involved in his own experience. Plucky, willful, and sure of herself, fictional nineteen-year-old Lois (like the actual nineteen-year-old Zelda Sayre at the time) holds back from momentous decisions about her romantic future because her lover may be unable to provide enough "things" calculated to ensure marital success. In what might otherwise be dismissed as cloying sentimentalism, Kieth, who is largely uninformed concerning Lois's relationship with Howard, nevertheless diagnoses the problem threatening her "little white soul." He views it not in terms of sexual temptation but in terms of her need to grow outside herself: "that white innocence of yours changing to a flame and burning to give light to other weaker souls" (155). The line artfully sustains the imagery of the benediction altar scene. There, evil had seemingly inhabited a pure white candle, until it was overcome by the red light emanating from the stained glass figure of Francis Xavier (152), another Jesuit figure who had surrendered himself unquestioningly for the love of God. Poignantly if somewhat pedestrianly, Kieth hopes that the love-inspiring Lois can herself be moved to surrender to carnal love: "and then I wanted some day to take your children on my knee and hear them call the crabbed old monk Uncle Kieth. . . . I wanted the letters you'd write me and the place I'd have at your table" (155).

Sentimental or not, the passage conveys inescapably earnest feeling. Indeed, the strong emotion that pervades "Benediction" suggests Fitzgerald's continued susceptibility to religious inspiration. While it is true that Fitzgerald had left off the outward practice of Roman Catholicism by the time of his marriage in 1920, "Benediction" presents convincing evidence that the spiritual consciousness engendered by his religious training remained an active intellectual force. For a while he had even hesitated to market the story because of its orthodoxy (" 'Benediction' sounds too much like Catholic propaganda so I guess I'll have to let it go by the boards," he wrote the editor of *Scribner's Magazine*). Fitzgerald felt genuinely aggrieved that his story had received a "most terrible lashing from the American Catholic intelligentsia"; he wrote Irish novelist Shane Leslie that "Benediction" had received the "imprimatur" of the most intelligent priest he knew, Father Joseph Barron, and represented an effort to treat their church as a "living issue."[16]

In any event, Kieth's faith in his sister's capacity for love is almost enough to overcome the doubts that have Lois clinging to selfishness— and almost not. The brief final section of "Benediction" returns to the frame story of the lovers, and we find that Lois is wavering still. Ultimately she will keep her Wilmington appointment with the devoted Howard, but only after she tears up a roughly phrased note "in the way of a permanent goodbye" (156). Although this aborted telegram is routinely viewed as evidence of momentary "virtue" that crumbles before Lois's submission to compulsions of lust in a cynical ending, no critic has satisfactorily demonstrated why a "virtuous" Lois need be harsh or cruel to the lover previously described as possessing qualities akin to Kieth's exquisite "sweetness." It does make sense, on the other hand, that the brush-off telegram should be hard and uncompromising if it is meant to represent a last gesture of defiance and an unwillingness to submit even to the most lovingly ardent pressure. The almost-sent message reveals the independence and self-assertiveness that survive in

16. Bruccoli and Duggan, eds., *Correspondence*, 46; Turnbull, ed., *Letters*, 378.

this young woman, and shows how narrowly the cause of true love may be winning. In the fall of 1919, wondering how the Zelda Sayre affair would ultimately resolve itself, Fitzgerald could not refrain from dramatizing the precariousness of even the most happy ending his imagination could conceive.

FITZGERALD'S CHRISTMAS CAROL, OR THE BURDEN OF "THE CAMEL'S BACK"

ALAN CHEUSE

Writing only seems difficult to other writers, Thomas Mann once remarked. In the case of F. Scott Fitzgerald, in some of his stories at least, the writer seems to have produced such wonderful fiction in such effortless fashion that even practitioners of the art have to bow their heads in amazement at just how simple he makes it appear.

That's the effect that his story "The Camel's Back" had on a young student of literature at Rutgers—yours truly—some thirty-five years ago, and that's the effect this story has had on me after a recent rereading. Here is true genius, which makes such wonders come with such a little stirring of the pot. The history of the story's composition pictures a junior whirlwind at work. Just after Christmas of 1919, Fitzgerald moved to New Orleans in order to avoid the worst of the Minnesota winter. By the third week in January he was installed in a room on Prytania Street where at eight one morning he sat down and began to compose this story that he completed, as he told Maxwell Perkins, by seven in the evening. He recopied the manuscript in the middle of the night and mailed it early the next day to his agent Harold Ober who sold it immediately to the *Saturday Evening Post*. It was published in the issue of April 24, 1920. The five hundred dollars that Fitzgerald was paid for the tale he used to buy a six-hundred-dollar platinum-and-diamond wristwatch for Zelda.[1]

---

1. Matthew J. Bruccoli, *Some Sort of Epic Grandeur: The Life of F. Scott Fitzgerald,* 113.

What writer wouldn't have marveled at his own ease of concentration and success at production? The story was then selected for that year's *0. Henry Prize Stories* series and appeared in *Tales of the Jazz Age* in 1922. It was republished in England in *Borrowed Time* and in *Six Tales of the Jazz Age and Other Stories,* which in its paperback edition is now in its fourteenth printing.

"The Camel's Back" is a holiday story, the tale of a successful young fellow from Toledo named Perry Parkhurst who, at Christmas 1919, sues unsuccessfully for the hand of Betty Medill and, when refused, goes off on a drunk. In his altered state, he shows up at a swanky costume party dressed as the front part of a camel—with a cabdriver in the rear—and by a series of seeming misadventures finds himself in a supposedly mock marriage ceremony with the same Betty Medill. Some critics, possibly as the result of class bias, have dismissed the story because of its material. K. G. W. Cross offers only a slighting reference to the tale as one that "reveals, if nothing else, the indulgence with which he regarded the pranks of the very rich." Where praise comes forth, it seems slightly misdirected, as when John A. Higgins labels the story "good farce, although it fails to reach the level of superior farce because it does not, as superior farces do, show the fundamental folly of human nature." Milton Hindus makes only a passing reference to the story as one of Fitzgerald's "humorous anecdotes" that "makes no pretense to 'deep' meanings or satiric overtones of an intellectual kind," though he adds—here's the praise—that the story "seems as assured of permanence as any of the more self-consciously 'serious' literary efforts of our time because it will cause hilarity in this or any century."[2]

The label of farce comes up again in a brief reference to the story by Sergio Perosa. Henry Dan Piper refers to it only as "a smooth little comedy," while Robert Sklar echoes Cross's charge that the story is a mean-spirited slur against "social inferiors," by which they mean the cabdriver who brings up the rear of the camel. Only Alice Hall Petry, the most recent of Fitzgerald's critics to write about the story, takes "The Camel's Back" seriously enough to spend at least several paragraphs

2. K. G. W. Cross, *F. Scott Fitzgerald,* 42; John A. Higgins, *F. Scott Fitzgerald: A Study of the Stories,* 24; Milton Hindus, *F. Scott Fitzgerald: An Introduction and Interpretation,* 106.

looking at the relation between the form—farce or fantasy, she calls it—and the subject of personal and social disillusionment that she sees as played out in Perry Parkhurst's dive into alcohol after his initial rejection by the object of his marital suit.[3]

If any of these readings in passing holds any truth for me, it is Hindus's assertion that the story seems assured of some kind of permanence. It held up for me more than thirty years ago, and it remains, in my view, a marvelous holiday fable—a winter's tale, if you will—not because of its bitterness and rue, but for reasons quite opposite. With its plot out of the tradition of new comedy—that of the disguised lover who turns his love suit around in the midst of dark confusion—it sounds the tune of "all's well that ends well" with a particular comic twist, since it is the cabdriver who brings up the rear of the camel.

So it is an old story that Fitzgerald puts up here in twentieth-century dress, a festival tale, a sequence of white romance, a story about change and transformation from one stage of life to another. Speaking of the champagne that he supplies to Parkhurst when Perry comes to him after being rejected by Betty and is ready to drink himself into another state, an acquaintance of Parkhurst's, "a bad man named Bailey, who had big teeth . . . and had never been in love," says, "This is the stuff that proves the world is more than six thousand years old. It's so ancient that the cork is petrified."[4] Playing the role of wizard in a hotel room, Bailey announces in a playful way the strong medicine that will preside over the rest of Perry's evening—the spirit of the Dionysian ripening of his love and life.

However, it is the fusion of old plots and details of the day that make the story the wonderful, if neglected, work that it is. The opening lines build this double vision directly into the discourse of the narrative:

> The glazed eye of the tired reader resting for a second on the above title will presume it to be merely metaphorical. Stories about the cup and

3. Sergio Perosa, *The Art of F. Scott Fitzgerald,* 31; Henry Dan Piper, *F. Scott Fitzgerald: A Critical Portrait,* 67; Robert Sklar, *F. Scott Fitzgerald: The Last Laocoön,* 67–68; Alice Hall Petry, *Fitzgerald's Craft of Short Fiction: The Collected Stories—1920–1935,* 84–85.

4. F. Scott Fitzgerald, *Six Tales of the Jazz Age and Other Stories,* 36. All subsequent page references to "The Camel's Back" are to this edition and will appear parenthetically in the text.

the lip and the bad penny and the new broom rarely have anything to do with cups or lips or pennies or brooms. This story is the exception. It has to do with a material, visible and large-as-life camel's back. (35)

It is no accident that Fitzgerald uses the traditional address to the reader in order to announce the ironic entrance of a "large-as-life" camel's back rather than the one broken by the proverbial straw. All of the acutely accurate social observation of the holiday social scene among the Toledo rich that follows—the story of Perry Parkhurst's almost misspent but ultimately gloriously successful evening at a circus party during the Christmas of 1919—makes for a large-as-life tale that is also a fable about the trials of romantic love whose airy superstructure is supported by naturalistic stonework.

"Now during the Christmas holidays of 1919," our narrator informs us, "there took place in Toledo, counting only the people with the italicized *the*, forty-one dinner parties, sixteen dances, six luncheons, male and female, twelve teas, four stag dinners, two weddings, and thirteen bridge parties" (35). This active festival calendar moves Perry Parkhurst to propose to Betty Medill, an action that in turn initiates Perry's idea to attend a winter circus party dressed in the front part of the "large-as-life" camel suit. This results in his winning the prize for most original costume, which leads to the mock wedding to the other costume-winner Betty Medill (who wins for her snake charmer's outfit) presided over by the obese black waiter named Jumbo who turns out to be an ordained minister.

Aside from the deft sketching in of characters and the easy management of the mob scene at the circus party (as well as a scene at an earlier party that serves as a kind of curtain raiser to the story's main spectacle), the most striking achievement of "The Camel's Back" remains the fusion of twentieth-century detail and mythic implication. The story opens in the Toledo of the social register, but it soon transcends the quotidian round by means of the introduction of alcohol—the "stone-age champagne" (37)—and enters the realm of inebriated or festival reality. From the inebriation scene in the hotel we follow Perry and a cabdriver to the "dim and ghostly" (40) setting of the costume shop run by the European—for Fitzgerald this apparently suggests some sort of wizardlike, alien stature—Mrs. Nolak.

The costume shop holds numerous portents of change to come—
"glass cases full of crowns and scepters, and jewels and enormous
stomachers, and paints, and crape [*sic*] hair, and wigs of all colors" (40).
When the costume shop owner produces the two-piece camel suit and
Perry tries to wear both sections of it himself, more auguries show forth.
Because of the hind legs of the costume tied "as a girdle around his waist,"
Perry gives the appearance "of one of those mediæval pictures of a monk
changed into a beast by the ministrations of Satan. At the very best the
ensemble resembled a humpbacked cow sitting on her haunches among
blankets" (41). Mrs. Nolak urges Perry to make a decision about the
costume because she wants to close the shop. The cabdriver wanders in
out of the cold and Perry gets the idea to hire the cabbie to wear the hind
part of the camel. Off they go to the party, except that Perry has forgotten
the location. He thinks to ask Mrs. Nolak, since she has stayed open late
in order to service the guests for this masked affair, but when he looks
out the car window at the shop, it has gone dark, and "Mrs. Nolak had
already faded out, a little black smudge far down the snowy street" (44).

So the transition from the mundane to the magical is nearly complete.
Perry, changed by imbibing the ancient drink and, as he arrives at the first
party, donning the camel costume, loses his identity to the beast who,
"as he walked . . . alternately elongated and contracted like a gigantic
concertina" (45). With his appearance, his identity, and, indeed, his
very movement transformed from the everyday into the magical—into
music—Perry moves into the festival round, first at the Tate house where
he mistakenly crashes a debutante party and is seen as a misfit, as a
beast, and then merely as a guest from out of town. He becomes the star
attraction, the young lawyer transformed, as if by the puckish powers of
some hidden god of festival, into a beast with two parts (and his actions
on the dance floor are a parody of Freudian schematics—with the taxi
driver showing at first a will of his own that seems out of synch with
Perry's desires to move in another direction).

The big party itself is a wonderful assembly of heated misrule under
the sign of perpetual change—a sign over the bar that bears the slogan
"Now follow this!"

A great tent fly had been put up inside the ballroom and round the walls
had been built rows of booths representing the various attractions of a

circus side show, but these were now vacated and over the floor swarmed a shouting, laughing medley of youth and color—clowns, bearded ladies, acrobats, bareback riders, ringmasters, tattooed men, and charioteers. (48)

In the midst of this festival, Perry, looking out through his camel's head, spies Betty Medill, who has so recently spurned him, "talking to a comic policeman" (48). Betty is dressed as a snake charmer, which gives the impression, as Fitzgerald tells it, that she is already halfway along toward transformation into another form herself since "Her fair face was stained to a warm olive glow and on her arms and the half moon of her back writhed painted serpents with single eyes of venomous green. Her feet were in sandals and her skirt was slit to the knees, so that when she walked one caught a glimpse of other slim serpents painted just about her bare ankles. Wound about her neck was a glittering cobra" (49).

In this state—which some of the older and more reserved women at the party recognize as "perfectly disgraceful" (49)—Betty is more than halfway ready to find herself matched up once again with Perry who earlier that day had pled his troth to her, complete with marriage license in hand, only to be turned away. But since one of the conventions of comedy, as Prospero announces in *The Tempest*, is that "light winning makes the prize seem light," Perry must still struggle a bit more before ending up with his intended. That struggle comes in the form of the mock wedding in which Perry and Betty, after both winning first place for their costumes, must take front and center.

"Form for the grand wedding march," the costumed ringmaster of the party declares, "the beautiful snake-charmer and the noble camel in front!" (53). Unaware that beneath the camel costume is the same man whom she had rejected earlier in the day, Betty steps up, as does Perry, still bearing with him the very marriage license he had carried to Betty's house some hours before. Music sounds: "The voluptuous chords of the wedding march done in blasphemous syncopation . . . in a delirious blend from the trombones and saxophones" (53). Perry fits right in. Remember that he's already moving like a living concertina. And Betty is halfway there—half serpent, half woman. When Jumbo the black waiter is called on to serve as minister for what everyone has planned to be a mock wedding ceremony, everything has moved into place for the final major movement of the story.

Jumbo—bearer of the name of another beast—produces a Bible and proceeds to officiate, asking the camel for his marriage license. Perry fumbles in his pocket, finds a folded piece of paper (the marriage license), and pushes it out through the camel's mouth. When Jumbo asks for a ring, Perry cadges one from the cabdriver to his rear and, in an action even more bizarre than the way in which he produced the marriage license, pushes the rhinestone "through a tear in the camel's coat" in a mythic variation of vaginal birth and slips the ring on the snake charmer's finger, "muttering ancient and historic words after Jumbo" (55).

At this point in the scene everyone participating in it—except for Jumbo, who knows more than he is saying—believes the event to be merely an empty ritual, a ceremony that is mere decoration rather than a serious moment in the truth of passage from one season to the next, in this case from the dark heart of winter to the possibility of heat and light in spring and summer. With the discovery that the marriage license is authentic and that Jumbo actually possesses the power to perform a marriage ceremony, the illusion flips over into reality, and within moments Betty passes from fury to acceptance. Just as Perry, ready to admit that he has failed miserably in his pursuit of Betty even in the playful form of the ceremony turned real, exits from the party, Betty, all "snakes and silk and tawny hair" (59), avows her love for him. Exit camel accompanied by true love. The transformation is complete. The two parts of the camel, recognizing that their complicity, crossing over social boundaries and a number of difficult obstacles, has won Perry his success in love, exchange "a particularly subtle, esoteric sort of wink that only true camels can understand" (59). The glazed eye of the tired reader that Fitzgerald alluded to in the first line of the story has been transformed as well into the complicity between writer and reader that allows such a "midwinter night's dream," a heated revel at the darkest part of the year, to seem true enough to win our attention and deserve our praise.

Of course none of this would work if it weren't for the meticulous buildup of naturalistic detail and sharply observed social gesture. This is not just any Christmas—this is the Christmas of 1919 through which Fitzgerald had just passed before he left for New Orleans and sat down to write the story. And "The Camel's Back" is not just any sentimental

Christmas story but, rather, a pagan fantasy, the suggestion of the possibility of a new and happy beginning in the middle of what Blake calls in his ode to St. Lucy "the year's deepe midnight" that seems deeply rooted in the peculiar holiday antics of the American midwest upper class. Coming from a twenty-four-year-old writer with a sharp sense of form, a fine eye for detail, and a great heart for comedy appropriate to the season, the story is a rather marvelous gift in itself.

"BERNICE BOBS HER HAIR": FITZGERALD'S JAZZ ELEGY FOR *LITTLE WOMEN*

SUSAN F. BEEGEL

In 1915 nineteen-year-old F. Scott Fitzgerald wrote a remarkable letter to his younger sister Annabel, criticizing her social deportment and arguing that a successful debutante's popularity is composed of a concerted appeal to male egotism ("Boys like to talk about themselves . . . always pay close attention to the man.") and accomplished acting ("Your natural laugh is good, but your artificial one is bum.") Abandoning the traditional role of elder brother as protector of innocence, he both instructs Annabel in the rudiments of sex appeal and endeavors to inoculate her with cynicism: "Learn to be worldly. Remember that in society nine girls out of ten marry for money and nine men out of ten are fools." Fitzgerald saved the letter and between November 1919 and February 1920 transformed it into a short story for the *Saturday Evening Post*—"Bernice Bobs Her Hair." Lest anyone doubt the short story's origin, Fitzgerald scribbled "Basis of Bernice" on the letter to Annabel.[1]

Published in the *Post* on May 1, 1920, and gathered almost immediately into Fitzgerald's first collection of short stories, *Flappers and*

---

1. Matthew J. Bruccoli and Margaret M. Duggan, eds., *Correspondence of F. Scott Fitzgerald*, 15–18; Matthew J. Bruccoli, *Some Sort of Epic Grandeur: The Life of F. Scott Fitzgerald*, 112.

Philosophers, "Bernice Bobs Her Hair" has since received little critical attention and less respect. Writing to H. L. Mencken, Fitzgerald labeled the story "trash."[2] Many critics, while admiring its lively plot development, sharply drawn characters, Wilde-like dialogue, whimsical imagery, and comic denouement, appear to accept Fitzgerald's disparaging estimate of "Bernice Bobs Her Hair." Matthew J. Bruccoli has called it "not one of Fitzgerald's greatest short stories," "obviously commercial," "written as an entertainment." Henry Dan Piper allots the story two sentences in a book-length study of Fitzgerald's work. John A. Higgins ranks it as "juvenilia." Brian Way views "Bernice" as "marred by immaturities of style and a sentimental ending." Sergio Perosa dismisses it as "purely humorous." Bryant Mangum labels the story "light." And John Kuehl, who believes that Fitzgerald "underrated" "Bernice Bobs Her Hair," nevertheless has little to say about it. Only Alice Hall Petry has called "Bernice Bobs Her Hair" "excellent."[3]

Yet Fitzgerald's valuation of "Bernice Bobs Her Hair" as "trash" was almost certainly insincere, an attempt to appease Mencken, then editor of *The Smart Set* and interested in more self-consciously "literary" fiction. In 1935 Fitzgerald expressed an entirely different opinion of "Bernice" when he suggested that Chatto and Windus include it in a collection of his best stories. It must be noted that the critics accepting Fitzgerald's remark to Mencken are exclusively male and perhaps ill-equipped to appreciate a short story about the gender socialization of young women, written for the predominantly female market of the *Saturday Evening Post.*[4]

2. Bruccoli and Duggan, eds., *Correspondence,* 68.
3. Matthew J. Bruccoli, "On F. Scott Fitzgerald and 'Bernice Bobs Her Hair,'" 217–23; Henry Dan Piper, *F. Scott Fitzgerald: A Critical Portrait,* 67; John A. Higgins, *F. Scott Fitzgerald: A Study of the Stories,* 23; Brian Way, *F. Scott Fitzgerald and the Art of Social Fiction,* 57; Sergio Perosa, *The Art of F. Scott Fitzgerald,* 31; Bryant Mangum, *A Fortune Yet: Money in the Art of F. Scott Fitzgerald's Short Stories,* 35; John Kuehl, *F. Scott Fitzgerald: A Study of the Short Fiction,* 33; Alice Hall Petry, *Fitzgerald's Craft of Short Fiction: The Collected Stories—1920–1935,* 10. Significantly, Petry, the story's lone female critic, is the only one to note Fitzgerald's reference in "Bernice Bobs Her Hair" to Annie Fellows Johnston and Louisa May Alcott (19). However, Petry misses the importance of Fitzgerald's allusion to Alcott by dismissing her work as "saccharine."
4. Bruccoli and Duggan, eds., *Correspondence,* 401. According to Mangum in *Fortune Yet,* magazine president Cyrus Curtis founded the *Post* on the financial success of the

Neglect of "Bernice Bobs Her Hair" may be reinforced by the story's rich structure of allusion to a source unacknowledged by Fitzgerald and still unrecognized by critics—a classic novel traditionally handed down from mother to daughter in American culture, seldom or never read by males of any age, and undoubtedly borrowed by Fitzgerald from Annabel's shelf—Louisa May Alcott's *Little Women*. In *This Side of Paradise*, Fitzgerald lists the books his autobiographical hero Amory Blaine has read in his childhood. There, among such boyish favorites as *For the Honor of the School, Dangerous Dan McGrew*, and *The Police Gazette, Little Women* is conspicuous as a book Amory has read not once, but twice. When, in "Bernice Bobs Her Hair," Fitzgerald has Bernice quote Alcott, one suspects that he too read *Little Women* more than once. Indeed, comparison of the short story and the novel reveals that Fitzgerald borrowed his major plot elements and themes from *Little Women*, turning them upside down in a Jazz Age revision of what Amory Blaine calls "the dull literature of female virtue."[5]

Fitzgerald mentions *Little Women* directly only once in his short story, when Marjorie urges her burdensome cousin, Bernice, to go home, and Bernice tries to make Marjorie see her rudeness:

> "Don't you think that common kindness . . . ?"
> "Oh, please don't quote *Little Women*!" cried Marjorie impatiently. "That's out of style."
> "You think so?"
> "Heavens, yes! What modern girl could live like those inane females?"
> "They were the models for our mothers."
> Marjorie laughed.
> "Yes, they were . . . not! Besides, our mothers were all very well in their way, but they know very little about their daughters' problems."[6]

Ladies' Home Journal (29). Curtis was adept at appealing to the middle-class morality and domestic values of the wives and mothers who purchased the *Saturday Evening Post* for family reading, and the magazine's female readership should be considered largely responsible for its rise from a circulation of two thousand in 1899 to three million in 1937.

5. F. Scott Fitzgerald, *This Side of Paradise*, 17. See also *Tender Is the Night*, 71, where Rosemary notices that the sinister women in Cardinal de Retz's palace appear to be "fashioned by Louisa May Alcott."

6. F. Scott Fitzgerald, *Flappers and Philosophers*, 125. All subsequent page references to "Bernice Bobs Her Hair" ("BBHH") are to the 1920 edition and will appear parenthetically in the text.

Marjorie and Bernice do experience problems (how to be popular, how to attract an eligible suitor, how to compete with other girls in the marriage market) experienced by their mothers and by all adolescent women before them. Yet "Bernice Bobs Her Hair" demonstrates that modern girls, whatever their mothers might have done, no longer solve such problems by emulating *Little Women*.[7]

"Bernice Bobs Her Hair" begins with two minor but significant allusions to Alcott's novel. In the story's opening paragraphs, middle-aged ladies with "sharp eyes and icy hearts" watch the country-club dances and postulate "that every young man with a large income leads the life of a hunted partridge."[8] In *Little Women*, when Meg considers marriage to an impoverished tutor, another middle-aged lady with sharp eyes and an icy heart, Aunt March, puts forth the same postulate: "You ought to marry well and help your family. It's your duty to make a rich match and it ought to be impressed upon you."[9] "Marmee," mother of *Little Women*'s four female protagonists, sounds the novel's moral keynote by overruling Aunt March's advice: "I'd rather see you poor men's wives, if you were happy, beloved, contented, than queens on thrones without self-respect and peace" (*LW*, 116).

A second borrowing from *Little Women* is the three-year engagement of Fitzgerald's Jim Strain and Ethel Demorest. In Alcott's novel, Meg consents to a three-year engagement in which she and the poor tutor, her beloved John Brooke, work to afford marriage. After doing his duty "manfully" in the Civil War, John devotes himself to "preparing for business, and earning a home for Meg," while she spends the three years "in working as well as waiting, growing womanly in character, wise in housewifely arts, and prettier than ever, for love is a great beautifier" (*LW*, 268). Alcott's characters contrast sharply with Fitzgerald's " . . . Jim Strain and Ethel Demorest, who had been privately engaged for three years. Everyone knew that as soon as Jim managed to hold a job for

7. Marjorie's mother, Mrs. Harvey, is named Josephine, perhaps for the protagonist of *Little Women* (137).

8. Of course, Fitzgerald is paraphrasing the famous opening sentence of Jane Austen's *Pride and Prejudice:* "It is a truth universally acknowledged, that a single man in possession of a good fortune, must be in want of a wife."

9. Louisa May Alcott, *Little Women*, 116. All subsequent page references to *Little Women* (*LW*) are to the 1962 reprint edition and will appear parenthetically in the text.

more than two months she would marry him. Yet how bored they both looked, and how wearily Ethel regarded Jim, as if she wondered why she had trained the vines of her affection on such a wind-shaken poplar" ("BBHH," 117).

One Victorian ideal, then, that Fitzgerald intends to shatter by revising *Little Women* as "Bernice Bobs Her Hair" is the notion of "love in a cottage," of sentimental poverty. The middle-aged ladies with their "hunted partridge" postulate prove Marjorie's point that their mothers were never so unworldly as their lip service to Alcott's novel might suggest. Fitzgerald's modern girl appreciates the inestimable advantage of a large income in sustaining married bliss. Even Bernice, reared on *Little Women,* has nothing but contempt for Jim and Ethel, "mooning around for years without a red penny" ("BBHH," 120).

Fitzgerald drew a large portion of his plot from chapter 9 of *Little Women,* "Meg Goes to Vanity Fair," where unspoiled and innocent Meg goes to stay for a fortnight with her sophisticated friend Annie Moffat, just as gauche and unworldly Bernice goes to visit her worldly wise cousin Marjorie Harvey. Meg overhears the Moffat girls and their mother discussing her dowdy clothes and inability to capture a desirable suitor, just as Bernice overhears Marjorie and Mrs. Harvey discussing her social shortcomings and unpopularity. Humiliated, Meg allows herself to be "made over" by Belle Moffat and her French maid, Hortense:

> They crimped and curled her hair, they polished her neck and arms with some fragrant powder, touched her lips with coralline salve, to make them redder, and Hortense would have added "a soupçon of rouge," if Meg had not rebelled. They laced her into a sky-blue dress, which was so tight she could hardly breathe, and so low in the neck that modest Meg blushed to see herself in the mirror. . . . A laced handkerchief, a plumy fan, and a bouquet in a silver holder finished her off; and Miss Belle surveyed her with the satisfaction of a little girl with a newly dressed doll. (*LW,* 106–7)

Bernice, too, allows herself to be "made over." Marjorie chooses a dark red dress to set off Bernice's "shadowy eyes and high coloring," arranges her cousin's hair, and sets it glistening with brilliantine ("BBHH," 130). Just as the Moffat girls "drill" Meg on the proper management of her skirt and "those French heels," so Marjorie coaches Bernice on graceful deportment, instructing her not to lean on a man when she dances and to develop more "ease of manner" (*LW*, 107; "BBHH," 126–27).

Meg is a social success in her borrowed finery. Several young ladies, who have not noticed her before, become "very affectionate all of a sudden," while several young gentlemen, who have hitherto only stared, ask "to be introduced," and say "all manner of agreeable but foolish things" (*LW*, 108). Meg's normally modest demeanor dissolves. She drinks champagne, dances and flirts, chatters and giggles, and "romps" in a scandalizing way. "I'm not Meg tonight," she tells a friend. "I'm a 'doll' who does all sorts of crazy things" (*LW*, 112). Meg in her new persona inspires her good friend Sallie Gardiner's jealousy by attaching the affections of Sallie's beau, Ned Moffat.

Like Meg, Fitzgerald's Bernice scores a social success by "follow[ing] instructions exactly," and is cut in on so frequently that she is "danced tired" for the first time in her life ("BBHH," 131). Bernice, who in Marjorie's view is "no case for sensible things," also behaves crazily. In her new persona, Bernice inspires her cousin's jealousy by attaching the affections of Warren McIntyre, "Miss Marjorie's best fella" ("BBHH," 132).

Here the similarities between "Meg Goes to Vanity Fair" and "Bernice Bobs Her Hair" end. After her makeover, Meg fails to have a "good time" (*LW*, 112). The champagne gives her a "splitting headache," and two men she admires, the dignified Major Lincoln and the charming Teddy Laurence, disapprove of her "fuss and feathers" (*LW*, 109, 113). Meg feels "uncomfortable and ashamed" and wishes she had been "sensible" (*LW*, 109). After being sick all the next day, Meg returns home and confesses all to Marmee, who draws a moral from Meg's unhappy experiment in vanity: "[Enjoying praise and admiration] is perfectly natural, if the liking does not become a passion and lead one to do foolish or unmaidenly things. Learn to know and value the praise which is worth having, and to excite the admiration of worthy people by being modest as well as pretty, Meg" (*LW*, 115). Alcott makes it clear that Meg is more happy and attractive at a "small party" she attends before her makeover. Clad in her shabby but spotless white tarlatan, adorned solely by flowers from Teddy, Meg dances "to her heart's content"; receives three compliments from worthy admirers on her fine voice, fresh appearance, and lively dancing; and enjoys herself "very much," achieving an inner contentment she cannot find when preening "like the jackdaw in the fable" (*LW*, 107).

Unlike Meg, Bernice is "sorta dopeless" before her metamorphosis into a "society vampire" ("BBHH," 118, 129). Despite her "dark hair and high color," Bernice's dresses are "frights" and her "straggly" eyebrows are a blemish ("BBHH," 123). She never says "anything to a boy except that it's hot or the floor's crowded or that she's going to school in New York next year," and "turns an ungraceful red," exclaiming "Fresh!" when Warren McIntyre tells her that she has "an awfully kissable mouth" ("BBHH," 119–20, 122). Marjorie must coax her own beaux to dance with the "lame-duck visitor," and Bernice, feeling "a vague pain that she is not . . . popular," has "a bum time" ("BBHH," 121, 122).

Under Marjorie's tutelage, Bernice, like Meg at Vanity Fair, becomes " 'a doll' who does all sorts of crazy things" (*LW*, 112). Adopting Oscar Wilde's principle that "you've either got to amuse people or feed 'em or shock 'em," Bernice amuses men with invitations to a fictitious bobbing ("Of course I'm charging admission, but if you'll come down and encourage me I'll issue passes for the inside seats" ["BBHH," 129]), feeds them with flattery ("I want to ask your opinion of several people. I imagine you're a wonderful judge of character" ["BBHH," 129]), and shocks them with sexual suggestion ("I always fix my hair first and powder my face and put on my hat; then I get into the bathtub and dress afterwards. Don't you think that's the best plan?" ["BBHH," 132]).

Meg learns that virtuous and modest behavior is its own reward; Bernice learns that "foolish and unmaidenly" antics pay enormous dividends in popularity, which is "everything when you're eighteen" ("BBHH," 121). Exchanging Louisa May Alcott's mores for Oscar Wilde's, Bernice finds herself a "gardenia girl" like Marjorie, with "three or four men in love with her," cut in on "every few feet" ("BBHH," 122). Glowing with gratified vanity, Bernice becomes attractive and genuinely enjoys herself: "Yes, she was pretty, distinctly pretty; and tonight her face seemed really vivacious. She had that look that no woman, however histrionically proficient, can successfully counterfeit—she looked as if she were having a good time" ("BBHH," 130).

Fitzgerald inverts *Little Women* in "Bernice Bobs Her Hair" in part to portray a generation adrift without moral guidance. In his country-club world, where parents are socially ambitious for their children, the moral destiny of little women who "give their hearts into their mother's keep-ing" is ambiguous at best (*LW,* 268). Meg, in a moral or social quandary, turns to her mother for advice. Even when Meg cannot "cry and rush home to tell her troubles," her mother's influence is omnipresent— Meg carries a note from Marmee in her pocket as a "talisman against envy, vanity, and false pride" (*LW,* 103). Bernice, on the other hand, has no intention of rushing home and telling her troubles. Meg visits the worldly Moffats in spite of her mother's misgivings; Bernice's visit with her cousin is "parent-arranged" ("BBHH," 120). Instead of longing for maternal advice, Bernice fears her mother's reaction to her social disgrace: "'You're my cousin,' sobbed Bernice. 'I'm v-v-visiting you. I was to stay a month, and if I go home my mother will know and she'll wah-wonder . . .'" ("BBHH," 124).

Young men, as well as mothers, can be sources of moral guidance in *Little Women.* Meg is especially devastated by Teddy's disapproval of her tight, low-cut dress and gaudy makeup. He is handsome, charming, and rich—a boy whose good opinion even a Fitzgerald flapper might value. In Fitzgerald's world, however, young men who offer moral guidance to debutantes are priggish figures of fun. Draycott Deyo, studying for the ministry, cuts in on Bernice because he thinks she is a "quiet, reserved girl" ("BBHH," 131–32). Bernice earns his disapproval by treating him "to the line which began 'Hello, Shell Shock,'" and to her story about doing her hair before getting into the bathtub: "Though Draycott Deyo was in the throes of difficulties concerning baptism by immersion and might possibly have seen a connection, it must be admitted that he did not. He considered feminine bathing an immoral subject, and gave her some of his ideas on the depravity of modern society" ("BBHH," 132). Draycott Deyo is no Teddy Laurence. To Bernice, his disapproval is merely an "unfortunate occurrence," more than offset by her "signal successes" with desirable young men like the Harvard lawyer G. Reece Stoddard ("BBHH," 132).

In Alcott's fictional world, active resistance against "envy, vanity, and false pride" ensures young women not only present happiness, but also future success in the marriage market. While Marmee warns her daughters that they had "better be old maids than unhappy wives, or unmaidenly girls, running about to find husbands," she also assures them that "poverty seldom daunts a sincere lover. Some of the best and most

honored women I know were poor girls, but so love-worthy that they
were not allowed to become old maids" (*LW*, 116). The novel bears her
out as Meg, Amy, and Jo each find husbands attracted by their "love-
worthiness," their ability to fulfill "woman's special mission" of "drying
tears and bearing burdens" (*LW*, 531).[10]

In "Bernice Bobs Her Hair," the world in which women were married for "mysterious womanly qualities, always mentioned but never
displayed," is a thing of the past ("BBHH," 121). While Mrs. Harvey
remembers that "when she was a girl all young ladies who belonged
to nice families had glorious times," her daughter pronounces that
"these days it's every girl for herself" and sneers at Bernice's reliance on
Little Women as a moral guidebook: " 'The womanly woman!' continued
Marjorie. 'Her whole early life is occupied in whining criticisms of girls
like me who really do have a good time' " ("BBHH," 122, 125).

In addition to Alcott's "Vanity Fair" scenario, Fitzgerald borrowed the
central episode of "Bernice Bobs Her Hair" from *Little Women*. In both
works, a young girl impetuously visits a barber shop and orders her long
hair cut off. Jo March's decision comes in chapter 15 of *Little Women*,
when Marmee receives a telegram informing her that her husband,
a chaplain in the Union Army, lies dangerously ill in a Washington
hospital. The family is too poor to purchase a train ticket, and Marmee,
who is "not too proud to beg for Father," humbles herself to borrow
money from a grudging Aunt March (*LW*, 180–82).

Jo, who identifies strongly with her mother's proud hatred of borrowing, finds herself "wild to do something for Father" and "bound to
have some money, if I sold the nose off my face to get it." Sent out to
buy nursing supplies, she passes a barber shop with "tails of hair with
prices marked" displayed in the window. Here she encounters a shrewd
and miserly barber: "He rather stared at first, as if he wasn't used to
having girls bounce into his shop and ask him to buy their hair. He said
he didn't care about mine, it wasn't the fashionable color, and he never
paid much for it in the first place. . . . I begged him to take it, and told
him why I was in such a hurry" (*LW*, 185). Jo finally sells her hair for
twenty-five dollars.

10. The saintly Beth meets a different bridegroom by dying young.

After her makeover, Bernice's "line about the bobbing of her hair" is "the best known and most universally approved element" of her conversation, though her "tonsorial intentions" are strictly dishonorable ("BBHH," 132). Marjorie, outraged by Warren McIntyre's sudden interest in her cousin, publicly calls Bernice's bluff, hoping to expose her as a fraud without title to either Warren or popularity ("BBHH," 133). Bernice tries to save face by reaffirming her intentions of bobbing her hair, but Marjorie and her friends demand immediate proof of sincerity. Bernice accepts their challenge:

> Out of the group came Marjorie's voice, very clear and contemptuous. "Don't worry—she'll back out."
> "Come on, Bernice!" cried Otis, starting toward the door.
> Four eyes—Warren's and Marjorie's—stared at her, challenged her, defied her. For another second she wavered wildly.
> "All right," she said swiftly, "I don't care if I do." ("BBHH," 135)

Jo's decision to sell her hair to help her family is a conquest of personal vanity as well as an exercise in humility. The least attractive of the four March sisters, Jo is thoroughly unfeminine in person. "Very tall, thin, and brown," she resembles "a colt," and has "round shoulders," "big hands and feet," and "long limbs which were very much in her way" (*LW*, 14). Her "long, thick hair" is "her one beauty" (*LW*, 188). Jo does shed a tear for her shorn hair, but proclaims "it will be good for my vanity, I was getting too proud of my wig" (*LW*, 184). Her mother congratulates her on sacrificing her "vanity . . . to her love" (*LW*, 184).

Jo cuts her hair out of altruism, imitating her mother and swallowing her pride to assist her beloved father. Bernice bobs her hair out of narcissism, braving maternal disapproval ("Even the thought of her mother was no deterrent now" ["BBHH," 133]) to salvage her pride. While hitherto Bernice has justified Marjorie's contempt for "the womanly woman" by whining and taking refuge in her mother's opinions when criticized, she stands firm when Marjorie makes her sincerity about bobbing her hair a public question. Viewing Marjorie's thrown gauntlet as "the test supreme of her sportsmanship, her right to walk unchallenged in the starry heaven of popular girls," Bernice undergoes her bobbing with lifted chin and clenched fists ("BBHH," 135).

Jo sacrifices her vanity to her love when she cuts her hair; Bernice sacrifices her vanity to her pride. Both sacrifices are considerable, for both girls dread the mutilation of their looks as they would physical dismemberment. When Jo sees "the dear old hair laid out on the table," she feels "as if I'd had an arm or leg cut off" (*LW,* 187). Fitzgerald borrows an even stronger image from *Little Women* to describe Bernice's dread—Jo's sister Amy is particularly horrified because she "would as soon have thought of cutting off her head as her pretty hair" (*LW,* 223). Bernice also equates the bobbing of her hair with decapitation: "It was a guillotine indeed, and the hangman was the first barber, who, attired in a white coat and smoking a cigarette, leaned nonchalantly against the first chair. . . . Would they blind-fold her? No, but they would tie a white cloth round her neck lest any of her blood—nonsense—hair—should get on her clothes" ("BBHH," 135). Fitzgerald embellishes and extends Alcott's decapitation imagery for his own purposes. Bound for the barbershop in Warren's car, Bernice has "all the sensations of Marie Antoinette bound for the guillotine in a tumbrel" ("BBHH," 135). As Marie Antoinette, last queen of a doomed aristocracy, was dragged to her execution by savage rebels of the new republic, so Bernice, the last "quiet, reserved girl" raised on *Little Women,* is dragged to her bobbing by the cruel adolescents of the "jazz-nourished generation" ("BBHH," 117, 132, 121). When Bernice bobs her hair, a "little woman" dies in the barber's chair and a flapper is born.

For Alcott, long hair worn elaborately restrained is a badge of mature womanhood, which the wearer must strive to merit through equally restrained behavior. In Victorian times, little girls wore their long hair loose or in pigtails; young women who were "out" wore their long hair bound in nets or snoods, or braided and pinned atop their heads. In the opening chapter of *Little Women,* Meg chides Jo for whistling when she is old enough to wear her hair "turned up" in a net, and Jo responds by unleashing both her bundled-up hair and her pent-up frustration with the behavioral restraint expected of her as she approaches womanhood: "I hate to think I've got to grow up, and be Miss March, and wear long gowns, and be as prim as a China aster! It's bad enough to be a girl" (*LW,* 13).

Alcott treats Jo's decision to cut her hair as her initiation into the womanhood she has rebelled against. When her father returns home from the war, he congratulates Jo on her new "womanliness," a state of feminine virtue she has attained not merely by binding up her hair, but by cutting it off altogether. Along with her chestnut mane, Jo has sacrificed her tomboyish demeanor:

> "I see a young lady who pins her collar straight, laces her boots neatly, and neither whistles, talks slang, nor lies on the rug as she used to do. Her face is rather thin and pale just now, with watching and anxiety, but I like to look at it, for it has grown gentler, and her voice is lower; she doesn't bounce, but moves quietly, and takes care of a certain little person [Beth, recovering from scarlet fever,] in a motherly way which delights me." (*LW*, 250)

"Womanliness" for Alcott is an asexual and subdued condition. Jo is most "womanly" when she has divested herself of her long, thick, beautiful hair, the emblem of her sex. "Womanliness" also involves conformity to societal norms of virtuous feminine behavior: Unlike young men, young ladies must pin their collars straight and lace their boots neatly; they must not whistle or talk slang. In *Little Women*, femininity is a ruthless suppression of sexual and personal identity.

In 1920, when Fitzgerald composed his short story, American attitudes toward women—and their hair—were in transition. Although popular dancer Irene Castle began the vogue for bobbed hair in 1918, short hair for women was not generally accepted until 1924. In 1920 "young ladies who belonged to nice families" still had long hair, worn atop their heads in the Victorian manner if they were "out" ("BBHH," 122). Fitzgerald lets us know that "little Madeleine Hogue" is very young by remarking that her hair "still feels strange and uncomfortable on top of her head," but the rage for bobbed hair is spreading—Mrs. Deyo devotes fifteen minutes to the subject in her speech on "The Foibles of the Younger Generation" ("BBHH," 116, 137). Yet not even the fearless and unsentimental Marjorie can number herself among the avant-garde young women who dared to bob their hair in 1920. When Bernice bobs her hair, then, she severs herself symbolically from the Victorian ideal of womanliness that Alcott reluctantly espoused.

When Jo cuts her hair, she exchanges her one physical beauty for spiritual beauty. Bernice exchanges an illusion of spiritual beauty for physical ugliness. The hair that once "hung in a dark brown glory down her back" now lies shorn in "lank, lifeless blocks on both sides of her suddenly pale face." The "Madonna-like simplicity" of her appearance gone, Bernice looks "well, frightfully mediocre—not stagy; only ridiculous, like a Greenwich Villager who had left her spectacles at home" ("BBHH," 136).[11] Neither poet nor reformer, Bernice has abandoned the pretty, virginal appearance of a "little woman" for the hard, experienced appearance of a New Woman. Her bobbed hair is "ugly as sin"—a phrase Fitzgerald repeats twice to underscore his misgivings about the flapper's moral destiny ("BBHH," 136).

Revenge is one of the first evils Jo rejects in *Little Women*, long before she cuts her hair. When, after a quarrel, Amy burns the sole manuscript of Jo's book, Jo refuses to accept an apology and deliberately does not warn her sister when she skates onto thin ice in the middle of a river: "The little demon [Jo] was harboring said in her ear . . . 'let her take care of herself'" (*LW*, 94). Amy does fall through the ice and is rescued unharmed, but Jo is overcome with remorse and confesses all to her mother. Marmee offers her usual sympathetic counsel, and Jo struggles from that day forward to hold her substantial temper in check. For Alcott, the ability to suppress anger is an important step toward womanliness.

By contrast, when Bernice cuts off the hair that is the emblem of "appropriately and blessedly feminine" qualities she once admired, her capacity for vengeance is unleashed ("BBHH," 120). For a short time, Bernice silently endures injury after injury—the bobbing has made her ugly, Marjorie wears a mocking smile, Warren deserts her, her aunt and uncle reproach her, she burns her hair and fingers in an unsuccessful attempt to repair her looks with a curling iron. Bernice's gathering rage spills over when Marjorie comes into her room to prepare for bed:

11. In 1920, Greenwich Village was a flourishing center of Bohemianism, whose notable women included (or had recently included) Emma Goldman, proponent of birth control, pacifism, and anarchy; Mabel Dodge, critic of New York's high society and leader of intellectual and aesthetic movements; and Edna St. Vincent Millay, cynical poet and playwright. From a Victorian moral standpoint, these women paid the unthinkable price of promiscuity, divorce, and alcoholism for their independence and substantial achievements.

Bernice winced as Marjorie tossed her own hair over her shoulders and began to twist it slowly into two long blond braids until in her cream-colored
negligee she looked like a delicate painting of some Saxon princess.
Fascinated, Bernice watched the braids grow. Heavy and luxurious they
were, moving under the supple fingers like restive snakes—and to Bernice
remained this relic and a curling iron and a tomorrow full of eyes. . . .
Marjorie had made a fool of her. ("BBHH," 138)

"Something" in Bernice—perhaps the last restraint of her Victorian
upbringing—"snaps" at the sight of Marjorie braiding her hair. An
expression flashes into Bernice's eyes "that a practiced character reader
might have connected vaguely with the set look she had worn in the
barber's chair—somehow a development of it. It was a new look for
Bernice and it carried consequences" ("BBHH," 139). After packing
her clothes for flight, she creeps into her sleeping cousin's room and
"amputate[s]" Marjorie's braids. Escaping into the night, Bernice flings
the severed remains of his "crush's" beauty onto the fickle Warren's front
porch. Unlike Jo, Bernice feels no remorse for her act of vengeance. After
disfiguring Marjorie, she is "oddly happy and exuberant," and, having
conceived Warren's punishment, she must "shut her mouth hard to keep
from emitting an absolute peal" of laughter ("BBHH," 139–40).

Formerly able only to imitate Alcott's idea of a "little woman" or
Marjorie's notion of a "modern girl," Bernice now makes decisions
of her own without regard for convention. Before her bobbing, she
dreaded the idea of returning home early and making explanations
to her mother. Now, with only a note to her aunt and no thought
of her mother's reaction, she leaves secretly and unescorted, catching
a taxi at the Marlborough Hotel and departing on a 1:00 A.M. train.
Bernice has lost the "dark brown glory" of her hair but has gained
a new independence of thought and action. The bobbing releases her
essential nature. Earlier, Marjorie attributes Bernice's unpopularity to
her reputed American Indian ancestry: "I think it's that crazy Indian
blood. . . . Maybe she's a reversion to type. Indian women all just sat
around and never said anything" ("BBHH," 122). After her barbershop
trauma, Bernice does indeed revert to type and goes on the warpath.
Running down the moonlit street, Bernice is never more like a savage:
" 'Huh!' she giggled wildly. 'Scalp the selfish thing!' " ("BBHH," 140).

Despite their differences, what *Little Women* and "Bernice Bobs Her Hair" have most in common is their intense ambivalence about the gender socialization of young women. Modeling her novel on *Pilgrim's Progress*, Alcott intended each incident in *Little Women* to illustrate a moral lesson. Yet the metaphors surrounding Jo's hair express Alcott's uncertainty about the "womanly woman" that Fitzgerald's Marjorie derides. In chapter 1, Jo is a "colt" with a free-flowing chestnut "mane," a wild animal rebelling against restraint, reveling in liberty (*LW,* 13). After her visit to the oily little barber, Jo is a shorn "black sheep," humiliatingly bereft of the fleece that endowed her with a separate identity (*LW,* 250). Her new "womanliness" seems a regrettable taming, a sad domestication. Patricia Meyer Spacks points out that Jo's "fictional vitality" stems from "her deep awareness of how the limitations of feminine possibility make it difficult to express what's in her."[12] *Little Women* is a classic precisely because generations of female readers have identified with Jo's suppressed rage against the behavioral restraints imposed on women.

Jo March, who wrote sensational stories like "The Phantom Hand" and "The Curse of the Coventrys" for pulp magazines titled the *Weekly Volcano* and the *Blarneystone Banner,* would have exulted guiltily over the *Saturday Evening Post* conclusion of "Bernice Bobs Her Hair," which sees Bernice transformed from silent, passive squaw into whooping warrior. As Bernice avenges herself by chopping off Marjorie's braids and flinging them on Warren's porch, as she dashes giggling into the moonlight, readers gloat over her unholy triumph for the same reason that they agonize over Jo March's sacrifice—Bernice has broken the yoke that Jo has determined to shoulder.

Like Jo March, Louisa May Alcott herself, using the pseudonym A. M. Barnard, wrote romantic thrillers such as "Behind a Mask" and "Pauline's Passion and Punishment" for pulp weeklies, including *Frank Leslie's Illustrated Newspaper* and the *Flag of Our Union.* Nearly all these stories, recently recovered by Madeleine Stern, feature wicked heroines who wreak vengeance on various oppressors while masquerading as virtuous women.[13] Behind the mask of A. M. Barnard, Alcott could

12. Patricia Meyer Spacks, *The Female Imagination,* 99–100.
13. Madeleine B. Stern, ed., *Behind a Mask: The Unknown Thrillers of Louisa May Alcott.*

express a feminist rage imperfectly suppressed in *Little Women*. Instead of automatically denigrating Fitzgerald's attempts at commercial fiction, scholars might well ask whether pulp formulae permitted *him* certain kinds of expression forbidden the serious novelist.

Fitzgerald's very choice of *Little Women* as an allusive subtext for "Bernice Bobs Her Hair" suggests his own ambivalence about the gender socialization of the 1920s' debutantes. Only superficially comic, the short story does little to conceal profound misgivings about a world where popular girls are "dangerous," young men are "stags" and "partridges" to be hunted, and couples with "artificial, effortless smiles" and "the very worst intentions" dance "weird barbaric interludes" to "African rhythm[s]" ("BBHH," 116–17). Marjorie Harvey, hard and selfish and without a feminine quality, reigns supreme in this "shifting, semi-cruel world" ("BBHH," 116), and each of Fitzgerald's allusions to *Little Women* underscores its sinister features. We cheer Bernice as much for counting coup on the individuals who would make her a "doll" and a sex object as we do for casting off her lame-duck dullness.

Finally, Fitzgerald combined a fatal obsession with glamour and an unbending morality worthy of Bronson Alcott. His mothlike attraction to and moral revulsion from alluring, convention-flouting women is the source of "Bernice Bobs Her Hair"'s dialogue with *Little Women*. While Bernice has freed herself from the mores of Louisa May Alcott, readers cannot know where she is going as she dashes recklessly into the night. Her new freedom is merely license. Bernice has exchanged dullness for glamour, but she has nothing to replace the past's "prosy morals." She is not so much running free as running wild. This ambivalence of Fitzgerald's makes "Bernice Bobs Her Hair" his jazz elegy for *Little Women*, for the passing of Victorian womanhood, regretted and not regretted. The adolescent savagery of this early work has not yet gone trending into the senseless violence of *The Great Gatsby*; its sparkling zaniness has not yet become the dark insanity of *Tender Is the Night*. But the seeds have been sown, making "Bernice Bobs Her Hair," written on the eve of Fitzgerald's tragic marriage to Zelda Sayre, something more than "purely humorous."

"JOHN JACKSON'S ARCADY": THE LAMENTABLE F. SCOTT FITZGERALD

JAMES J. MARTINE

> Nel mezzo del cammin di nostra vita
> mi ritrovai per una selva oscura,
> chè la diritta via era smarrita.
> —Dante, *The Divine Comedy*

Both the failure of Fitzgerald's play *The Vegetable* at its November 1923 Atlantic City tryout and a notoriously extravagant lifestyle left the writer in debt and set him off into a burst of composition that led to his publishing ten stories in 1924, four of which would be sold to the *Saturday Evening Post* for $1,575 each. The last short story that Fitzgerald wrote in the fabled Great Neck house before he sailed on May 3, 1924, aboard the *Minnewaska* from New York for the Riviera where he would concentrate on concluding *The Great Gatsby* was "John Jackson's Arcady," which he wrote in April 1924 and which appeared in the *Post* on July 26, 1924. The story was republished as a pamphlet in 1928 for public reading contests, earning small royalties until 1936, including some as tiny as two dollars for 1931 and nineteen dollars for 1932. However, the story was never gathered in any collection of Fitzgerald short stories until Matthew J. Bruccoli included it in *The Price Was High*.

"John Jackson's Arcady" has been largely dismissed or ignored by scholars. In the last four decades, representative scholarship on this particular piece of fiction has dwindled. Kenneth Eble mentions "John

Jackson's Arcady" in three sentences and only then to remark upon the hero's attempt at time dominance, which strongly suggests an essential theme of *The Great Gatsby*. John A. Higgins in his study of the stories expands Eble's three sentences to six paragraphs; conceding that the search for the past holds all the tale's significance, he concludes that the "outside story" of Jackson is "pure trash." Following this dismissal by Higgins, André Le Vot does nothing more than acknowledge the story's existence. Bryant Mangum later devotes two paragraphs to the tale, but the highly respected John Kuehl in his recent study of the short fiction does not mention the story at all.[1]

Even as there is little scholarship to survey, the story's basic plot itself is quickly summarized. At its most overt textual level, the story of John Jackson unfolds in what through a cursory reading would seem five melodramatic acts. In the first section, the reader meets John Jackson, the community's most respected citizen, brooding at home over two letters in the morning's post. The first is an invitation from the Civic Welfare League to speak at its annual meeting on the topic of "What Have I Got Out of Life." The second dispatch is from the dean of the college at Jackson's alma mater informing him that his son, Ellery Hamil Jackson, has been requested to withdraw from the university. Distressed and feeling hollow, Jackson vows to leave his home and the city to seek the happiness he once knew when he was young. The story's second section follows Jackson to his office where the reader meets his chief clerk, Fowler; an intrusive and persistent solicitor for various charities, Mrs. Ralston; and Jackson's arch rival and antagonist, Thomas J. MacDowell. Jackson leaves directions to close up his house, pay off his servants, and cancel every one of his engagements.

In the story's third section, Jackson sets out on his mission, traveling seventy miles to the little town where he had been born but had not visited for twenty years. Absorbed with memories at this time of crisis in his life, Jackson returns unannounced and unexpected to the deserted home of his childhood, where he finds, *mirabile dictu*, Alice, the first and

---

1. Kenneth Eble, *F. Scott Fitzgerald*, 99–100; John A. Higgins, *F. Scott Fitzgerald: A Study of the Stories*, 75–76; André Le Vot, *F. Scott Fitzgerald: A Biography*, 139; Bryant Mangum, *A Fortune Yet: Money in the Art of F. Scott Fitzgerald's Short Stories*, 52–53; John Kuehl, *F. Scott Fitzgerald: A Study of the Short Fiction*.

only true love of his life. After a delicious, if momentary, experience of dominance over time during which he feels as if he were holding his own lost youth in his arms in the person of Alice, he must face the reality of the fourth section, in which he meets Alice's husband, George Harland, and their children. Jackson's mood of ecstasy slips away, leaving him to conclude that what he has gotten out of life is nothing.

In the story's fifth and final section, Jackson returns to the city of his maturity and finds himself in the Civic Club hall, secreted from sight or notice, unobserved, himself observing and listening to the sincere testimonials to him from friends and foes alike. Eventually recognized and acknowledged, he finds himself accepting the approbation of his fellow citizens; he understands and admits that what he has gotten out of life is everything. Thus refreshed, the less sad but wiser John Jackson is prepared for the ultimate reconciliation with his chastened son in the tale's closing paragraphs.

It must be said that this schematic summary reduces "John Jackson's Arcady" to melodrama and misses the depth and merit of the story. If the *Saturday Evening Post*'s money was the immediate cause of the tale's existence, its compositional roots may reside elsewhere and provide insights into previously overlooked values.

The ultimate of the lightbulb riddles asks: How many Irishmen does it take to change a lightbulb? And the answer: Ten. One to change the lightbulb and nine to stand around rememberin' how beautiful the old bulb was.

Many teachers of Fitzgerald's works instruct their students that, though Fitzgerald's heritage was, in part, Irish, none of his principal protagonists are noticeably Irish. Well, is that really so? Fitzgerald's dominant vision, the double vision, may well be informed by his Irish forebears. Fitzgerald himself may have been one of those nine Irishmen standing around remembering how beautiful that old bulb was, but, once in a great while, his main character will be one who will up and change that bulb.

Fitzgerald himself noted that the family of his mother, Mollie McQuillan Fitzgerald, was straight 1850-potato-famine Irish, about which a very young Scott may not have been especially enthusiastic. A particularly oft-quoted line is one from a July 18, 1933, letter to John O'Hara in which the adult F. Scott Fitzgerald identified himself as "half black Irish." This "black Irish" is a reference to the lineage of those Irish along the southeast coast of Ireland who reputedly intermingled with the survivors of the defeated Spanish Armada. Fitzgerald's remark came as a response to O'Hara's warmly Irish inquiry about Fitzgerald's skill at presenting the assertive upwardly mobile character: "I wonder why you do the climber so well. Is it the Irish in you?"[2] While no one makes excessive claims for Fitzgerald as an Irish-American writer, there may be something in the lightbulb joke that will illuminate a second look. The pith in the lightbulb riddle, to which Irishmen and Irish Americans invariably respond with knowing laughter, captures the melancholy and brooding reflection of the stereotypical Celtic posture. This melancholy, informed by black bile and originally one of the four chief humors, often shapes a lament, a "lamentable" literary or musical composition mourning some loss. It is this sadness, a gloomy and thoughtful reflection, that lurks in the unswept corners of many of Fitzgerald's tales: some minor, such as "Two for a Cent" (1922), "The Love Boat" (1927), "Diagnosis" (1932), or "John Jackson's Arcady" (1924); some major, such as "Winter Dreams" (1922) and "Babylon Revisited" (1931). Can it be that melancholy marks a portion of Fitzgerald's best writing? Reread the last page of *The Great Gatsby* with this is mind. If Fitzgerald's stories are not exactly tragic, they are often laments, and the lament may be both Charlie Wales's "Gone!" and Fitzgerald's.

Fitzgerald records with, and for, them all—John Jackson, Charlie Wales, Dexter Green—whether what they experience ever really happened in a nominal sense in the author's, not the narrator's, tale. Whether or not they *were* in Fitzgerald's life, they have a life of their own in the reader's imagination. The lamentations of Fitzgerald contain both joy and sadness, happiness and tears. It is sad that the things celebrated are gone. But isn't it fine that they were at all! It is sad and fine, and the protagonists of many of Fitzgerald's short stories are both, all the sad young men and all the fine young men—and an occasional man who is not so young. Aren't we lucky that, after the beautiful things we joyfully and sadly remember, they live in our memories, in our stories?

2. Le Vot, *Fitzgerald: A Biography*, 7; Andrew Turnbull, ed., *The Letters of F. Scott Fitzgerald*, 503; Matthew J. Bruccoli, ed., *Selected Letters of John O'Hara*, 75–76.

Isn't it a joy? Isn't it sad? Of such stuff are the Celtic character and tale made.

Some of Fitzgerald's stories, such as "John Jackson's Arcady," might be compared to an indigenous Irish musical instrument, the clairseach, an ancient wire-stringed harp. The clairseach is different from the standard harp in that it is bowed forward, straining in its yearning—a key word to describe and summarize many of Fitzgerald's tales. The notes of the clairseach linger longer than those of the harp, and it is the lingering, echoing sounds that make it both difficult to play and unique. A musician playing this brass-stringed instrument must learn to live with his or her mistakes, because the sound resonates so long—far longer than that of the more common European gut- or hair-stringed harps. The rich, lingering quality of the instrument's music is characteristic of what might be called the Irish sense, whether it is in their music, their jokes, or their tales. So it is with Fitzgerald's melancholy stories. Whether it is the clairseach or the cittern, bodhran, tin whistle, or button accordion, the Celtic sound is never confused with the zampogna or mandolin of Italian music, say, with its passion or violence, the operatic quality present not only in its opera but also in its folk tunes and folktales alike. It is the aural articulation of melancholy that is the quintessence of the Irish character.

It is the yearning, the living with mistakes, and the melancholy that might serve to place some of Fitzgerald's short stories in a tradition of Gaelic tale tellers extending from the northern melancholy of the Ossianic poems to the tragic and liberating stories of the subsequent longing after leaving home and suddenly (or not so suddenly) seeing clearly the effects known to the Irish tale tellers as the American wake—that long farewell told of by classic storytellers such as Killarney's Eamon Kelly. What has come to be called Fitzgerald's roots-pilgrimage theme has, in turn, its roots in the stories of emigration sometimes known as the American wake. This wake has nothing to do with death or dying but with leaving a place to which you may never return. Like those tales, Fitzgerald's stories of leaving home and the desire (whether John Jackson's or Jay Gatsby's) to return to a certain spot are imbued with the spirit of an almost vanished ambience. It is, however, the going away that inspires insight and illumination.

The question, of course, is how Fitzgerald came to this Irish understanding of the sadness of parting. Various biographers are helpful in providing a hint here. None of Fitzgerald's major biographers place special emphasis on the importance of his Celtic heritage; in fact, most would agree that early on he identified himself more closely with his paternal ancestors, the Fitzgeralds and the Scotts whose "sympathies were Southern." Fitzgerald's father, Edward, was a dapper man with excellent southern manners; the family of his mother, Mollie McQuillan, like most of the Irish in St. Paul, was "regarded as common," though it was the McQuillan money that gave Fitzgerald the advantages of the exclusive residential Summit Avenue neighborhood in St. Paul and, eventually, Fitzgerald's expensive education.[3] Fitzgerald's disaffection with his parents ironically may have been due to his judgment of them as mediocre, the more curious because Mollie's hopes and ambitions for her son increased as she accepted her husband's business failures. Mollie Fitzgerald "bitterly resented the fall from status her husband's business failures had caused, and she was determined that her son would suffer no social disadvantage because of them."[4]

About his parents, Fitzgerald could be cruel: "My father is a moron and my mother is a neurotic, half-insane with pathological nervous worry . . . . Between them they haven't and never had the brains of Calvin Coolidge." Whatever else, it was certain that "the Catholic father of this household was a universally acknowledged failure." If "John Jackson's Arcady" has any autobiographical underpinnings at all, it is that Jackson is a reversed projection of some aspect of Fitzgerald's father, at once an idealized apotheosis (John Jackson in deed, Edward Fitzgerald in his son's mind) and a "universally acknowledged failure" (John Jackson in his own view, Edward Fitzgerald to the McQuillans), inspired by his son's academic debacle. The son, Ellery, would be a further projection of F. Scott Fitzgerald himself returning not from New Haven but from Princeton in December 1915. In a final analysis, however, it may be,

3. Matthew J. Bruccoli, *Some Sort of Epic Grandeur: The Life of F. Scott Fitzgerald,* 11, 13.

4. Joan M. Allen, *Candles and Carnival Lights: The Catholic Sensibility of F. Scott Fitzgerald,* 9.

as Matthew J. Bruccoli observes, that there "is little documentation for young Scott's relationship with his parents. . . . Scott rarely spoke about them . . . it is as if they scarcely existed."[5]

As young Fitzgerald shared intensely the embarrassment of his father's being fired from his job with Proctor and Gamble in Buffalo, New York, he found there the first of three new and important male role models. As a boy of seven living in Buffalo, Fitzgerald "fell under the spell" of Reverend Michael Fallon of the Church of the Holy Angels, an educated scholar, able administrator, skilled rhetorician, and mesmerizing homilist—quite a different priest and Irishman from the peasant-class Irish clergy the Fitzgerald and McQuillan families were accustomed to in St. Paul. The class-conscious young Fitzgerald's nascent interest in the Emerald Isle, and County Fermanagh in particular, of his McQuillan grandparents began to stir. Its full liberation came in September 1911 when Fitzgerald entered the Newman School in Hackensack, New Jersey, and a year later met Father Cyril Sigourney Webster Fay, a trustee of Newman and later its headmaster; through Father Fay he met the Anglo-Irish novelist Shane Leslie, a "romanticist on the Irish question." According to James R. Mellow, "Both Fay and Shane Leslie, with whom Fitzgerald became friendly during these years, effected something like a religious conversion in Fitzgerald, who was weary of the glum, varnished-oak Irish Catholicism of his St. Paul childhood. They brought to him a sense of a Catholic elite, a society of money and style . . . . [Leslie's] romantic faith in the cause of Irish nationalism stirred Fitzgerald's interest in his own ancestry."[6]

Fitzgerald never made an accommodation to his Irish Catholicism, but, carrying the scars of the financial roller-coaster ride of his youth, he recognized a part of his yearning, the elite, that society of money and style. Monsignor Fay and Shane Leslie opened to him "a romantic and literary sort of Irish heritage" later embellished by Edmund Wilson such that Fitzgerald "would begin to speak with pride of his own Celtic background." Fitzgerald discovered Celtic music and literature, and

5. James R. Mellow, *Invented Lives: F. Scott and Zelda Fitzgerald,* 22; Allen, *Candles and Carnival Lights,* 1; Bruccoli, *Epic Grandeur,* 24.
6. Allen, *Candles and Carnival Lights,* 7; Mellow, *Invented Lives,* 25, 27.

"Fay and Leslie suggested that Ireland was a romantic lost cause." The attraction for the romantic young man of lost causes was overwhelming. Fitzgerald "never allowed his religion and ancestry to become part of his public image; . . . yet his Irishness was an essential part of him."[7] Fitzgerald so assimilated the characteristic tenor of Gaelic literature into himself that he transformed it, as he did with every other influence, into something autochthonously American and his own. The spirit and tone of the Irish are subsumed into subject matter uniquely his own—from the "profound melancholy" of "Winter Dreams" to the incremental refrain "Gone!" of "Babylon Revisited." Thus appears the Fitzgeraldian Irish American pensive brooding that subtends many of his tales, including "John Jackson's Arcady."

Like Jeanne Crain's 1949 film, *Pinky,* the bulk of Fitzgerald's heroes, of course, pass as pabulum-pure Americans, eastern-educated midwesterners with nary a brogue in the lot. But careful examination discovers the shamrock in the soul of Dexter Green, the Irish mobility in the face of Charlie Wales. Yet "John Jackson's Arcady" and its hero escape the lingering melancholy of "Winter Dreams" and "Babylon Revisited." Why? Of the ten stories Fitzgerald published in 1924, recall that he sold four to the *Saturday Evening Post.* It is more than an astute author tailoring his material to suit the requirements of the *Post* audience that is responsible for the upbeat conclusion of "John Jackson's Arcady." The reason simply may be that Fitzgerald was at the peak of his power; in April 1924 he was preparing to leave for France, and "John Jackson's Arcady" was the last of the ten stories that earned a total of $15,750 and would enable him to be, as he wrote in his *Ledger,* "out of the woods at last and starting novel." Even as he was "writing stories that were supposed to free him from the necessity of writing more stories," that sense of a necessary job well done as he returned his attention to his masterpiece *The Great Gatsby* is reflected in the exuberance of the story's last two pages.[8]

Moreover, let's say, for convenience sake, there are two sorts of heroes in Fitzgerald. There are those like Charlie Wales, Dexter Green, and

7. Allen, *Candles and Carnival Lights,* 21, 22.
8. Bruccoli, *Epic Grandeur,* 530–31; Le Vot, *Fitzgerald: A Biography,* 139; Matthew J. Bruccoli, ed., *The Price Was High: The Last Uncollected Stories of F. Scott Fitzgerald,* xv.

John Jackson who know that "it" or "she" is "gone" and are painted in shades of melancholy blue, pastel to deepest indigo. Identify them as Anglo-Irish. There is another sort, perhaps more famous, like Jimmy Gatz, who never knows and never accepts the fact that one cannot relive the past. He does not know as much as the first hero, but he is heroic precisely because if he appears naïve and innocent, then he is loyal to his quest; he is engaged in the pursuit. If characters like Wales and Green know better, they still, in their retrospection, bear the outraged fortune of the melancholy Irishman. They are, finally, cut from the same peat, both sorts.

Most frequently, the ones who do not suffer, or suffer less, are the narrators like Nick Carraway, who neither believe in the importance of "gone" nor are melancholy. They are not pursuers, not of life at full throttle, but are the witnesses, the recorders and reporters, and are detached and sans delusions, illusions, or dreams. They believe they suffer not, intellectuals all, the quintessential craftsmen. Like Harry, the dying writer in Hemingway's "The Snows of Kilimanjaro," in his contempt for those "who wrecked," ironically placed in the paragraph immediately after the celebrated "poor Julian" passage, they believe nothing could hurt them if they did not care. So some Fitzgerald characters who are writers, Nick Carraway for example, may sit safely behind the barricade of their typewriters or climb high into an ivory tower and purchase a sliver of greater intellectuality with a chip of their true heart. There is no mud high up, nor is there hurt, nor, at last, melancholy. In case of an attack to the heart, the safest place to be is in one's own mind. Dexter Green cares and suffers; Charlie Wales cares and suffers; John Jackson cares, suffers, and transcends.

Here, the ages of Fitzgerald's characters are, as always, instructive. "John Jackson's Arcady" does not provide a tale of midlife crisis. It is no male menopause myth. At the end of their stories, Wales is thirty-five and Green is thirty-two; most of Fitzgerald's memorable characters are about that age. John Jackson is forty-five, which is ancient in the Fitzgerald canon where it sometimes seems as if almost all the women are between seventeen and twenty-three, and the men—Tom, Jay, and Nick, for example—reach their peak of power, affluence, and influence at thirty. Thus, "John Jackson's Arcady" is unlike most of the celebrated and better-known Fitzgerald stories, because its hero is older than most representative Fitzgerald males. His memorable men are obviously those who were about Fitzgerald's age at the time of composition. The romantic Gordon Sterrett is "about twenty-four" in "May Day," which was published in *The Smart Set* in July of 1920; Fitzgerald turned twenty-four in September of that year. George Hannaford who appears in "Magnetism" in the *Saturday Evening Post* for March 3, 1928, "was thirty"; Fitzgerald at the time was thirty-one. Fitzgerald has created few memorable men over forty-five—perhaps because he was dead at forty-four. Thus, John Jackson, while not exclusively so, is something of an anomaly in the Fitzgerald canon.

There is, however, a more curious problem with "John Jackson's Arcady" that may be unique in all Fitzgerald's short stories: that is, determining its genre. If the audience of the story is asked to accept it as realism, it is a far stretch. The proposition that Jackson returns unannounced and unexpected—indeed on the spur of the moment—to his hometown, in fact, almost directly to the home of his boyhood where he meets Alice, the lost love of his youth, demands more suspension than most readers will be able to require of their disbelief. The story tumbles victim in that case to a coincidence that is outrageously unbelievable.

Yet there is to that central scene in section 3 of the story that which suggests it is not quite to be taken literally or realistically. There is a blue, illusory quality to suggest that this "bright, warm afternoon, and the silver sliver of the moon riding already in the east" is something beyond realism.[9] It is not science fiction or fantasy like "The Diamond as Big as the Ritz" (1922), but there is a sense that this section takes place *presque vu*, or perhaps even *jamais vu*, in the mind of Jackson as he imagines walking the road, "a short green aisle crowded with memories" (149). It is too much to ask a mature reader to accept this section as literal. But as an introspective journey into the dark woods of self—much like that of Nathaniel Hawthorne's "Young Goodman Brown," the brilliant flashes of clarity when the chaplain almost saw absolute truth in Joseph Heller's *Catch-22*, or the introspective journey to self-knowledge so strongly implied in Dante's opening terza rima to canto 1 of *The*

9. Bruccoli, ed., *Price Was High,* 149. All subsequent page references to "John Jackson's Arcady" are to this edition and will appear parenthetically in the text.

Inferno (which provides the epigraph for this essay)—the story opens itself to its audience. Thus we are not asked to see Jackson's first love, Alice, literally in the house where he was born, but it is "her ghost who was most alive here," not in a shuttered and vine-tangled dwelling that "was no longer a dwelling," but as he calls to her, embraces her, and kisses her, it is in his reverie, and John Jackson is "convinced that his own imagination had evoked the reality" (150). There is a touch of Henry James's "The Jolly Corner" as well as "Young Goodman Brown" at work here. Like Spencer Brydon, Jackson conjures up his "might-have-been," but, unlike Jay Gatsby, Jackson knows that he cannot relive that past—or any other—with Alice, who is, if not happily then at least solidly and securely, married to George Harland (152).

That this journey is not to be taken as realistic is apparent to the careful reader who notes that the hometown to which Jackson "returns" is Florence, an American locale that bears the name of the Italian city noted for fine art characterized not by realistic but by idealized portrayal. Fitzgerald's intention on this point is apparent as early on as the story's title. Most contemporary users of the word "arcady" understand it to be an ideal rather than a real place. That same reader is reminded that the "Arcady" of this story's title, more than a place of rural peace and simplicity, is a pastoral district of ancient central Peloponnesus, Greece, scarcely to be reached in a train ride of seventy miles. To reach it, John Jackson must cross over "the border of the next state" (149), and that next state is a state of consciousness.

John Jackson has an experience not of *presque vu* (almost seen), or of brilliant flashes of clarity that almost come to him, but an optical phenomenon corollary of both *presque vu* and *déjà vu* (already seen). It is, in fact, the opposite of *déjà vu* called *jamais vu,* which is, simply put, something you think you've seen but you've never seen. This subtle confusion between illusion and reality is characteristic of paramnesia. Like its more famous opposite number, *jamais vu* is an illusion of memory rather than of the senses, and it corresponds in simplified Freudian terms to the memory of an unconscious fantasy and occurs when healthy, normal people are in a state of exhaustion—all of which might be said to apply to Jackson, a normal and healthy man. Other gifted American writers of fiction have been fascinated by these states. As Heller explored *presque vu* in *Catch-22,* David Morrell expands significantly on *jamais vu* in *The Fifth Profession. Jamais vu,* then, may be cataloged as part of a normal man's panoply of defense mechanisms. It is not difficult to see how this might apply to Jackson. In psychological terms generally, it is a case of the subconscious mind working faster than the conscious mind.

To demonstrate that something unique happens in the central sections of "John Jackson's Arcady," the reader need only compare these passages with less skillfully handled situations that are thematically identical, those in which successful men make pilgrimages to the homes—the physical houses—of their youth. The vast nostalgia Fitzgerald presents in the sentimental excursions of Abercrombie in "Two for a Cent," Bill Frothington in "The Love Boat," and Charlie Clayhorne in "Diagnosis" are examples. "John Jackson's Arcady" is superior to any of these. If there is anything missing from "John Jackson's Arcady," it is the brilliantly crafted poetic prose of "Winter Dreams" or *The Great Gatsby,* but Fitzgerald's presentation here of the flight of the subconscious sets it apart from his run-of-the-mill work for *Metropolitan Magazine* or the *Saturday Evening Post.*

The reader notes that Jackson's decision to return home after twenty years is spontaneous and serendipitous. That Alice is there upon his arrival can only be acceptable if it takes place in Jackson's mind. Much the same might be said for his return in the story's fifth section to the surprise testimonial prepared for him by the grateful town's Civic Welfare League. Jackson sits unseen behind a pillar and listens to the praise of everyone to whom the reader has been introduced in section 1: Fowler, his chief clerk; Mrs. Ralston, who has often prompted Jackson into some of his many charities; and even, unexpectedly, Jackson's nemesis, Thomas J. MacDowell. All come forward in the story's final section to articulate their appreciation of Jackson's generosity and value to his fellow man. What a triumph for Jackson, who has been provoked into his earlier contemplation by the news of his son, Ellery, being dismissed by the dean of his college at New Haven, Jackson's alma mater, to hear the "storm of applause" (159), and even the words of his archenemy that he would be honored to call John Jackson a friend (159).

The reconciliation that takes place in the final scene of "John Jackson's Arcady" is not merely a reconciliation between Jackson and his ne'er-do-well son, Ellery; the more significant reconciliation is in Jackson's reconciling himself to the facts of his life. Jackson's wife "ran off one windy night" (143); his son has been expelled from college (144); young men in the city look to Jackson to "disclose some secret formula that would make their lives as popular and successful and happy as his own" (145). All of this occurs at exactly the moment he is seized by the thought that his life may have been meaningless. The significance of this will become clear if readers reflect on how broadcast and universal a phenomenon is portrayed here. Walt Whitman captured it perfectly in "Crossing Brooklyn Ferry":

> It is not upon you alone the dark patches fall,
> The dark threw its patches down upon me also,
> The best I had done seem'd to me blank and suspicious,
> My great thoughts as I supposed them, were they
>   not in reality meager?

As it was for Whitman, so it was for John Jackson. In moments of candor, we all will suspect, and acknowledge, ourselves capable of exactly the same sort of momentary—sometimes not-so-brief—self-doubt.

John Jackson wants life to mean. He wants *his* life to mean. At a time when Fitzgerald's peers, like Hemingway, had established a dominant philosophical mood of "*nada e pues nada*," Fitzgerald's tale is hopeful and hope-filled. It is life-affirming. It is almost as though this story's "Everything!" is an anticipation and antidote to the culmination of Hemingway's "nothing" that would come nine years later in "A Clean, Well-Lighted Place." Early on, Jackson has determined that he expects he will answer the question "What have I got out of life?" with a single word—"Nothing!" (144). When the time comes, Jackson changes that "Nothing!" to "Everything!" (161). It is possible that by 1933, Fitzgerald would have had enough of life to agree with Hemingway's view, but Fitzgerald's 1924 tale of John Jackson presents an optimistic view that is as representative of the moment of its publication and its audience as Hemingway's is of his.

Fitzgerald's friend Ernest Hemingway did not invent the nihilism of the lost generation. He gave it its most succinct articulation. Perhaps the best thing to have lighted that clean, well-lighted place would have been a new bulb. "John Jackson's Arcady" suggests that it is better to change the bulb than to curse the darkness. Fitzgerald seems to say that we all have panicked moments of insight, dark introspection, and self-doubt. Jackson is unique among Fitzgerald heroes in that he discovers, unlike Jay Gatsby (whose story is published exactly one year to the month later), that one cannot relive the past. But the point of the novel and Jackson's short story is the same: One cannot relive the past. And if the past cannot be relived, what is it for? It is, Fitzgerald suggests, to acknowledge, appreciate, and accept. The old bulb is *not* more beautiful than the "changed" bulb, but it does illuminate the "what we were" that makes possible the "who we are"—if we accept that which is gone and see our way in the light of who we are now.

Moreover, unlike Dexter Green and Charlie Wales, John Jackson is able to transcend the melancholy that infects them and rise again to see the richness and possibilities, accomplishments and rewards of life, as well as its aborted relationships and failed attempts—as husband, father, lover . . . whatever. Thus Fitzgerald presents here not an excessively romantic vision, nor the fashionable philosophical funk of the 1920s, but a balanced portrait replete with human understanding.

Is the story marred by its patently sentimental ending? The prodigal son returning home to a welcoming father is at least as biblical as it is sentimental. Is the story itself sentimental? No more than another story of a generous human being who is so involved in doing good for others that he feels his own life has passed him by: Frank Capra's 1946 film *It's a Wonderful Life,* which so much resembles "John Jackson's Arcady." The story of George Bailey in Capra's film was anticipated by twenty-two years in Fitzgerald's creation of John Jackson. They both make similar discoveries, and Fitzgerald's tale requires even less willing suspension of disbelief than that required of Capra's audience.

Why then has "John Jackson's Arcady" not been a popular story? Not as popular as *It's a Wonderful Life,* but why not as well known or accepted as "Winter Dreams" or "Babylon Revisited," both of which have been anthologized many times? The more inspired prose of these two short stories aside, perhaps it is because while melancholy can be fashionable, sentimentality almost never is, at least among intellectuals. I knew a girl once who fancied herself a throwback to the flappers of the 1920s, and she bragged that she was completely without sentimentality, as if that fact were some clever badge of honor. There is something in sentiment that cloys for intellectual and sophisticated readers. These are the same people, by the way, who affect the pose of high disdain for *It's a Wonderful Life* but who love to wallow in "*nada e pues nada.*"

Yet it is the *Post* audience for this Fitzgerald short story and the unabashedly sentimental audience for Capra's film who are far larger in numbers. It is not Hemingway's code hero alone who may survive. It is John Jackson, with his dreams of the past dashed and a new, balanced view of the human, and his own, situation, who, in the story's last words, "could stand anything now forever—anything that came, anything at all" (161). John Jackson remembers how beautiful the old bulb was, but in the story's final section, in his new arcady, he steps out from among the rest of the crowd and changes the bulb.

CLIMBING "JACOB'S LADDER"

ALAN MARGOLIES

"Jacob's Ladder," written in June 1927 while the Fitzgeralds were living at "Ellerslie," their rented mansion in Edgemoor, Delaware, was the result of Fitzgerald's trip to Hollywood that previous January where he was working on the script for the never-to-be-made film "Lipstick." The story was published in the *Saturday Evening Post* on August 20, 1927, but was not collected in book form until 1973 when it was included in *Bits of Paradise,* stylized for British readers with single quotation marks (and double quotation marks for quotes within quotes) and the omission of periods after "Mr." and "Mrs." In 1989 it was republished without these changes in Matthew J. Bruccoli's edition of *The Short Stories of F. Scott Fitzgerald: A New Collection.*

A number of critics have suggested an autobiographical interpretation of the story. Nancy Milford notes that "Fitzgerald's attitude toward [actress] Lois Moran took material form" in "Jacob's Ladder." Bruccoli states, "Full of regret, loss, and loneliness, 'Jacob's Ladder' is a projection of Fitzgerald's feelings at thirty." André Le Vot claims that it "reveal[s] how persistent were the feelings triggered in him by Lois Moran." Scott Donaldson sees "Jacob's Ladder" as one of a number of stories in which Fitzgerald "sublimated his yearning" for the young Moran "by emphasizing the inappropriateness of a 'middle-aged' man . . . falling heels over head for a girl about half his age." Robert A. Martin observes: "In one sense, the story is a modified version of *Pygmalion,* stripped down from

Bernard Shaw's play and transferred to a new circumstance and Holly-wood setting. In quite another sense, it is Fitzgerald using Hollywood as a metaphor for his own romantic attraction to Lois Moran . . . and as a fictional equivalent for his own sublimated passion." Earlier, both John A. Higgins and Bruccoli had also suggested a "*Pygmalion*-like" relationship between the two major characters in the story.[1]

Although no critic has ranked "Jacob's Ladder" among Fitzgerald's best short stories, a number feel that it is one of the better ones. Robert Sklar calls it "powerful and sensitive," while Bruccoli refers to it as one of a number of "good stories" omitted from *Taps at Reveille*.[2]

Some have chosen to point out the story's flaws too. James R. Mellow sees "touches of mawkishness at the end of the story" but a "genuinely affecting final moment." Bryant Mangum notes that the unhappy ending, while new for a Fitzgerald *Saturday Evening Post* story, was not a radical change since "what the editors had done, in effect, was to approve the replacement of one kind of sentimentality—the virtue-is-always-rewarded variety in 'The Third Casket,' for example—for another which, as in 'Jacob's Ladder,' invites sympathy for the hero's sad plight." Earlier, in 1971, before "Jacob's Ladder" appeared in *Bits of Paradise*, John A. Higgins had written that "though it cannot be ranked among Fitzgerald's finest pieces, [it] is probably the best of his stories yet uncollected." Higgins continued: "The story's plausibility is weakened by Fitzgerald's failure to explore Jacob's background and initial motivation, by Jenny's ludicrous dialog in the opening scenes, by an extraneous, melodramatic scene with a blackmailer, and by the incorporeality of the lover Jenny chooses over Jacob. Nevertheless, the story succeeds because the emotion is there and because the denouement is both plausible and appropriate."[3]

Fitzgerald himself recognized at least some of these flaws. In 1929, when Scribner's refused to let Bennett Cerf and Random House use

1. Nancy Milford, *Zelda: A Biography*, 129; Matthew J. Bruccoli, *Some Sort of Epic Grandeur: The Life of F. Scott Fitzgerald*, 262; André Le Vot, *F. Scott Fitzgerald: A Biography*, 227; Scott Donaldson, *Fool for Love: F. Scott Fitzgerald*, 55; Robert A. Martin, "Hollywood in Fitzgerald: After Paradise," 140; John A. Higgins, *F. Scott Fitzgerald: A Study of the Stories*, 96; Bruccoli, *Epic Grandeur*, 262.

2. Robert Sklar, *F. Scott Fitzgerald: The Last Laocoön*, 228; Bruccoli, *Epic Grandeur*, 394.

3. James R. Mellow, *Invented Lives: F. Scott and Zelda Fitzgerald*, 290; Bryant Mangum, *A Fortune Yet: Money in the Art of F. Scott Fitzgerald's Short Stories*, 86; Higgins, *Fitzgerald: Study of the Stories*, 97.

for a Modern Library anthology any of his short stories that had previously been collected, Fitzgerald felt that "Jacob's Ladder" was "the
best available." "But it will look rather sentimental beside Conrad E.
M. Forster ect. [sic]," he wrote. "Still it is a pretty darn good story,"
he added. Then, in 1935, while planning a never-to-appear anthology
of previously uncollected stories, one of which was "Jacob's Ladder," he
wrote that "each story contain[ed] some special fault—sentimentality,
faulty construction, confusing change of pace—or else was too obviously
made for the trade."[4]

But he had come very close to including "Jacob's Ladder" earlier that
year in Taps at Reveille, so close that it had been set in galleys, then briefly
corrected and emended. Soon after, he wrote Lois Moran: "I have a book
of short stories called 'Taps at Reveille' coming out in a few weeks and
I thought of including that old piece 'Jacob's Ladder' but I found that I
had so thoroughly disemboweled it of its best description for 'Tender is
the Night' that it would be offering an empty shell."[5]

"Disemboweled" was far too strong a word to describe what he had
done. In his copy of the discarded galleys from Taps at Reveille, Fitzgerald
marked some six passages that he used, with some changes, in Tender Is
the Night. Even the few others that the reader can spot do not add up to
disembowelment.

Three passages in romantic scenes between Jacob Booth and Jenny
Prince early in the short story reoccur in book 1, chapter 15, a scene
with Dick Diver and Rosemary Hoyt in a taxi in Paris:

(1) Driving homeward through the soft night, she put up her face quietly
to be kissed. Holding her in the hollow of his arm, Jacob rubbed his
cheek against her cheek's softness and then looked down at her for a long
moment.
"Such a lovely child," he said gravely.[6]

4. Matthew J. Bruccoli, ed., As Ever, Scott Fitz—: Letters between F. Scott Fitzgerald and
His Literary Agent, Harold Ober—1919–1940, 130; Matthew J. Bruccoli and Margaret M.
Duggan, eds., Correspondence of F. Scott Fitzgerald, 406.
5. Bruccoli and Duggan, eds., Correspondence, 403.
6. Matthew J. Bruccoli, ed., The Short Stories of F. Scott Fitzgerald: A New Collection,
354. All subsequent page references to "Jacob's Ladder" are to this edition and will appear
parenthetically in the text.

(2) He kissed her, without enjoying it. There was no shadow of passion in her eyes or on her mouth; there was a faint spray of champagne on her breath. She clung nearer, desperately. (356)

(3) Hesitating tentatively, he kissed her and again he was chilled by the innocence of her kiss, the eyes that at the moment of contact looked beyond him out into the darkness of the night, the darkness of the world. She did not know yet that splendor was something in the heart; at the moment when she should realize that and melt into the passion of the universe he could take her without question or regret. (357)

Another reused passage from "Jacob's Ladder" takes place in Hollywood when Jenny tells Jacob of her movie success:

"Everybody that's seen the rushes says it's the first one I've had sex appeal in."
"What are the rushes?"
"When they run off what they took the day before. They say it's the first time I've had sex appeal."
"I don't notice it," he teased her.
"You wouldn't. But I have." (360)

In *Tender Is the Night,* Dick and Rosemary have a similar conversation on the set for the film "The Grandeur That Was Rome."[7]

In addition, some shorter passages were reused. A description of Jenny—"Her face, the face of a saint, an intense little Madonna" (352)—was used for Nicole in *Tender Is the Night:* "Her face, the face of a saint, a viking Madonna" (33); Jacob's jealousy of the actor Raffino ("He was a gruff white bird now." [364]) was transformed into Dick's jealousy of the actor Nicotera ("He was a gruff red bird." [218]); and the argument over Raffino, " 'Oh Jake,' she cried, 'please lemme go. I never felt so terrible and mixed up in my life' " (364), was changed to "Dick, let me go. I never felt so mixed up in my life" (218).

There was even a passage similar to one previously used in *The Great Gatsby.* At one point Jacob wires Jenny in Hollywood, "New York

7. F. Scott Fitzgerald, *Tender Is the Night,* 212. All subsequent page references to *Tender Is the Night* are to the 1960 reprint edition and will appear parenthetically in the text.

desolate. . . . The night clubs all closed. Black wreaths on the Statue
of Civic Virtue. Please work hard and be remarkably happy" (359).
Didn't Fitzgerald recall that when Daisy Buchanan asked if her friends
in Chicago missed her, Nick Carraway replied, "The whole town is
desolate. All the cars have the left rear wheel painted black as a mourning
wreath and there's a persistent wail all night along the North Shore"? Of
course, it is likely that the novelist was thinking more of Moran than *The
Great Gatsby* here. Moran had sent Fitzgerald a telegram with a similar
motif from the West Coast on March 14, 1927: "HOLLYWOOD COMPLETELY
DISRUPTED SINCE YOU LEFT . . . BOOTLEGGERS GONE OUT OF BUSINESS COTTON
CLUB CLOSED ALL FLAGS AT HALF MAST EVEN JOHN BARRYMORE HAS GONE
OUT OF TOWN BOTTLES OF LOVE TO YOU BOTH." The actress had been
reading novels suggested by Fitzgerald (she mentions David Garnett's
The Sailor's Return and Hemingway's *The Sun Also Rises*), and one can
easily surmise that *The Great Gatsby* had at one time been on her reading
list too.[8]

But it was the reuse of material in *Tender Is the Night* that bothered
Fitzgerald. Was he also concerned about some similarities in plot? In
early drafts of his novel, Fitzgerald even gave his actress the same
surname, Prince, and the actor the same surname, Raffino, but later
he changed the names to Hoyt and Nicotera.

There is no reason to dispute Bruccoli's statement that Fitzgerald was
thinking of "Jacob's Ladder" when he wrote Maxwell Perkins sometime
in the middle of 1929 that he was "working night and day on novel from
new angle. . . ." Bruccoli states that the " 'new angle' can be traced back
to 1927 when [Fitzgerald] had written 'Jacob's Ladder,' a story which
deals seriously with an affair between a cultured man of thirty-three
and a seventeen-year-old actress." And there is no reason to disagree
with Bruccoli in his evaluation of the influence of the short story upon
the novel. The sequence in the holograph draft of *Tender Is the Night* that
later became chapters 20 and 21 of book 2 does draw "rather heavily on
'Jacob's Ladder' for the feelings of an older man about a young actress."
And "[i]n the story—as in *Tender is the Night*—the man had previously

---

8. F. Scott Fitzgerald, *The Great Gatsby*, 11; Donaldson, *Fool for Love*, 54. Moran's letter
mentioning the two books is in Bruccoli and Duggan, eds., *Correspondence*, 206.

failed to reciprocate the girl's passion, and now he is jealous of her young suitor. . . ."9

But there is hardly any similarity in personality or background between Jacob Booth, a bored playboy who helps Jenny become a Hollywood star and falls in love with her, and the sophisticated psychiatrist Dick Diver. And Jenny, when we first meet her at the age of sixteen, bears more resemblance in her lower-class background to Tom Buchanan's mistress Myrtle Wilson (in *The Great Gatsby)* than to Rosemary Hoyt. When Jenny says, "Geeze! I hope I never have to go to court again" after Jacob denies her that first kiss (354), we know this is not the much-more-refined Rosemary. Even after her Hollywood success, Jenny is not a carbon copy of Rosemary Hoyt. In effect, while there *are* similarities between the two stories, "Jacob's Ladder" is a much different tale from *Tender Is the Night.*

Actress Moran's life had been intertwined in a number of ways with Fitzgerald's. There is general agreement that she was a model for Rosemary, but obviously not the only one. In his plan for the novel Fitzgerald had written:

> The actress was born in 1908. Her career is like Lois or Mary Hay— that is, she differs from most actresses by being a lady, simply reeking of vitality, health, sensuality. Rather gross as compared to the heroine, or rather *will be* gross for at present her youth covers it. Mimi-Lupe Velez.
>
> We see her first at the very beginning of her carreer [*sic*]. She's already made one big picture.
>
> We follow her from age 17 to age 22.10

Moran was also in some way a model for Jenny Prince in Hollywood. But Moran's early life as a ballet dancer in Paris bore no resemblance to the coarse, uneducated Jenny. Whatever their relationship in Hollywood or later, the novelist's correspondence as well as his nonfictional writing

---

9. Matthew J. Bruccoli, *The Composition of "Tender Is the Night": A Study of the Manuscripts,* 59, 66, 127.

10. Ibid., 81.

suggests in no way that the relationship reached the emotional intensity found in "Jacob's Ladder." Moran's correspondence with biographer Arthur Mizener in 1950 seems to verify this, suggesting that Fitzgerald thought of her mainly as a young disciple.[11]

Further, in using the name Jenny Prince, Fitzgerald may also have been thinking of Ginevra King, his early love (Jenny = Ginevra; Prince = King), and may have used some of the emotion from that relationship, too, while writing "Jacob's Ladder." But Jenny's lower-class background, her speaking mannerisms, and her Hollywood success are in no way meant to be reminders of Ginevra King either.

Finally, Jacob's emotional quest for Jenny was not a new one for Fitzgerald's fictional characters. Richard Lehan's description of Gatsby's quest for Daisy Buchanan can also be applied here: "The desire for Daisy energizes his world, fuels his very being; and when he loses her, romantic possibility is exhausted, a romantic state of mind depleted."[12]

Was Jacob Booth named for John Wilkes Booth? One of Fitzgerald's ancestors, Mary Surratt, first cousin of Edward Fitzgerald, Scott's father, was hanged for conspiring in the Lincoln assassination. In addition, Edward Fitzgerald, as a boy, supported the Confederacy and, according to Andrew Turnbull, "rowed Confederate spies across the river."[13] As a youngster, Fitzgerald wrote at least three works with a Civil War background: two short stories, "A Debt of Honor" (1910) and "The Room with the Green Blinds" (1911), the latter an unbelievable story about the shooting of John Wilkes Booth, and a play, "Coward" (1913). After "Jacob's Ladder" there were two more stories about the Civil War, "The Night before Chancellorsville" (1935) and "The End of Hate" (1940), the latter including a scene in which Lincoln's assassination is mentioned. Furthermore, it was not unusual for Fitzgerald's characters to have familiar historical names. Basil Duke Lee, the young hero of eight *Saturday Evening Post* stories, Braddock Washington, the richest

11. Bruccoli (*Epic Grandeur*, 257–58) and Mellow (*Invented Lives*, 284) say that Moran was always chaperoned whenever she was with Fitzgerald. The correspondence with Mizener is in the Arthur Mizener Papers at the Princeton University Library.

12. Richard D. Lehan, *"The Great Gatsby": The Limits of Wonder*, 73.

13. Andrew Turnbull, *Scott Fitzgerald*, 6.

man in the world of "The Diamond as Big as the Ritz" (1922), and Tom Buchanan are only a few.

Or did Fitzgerald have novelist Booth Tarkington in mind? Tarkington had founded the Princeton Triangle Club, one of Fitzgerald's major interests while in college, and later Fitzgerald told Edmund Wilson that Tarkington was one of the influences on an early version of his first novel.[14] In *Tender Is the Night,* while hurrying to meet Rosemary Hoyt at a Paris film studio, Dick Diver is described as walking "briskly around the block with the fatuousness of one of Tarkington's adolescents" (91).

Since Jacob Booth is like other rich young men in Fitzgerald's stories, self-made and bored, is it possible that Fitzgerald wanted to show how he, like John Wilkes Booth, reflects an older, dying United States? If he thought of Jacob Booth as juvenile in some ways, was he thinking of Booth Tarkington's work?

Or was Jacob Booth named after Jake Barnes of *The Sun Also Rises,* as suggested by James R. Mellow? In 1934 Fitzgerald wrote Hemingway that he had purposely avoided reading Hemingway's work for a year and a half while writing *Tender Is the Night,* because he had been drawn to his style at times "by process of infiltration." While one can find a few passages in the drafts and published version of *Tender Is the Night* that reflect Hemingway's influence, there is none in "Jacob's Ladder." Jake Barnes and Jacob Booth do share first names and first initials of surnames in common, but their only other similarities are disappointment in love, an absence of progeny, and the irony that Jacob of Genesis had twelve sons who lent their names to the twelve tribes of Israel. ("You've a hell of a biblical name, Jake," Brett Ashley says in *The Sun Also Rises* when she avoids Robert Cohn's request for a dance and then dances with Jake Barnes instead.)[15]

When Jacob Booth first meets Jenny, the reader's expectations are that Jacob and Jenny are meant for each other because of the alliteration in their names, like Jack and Jill of our childhood; or because of the

14. Andrew Turnbull, ed., *The Letters of F. Scott Fitzgerald,* 323.

15. Mellow, *Invented Lives,* 290; Turnbull, ed., *Letters,* 309; Ernest Hemingway, *The Sun Also Rises,* 22. The influence of Hemingway on Fitzgerald in *Tender Is the Night* is discussed in my article " 'Particular Rhythms' and Other Influences: Hemingway and *Tender Is the Night.*"

similarity of names, like "anyone" and "noone," the lovers in e. e. cummings's "anyone lived in a pretty how town"; or even like Milly Cooley and Bill Driscoll—Milly and Billy—in Fitzgerald's "Not in the Guidebook" (1925). But of course, ironically, it is Jacob who names Jenny, who gives her a first name that would couple nicely with his, yet a last name more masculine than feminine, reflecting his absence of sexual attraction toward her at the beginning of the story and, in addition, reflecting her lack of sexual attraction for him throughout the tale.

Thirty-three-year-old Jacob C. K. Booth earned his money during the 1920s in a way similar to a number of other Fitzgerald gentlemen. A bout of laryngitis having frustrated his desire to become a world-famous tenor, he purchased a Florida plantation, turned it into a golf course, and then sold it for eight hundred thousand dollars during the 1924 land boom. Then he tried but failed to marry a wealthy woman. "Like so many Americans, he valued things rather than cared about them," the narrator tells us. "His apathy was neither fear of life nor was it an affectation; it was the racial violence grown tired. . . . Except when he was overcome by a desperate attack of apathy, he was unusually charming; he went with a crowd of men who were sure that they were the best of New York and had by far the best time. During a desperate attack of apathy he was like a gruff white bird, ruffled and annoyed, and disliking mankind with all his heart" (353).

In effect, Booth's wealth has brought him no joy. Similar to such Fitzgerald characters as Dexter Green of "Winter Dreams" (1922), a self-made man who borrows a thousand dollars, goes into the laundry business, at twenty-seven sells out the "largest string of laundries in his section of the country," and ends up "probably making more money than any man of [his] age in the Northwest," Anson Hunter of "The Rich Boy" (1926), who would some day inherit a sixth of a fifteen million dollar fortune, and Jay Gatsby, Booth fails to find happiness.[16]

At the beginning of Fitzgerald's tale, Booth is grasping for anything in life to relieve his apathetic existence. We see him finding pleasure yet disgust while watching "a particularly sordid and degraded murder

16. Bruccoli, ed., *Short Stories,* 221, 226.

trial" on a hot day when one must be careful to avoid the "obvious sweat in large dewy beads" from the "hundred people, inhaling and exhaling with difficulty" (350). The murderer, a Mrs. Choynski née Delehanty, has killed her sailor lover with a meat ax.

By contrast, there is Mrs. Choynski's sister, Jenny, described as having "the face of a dark saint with tender, luminous eyes and a skin pale and fair" (350–51). Soon after, Fitzgerald uses similar religious imagery to describe her, repeating the phrase "the face of a saint" and adding "an intense little Madonna" (352).

Jacob is attracted to the vitality and youth of this sixteen year old, a vitality that he does not find elsewhere in life. When a newspaperman bothers her at the trial, she reacts with a forcefulness that Jacob reacts to positively:

> "Go jump in the river!" said Miss Delehanty, sitting in Jacob's car. "Go—jump—in—the—river!"
>
> The extraordinary force of her advice was such that Jacob regretted the limitations of her vocabulary. Not only did it evoke an image of the unhappy journalist hurling himself into the Hudson but it convinced Jacob that it was the only fitting and adequate way of disposing of the man. (352)

Mesmerized, Jacob is not taken aback by Jenny's lower-class background and her complete lack of sophistication. Of the agreement she has made with a newspaper to give information regarding her sister's trial, she tells Jacob: "Oh, I'm sicka the whole thing. . . . It gives me a pain in the eye" (351). Of her job in a department store, she reports, "That's where I work. Back to the old pick and shovel day after tomorrow" (353). And when Jacob offers her a ride home, she tells him that she lives on "Eas' Hun'erd thuyty-thuyd. Stayin' with a girl friend there" (352).

Contrary to what one might expect, Jacob sees in Jenny something that has been lacking in his own existence. Jenny's words "vibrated with life" (352). Fitzgerald once again uses religious imagery to emphasize Jacob's attraction to Jenny: "On the pure parting of her lips no breath hovered; he had never seen a texture pale and immaculate as her skin, lustrous and garish as her eyes. His own well-ordered person seemed for the first time in his life gross and well worn to him as he knelt suddenly at the heart of freshness" (352).

Thus begins the change in Jacob's life. At first he fears passion with a puritanical streak and cannot allow himself to feel anything for Jenny. During a most romantic setting—summer moonlight, flower scents, and champagne—he talks to her in a stilted manner, reflecting his old-fashioned moral integrity: "You are the most beautiful thing I have ever seen . . . but as it happens you are not my type and I have no designs on you at all" (353). When Jenny expects him to kiss her goodnight, he reflects on her extreme youth instead and changes the subject. Jenny's reaction, "You're a card, handsome," indicates her surprise (354). But there is an absence of sensuality on her part. When Jacob does kiss her a few days later, he finds no passion in her and is "chilled by the innocence of her kiss" (357).

Until now, Jacob had remained relatively secure in a life devoid of any close contact with those not in his own social or economic class. But there have been frustrations too, one of which is his desire to become a great singer. Thus, while Jenny is in Hollywood, he goes once again to a specialist. "There's no change," he is told. "The cords are not diseased—they're simply worn out. It isn't anything that can be treated" (359). This has not only contributed to his sense of apathy, but it is also one of the reasons he has been helping Jenny enter the world of entertainment, a field in which he has not succeeded. In entering Jenny's life, however, he encounters a world of seduction and blackmail, of Irish and Latin rivals for Jenny's affection, of uneducated Poles and Irish, of a Jewish (or German) villain who attempts to blackmail Jenny, and especially a world of sensuality and feeling. This is the new America, a world foreign to the older America that Jacob represents, one that will eventually defeat him. While Jacob is not of the social class of the extreme American rich represented by such Fitzgerald characters as Anson Hunter ("The Rich Boy"), Tom Buchanan *(The Great Gatsby),* and the Warrens *(Tender Is the Night),* they share some characteristics. All represent the failed American class discussed in Brian Way's *F. Scott Fitzgerald and the Art of Social Criticism:*

> The social habits of the Gilded Age lingered on into the early 1920s; and the great changes which took place during the postwar decade confirmed rather than altered his [Fitzgerald's] conviction that the American rich were a class who had been given the opportunity to become an aristocracy

and had failed. Like Edith Wharton, he appears to have felt that the worst aspect of their failure was their capacity to obstruct or injure the very manifestations of life towards which they should themselves have been aspiring. . . .

But—unlike the Buchanans who ruin Gatsby, the Warrens who contribute to Dick Diver's decline, and Anson Hunter who "brings unhappiness if not disaster to almost everyone he meets"—Jacob Booth only brings disaster upon himself.[17]

To get a movie part for Jenny, Jacob introduces her to film director Billy Farrelly, "a wild Irishman" (355). Farrelly contrasts in many ways with Jacob and Jacob's world, especially his outgoing personality and self-confidence. He does not disguise his contempt for the type of pictures he is making and the actresses and actors he works with: "I'm sick of these lousy actresses. I'm going out to the Coast next month. I'd rather be Constance Talmadge's water boy than own most of these young—" (355). Soon after, when he repeats himself, Fitzgerald emphasizes his self-confidence. Of his stars he says: "They're all the same. . . . Shucks! Pick 'em up out of the gutter today and they want gold plates tomorrow. I'd rather be Constance Talmadge's water boy than own a harem full of them" (355).

Despite Farrelly's obvious sexual bluster, Jacob's puritanical streak only comes to the surface later when he discovers that Jenny is aware of the director's roaming eye. "You can tell when a guy wants to make you," she tells Jacob. "I don't mean he wanted to make me, handsome. But he's got that look about him, if you know what I mean" (355–56). Jacob, overly protective of Jenny, not only warns off Farrelly, at the same time denying his own amorous interests, but also warns Jenny against alcohol.

In Hollywood, the relationship changes as Jacob falls in love with Jenny, and Jenny, growing older, learns to project sex appeal in films and eventually to find passion in her relationships with men. Her relationship with Raffino results in Jacob's anger—"An actor!" he fumes (364)—especially when she denies loving Raffino. Jenny even agrees to marry Jacob, but Jacob decides against it when Jenny reveals that she

17. Brian Way, *F. Scott Fitzgerald and the Art of Social Fiction*, 37, 38.

feels no passion for him: "You don't—thrill me, Jake," she admits. "I don't know—there have been some men that sort of thrilled me when they touched me, dancing or anything" (365). Eventually she falls for a director. If an actor is to Jacob an illogical choice for Jenny, this causes Jacob even more disappointment.

Jacob now realizes that he will never have Jenny and that he has lost his only chance for pleasure in life: "The wave appeared far off, sent up whitecaps, rolled toward him with the might of pain, washed over him. 'Never any more. Never any more.' The wave beat upon him, drove him down, pounding with hammers of agony on his ears" (371). The passage is reminiscent of the end of "Winter Dreams" where Fitzgerald illustrated disillusionment and loss by alluding to nature ("the sun was gone down") and by using repetition to emphasize the moment ("Long ago," Dexter Green says, "long ago, there was something in me, but now that thing is gone. Now that thing is gone, that thing is gone. I cannot cry. I cannot care. That thing will come back no more").[18]

For Jacob, all that remains is fantasy, only dreams. Jenny Prince can belong to him—as well as to all of her fans—only on a movie screen, where Jacob, like all moviegoers, can be enveloped in fantasies and be one with the shadows on the screen. Jacob sees the name "Jenny Prince" on the marquee of the movie house: "It hung there, cool and impervious, in the night, a challenge, a defiance." Then, in language reminiscent of the King James Bible, possibly of the Song of Solomon, Fitzgerald reminds us of the seductive power of Jenny Prince on the screen and, more specifically, of the seductive power of film: " 'Come and rest upon my loveliness,' it said. 'Fulfill your secret dreams in wedding me for an hour' " (370). Jacob's search for love has ended, and he becomes just another moviegoer hoping to find solace for an empty life in a movie house. He gazes up at the marquee and then strolls in with the remainder of the crowd:

> Proud and impervious, the name on high challenged the night.
> Jenny Prince.
> She was there! All of her, the best of her—the effort, the power, the triumph, the beauty.

18. Bruccoli, ed., *Short Stories,* 235–36.

Jacob moved forward with a group and bought a ticket at the window. Confused, he stared around the great lobby. Then he saw an entrance and walking in, found himself a place in the fast-throbbing darkness. (371)[19]

It is fun to speculate that when Fitzgerald named his protagonist Jacob Booth, he was thinking not of John Wilkes Booth nor of Booth Tarkington nor of Jake Barnes but of Jacob in Genesis where Jacob's dream as well as the booths he builds are mentioned: "And he dreamed, and behold a ladder set up on the earth, and the top of it reached to heaven; and behold the angels of God ascending and descending on it" (Gen. 28:12). Soon after his dream, "Jacob journeyed to Succoth, and built him an house, and made booths for his cattle: therefore the name of the place is called Succoth" (Gen. 33:17).

Of course, Jacob Booth's dream is not of angels going to and coming from heaven, but of another angel, Jenny Prince, who he hoped would rescue him from his humdrum life and, in effect, take him to heaven. In the *Taps at Reveille* galleys, Fitzgerald even changed his first description of her from that of a "saint" to that of an "angel."

But there is no proof that despite the title Fitzgerald had this analogy consciously in mind when he composed the story. Since he was to say that Jenny had the "face of a saint" soon after, the change in the manuscript from "saint" to "angel" may have merely been his desire to avoid using the same description twice within a few pages. Further, the title is penciled in large caps on the top of page 1 of his typescript as though it were an afterthought. And, in addition, this was not the first time that Fitzgerald had used the image of climbing or a ladder to suggest a goal. For Jay Gatsby, the goal can only be reached if he rejects the woman:

Out of the corner of his eye Gatsby saw that the blocks of the sidewalk really formed a ladder and mounted to a secret place above the trees—he could climb to it, if he climbed alone, and once there he could suck on the pap of life, gulp down the incomparable milk of wonder.

19. In Fitzgerald's typescript at the Princeton University Library, Jenny Prince is in caps and centered. Fitzgerald's marginal note asks that it be printed this way.

His heart beat faster and faster as Daisy's white face came up to his own. He knew that when he kissed this girl, and forever wed his unutterable visions to her perishable breath, his mind would never romp again like the mind of God.[20]

And neither is there any other evidence that Fitzgerald had John Wilkes Booth, Booth Tarkington, or Ernest Hemingway consciously in mind while composing this work. Even if he did, the metaphors do not add much to our understanding of Fitzgerald's purpose here. They are the minor threads in Fitzgerald's tapestry, not too important when isolated from the entire work.

Fitzgerald once again had written a story in which a representative of an older moneyed American society is unable to cope with a newer contemporary world. He had used the theme of a man's failed quest for a woman much more successfully in such works as "Winter Dreams," "The Rich Boy," and *The Great Gatsby,* and would repeat the theme of an older man's attraction for a younger woman in *Tender Is the Night.* He was to use Hollywood for a background soon after in "Magnetism" (1928), for a few scenes in *Tender Is the Night,* as well as much more creatively in both "Crazy Sunday" (1932) and *The Last Tycoon.* The blackmail theme would also appear in "Magnetism" and was projected for the unfinished portion of *The Last Tycoon.*

Fitzgerald was right when he saw "Jacob's Ladder" as flawed. It is overly sentimental in spots and is probably overplotted. However, because of Fitzgerald's statement that he had "disemboweled" it, because Fitzgerald did not collect it in *Taps at Reveille,* and because critics have placed too much emphasis on the story's autobiographical characteristics, it has not been given sufficient attention.

20. Fitzgerald, *The Great Gatsby,* 86.

DISTANT IDOLS: FATE AND THE
WORK ETHIC IN "THE BOWL"

BRYANT MANGUM

Narrator Jeff Deering begins F. Scott Fitzgerald's "The Bowl" with details about a former classmate at Princeton who never attended football games and who "spent his Saturday afternoons delving for minutiae about Greek athletics and the somewhat fixed battles between Christians and wild beasts under the Antonines."[1] Jeff chides this man for having been "unresponsive to the very spectacle at his door," though now he makes etchings of football players, a fact that causes Jeff to view with suspicion the man's originality in judging "what is beautiful, what is remarkable and what is fun" (256). After the first paragraph, Jeff never refers to this man again. But with this beginning he has suggested connections between ancient and contemporary contests that test the strength of the human spirit, sometimes against difficult odds; and he has raised questions about the need for personal involvement in these rituals.

In the final paragraph of the story Jeff reflects philosophically on football star Dolly Harlan as he walks "oblivious alike to the fate ahead of him or the small chatter behind" (277) toward the room of Daisy Cary,

---

1. "The Bowl" was first published in the *Saturday Evening Post* 200 (January 21, 1928): 6, 7, 93, 97, 100, and then collected in England in *The Bodley Head Scott Fitzgerald*, vol. 5. It was reprinted in Matthew J. Bruccoli, ed., *The Price Was High: The Last Uncollected Stories of F. Scott Fitzgerald*. All page references to the story will be to the *Price Was High* version and will appear parenthetically in the text.

the successful young movie star whose admiration he has won through a combination of determination, hard work, and luck. With these odd couplings of trivial chatter and sublime fate, Jeff hints at the complex forces that are a part of the human quest for victory. Between the first and last paragraphs he fashions a narrative that he understands better than Dolly, and one in which he is more involved than his classmate who could not see the mythic content in everyday life. Jeff's story of Dolly Harlan's heroic struggle is, in fact, elaborately conceived, richly textured, and delicately balanced, a story apt to reveal its complex insights only after careful readings, and even then not without thoughtful analysis.

I.

Looking at the scant critical attention that "The Bowl" has received (less than a dozen paragraphs), one would scarcely suspect that it deserves more than the quick reading it probably received from casual readers of the *Saturday Evening Post* when it appeared in the January 21, 1928, issue. It completely escaped critical notice until 1965, when Henry Dan Piper noted the scene in which Daisy Cary "jumps into a swimming pool with a high fever because it is part of her job as an actress" as being closely related to a similar scene with Rosemary Hoyt in *Tender Is the Night*. Robert Sklar pointed to it as written from "Fitzgerald's mature perspective." John A. Higgins coupled it with "Jacob's Ladder" (1927) and "The Love Boat" (1927) as narrowly missing "being major achievements." He observed that the story had "a serious theme, a high degree of atmosphere, some excellent passages, and foreshadowings of *Tender Is the Night*," all finally undercut by "weakness of execution" and "ending trouble." Bruccoli's headnote in *The Price Was High* described the circumstances of the story's composition and its publication history, as well as commented on the connection between Daisy Cary and Rosemary Hoyt. An anonymous reviewer of *The Price Was High* in *Kirkus* singled out "The Bowl" as the best story in the collection—the only one not "churned out under obligation."[2]

---

2. Robert Sklar, *F. Scott Fitzgerald: The Last Laocoön*, 230; John A. Higgins, *F. Scott Fitzgerald: A Study of the Stories*, 100; Bruccoli, ed., *Price Was High*, 256; Jackson R. Bryer, *The Critical Reputation of F. Scott Fitzgerald: A Bibliographical Study—Supplement One through 1981*, 69.

The most probing discussion of the story to date is Brian Way's three-paragraph discussion, in which he notes that "The Bowl" makes good use of "well worn material [and] at times . . . gives intimations of something far more subtle and original—a penetrating insight into the nature of achievement and popular success." Ultimately though, to Way, "no one anxious for Fitzgerald's reputation would place it unhesitatingly in the canon of his best work." Only Bruccoli in *Some Sort of Epic Grandeur,* André Le Vot, and James Mellow have mentioned the story since Way's analysis: Bruccoli and Le Vot to make points about Fitzgerald's interest in football, and Mellow to capture Fitzgerald's difficulties in making money while he was at Ellerslie, as reflected in his correspondence with his agent, Harold Ober, regarding the story. And though there are tantalizing bits of information in every discussion of "The Bowl" to date, there is scarcely a hint that it merits rigorous debate as an important, pivotal story.[3]

The most obvious factor that has contributed to the critical neglect of "The Bowl," as it has contributed to similar neglect in the cases of many good Fitzgerald stories, has been its unavailability to American readers after its first magazine publication in the *Saturday Evening Post* until its collection in *The Price Was High* in 1979. Also, conventional wisdom has had it that the Fitzgerald stories worth rereading were those he selected himself for the four authorized collections published in his lifetime. However, many fine stories were excluded from those volumes for complex reasons, and this is particularly true for many stories excluded from *Taps at Reveille,* the volume that would have contained "The Bowl" if Fitzgerald had chosen to include it. It is also true that those Fitzgerald stories to have received most attention, aside from the unanimously acclaimed masterpieces such as "Babylon Revisited" (1931) and "The Rich Boy" (1926), are the stories that are the best and most illustrative of a particular group or type of story: "The Ice Palace" (1919) for the Tarleton trilogy, or "Bernice Bobs Her Hair" (1920) for the flapper stories, or "One Trip Abroad" (1930) for the *Tender Is the Night* cluster stories.

---

3. Brian Way, *F. Scott Fitzgerald and the Art of Social Fiction,* 74; Matthew J. Bruccoli, *Some Sort of Epic Grandeur: The Life of F. Scott Fitzgerald,* 263; André Le Vot, *F. Scott Fitzgerald: A Biography,* 44–46; James R. Mellow, *Invented Lives: F. Scott and Zelda Fitzgerald,* 300.

Part of the neglect of "The Bowl" has resulted from the fact that it does not easily or neatly fall into or illustrate the characteristics of a single group as do such stories as those mentioned above. In one sense, "The Bowl" belongs to a group of retrospective stories that Fitzgerald began shortly after *The Great Gatsby*, in which he creates adolescent and college-age protagonists similar to the ones in his early *Post* and *Smart Set* stories, such as "The Camel's Back" (1920) and "Babes in the Woods" (1919), but in the later stories he achieves a degree of aesthetic distance from his subjects that did not characterize the early ones. For this reason among others, "The Bowl" would qualify as belonging to what Alice Hall Petry calls the "final blooming" of Fitzgerald's talent. Also, because "The Bowl" contains, in Daisy Cary, a young movie star who believes in the work ethic, and who is what Bruccoli calls "a trial sketch" for Rosemary Hoyt, the story belongs to the group of *Tender Is the Night* cluster stories.[4] But, on both counts, numerous other stories have received more attention than "The Bowl" because they provide clearer illustration of the characteristics of these two groups.

It is true as well that critics, from contemporary reviewers of the story volumes such as H. L. Mencken to the present, have been suspicious of stories that Fitzgerald wrote for the slick magazines. As Way observes, "It is reasonable to think of 'The Bowl' as one of those pieces of 'best selling entertainment,'" a work "conceived in the first place as entertainment."[5] Fitzgerald's correspondence with Ober regarding "The Bowl" contains virtually all the factual information available on the composition and marketing history of the story, and it affirms that Fitzgerald saw it almost from the beginning as "best selling entertainment." These exchanges with Ober reflect a familiar pattern that emerges from their correspondence over the more than twenty-year span of their relationship: Fitzgerald often began thinking of stories in early stages of composition in terms of whether they would entertain a particular magazine such as the *Post* and then tailoring the stories to the requirements of the audience for

4. Alice Hall Petry, *Fitzgerald's Craft of Short Fiction: The Collected Stories—1920–1935*, 154; Bruccoli, ed., *Price Was High*, 257.
5. Way, *Social Fiction*, 75.

which he was writing, discussing with Ober along the way his ideas about strengths and weaknesses of individual stories for various markets. "The Bowl" is certainly one story that fits this pattern.

But perhaps the most telling fact about the composition of "The Bowl" revealed in the correspondence with Ober is the great difficulty Fitzgerald experienced in writing it. He began the story in the fall of 1927 after returning from Hollywood and while living at Ellerslie. He informed Ober in September 1927 that he was "WORKING ON A TWO PART SOPHISTICATED FOOTBALL STORY," and he requested that Ober see if the *Post* could take it for the fall if he could finish it in one week. Ober immediately wired him that the *Post* was interested. The two weeks that followed Ober's reply brought telegrams requesting advances against the story and reported that it was "FINISHED." In the remaining weeks of September, Fitzgerald had problems with the story and was unable to send along even a part of it so that the *Post* could begin having it illustrated. During this time he visited Princeton to "WATCH FOOTBALL PRACTICE AND SEE IF I COULD GET A LITTLE LIFE INTO THAT WHICH IS THE WEAK PART OF MY STORY." On October 3, he wired Ober that the story was "AN AWFUL MESS" and expressed the hope that the *Post* would buy it after it was finished, perhaps for the next football season. Fitzgerald then took a break from "The Bowl" and wrote "A Short Trip Home," which the *Post* bought and published; he finally completed "The Bowl" as a one-part story in early December. Understandably excited that Fitzgerald had resolved his difficulties with the story, Ober reported to him that *Post* editor Thomas B. Costain said that "they feel that you have got the real spirit of the game as it has perhaps never been done before."[6]

Reflecting on the painful difficulty surrounding the composition of "The Bowl," many will recall Fitzgerald's comment to Ober regarding "Not in the Guidebook" (1925): "Good stories write themselves—bad ones have to be written so this took up about three weeks." But Fitzgerald also had trouble with his best stories, as is obvious in his comment to Ober in 1925 that "*The Rich Boy* has been a source of much trouble but its [*sic*] in shape at last."[7] Fitzgerald's problems with "The Bowl," as

6. Matthew J. Bruccoli, ed., *As Ever, Scott Fitz—: Letters between F. Scott Fitzgerald and His Literary Agent—Harold Ober, 1919–1940*, 100–104.
7. Ibid., 76, 79.

he no doubt realized at the time, more closely resembled his problems with "The Rich Boy" than "Not in the Guidebook." They resulted from conflicts and tensions that ultimately worked their way into the deepest levels of the story. And though the story itself must provide the final word as to how well he had begun to resolve the conflicts, knowing them before going into "The Bowl" helps one appreciate what is happening at the story's deepest levels.

Fitzgerald's proximity to Princeton and his visits to the campus and football practice during the fall of 1927 had rekindled his interest in the sport, an interest that Le Vot notes consumed him even until the moment of his death, at which time he was making notations in an article in the *Princeton Alumni Weekly*. Le Vot dramatically describes it this way: "His dying thought was for his college's football season. . . . In his copy of the magazine, a pencil line still runs wildly down a page of a story about the current football season."[8] But on a deeper level, Fitzgerald in 1927, approximately a decade removed from the days of his undergraduate participation as a spectator, was attempting to understand the symbolic and mythic components of the game. Ultimately these reflections led him to a reconsideration of the romantic hero and of the heroic quest itself, concerns that are being worked through in "The Bowl."

Having recently returned from Hollywood where he had met Lois Moran, Fitzgerald was in the process of reexamining his ideas about those qualities in women that make them worthy of admiration— suitable objects of the heroic quest. Lois Moran, who had already provided inspiration for Jenny Prince in "Jacob's Ladder" (1927) and who had sparked Zelda's jealousy, becomes the embodiment of the new Fitzgerald heroine as Daisy Cary in "The Bowl" and will become the prototype for Rosemary Hoyt in *Tender Is the Night.* In "The Bowl," Fitzgerald is pitting this character against his earlier heroines, embodied in the story in the beautiful and callous Vienna Thorne, who, as Higgins notes, "marks the return for the first time since 'The Adjuster' and *The Great Gatsby* of the callous, selfish *femme fatale.*"[9] Between Vienna Thorne and Daisy Cary falls the relatively innocent Josephine Pickman,

8. Le Vot, *Fitzgerald: A Biography,* 86.
9. Higgins, *Fitzgerald: Study of the Stories,* 100.

a respectable girl with little spark or conviction. It is significant that Fitzgerald interrupted his work on "The Bowl" and wrote "A Short Trip Home," in which Eddie Stinson, the narrator, risks his safety to save Ellen Baker, a respectable and innocent midwestern girl who is closer to Josephine than to Vienna or Daisy. Fitzgerald's "A Short Trip Home" is symbolically a detour in which he affirms the validity of the hero's quest to save the innocence of young virginal girls. "The Bowl" becomes a forum in which the qualities that these women represented to Fitzgerald are debated.

It is revealing in this regard that Fitzgerald uses character names in the story that look both back to early material and forward to work not yet begun. Devlin, who scores a touchdown in "The Bowl," looks back to Devlin, from "Winter Dreams" (1922), who gives Dexter the information about Judy Jones that shatters his winter dreams. Daisy Cary's name, of course, recalls Daisy Buchanan, symbolically an interesting change since the new heroine Daisy is the antithesis of Daisy Buchanan. Devereaux, a Yale punter in "The Bowl," anticipates in name Nicole's father Devereux Warren in *Tender Is the Night* (with a slight spelling change); and Fitzgerald uses Josephine Pickman's first name for Josephine Perry. Dolly Harlan has come from St. Regis, which will be Basil Duke Lee's school. Although minor, these details suggest a richness of association, perhaps unconscious on Fitzgerald's part, that hints at the collision of Fitzgerald's old and new worlds, providing the dramatic tension in "The Bowl."

II.

It is perhaps no coincidence that the strategic games in "The Bowl" occur in New England, traditional territory of the Puritans, whose moral system pitted divine fate against the work ethic, two important conflicting elements in the story. Jeff Deering, who knows more by the time he shapes the narrative than the football hero Dolly probably ever will know, and whose vision is more original than that of his former classmate who avoided the games altogether, understands the complexities of the worlds in conflict in the story. And he reveals them only after painstaking firsthand observations, a fact that itself suggests one of the story's main truths: Knowledge begins with close observation. Jeff is a spectator who, as he describes himself, "reveled in football, as audience, amateur statistician and foiled participant" (256). Ill-suited to play because of his size, Jeff becomes "a very fair pole vaulter" (257), to him a poor substitute for gridiron glory, but to the reader a perfect metaphor for his visionary role. He vaults to heights that allow him to observe what others cannot, as his view from high in the stands affords him perspective. A revealing example of his insistence on personal observation is in the story's fifth paragraph as he begins to describe the fears that overtake Dolly when he plays in the Bowl. Jeff offhandedly mentions that his psychoanalyst friend, Dr. Glock, would easily explain Dolly's frame of mind as "agoraphobia—afraid of crowds" (257). Then, just as offhandedly, he dismisses Dr. Glock's diagnosis as not worth exploring, perhaps because it is based on generalization and theory. Instead he opts for the details that Dolly related to him: "But here's what Dolly told me afterward" (257), he says as preface to Dolly's recounting of his fears about the Bowl.

Jeff is always observing the spectacle before his eyes. Even "between quarters I watched Dolly" (258), he says. The story is filled with scenes in which Jeff sees things before others, particularly before Dolly does and always more clearly. When the drama between Carl Sanderson and Vienna unfolds in front of them all at the old Frolic, and Jeff overhears that Carl has tried to kill himself, Jeff has to explain to Dolly what has happened. Dolly jumps to a quick conclusion stereotyping Carl: "Just some souse. . . . He probably tried to miss himself and get a little sympathy. I suppose those are the sort of things a really attractive girl is up against all the time" (264–65). Jeff reflects to himself, "This wasn't my attitude" (265). In an episode later in the evening, Jeff explains to Dolly that Vienna had not complimented him on his performance in the game because she has hated the game since her brother's death on the field the year before. Still, a half hour passes in the darkness of their room before Jeff finally hears him say loudly, "I see" (265), having had Jeff point the way for his understanding.

So dependent does the reader become on Jeff's firsthand observations that he comes to feel that if Jeff has not seen the event, it may not have happened or that it is somehow less important than the things he does see. This is particularly true of the climactic scene of the story, Dolly's interception of the pass that allowed him to make the tying score in the final Yale Bowl. Just before the interception, Jeff says, "my view was blocked out for a minute" (275). Dramatically, of course, this is an effective device in that such important scenes described directly can seem anticlimactic, but in this case the thematic point is more significant: Dolly's score was much less important itself than were the quirks of fate that led up to it and the ironies of the heroic status that he achieved in the wake of the scene, things that Jeff certainly does see, though the actual workings of fate were obscured.

All of this is not to say that the story is a parable on empiricism. It does suggest over and over, however, that close personal observation is the foundation for truth, an observation the narrator of "The Rich Boy" makes less subtly in the famous "Begin with an individual" first paragraph of that story. Jeff's observations establish him as a reliable narrator, and as the story's deeper implications unfold through him they have the authority of truth because Fitzgerald has so carefully established his balanced perspective and reliability. This quality becomes especially important in Fitzgerald's creation of a believable conflict between representatives of his old heroine embodied in Vienna Thorne and the new one in Daisy Cary.

Jeff is able to present Vienna with very little bias because he typically describes her indirectly, as she might be perceived by others. When she returns from Europe during the New Year's holiday, Jeff describes her as "even prettier than she had been before" (266). But then quickly he follows this with a view from outside: "People passing her on the street jerked their heads quickly to look at her—a frightened look, as if they realized that they had almost missed something" (266). He reveals his suspicions about her very softly: "I'm not arguing, but—would you have taken this stand if it hadn't been for Vienna?" (268), he asks Dolly when he believes that she has caused him to compromise his convictions by giving up football. Time after time he lets Vienna reveal her own character without commenting on it or judging her. When she tells him, "I approve of you Jeff. . . . I want Dolly to have more friends like you. . . . I told Dolly he could probably find others like you if he looked around his class" (267), the reader perhaps feels Jeff cringe at being typecast, but Jeff says not a word.

He reserves his few judgments in the story to reinforce the most important issues. A case in point is in his presentation of Daisy Cary, who will become a prize of sorts at the end of Dolly's heroic triumph:

"She was eighteen and I compared her background of courage and independence and achievement, of politeness based upon the realities of cooperation, with that of most society girls I had known. There was no way in which she wasn't inestimably their superior . . ." (276). Here, of course, he presents the standard for women of Fitzgerald's mature vision. At least on the most superficial level, the story is constructed around three Princeton-Yale games during Dolly's sophomore, junior, and senior years to communicate the point that such a prize as Daisy Cary will rightly go to the triumphant hero, Dolly Harlan, who by the end of "The Bowl" has regained the moral courage that Vienna had taken from him and who has at last, through a fluke of fate, been elevated for the first time in his life to the status of star.

In the dramatic first game, one destined in Jeff's words to be "a historic game" (258), Dolly played true to form, acting on instinct to throw the block that allowed Devlin to score the winning touchdown. After the block, Jeff heard the radio man behind him ask, "Who's Number 22?" And the simple reply came back, "Harlan" (259). It was Devlin, of course, who made the headlines in the morning paper. We learn only that the second game, though Dolly played in it, was "disastrous" (266). Then between that game and the final one, Dolly intentionally breaks his ankle as a ploy that will allow him to quit football, since Vienna has demanded he do so as a condition of their continued relationship. But finally he regains his commitment to the team, plays in the Yale Bowl on a painful ankle, and catches the pass intended for someone else that allows him to score, tying the game. For all of this he becomes a star, and wins, at least for the moment, the beautiful Daisy Cary. His transformation from competent member of his team—from simply Number 22—to star is marked by a brief scene near the end of the story in which he asks the hotel desk clerk to connect him with Daisy Cary. An unpleasant underclassman asks, "Just who are you?" to which Dolly replies, "Why I'm Dolly Harlan. . . . What do you think of that?" (277). Through a combination of determination, hard work, and fate he has earned not only Daisy Cary but his own name as well.

On this level "The Bowl" is a fairy tale. And Jeff would not deny it: "All that is childish?" (275), he asks after his detailed description of the game and his admission of belief in the communal superstition that a tied game with Yale guaranteed a year lived out of the shadow of defeat.

But Jeff is not much interested in dignifying the sensational aspects of the story with worn clichés about heroism. This he leaves to Dolly, who thinks he comprehends the meaning of this fairy tale he has lived in and who summarizes the meaning for Daisy in this way: "For two years I was pretty good and I was always mentioned at the bottom of the column as being among those who played. This year I dropped three punts and slowed up every play. . . . But a pass not even aimed at me fell in my arms and I'll be in the headlines tomorrow" (276).

Jeff sees more profound implications for the meaning of "The Bowl," and only twice does he directly state his conclusions. In the first instance, discussed above, he declares his absolute approval of the qualities "of courage and independence and achievement" (276) that he sees in Daisy. In the second, he generalizes about the status of idols. His statement comes during a lull in which Dolly has become lonely and requires the company of his peers, a point appropriately at the center of the narrative since Jeff's statement articulates what is perhaps the main theme of "The Bowl": "But people want their idols a little above them" (269). It is worth noting that Jeff does not make this statement without accumulating considerable detail to illuminate it. Nor can the statement be as simply understood in the context of "The Bowl" as it may seem at first glance. In many ways, the entire story explores the subtle implications of this statement, finally presenting the view that people need communal rituals that allow them to experience victory vicariously through distant idols. In this case, the ritual centers on the story's controlling metaphor, the Bowl itself, which serves finally as a kind of communion vessel around which gather those who would unite in the pursuit of victory, as Jeff's description of the spiritual union of spectators during the final game makes clear: "With the first play pandemonium broke loose and continued to the end of the game. At intervals it would swoon away to a plaintive humming; then it would rise to the intensity of wind and rain and thunder, and beat across the twilight from one side of the Bowl to the other like the agony of lost souls swinging across a gap in space" (274). Clearly, redemption of some sort hangs in the balance of what occurs that day in the Bowl.

"People want their idols a little above them." The temptation is to look for a way to restate Jeff's observation, a paraphrase perhaps, suggesting simply that people prefer their heroes aloof so that they can be looked up to as a "star" (259), which Dolly was not at the beginning but became at the end. This level of deconstruction of the concept of heroism, however, occurs near the surface layer of the story as fairy tale. Jeff is looking more deeply than this for a spiritual truth in the details of the events he recounts. Irving Malin is absolutely correct in maintaining that Fitzgerald, as is evidenced in "Absolution" (1924) and more subtly in *The Great Gatsby*, "is often concerned with the unseen, spiritual dimensions." Le Vot suggests that the game of football had these religious dimensions for Fitzgerald, that it was "a collective ritual . . . intensely personal," that it was a ceremony that produced "a feeling of communion."[10] With these things in mind, it is clear that Jeff chooses the word "idol" advisedly, not once exchanging it with the word "hero." Idols are images that people worship in the place of deities or divinities. And idols do not interact in the physical world with communities of worshippers. Jeff's language in describing the team on the day of the final Yale game captures the religious dimension of the ritual and the absolute isolation of those who have assumed the burden of idol in this ritual: "The eleven little men who ran out on the field at last were like bewitched figures in another world, strange and infinitely romantic, blurred by a throbbing mist of people and sound. One aches with them intolerably, trembles with their excitement, but they have no traffic with us now, they are beyond help, consecrated and unreachable—vaguely holy" (272–73).

Because idols must remain "unreachable" and thus at least "vaguely holy," the reader is destined to learn little about them in the story. Jeff characterizes Dolly as having been "a sort of private and special idol" (269), who at Princeton was viewed by his classmates as "a moving shrine" (269). Part of his mystery, which Jeff can explain only by calling it "moral responsibility" (258), is that he continued to play in spite of the fact that he had always detested most things to do with football: "the long, dull period of training, the element of personal conflict, the demand on his time, the monotony of the routine and the nervous apprehension of disaster just before the end" (258).

Understandably, Jeff, for all his careful observation of Dolly and reporting of his appearance, movements, and habits, is little help on

10. Irving Malin, " 'Absolution': Absolving Lies," 209; Le Vot, *Fitzgerald: A Biography,* 46.

the score of what makes him or his teammates idols, avoiding a close look at their motives, because to understand them would be to remove the distance between idols and those who need them. When Dolly takes time off from the game and wants to spend more time with him, Jeff reports, "I didn't enjoy Dolly so much in those days" (269), reflective of a need for distance that helps explain Jeff's resistance to a psychoanalytic view of Dolly's "agoraphobia" in the Bowl. Jeff needs Dolly a little above him, a little unknowable so that he can participate through Dolly as a communicant in the quest for victory. His awareness of the separateness of worshippers and idols in the physical world comes near the end of the story when he describes the beauty and desirability of the movie star, Daisy Cary: " . . . if she had looked for a moment my way—but it was Dolly's shining velvet eyes that signaled to her own." Both of them, he had said, were workers; and they "understood each other" (276). Unlike Vienna, for whom Dolly breaks his ankle and gives up football— symbolically revealing his feet of clay—Daisy accepts Dolly as an idol as she accepts her own role. Theirs was a community of idols separate from the community of idolaters.

But Jeff, the reliable narrator, who painstakingly observes life and bears personal witness to the spectacle before his eyes, who is knowing and wise, reveals finally to the reader that he is a mystic who believes that sometimes one must leap into the unknown, surrendering one's consciousness and hard-earned knowledge in order to achieve victory; that one cannot finally understand mystery and must instead "become" part of it, a truth that Jeff's schoolmate in the story's first paragraph could not know simply by delving for minutiae in history books. This is demonstrated first in a sentence leading up to the story's final paragraph and then in the final paragraph itself. Jeff reports that when Dolly, in the scene referred to earlier, was asked the question, "Just who are you?" a profound change occurred: "Something happened inside Dolly; he felt as if life had arranged his role to make possible this particular question—a question that now he had no choice but to answer" (277), an affirmation, as reported by Jeff, of the role of fate in human destiny. Then in the last paragraph Jeff describes the process and Dolly's role in this way: "Dolly turned away, alone with his achievement, taking it for once to his breast. He found suddenly that he would not have it long so intimately; the memory would outlive the triumph and even the triumph would outlive the glow in his heart that was best of all. Tall and straight, *an image of victory and pride,* he moved across the lobby, oblivious alike to the fate ahead of him or the small chatter behind" (277; emphasis mine).

The most remarkable thing about these two passages is that they seem to violate the point of view that Fitzgerald has faithfully maintained up to now. Jeff has never reported to us things that he cannot account for. He is careful to remind us of those things that were told to him after the fact by firsthand observers, and he tells us each time his view is blocked by other spectators. Yet here he presumes to know precisely how Dolly felt, and which aspects of Dolly's achievement would outlast the others. This seeming flaw in the story, however, appears on closer analysis to be a conscious shift intended by Fitzgerald to underline a major point. In Jeff's words, "Dolly was abstracted"; and Jeff has merged with him. His presumption is the final proof of the transcendent power of the communal ritual in which Jeff has effected a mysterious union with the idol: "an image," he says, "of victory and pride" (277). And like the idol, Jeff can, for a time at least, be oblivious to the fate ahead or the chatter behind. He can know that the glow in his heart is the victory of the moment, that it will fade into triumph, that the triumph will become memory. And if we consider all of this childish, Jeff says, "Find us something to fill the niche of victory" (275), the charge that is finally Fitzgerald's main challenge to readers of "The Bowl."

"OUTSIDE THE CABINET-MAKER'S": FITZGERALD'S "ODE TO A NIGHTINGALE"

BRUCE L. GRENBERG

Like many of Fitzgerald's lesser known, seldom anthologized short stories, "Outside the Cabinet-Maker's" has a somewhat baffling critical history. Written in 1927 during the Fitzgeralds' turbulent stay at Ellerslie, outside Wilmington, Delaware, and offered to seven different magazines before finally being published by *Century* magazine in December 1928, the story was not included in *Taps at Reveille* and remained virtually unnoticed until Arthur Mizener reprinted it in *Afternoon of an Author,* with a brief but suggestive interpretive headnote.[1] With its rebirth in Mizener's widely read collection, and its additional reprinting in volume 5 of *The Bodley Head Scott Fitzgerald* and in Mizener's edition of *The Fitzgerald Reader,* the story finally began to receive some critical notice in the 1960s and early 1970s.

Indeed, in the nine-year period from 1962 to 1971, Andrew Turnbull, Henry Dan Piper, Sergio Perosa, and John A. Higgins all made favorable comment upon the story in one way and another; nevertheless, for the past twenty years, "Outside the Cabinet-Maker's" has been almost totally neglected in critical studies of Fitzgerald's work. Matthew J. Bruccoli's *Some Sort of Epic Grandeur,* notable for its inclusiveness of detail, does not mention the story, and in Alice Hall Petry's *Fitzgerald's Craft of Short*

---

1. Henry Dan Piper, *F. Scott Fitzgerald: A Critical Portrait*, 173.

Fiction (which deals with Fitzgerald's *collected* short stories) the story is summarily treated in a single sentence with four other "pre-1935 stories that had not been included in the four collections." More recently, the story has received "honorable mention" in two books on Fitzgerald. Bryant Mangum finds in the story's "brevity and compactness" a precedent for Fitzgerald's "new style" in the 1930s. John Kuehl holds a similar view of the story's stylistic significance, seeing in the "detached exclusive" style of "Outside the Cabinet-Maker's" the precursor of the ironies found in "Babylon Revisited."[2]

In his headnote to the story in *Afternoon of an Author*, Mizener sets the basic assumptions and terms of reference for all the early commentators. Citing the autobiographical origins of the story, he rightly notes Fitzgerald's "intense and incommunicable" love for his daughter and sees the story as a "characteristic example of the way Fitzgerald transmuted actuality to make it true." And certainly Mizener is also right when he observes that the story is a "brilliant manifestation of the acceptance of the loss Fitzgerald would never cease to feel." But he also sets a dangerous and misleading precedent for the criticism to follow by concluding that "the story has the basic simplicity of plan and the care to be explicit, to make no unnecessary mysteries for the reader, that Fitzgerald always aimed at."[3] This assumption of the story's "simplicity" is erroneous in itself, and, more seriously, it has debilitated all subsequent criticism.

Andrew Turnbull was the first to reflect Mizener's reductive assumptions and reading. Ignoring the boundary between life and art, Turnbull mistakenly views "Outside the Cabinet-Maker's" as an exclusively autobiographical sketch recounting a pleasurable moment between Fitzgerald and Scottie during their time at Ellerslie: " 'You're my good fairy,' said Fitzgerald [*sic*] smiling and touching Scottie's [*sic*] cheek." Sergio Perosa is more perceptive, viewing "Outside the Cabinet-Maker's" as a "beautiful little sketch, which shows what delicacy of feeling and bareness of

---

2. Alice Hall Petry, *Fitzgerald's Craft of Fiction: The Collected Stories—1920–1935*, 190; Bryant Mangum, *A Fortune Yet: Money in the Art of F. Scott Fitzgerald's Short Stories*, 153; John Kuehl, *F. Scott Fitzgerald: A Study of the Short Fiction*, 113–14.

3. F. Scott Fitzgerald, *Afternoon of an Author: A Selection of Uncollected Stories and Essays*, 137. All subsequent page references to "Outside the Cabinet-Maker's" are to this edition and will appear parenthetically in the text.

style Fitzgerald could attain." Perosa relates the story not to Fitzgerald and Scottie, but to Dick Diver and his children in *Tender Is the Night.* And Henry Dan Piper views "Outside the Cabinet-Maker's" as one of Fitzgerald's "most perfect stories," finding in "its charm, its precision of language and image, its cool detached humor and affection" a foreshadowing of "such notable essays as his 'Crack-up' [*sic*] pieces, 'The Lost Decade,' 'Author's Home,' and 'Afternoon of an Author.'"[4]

John A. Higgins presents some cogent reasons for viewing this neglected short story as a superb example of Fitzgerald's fiction. Higgins argues that "Outside the Cabinet-Maker's" is "unlike any other piece of its author's short fiction before 1935," and sees in the story's "objectivity, implication, and ratio of dialog" an "almost . . . complete reversal of [Fitzgerald's] typical pattern." Higgins attributes this radical change to the influence of Hemingway upon Fitzgerald at that time and cites signal similarities between Fitzgerald's story and Hemingway's "episode pieces" such as "A Clean, Well-Lighted Place." Higgins claims, finally, that Fitzgerald, indeed, "had manifested the whole of what would become his 'new' technique in 'Outside the Cabinet-Maker's.'"[5] But Higgins adheres tightly to his main concern with Fitzgerald's techniques and confines his comments on the story to matters of style, scarcely discussing the story's themes or dramatic power.

Even though these "early" commentaries by Mizener, Turnbull, Perosa, Piper, and Higgins are progressively laudatory—suggesting intricate connections between the story and Fitzgerald's life, artistic theory, and practice in the late 1920s—the seeds of these ideas have been slow to germinate. Even Kuehl and Mangum, who genuinely admire the story, use it merely as a springboard to their critical comments about Fitzgerald's style, apparently assuming that such a simple little story is essentially self-explanatory, however finely constructed. The reason for this untoward suspension of critical activity, I think, is that we have placed the critical cart before the horse; we have had premature agreement about the story's autobiographical, canonical, and stylistic implications before we have

---

4. Andrew Turnbull, *Scott Fitzgerald,* 174; Sergio Perosa, *The Art of F. Scott Fitzgerald,* 95; Piper, *Fitzgerald: Critical Portrait,* 173.

5. John A. Higgins, *F. Scott Fitzgerald: A Study of the Stories,* 147.

adequately debated its intrinsic concerns and values. What is ultimately lacking in the existent criticism, and what I hope to provide in this essay, is a detailed analysis of the story's central thematic concerns. For far from being simple, "Outside the Cabinet-Maker's" is intricately wrought; and though I cannot hope to find the bottom of Fitzgerald's art in the story, I do hope that my comments will stimulate further inquiry into a work that has been allowed to lie fallow for far too long.

For the most elemental reasons, "Outside the Cabinet-Maker's" should be of more than casual or peripheral interest to Fitzgerald scholars, for it was written almost exactly midway between the publication of *The Great Gatsby* and Fitzgerald's settling upon the plan for the new novel, which would become *Tender Is the Night,* that was giving him "the terrible incessant stop[p]ies" in 1927.[6] Accordingly, then, within the compass of this very short story Fitzgerald explores many of the themes that were at the center of *The Great Gatsby,* with its focus upon the dreamworlds of imagination and expectation (Gatsby's, Nick's, and Myrtle's) and their collisions, frequently violent, with the real worlds of experience and fact. The story also reveals Fitzgerald's preoccupation with the themes and values that become the center of *Tender Is the Night,* where the reality of mindless will and money clashes with idealism and a "willingness of the heart" to suspend belief in one's own experience. The story, in fact, succinctly expresses Fitzgerald's creative concerns in this most critical period in his career; for, ultimately, "Outside the Cabinet-Maker's" is about imagination itself—about its power and its limitations. It is Fitzgerald's latter-day "Ode to a Nightingale," in which he captures the essence of the "waking dream" of imagination and the forlorn nature of what Keats called "the sole self"—when that music is fled.

I agree with Piper and Higgins that "Outside the Cabinet-Maker's" is a most carefully crafted short story, and its brevity allows us a very sharply focused view of Fitzgerald's commitment at this point in his career to a fiction of form, exclusion, suggestion, and splendid intimation. Although Perosa is right when he says that "there is practically no action" in the story, he is right in a misleading way, for the story powerfully demonstrates Fitzgerald's sense of just how much can take place when

---

6. Matthew J. Bruccoli, *Some Sort of Epic Grandeur: The Life of F. Scott Fitzgerald,* 263.

there is "nothing happening."[7] Indeed, the story flourishes, and can flourish, only when the reader is willing to witness and accept Fitzgerald's incalculable "trick of the heart" that leads us through the minimal, indeterminate surface plot to the thematic center of the story. We, like the imaginary Prince of the story's fairy tale, are charged with the task of rescuing the beautiful Princess—imagination—from the curtained surface reality of the narrative.

We needn't dispute an autobiographical provenance to recognize that Fitzgerald intended a much broader and deeper significance in "Outside the Cabinet-Maker's." He purposefully expands the story's values by leaving the main characters unnamed—referring to them throughout the story as "the man," "the lady," and "the child," thus universalizing their roles and the values of their relationship. Fitzgerald expands the story yet further by placing the story's superficial "reality" in opposition to the subjective expectations and imaginings of the central characters. The most evident expression of this theme, of course, is the encompassing opposition between the actual events of the narrative and the imaginary world the man creates for the child while waiting for the lady to return to the car. But throughout the story there is a persistent, emphatic leitmotiv of oppositions, or interpenetrations, between reality and imagination that serves as a repeating pattern of the story's central concerns.

Thus, we note the anomalous contrast between the story's initial setting "at the corner of Sixteenth and some dingy-looking street" (137) and the conversation in French between the man and the lady as they decide upon a "maison de poupée" for their child. Similarly, the neighborhood is described both as "red brick" (138; or solid, fixed, immovable) and as "vague, quiet" (138; or indeterminate, suggestive). Furthermore, this neighborhood's ambiguous character gives rise to the man's fairy tale, which is in itself insubstantial yet founded upon the objective details of the neighborhood scene. "Darkies," clerks, and passersby become King's soldiers, a little boy becomes the Ogre, and, to cite a classic example of Fitzgerald's method of mingling fancy with fact, the man in the story affirms that the Prince in the fairy tale found one of the blue stones "in President Coolidge's collar-box" (139).

---

7. Perosa, *Art of F. Scott Fitzgerald*, 95.

The dollhouse as central motivation in the story is, in itself, an object both of reality (with a set price of twenty-five dollars) and of imaginative promise (for the lady who never had one as a child, and for her child, who doesn't know she is getting one made for her). Further, and more conclusively, the whole imaginary world the man creates for the child means something far different to him than to the child, who actually *sees* the soldiers that her father can only imagine. In all these instances (and in many others throughout the story), Fitzgerald establishes a complex interdependency between a reality that appears fixed and a subjectivity of imagination and expectation that nevertheless attempts to give new shapes and purposes to that reality. And the dynamic modulations and displacements of the "objective" and the "subjective" in the story express Fitzgerald's definition of both the power and the limitations of imagination.

The protagonist and focal point of the story is the man, who, like the poet in "Ode to a Nightingale," clearly recognizes the ambiguity of living at once in the related but distinct worlds of reality and imagination. Almost always in Fitzgerald's fiction the dreams that are so compelling for the dreamers prove to be Keatsian dreams—transient, incomplete, and thus, ultimately, unsatisfying; in "Outside the Cabinet-Maker's" the man's acute awareness of his situation produces in the story both an intensity and a fragility of tone as he attempts to accommodate both worlds in his experience.

The man's journey into the realm of imagination begins inauspiciously enough. Waiting outside the cabinet-maker's on the "vague, quiet" street, "the man and the little girl looked around unexpectantly." After the child and man exchange perfunctory and conventional declarations of love, the man begins to make up a fairy tale to pass the time for himself and the child: " 'Listen,' the man continued. 'Do you see that house over the way?' " (138). The story he makes up is, as a fairy tale, utterly derivative and conventional, or, if you will, archetypal. It includes an imprisoned Princess, an Ogre, a Prince who must complete a quest to free the Princess and restore order to the kingdom of the captive King and Queen, and so on. At the outset the man is only half-committed to his own creation, and his imagination falters: " 'She [the Princess] can't get out until the Prince finds the three—' He hesitated." And when he is prompted by the child to complete the conditions of the quest ("The three—the three stones that will release the King and Queen"), he is overtaken by ennui—"He yawned" (138).

At this point in the story a deep sea change takes place. The fabricating fancy of the man is outrun and taken over by the imagination of the child, and from this point to the end of the story, the man finds himself in an unequal contest with the child, who can experience directly what the man can only invent. The man embellishes his tale with the assertion that the room will turn blue every time the Prince finds one of the three stones and thinks to titillate the child with the remark, "*Gosh!* . . . Just as you turned away I could see the room turn blue. That means he's found the second stone" (139). On the surface, the child's response seems innocent enough: " 'Gosh!' said the little girl. 'Look! It turned blue again, that means he's found the third stone' " (139). But Fitzgerald is concerned with more than a child's echo of a parent's speech. Although the child's response reflects her father's fancy, as well as words (beginning with the exclamatory "Gosh!"), we are forced by Fitzgerald to recognize a critical distinction amid likeness. The child's echo, in fact, sounds more deeply and resonantly than her father's proclamation, for while he has merely represented the room as turning blue, she has *seen* it turn blue.

At this crucial juncture in the story, Fitzgerald underscores what is at stake for the man in an emphatic one-sentence paragraph: "Aroused by the competition the man looked around cautiously and his voice grew tense" (139). This sentence is at the center of the story and is, I think, the axis around which the story turns. Challenged by the child's envisioning imagination, the man is frightened by what he finds, or rather doesn't find, in himself—the capacity for believing in and directly experiencing a world of pure imagination. From this point in the story until the wife returns from the cabinet-maker's and reintroduces reality into the narrative, the man, like Nick in *The Great Gatsby* and Dick in *Tender Is the Night,* strains to recapture childhood's simple yet dauntless belief in a fairyland world that conforms to the expectations and anticipations of one's imagination.

The man's position is ambivalent, tenuous, and weighted with irony, yet Fitzgerald is able to compress the complex condition of his character in the simple question the man puts to his daughter: " 'Do you see what I see?' he demanded" (139). Of course she doesn't, but at this point in the story he does try to see what *she* sees. He creates an Ogre out of a little boy walking along the street, but now instead of being writer, producer, and director of the drama being played out, the man joins the little girl as part of the audience: "They both watched" (139). And "the little boy" most improbably construed as an Ogre finally becomes that Ogre—for the child, the man, and even for the third-person narrator. If only for a moment, the imagined becomes the reality of the scene: "The Ogre [not 'the little boy'] went away, taking very big steps" (139).

This struggle of imagination to exert itself upon reality and, in effect, transcend it informs the falling action of the story. The resolution of the fairy tale hinges upon the outcome of the conflict between the bad fairies and the good fairies, who struggle for control over the shuttered window of the Princess's prison room. In the story's thematic terms, the struggle is between the vague stolidity of the neighborhood scene and the values invested in that reality by fancy and imagination. Finally, the conflict is played out within the man's ambivalent consciousness of being an adult inextricably bound to a world of inflexible reality and, at the same time, being irresistibly drawn to the imagined world of the child.

All the implications of the man's predicament conflate into his summary statement of the conflict between the bad fairies, who "want to close the shutter so nobody can see in," and the good fairies, who "want to open it" (140). In the story's terms, bad fairies are prohibitive—the conservative guardians of a reality viewed as impenetrable surface; and good fairies are liberating—inviting one to look beneath and beyond the surface of things to a richness of meaning that is as compelling as it is fleeting. Thus, the child's observation that "The good fairies are winning now" marks the ascendancy of creative imagination as it gives form to resistant reality, both in the fairy tale and in the story itself. And the man's response (" 'Yes.' He looked at the little girl. 'You're my good fairy' " [140]) emphasizes Fitzgerald's abiding romantic conviction that the liberating, creative imagination is never and nowhere stronger than in the innocence of childhood.

As in Keats's "Ode to a Nightingale," however, that deceiving elf, imagination, "cannot cheat so well as he is famed to do," and the man is stricken by the realization that even while the little girl sits upon the throne of Queen Mab, "clustered around by all her starry Fays," *he* is doomed to "the weariness, the fever, and the fret" of his adult world: "The man was old enough to know that he would look back to that time—the tranquil street and the pleasant weather and *the mystery playing before the child's eyes, mystery which he had created, but whose luster and texture he could never see or touch any more himself.* Again he touched his daughter's cheek instead and in payment fitted another small boy and limping man into the story" (140; emphasis mine).

The man thus realizes he is exiled forever from the true mystery (that is, the miracle) of the child's imagination, and this realization produces in him a spontaneous declaration of love: " 'Oh, I love you,' he said" (141). The words "I love you" are the same as those uttered at the beginning of the story, but they are now invested with a rich meaning, for the declaration of love springs not from the imprisoning authority of the parent ("Listen, . . . I love you") but from the man's recognition that the child is, as Wordsworth would have it, "abundant recompense" for his own lost childhood. Or perhaps it is more accurate to say that for Fitzgerald the child is *almost* recompense for the man's lost youth: "For a moment he closed his eyes and tried to see with her but he couldn't see—those ragged blinds were drawn against him forever. There were only the occasional darkies and the small boys [not soldiers and not Ogres anymore] and the weather that *reminded* him of more glamorous mornings in the past" (141; emphasis mine).

This shock of self-recognition abruptly cuts off the flight of fancy that has taken him momentarily to the fairyland of the child's imagination, and it is precisely at this moment that "the lady came out of the cabinet-maker's shop" (141). Earlier, the man had described the lady on the street as "a Witch, a friend of the Ogre's"(140), and that definition has a resonant effect upon our view of *the* lady in the story. For her return to the car from inside the cabinet-maker's signals the man's irrecoverable return to the world of reality, his conversation with his wife turning immediately to matters practical and mundane, focusing upon the price of the dollhouse. The man's fall from grace is emphasized yet further by the fact that he must leave behind him the child, who remains in fairyland. With great concision, but bearing the cumulative force of the entire narrative with it, the final line of the body of the story is the haunting plea of the child: "Look, Daddy, there go a lot more soldiers!" (141).

The closing section of the story emphasizes a dualistic world in which reality and imagination, adulthood and childhood, are essentially discrete. And the last "paragraph-epilogue" serves not only as a narrative conclusion to the story but also as a summary gloss upon the values of the man, the lady, and the child: "They rode on abstractedly. The lady thought about the doll's house, for she had been poor and had never had one as a child, the man thought how he had almost a million dollars and the little girl thought about the odd doings on the dingy street that they had left behind" (141). This conclusion, however, provides an "overture" rather than a "closure" to the story's ultimate values, for it invites us to rethink and revalue the story from an altered perspective. The lady, who for the most part has been given form by her absence throughout the story, is now given a presence and at least a hint of definition. The man, who has been seen essentially as father of the child, now is seen as his "sole self." And the child, who has been depicted as responding to, though dominating, her father, is seen, for the first time, to be reflective. In these hints toward new directions, the final paragraph invites us to inquire more deeply into the "odd doings on the dingy street."

The salient revelations in this last paragraph are that the man has money and that the woman has had a "deprived" childhood. It is commonplace to comment upon Fitzgerald's preoccupation with money, but I am not sure we have valued properly yet the metaphorical, even symbolic, value of money in his works. Although his short stories and his novels are to a large degree founded upon money—upon people who have it and people who don't, people who dream about it and people who dream with it—money never remains just money in Fitzgerald's works; it becomes, rather, a symbolic means of revealing personality. Thus, the mention of the man's money in the last paragraph of "Outside the Cabinet-Maker's" is intrinsic rather than peripheral to our understanding of the man's character throughout the story. The revelation that the woman "had been poor" gives color and substance to our late-blooming thoughts about who she is and who she has been. And the revelations together give at least some definition to the relationship between husband and wife that is not made clear elsewhere in the story.

In a direct inversion of Fitzgerald's more typical plot depicting "the struggle of the poor young man to win the hand of the rich girl,"[8] in

---

8. Scott Donaldson, "Money and Marriage in Fitzgerald's Stories," 75.

"Outside the Cabinet-Maker's" the poor young girl *has* won the hand of the rich boy, and perhaps because of this inversion it is easier to recognize Fitzgerald's symbolic use of money, not only in this story, but in his other fiction as well. Here, money is seen clearly, if implicitly, as a means of realizing one's dreams and giving substance to one's imagination. The lady who dreamed of, but never had, a dollhouse as a child can, thanks to her husband's wealth, buy one for her daughter and, we clearly sense, for herself. Indeed, in looking back upon the story we realize that all the lady's comments on the dollhouse are almost wholly restricted to its cost. Getting out of the car at the beginning of the story, she affirms, "I'm going to tell him it can't cost more than twenty dollars" (137); returning to the car at the end of the story, she says that it will cost "vingt-cinq" dollars and apologizes for taking so long (141).

If, in Fitzgerald's fiction, money is projected as the means of realizing personal dreams and is frequently depicted as an expression of the larger cultural American dream, he makes it clear in both story and novel that those individual dreams, like the national dream they embody, are inherently flawed. For Fitzgerald there is no reality, by definition, that can conform to the exquisite balance and harmony of winter dreams— or dreams outside the cabinet-maker's. The dollhouse in the mind of the lady and in the mind of the cabinet-maker will not and cannot be captured for twenty-five dollars or twenty-five thousand dollars.

As in all his great fiction, in "Outside the Cabinet-Maker's" Fitzgerald depicts money as a false lure that promises, but fails, to realize the soaring expectations of one's dreams. The man, who has been transported to the boundary of fairyland by his fairy child, returns with a crash at the end of the story to the anticlimactic reality of having "almost a million dollars," a phrase that at once conveys both completion and dissatisfaction; "almost a million dollars" is both a great deal of money and, we recognize with the man, not nearly enough. In Fitzgerald's fiction in general the adult's quest for material wealth is, indeed, a self-confounding attempt to supplant the lost ability of the child to experience dreams as actuality. Ultimately, in the ironic context of this story's final paragraph, "almost a million dollars" appears as the surviving fragment of an adult fairy tale with no fixed purpose and no happy destination in sight. At the story's end, the man, the lady, and the child "rode on abstractedly" (141).

The child, too, stands at the focal point of Fitzgerald's finalizing ironic vision, for the closing paragraphs suggest that the child is herself on the perilous brink of adulthood. Her resolution of the man's fairy tale is rooted in the death of the King, the Queen, and the Prince, and is expressed in her proclamation that "the Princess is Queen" and in her cheerful announcement that "she'll marry somebody and make him Prince" (141). The stakes involved in this transparently Freudian resolution are suggested by Fitzgerald quite clearly. The man, who "had liked his King and Queen and felt that they had been too summarily disposed of" (141), chastises his daughter: " 'You had to have a heroine,' he said *rather impatiently*" (141; emphasis mine). But his unease, I suggest, arises not simply from his sense of lost authority, but from his deeper awareness of the condition underlying that lost authority— his child's loss of innocence and passage into adulthood. She too will become—at the very moment *is* becoming—an adult all too much like her parents.

The final sentence of the story tells us that the child "thought about the odd doings on the dingy street that they had left behind" (141). In that suggestive, compressed statement we see the first diminution of the child's unquestioning capacity for wonder and the first chilling hint of the adult's pained awareness of the intricate inseparability of "odd doings" and "dingy street[s]"—of imagination and the reality it feeds upon but cannot be nourished by.

THE SOUTHERN AND THE SATIRICAL IN "THE LAST OF THE BELLES"

HEIDI KUNZ BULLOCK

"The Last of the Belles" completes Fitzgerald's Tarleton series, a trilogy of short stories—the others are "The Ice Palace" (1919) and "The Jelly Bean" (1920)—involving the imaginary town of Tarleton, Georgia. First published in the *Saturday Evening Post* on March 2, 1929, and later collected in *Taps at Reveille*, in *The Stories of F. Scott Fitzgerald*, in volumes 2 and 5 of *The Bodley Head Scott Fitzgerald*, and in *The Short Stories of F. Scott Fitzgerald: A New Collection*, "The Last of the Belles" has rightly enjoyed both critical and popular acclaim. Bryant Mangum places the story squarely in the author's "*Saturday Evening Post* period," explaining that its composition coincided with both the end of Fitzgerald's work on the Basil group and his intensifying focus on *Tender Is the Night*. Matthew J. Bruccoli remarks its "retrospective and reassessing" quality, which Herbie Butterfield ascribes to deteriorating personal conditions between Fitzgerald and his wife. While it does attract considerable scholarly attention—it has been called "the much-analyzed 'Last of the Belles' "—that attention virtually excludes narrative issues that affect the meanings of the story.[1]

---

1. The publication histories of these and indeed of all other Fitzgerald short stories is in Bryant Mangum, *A Fortune Yet: Money in the Art of F. Scott Fitzgerald's Short Stories.* His comments appear on pages 61 and 119. Matthew J. Bruccoli, ed., *The Short Stories of F. Scott Fitzgerald: A New Collection,* 449; Herbie Butterfield, " 'All Very Rich and Sad': A Decade of Fitzgerald Short Stories," 104; Alice Hall Petry, *Fitzgerald's Craft of Short Fiction: The Collected Stories—1920–1935,* 183.

Everybody seems to know that Ailie Calhoun is "The Last of the Belles." When Andy the narrator meets her, he declares, "I would have recognized Ailie Calhoun if I'd never heard Ruth Draper or read Marse Chan [sic]."[2] Readers similarly identify her: Ruth Prigozy sees the story as "a touching reminiscence of the lovely Southern girl" figure already established in Fitzgerald's fiction by 1928, while Scott Donaldson perceives Andy's account as Fitzgerald's "ultimate rejection of the Southern belle." C. Hugh Holman asserts Ailie personifies an "enchanting and hypnotizing tradition," that she is "wistful nostalgia made fresh." Alice Hall Petry counters that "essentially . . . she is a good imitation of a kind of figment of the Southern imagination" who is "not worth the trouble of the narrator or any other man." These and other critics "recognize" Ailie and confidently judge her.[3] Fitzgerald's satiric strategy operates so successfully that the reader, even the critical reader, involves himself in an object lesson.

The problem begins with the narrator's assumption of a universally apprehended South. The South of "The Last of the Belles" is "relentlessly" trite, assembled with clichés appropriated from popular fiction and regional convention. Atlanta provides an "elaborate and theatrical rendition of Southern charm" (449), for instance; the reader is left to evoke the detail for himself, since Andy assumes a shared understanding so precise as to distinguish unexplained degrees and extremes. Andy's standardized South is sultry, pastoral, almost surreal: It is "a little hotter" than any experience, it has "herds of cows drifting through the business streets," and, in this altered state, "you wanted to move a hand or foot to be sure you were alive" (449). It is a locality full of preconceived meanings. Andy becomes interested in the preeminent debutantes of Tarleton because "there was something mystical about there being three girls" (450). He finds it important enough to note that he meets Ailie on the evening of the third day of his interest and calls upon moonlight and

2. Bruccoli, ed., *Short Stories,* 450. All subsequent page references to "The Last of the Belles" are to this edition and will appear parenthetically in the text.

3. Ruth Prigozy, "Fitzgerald's Short Stories and the Depression: An Artistic Crisis," 124; Scott Donaldson, "Scott Fitzgerald's Romance with the South," 7; C. Hugh Holman, "Fitzgerald's Changes on the Southern Belle: The Tarleton Trilogy," 64; Petry, *Fitzgerald's Craft,* 156.

magnolias in his recalling "the flowery, hot twilight" (450). As Robert Roulston and others note, Fitzgerald held a multiple view of the South that diversifies its meaning in his texts. The heat that enervates may also impassion. The pastoral may be bucolic or ideal. Heightened sensibilities may enhance experience as well as distort it. Moreover, Fitzgerald saw the South as feminine in principle, both desired and dominated by a masculine North.[4] Andy's image scheme is suspiciously simple.

The problem intensifies with Andy's focus on Ailie. He first assigns her mythic stature as "the last of the belles" and then approaches her character through a series of presentations that become incrementally more specific but never quite individualized. After the title of the story, the reader encounters the outscale version of southern culture that is Atlanta; next a Lieutenant Warren tells Andy about the local Tarleton women; soon Bill Knowles delimits, "there're really only three girls here—" (449). Andy notes the obligatory white-pillared, vine-covered veranda on which Ailie makes her first appearance. He announces her from this proscenium as a concept: "There she was—the Southern type in all its purity" (450). He indulges his conventional imagination instead of taking the final crucial step into her individuality:

> She had the adroitness sugar-coated with sweet, voluble simplicity, the suggested background of devoted fathers, brothers and admirers stretching back into the South's heroic age, the unfailing coolness acquired in the endless struggle with the heat. There were notes in her voice that order slaves around, that withered up Yankee captains, and then soft, wheedling notes that mingled in unfamiliar loveliness with the night. (450)

Here at last the writer-narrator shapes his southern image, but he remains decidedly unoriginal.

Just as Andy assumes a codified South, he assumes a codified southern woman. His assumptions inevitably affect his perception; once one typecasts another, one tends to notice and remember the ways in which that person seems to fit the stereotype while resisting evidence that contradicts it. Andy's perception is further impaired by a confusion of

4. Robert Roulston, "Whistling 'Dixie' in Encino: *The Last Tycoon* and Fitzgerald's Two Souths," 157–65; Holman, "Fitzgerald's Changes," 55.

which he seems to be unaware: His version of the "belle" is garbled if it derives from "Marse Chan." Thomas Nelson Page's heroine is the dignified Miss Anne Chamberlain, whose unswerving devotion to the single love of her life and to a chivalric code of honor make her not a belle but rather a lady.[5] Andy is not entirely wrong in seeing the belle in Ailie. At first she behaves like one, skillfully manipulating the men on her porch, defusing their competitive antagonisms and eliminating Andy's awkward presence with flirtatious ease. With her white dress, her collection of admirers, and apparent respect for her parents' social values, Ailie deliberately approximates the stereotype: "How the Yankees did deceive us poor little Southern girls. Ah, me!" (461). And Ailie can act the lady. She exercises her superior "breeding" to social advantage (455). But by substituting a category for a characterization, however, Andy separates himself from his subject and sabotages his effort to know her.

The narrator's mistakes point up major issues in southern woman-hood: "Southern girls who take on the roles of belle and lady take on an entire history of the meaning of the South."[6] In this sense, Ailie risks being depersonalized when she incorporates stereotypes into her public persona. Yet her situation as an early-twentieth-century single white woman of some standing directs her to pursue certain social objectives, including the attraction of an appropriate husband. Officer Andy and his fellow Harvard graduate Knowles are initially "drawn to her" because they "recognized her"—as the belle (451). Southern scholar Peggy Whitman Prenshaw's explication of the stereotype illuminates its complexity: The role of the belle is "absurdly inconsistent with life," because it is fraught with "impossible contradictions" understood by familiars of southern culture. As a northern soldier, Andy is encamped in the South but is not at home in it; he assumes "that the admired traits are compatible, an assumption based on the uncritical acceptance

5. Mark Snyder's "Self-Fulfilling Stereotypes" explains this psychological phenomenon; see especially page 266. Criteria for the *belle* and *lady* and others appear in John Shelton Reed, *Southern Folk, Plain and Fancy: Native White Social Types;* in Patricia Sweeney, *Women in Southern Literature: An Index;* and in Charles Reagan Wilson and William Ferris, eds., *Encyclopedia of Southern Culture.*

6. Anne Goodwyn Jones deconstructs stereotypical southern womanhood in "Belles and Ladies," in Wilson and Ferris, eds., *Encyclopedia,* 1528.

of nineteenth-century stereotypes."[7] It follows that Ailie is caught in the "impossible contradiction" of her regional imperative. In order to distinguish herself as a potential mate—she looks at her new acquaintance Andy "as if she asked, 'Could it be you?'" (451)—she must first manage to be "recognized" as a generality.

The violent death of her frustrated suitor Horace Canby provides an occasion when Andy might individuate his perception of Ailie. She responds to the fatal accident by covering her face with her hands and groaning (452–53). Andy is positioned to connect with the Ailie behind the mask: He alone of her acquaintance knows Canby had threatened suicide, and the news comes to them in a moment of physical intimacy. In these pointedly personal circumstances, Andy considers her so impersonally that he does not ask himself why she has been kissing him instead of the man she ponders marrying; he does not wonder what feeling slows her exit from the car where they have been embracing. He then extends her no word of comfort or gesture of support. Rather, he dissociates himself by joining the news-bearing stranger to form an audience to her grief (453). The two officers keep their psychic distance, "watch[ing] her helplessly" for a full minute; Andy relieves his discomfiture by leaving the parking lot altogether (453). He passes the opportunity to participate in her emotion to her official escort Knowles, whom he tells on his own authority "she wanted to go home" (453). By the time Knowles arrives Ailie has stopped "gagging" and just "whimpers a little," but Andy takes her self-possession for self-preservation (453). He confesses he distrusts his senses, yet he is sure that, true to type, she merely imitates grief to "[call his] attention to her involuntarily disastrous effect on men" (453). He even feels competent to make moral judgments of her (453).

Now and again Andy senses Ailie is not so immediately comprehensible, as when he observes that "by degrees I saw that she was consciously and voluntarily different from these other girls" (451). But his insights never enlighten him; rather, he twists them to affirm his imagined understanding ("That's why Bill and I and the others were drawn to her. We

---

7. Peggy Whitman Prenshaw, "Southern Ladies and the Southern Literary Renaissance," 80, 82.

recognized her" [451]). He insists that he is her "confidant," but "some girl" unworthy of so much as a name in Andy's account teaches him a few things about Ailie's intimacies (451, 453). He mispredicts Ailie's responses (456–57); he "half-suspects" greater depths to her character than he has explored (457); and he even admits he cannot discern the operative priorities of her personal decisions. Nevertheless, he does not refine his perception of her or hesitate to interpret her in terms of it. He cannot account for her interest in Earl Schoen, for example; still he presumes she rejects Schoen because "the background of mill-town dance halls and outing clubs flamed out at you—or rather flamed out at Ailie. For she had never quite imagined the reality" (459). Her eventual refusal of Andy's proposal of marriage literalizes his inability to engage her.

"The Last of the Belles" is ostensibly a portrait of Ailie Calhoun, drawn by the man who claims to love her "deeply and incurably" (461), but the image is imprisoned in an outline and overpowered by the frame. Formally, the story is divided into three numbered sections arranged in chronological order. Instead of developing Ailie's character, however, the passing of time elaborates her predicament. Andy labels her on their first encounter and constrains her to type ever after; he presents her story as a sequence of romances, as though she could be characterized exclusively in relation to the men she entertains. Even so, in each case the relation goes unsubstantiated. Andy does not understand Ailie's idiosyncratic definition of *sincere*, so he cannot fathom the "sincerity" she finds in Knowles, Canby, and Schoen, but not in him. With each successive episode Andy finds himself further removed from the individual Ailie. The changes in his relation to her—from being her "experimental" lover to serving as her insufficiently informed apologist to losing touch with her entirely—result from the inflexibility of his logic (452, 461). The magnitude of his misjudgment increases section by section. When he does revise his perception in the last part, he comes no closer to characterizing her: "The modulations of pride, the vocal hints that she knew the secrets of a brighter, finer ante-bellum [sic] day, were gone from her voice; there was no time for them now as it rambled on in the half-laughing, half-desperate banter of the newer South" (460). Andy consigns her to the perpetual role of cultural representative. All three sections open and close on his interpretive experience; he effectively confines every glimpse of Ailie's character to a cell surrounded by powerfully biased narrative.

Alice Petry asserts, "Fitzgerald gradually instills in his reader the realization that the presentation of Ailie is satiric" because "the falling away of her mask [reveals] the chill-minded flapper under the alluring Southern belle." "The Last of the Belles" indeed demonstrates the unsuitability of the label—but the story is a study of Andy rather than of Ailie, about whom little actual information is provided. The reader comes to know far less about Ailie, whom critic John Kuehl calls an "ostensible protagonist," than about the framer of "her" story, whose perception predominates both spatially and structurally.[8] "The Last of the Belles" culminates in the rejection of Andy. Through him the reader feels the bite of Fitzgerald's satire.

The exposition of the story sets a satiric trap: "After Atlanta's elaborate and theatrical rendition of Southern charm, we all underestimated Tarleton" (449). The warnings are both contextual and grammatical. The narrator acknowledges the pervasiveness and extent of cultural pretense. "Southern charm" is too mutually familiar a concept to require description; the smoothly inclusive phrasing implicates the reader in the first-person plural. With becoming modesty, the persona simultaneously admits and rationalizes his mistake as part of a collective misjudgment. He maintains the attitude as he more boldly involves the reader: "It was a little hotter than anywhere we'd been—a dozen rookies collapsed the first day in that Georgia sun—and when you saw herds of cows drifting through the business streets, hi-yaed by colored drovers, a trance stole down over you out of the hot light; you wanted to move a hand or foot to be sure you were alive" (449). The speaker's candor about his own inexperience disarms the reader while it cultivates a sense of identification. When he assigns his own responses to "you," the trap is sprung. He undertakes to identify himself by name and by characterization only once the reader has been drawn into his point of view.

Andy functions as a cautionary model: He relies uncritically on the words of confiding men he hardly knows. He "lets" Lieutenant Warren

8. Petry, *Fitzgerald's Craft*, 156; John Kuehl, *F. Scott Fitzgerald: A Study of the Short Fiction*, 74.

tell him about the girls instead of learning about them himself; he can quote verbatim the feelings expressed by other characters, but he has "forgotten how I felt, except that the days went along, one after another, better than they do now" (449). By the time the narrator exhibits his unreliability, the reader's allegiance has been expertly secured. Andy's slip that he "guesses" (450) the emotional truth behind Knowles's words is not likely to weaken the reader's commitment—it certainly has not concerned Fitzgerald scholars, who neglect to consider the source of the evidence on which they base their evaluations of the title character. "The South would be empty for me forever," Andy concludes when his representation is exploded (463). He prefigures the critics, for whom Ailie also always represents something—"the gracious life," the South, Zelda Sayre Fitzgerald, or even a developmental "stage which inevitably is left behind."[9] Like Andy, everybody "knows" that Ailie Calhoun is "the last of the belles"—until Fitzgerald's satire reminds us that, like Andy, nobody really knows Ailie.

9. Richard D. Lehan, "The Romantic Self and the Uses of Place in the Stories of F. Scott Fitzgerald," 59; Butterfield, " 'All Very Rich and Sad,' " 104; Donaldson, "Fitzgerald's Romance," 4; Holman, "Fitzgerald's Changes," 64.

FITZGERALD'S VERY "ROUGH CROSSING"

WILLIAM H. LOOS AND
VICTOR A. DOYNO

F. Scott and Zelda Fitzgerald sailed on the *Conte Biancamano* from New York on Saturday, March 2, 1929, bound for Europe. The ship ran into a terrible ocean storm, and Scott Fitzgerald wrote a story about such a voyage. "The Rough Crossing" was purchased by the *Saturday Evening Post* in April for $3,500, earning Scott a purchasing power equal to at least $33,250 in 1995 American dollars, and, of course, the purchasing power of that $3,500 was greater in Europe. "The Rough Crossing" appeared in the June 8, 1929, edition of the *Post*. Subsequently the story was reprinted at least four times; Cowley's 1951 collection, *The Bodley Head Scott Fitzgerald*, volumes 4 and 5, and the Penguin *Stories of F. Scott Fitzgerald* have offered this elusive tale to generations of readers. Such respected Fitzgerald scholars and critics as Eble, Bruccoli, Higgins, Lehan, Perosa, Sklar, Kuehl, and Mangum have each offered helpful commentary about this puzzling story.[1]

---

1. F. Scott Fitzgerald, *The Stories of F. Scott Fitzgerald: A Selection of 28 Stories;* F. Scott Fitzgerald, *The Bodley Head Scott Fitzgerald,* vols. 4 and 5 ("The Rough Crossing" appeared in both volumes in the 1961 edition; in the revised 1967 edition, it appeared only in vol. 5); F. Scott Fitzgerald, *"Bernice Bobs Her Hair" and Other Stories,* vol. 4 of *The Stories of F. Scott Fitzgerald;* Kenneth Eble, *F. Scott Fitzgerald,* 124; Matthew J. Bruccoli, *The Composition of "Tender Is the Night": A Study of the Manuscripts,* 59, 66, 84; Matthew J. Bruccoli, *Some Sort of Epic Grandeur: The Life of F. Scott Fitzgerald,* 279; John A. Higgins, *F. Scott Fitzgerald: A*

In looking at this complex story through different, yet overlapping critical filters, we begin with an analysis of the structural conflicts, then progress to anthropological and folkloric approaches, and use a "new critical" examination of motifs and image patterns. In addition, we juxtapose information from Fitzgerald's biography with a revealing diary of the voyage kept by a beautiful woman on the ship whom Fitzgerald declared that he loved and who probably had a substantial emotional impact upon him. Finally, genetic criticism, which draws upon how Fitzgerald creatively revised his manuscript, leads to an assessment of the story's artistic and thematic achievement. This crucial and crucially indicative story deserves and repays the scholar/critic's careful attention.

"The Rough Crossing" deals with structural conflicts and transitions in the marital state by using the setting of an ocean voyage during a life-threatening storm. The hero and heroine, Adrian and Eva Smith, apparently gain some slight maturity as their marriage is severely tested by the husband's extramarital shipboard romance. The voyage itself presents a series of transitions from America to the world of a 1920s luxury liner bound for Europe and its differing culture, from notoriety or celebrity to hoped for but rejected anonymity. The story dramatizes conflicts between flirtatiousness or infidelity and familial commitments, between overindulgence in alcohol and attempted sobriety, between being unknown to others and having some very slight self-knowledge. Of course, during this period, spring 1929, Fitzgerald was himself fighting alcoholism—and losing the fight. The story traces one movement from party life to family life, from the author figure being adulated and captivated by a fan to his being committed to his marriage and his children. The parallel movements include a progression from near childishness to semimaturity, from self-indulgence to self-denial and self-renunciation. The story presents many rites of passage, many moments of change, and most of these crossings are, indeed, rough.

Study of the Stories, 110–11; Richard D. Lehan, *F. Scott Fitzgerald and the Craft of Fiction,* 57, 143–44; Sergio Perosa, *The Art of F. Scott Fitzgerald,* 100–101; Robert Sklar, *F. Scott Fitzgerald: The Last Laocoön,* 234–36; John Kuehl, *F. Scott Fitzgerald: A Study of the Short Fiction,* 103–9; Bryant Mangum, *A Fortune Yet: Money in the Art of F. Scott Fitzgerald's Short Stories,* 88–89.

An anthropologist would immediately comment that the story contains familiar situations and complex motifs. The beginning approach to the ship at night, through the loading pier, creates a sense of cultural displacement: " . . . you have come into a ghostly country that is no longer Here and not yet There."[2] The womblike image with the distant, brightly illuminated entrance to the ship marks the transition from America to a new microcosm. Fitzgerald was apparently quite taken with the first two paragraphs of this story because he put them in his notebook and used them again in a slightly different form in *Tender Is the Night* (chapter 19, paragraphs 3 and 4). The entire story thereafter occurs in special places with otherworldly aspects. The married couple experiences an originally desired isolation; their children and their nursemaid mysteriously drop out of the story and are ignored, magically requiring almost no attention despite a terrifying storm, until the family (mysteriously minus the nurse) is once more on land, in a train compartment bound for Paris.

The major anthropological theme of the story, of course, involves the testing of the marriage by Adrian's sexual attraction to a younger, "immaculate" woman, by Adrian's emotional need for and response to adulation, by the married couple's compounding alcoholisms, and by the severe ordeal of the ocean storm. Just as the ship is storm-tossed, the husband, wife, and their marriage endure both internal and external conflicts.

The Fitzgeralds experienced such a storm themselves on their voyage to Europe in March 1929, and undoubtedly the storm partially inspired the story. A few words may lend emphasis to the power of such a testing experience. Most readers have probably never encountered such a storm. But one of the authors of this essay can testify, from the personal endurance of a single night on a small Yugoslavian steamer without stabilizing devices now found on most modern large steamers, that an ordinary ocean storm is quite disorienting, creating an apparently life-threatening situation far beyond the merely frightening. The combination of tilting and vertigo, the shifting floors, the noise, the crashes of furniture, and the creaking of the ship, with both rhythmic

---

2. Fitzgerald, *The Stories of F. Scott Fitzgerald*, 254. All subsequent page references to "The Rough Crossing" are to this 1951 edition and will appear parenthetically in the text.

and arrhythmic shocks and thumps, can certainly disorient a person and can never be forgotten. In addition, one is surrounded by people in various stages of seasickness, ranging from a sullen, withdrawn quietness to a smelly, wretched desperation. One feels and fears incipient nausea while understanding the peculiar will-lessness, lethargy, or despair of the seasick, as well as the fragile arrogance and hyperactive recklessness of those who have temporarily escaped the sickness. A major hurricane must have been significantly worse! In sum, these conditions could lead to a conversion experience, to vows of reform, to extremes of thought and emotion, as occur when Eva kisses her week-old pearls goodbye and throws them into the sea, sacrificing her husband's expensive birthday gift to propitiate the angry sea gods and also to punish the husband who she fears has been unfaithful.[3]

The story also includes a second sacrifice to the sea. The sick steward, James Carton, who Eva is appalled to find mysteriously ill on her bed, does not survive his midstorm appendicitis operation and is buried at sea, an obvious reminder of death's power. Because Eva has angrily wished him dead when she finds him, she is accordingly horrified to learn that he does not survive the emergency operation. Other repeated references to death and to the threat of death throughout the story remain so muted that the serious theme can be easily overlooked.

As any folklorist would immediately recognize, the ocean voyage is a trial, a measuring of selves against a hostile natural force. The ocean liner provides an isolated, enclosed setting. In addition to the testing ordeal of the storm, the marriage of Adrian Smith, a promising playwright, and his wife Eva faces an attack in the form of an aggressive, attractive younger woman, a fictional version of Lois Moran. A deliberate ambiguity in the story leaves even a careful reader wondering if Adrian totally succumbs to the sexual temptation offered by Miss Betsy D'Amido. But there is no doubt that Adrian fully lusts for her with his heart and with his lips. Other organic contact remains a mystery, a subject for Fitzgeraldean scholars' speculation. After Eva Smith makes her sacrifice to the storm by

---

3. As Nancy Milford has noted in *Zelda: A Biography*, Zelda apparently threw her own diamond and platinum wristwatch from a train in 1927, when the Fitzgeralds quarreled over Scott Fitzgerald's relationship with the seventeen-year-old Lois Moran. The watch was the first valuable gift he had given her during their courtship (131).

throwing away her talismanic pearls, symbolic of past happiness, the ship makes it through the storm. Moreover, during the storm's height, after Adrian bravely goes to an exposed upper deck to seek Eva and rescues her from a monstrous wave, the at least temporary survival of the marriage seems assured. But Eva, during this episode, had actually been on her drunken way to the wireless room to send a message to Paris seeking the services of a divorce lawyer. How stable could the marriage be?

Because this short story concentrates on the moments of transition, on the fictional characters struggling across—and then back across—various thresholds, it may appear to an uninformed or hasty reader that little happens. But a "new critically" trained close reading would declare it noteworthy that the setting on the ship, with its naval architecture, emphasizes those liminal places and moments when people pass from one room to another, or into a passageway by stepping over the raised door sill of a ship's bulkhead. Of course, there is an inside "cramped" versus an outside "tempestuous" contrast on the ship. The usually enclosed setting of the ship functions through most of the story, but the final portion, part 4, also takes place in a similarly enclosed railway compartment as the entire Smith family travels safely toward Paris.

Fitzgerald is, as usual, brilliant in the details, such as his choice of names. Adrian and Eva Smith, an obvious fictionalization of F. Scott and Zelda Fitzgerald, as well as an evocation of the primal couple Adam and Eve, seem to have the possibility of being ordinary; "there are so many Smiths in the world."[4] Are they perhaps meant to represent "every couple"? The seductress in this nautical Eden is aptly named "Miss Betsy D'Amido," conveying a dark, glossy Mediterranean sensuality, with aural echoes of "Damn, I do" and, macaronically, "Miss, I do love." The couple's children remain nameless, quite unimportant really, until the last section, when we learn that one is named "Estelle," a *star*. But the couple certainly do not attribute value to or navigate by their children or by their own earlier commitments during most of the story. (Eva goes to check on the children only once. The second time she mentions them it is only as a cover when she goes drunkenly to radio Paris for a divorce

---

4. Herbie Butterfield, " 'All Very Rich and Sad': A Decade of Fitzgerald Short Stories," 106.

lawyer.) Miss D'Amido's chaperon on the ocean voyage is humorously named "Mrs. Worden," but the wardenlike guardian proves ineffective because her own seasickness completely prevents her from restraining the young seductress.

Close reading also reveals that the story includes a "betrayal" or infidelity motif. We learn toward the beginning that Mr. and Mrs. Smith are "unfaithful to the ships that had served their honeymoon" (255). The gradual temptation, male ego gratification, marital deception, and, later, guilty attentiveness are portrayed with a delicate brush that Fitzgerald must have dipped in acid. Close reading provokes serious questions. Is emotional infidelity a form of introductory adultery? How would a romanticizing, idealizing Fitzgerald react to such thoughts?

Clearly the voyage reminded Fitzgerald of his and his wife's first trip to Europe in 1921, before her brief affair with the French aviator Jozan. The fictional Adrian Smith has conflicting—Fitzgeraldean—emotions when he first reluctantly kisses the young seductress:

> When Adrian and Betsy D'Amido, soaked with spray, opened the door with difficulty against the driving wind and came into the now-covered security of the promenade deck, they stopped and turned toward each other.
>
> "Well?" she said. But he only stood with his back to the rail, looking at her, afraid to speak. She was silent, too, because she wanted him to be first; so for a moment nothing happened. Then she made a step toward him, and he took her in his arms and kissed her forehead.
>
> "You're just sorry for me, that's all." She began to cry a little. "You're just being kind."
>
> "I feel terribly about it." His voice was taut and trembling.
>
> "Then kiss me."
>
> The deck was empty. He bent over her swiftly.
>
> "No, really kiss me."
>
> He could not remember when anything had felt so young and fresh as her lips. The rain lay, like tears shed for him, upon the softly shining porcelain cheeks. She was all new and immaculate, and her eyes were wild.
>
> "I love you," she whispered. "I can't help loving you, can I? When I first saw you—oh, not on the boat, but over a year ago—Grace Healy took me to a rehearsal and suddenly you jumped up in the second row and began telling them what to do. I wrote you a letter and tore it up." . . . She was weeping as they walked along the deck. (261–62)

A sensitive reader may simultaneously feel Adrian's and Fitzgerald's passion while remaining aware of the hypocritical desire for an immaculate woman, while appreciating the imagery of lachrymose Catholic statuary, and while remembering Zelda Fitzgerald's intense, wild glances. In contrast to the famous Gatsby-Daisy kiss, this scene has the author's knowledge of life after the fall into knowledge of good and evil mixed with a tone of regret. Of course, Adrian and Miss D'Amido have more furtive doorway and hallway hugs and kisses and perhaps consummate their affair during the ship's party. But we also learn, to our astonishment, in part 4 of the story, that Miss D'Amido already has a fiancé, a revelation that presumably diminishes her prior interest in Adrian to no more than a wish for a romantic, if not sexual, adventure or exploit, for a one-night stand or a one-hour recline. Even the fictional mistress betrays the famous author.

Here we are at some depth in Fitzgerald's mind, because the temptress is an "immaculate" woman whose eyes are "wild" (262). Perhaps a sensitive reader may hear a portion of the dialogue as quite touching, even searingly acute. When the married couple are dressing for the ship's costume party they argue in a way that reminds us of the Fitzgeralds:

> "Ships make people feel crazy," she said. "I think they're awful."
> "Yes," he muttered absently.
> "When it gets very bad I pretend I'm in the top of a tree, rocking to and fro. But finally I get pretending everything, and finally I have to pretend I'm sane when I know I'm not."
> "If you get thinking that way you will go crazy."
> "Look, Adrian." She held up the string of pearls before clasping them on. "Aren't they lovely?"
> In Adrian's impatience she seemed to move around the cabin like a figure in a slow-motion picture. After a moment he demanded:
> "Are you going to be long? It's stifling in here."
> "You go on!" she fired up.
> "I don't want—"
> "Go on, please! You just make me nervous trying to hurry me."
> With a show of reluctance he left her. After a moment's hesitation he went down a flight to a deck below and knocked at a door.
> "Betsy." (263)

But the story does not deal only with Scott and Zelda Fitzgerald. Malcolm Cowley has noted that the Fitzgeralds were known to have "flirted with strangers" on their trip to Europe in 1929 on the Italian liner, the *Conte Biancamano*.[5] Striking confirmation of that fact came to light when a Buffalo, N.Y., bookseller, the late Thomas D. Mahoney, purchased the library of a deceased Buffalo society matron. Among the books Mr. Mahoney discovered were two travel diaries, one for 1922 and a second for 1929. When he read the 1929 diary and found that it included descriptions of shipboard meetings with the Fitzgeralds, he generously presented the diaries to the Rare Book Room of the Buffalo and Erie County Public Library. This private diary, a day-by-day account by an observant participant, puts the entire voyage and the autobiographical elements in Fitzgerald's short story into another—quite surprising—light.

Mrs. Geneva Thompson Porter of Buffalo sailed with her husband, Peter A. Porter Jr., on the *Conte Biancamano*. This American beauty, part of the economic aristocracy, conducted herself in a manner above reproach, but Fitzgerald did manage, in a romanticizing or awkward fashion, to kiss her "white hand." Also on board, forming a group, were several of her Buffalo area acquaintances, people from similarly socially prominent families, including Mr. and Mrs. Paul A. Schoellkopf and Dr. Frederick N. C. Jerauld of Niagara Falls, New York.

Geneva Thompson Porter was an intelligent, well-read, beautiful woman of forty-six. From available photographs it is apparent that she bore a resemblance to F. Scott Fitzgerald's first love, Ginevra King. The similarity in names must have caught his attention; we cannot know if there were any other physical similarities or shared gestures, inflections, or mannerisms in addition to a facial similarity between the two women. Perhaps an open-minded contemporary critic can imagine what it must have been like for Fitzgerald—drunk or sober—suddenly to find himself on an ocean voyage with a more mature reincarnation, in face and almost in name, of his teenage sweetheart.

We are fortunate that Mrs. Porter's diary has survived and is now accessible. The following excerpts from the unpublished journal are offered in edited form to present a contrasting, apparently factual, view of some revealing events. Mrs. Porter's behavior was consistently proper and, under the circumstances, gracious. It is, however, obvious from

5. Fitzgerald, *Stories of F. Scott Fitzgerald*, 175.

the repetitions and jumbling of chronology in her account that Mrs.
Porter was rather flustered or confused by what was occurring. In the
fictional version, Miss Betsy D'Amido boldly declares her love for the
talented playwright Adrian; but in the diary version F. Scott Fitzgerald
threw himself at Geneva Porter, who, while she knew who Fitzgerald
was, certainly could not have known that she resembled Ginevra King.
Mrs. Porter was probably nonplussed by the gallant or inappropriate or
drunken attentions of a man fifteen years her junior. But in writing
his story, Fitzgerald's imagination transformed the following events,
changing Mrs. Porter's graceful, polite deflections into actions more
desired by his male ego:

March 3, Sunday.
    We all staid in bed all day—a terrible storm has been raging all night
and all day. Some of the officers told Pete a hundred mile gale from two
to five in the morning. Our rooms kept us busy all night trying to save
things from smashing. The odor of a boat that is shut up tight is a ghastly
sweetish smell. I have been reading *Traveling Light* and finished it. Pete
and I went to sleep at eight. At ten a big wave hit the boat and Pete woke
up and went up to see what had happened to be asked to have a drink
with Scott Fitzgerauld [*sic*] & his wife. Both lit.—Scott asked a Mr. & Mrs.
Williams (older) and an Italian to join them. He ended by getting very
tight and smashing a glass of champagne on his head and being carried
up stairs kicking by the Italian.

March 4, Monday.
    We slept late. The boat has stopped some of its violent contortions.
We ordered breakfast at what we thought was nine to find it was eleven
o'clock. It seemed nice to be able to get into the bathtub. Had my first walk
on deck. Sat out until cold then played cards. Won again, fifty-five ahead
of Schoellkopf family. Met Scott Fitzgerauld [*sic*] and little wife with name
commencing with Z. Played bridge with Williams and wife. Later talked
to Fitz—and wife—both very tight. She was probably very pretty when
younger and very amusing. He ended by asking Mrs. Williams something
about men's private parts and Mrs. Fitzgerauld called him a fool—("Scott,
you fool, you better shut up. One can never talk about anything seriously
with people.") Everyone was paralysed. He turned to me and I said "if
I am silly I can never answer you." He followed me out saying I was
beautiful and he loved me but I was very silly and kissed my hand. Scott
and I had been talking about literature. He maintained that Mencken

was the greatest man of the age, and I standing up for George Bernard Shaw, James Branch Cabell, Anatole France—saying they were fun but that Mencken was silly and trivial—that greatness had to be constructive not destructive for the race. He turned from this to Mrs. W. and said, "Mrs. W. do women like men's private parts large or small?" He kept at her—then his wife spoke up. Then he turned to me and said, "Geneva won't you answer me" & I said "If you think I am silly how could I."

March 5, Tuesday.
    Another very stormy day—five dining room tables upset. An apple and an orange are chasing each other from Pete's bed to mine. Fred Jerauld came in and said, "I love you and you are beautiful but you are silly," and planted himself on my bed. He was very much impressed by my conversation with Fitzgerauld [*sic*]. It is such a dangerous day to try moving that we are all staying in bed all day. I finished *Traveling Light*.[6]

Fitzgerald has transformed his actual flirtation or conversation target to a fictional premarital, engaged status. He has omitted his crude and rude conversational seduction gambit about whether women like men's sexual parts large or small. (But this diary entry reveals that his genuine concern about this topic predated his private and possibly sober conversation later that same year with Hemingway, which Hemingway so brutally describes in *A Moveable Feast*.) Although repetitive, Mrs. Porter's diary is to be valued both for its record of literary opinions and for the evidence of a situation of male infatuation transformed by imaginative wish fulfillment into a fictional case of Miss D'Amido insistently throwing herself at the older, presumably wiser, more sophisticated, successful, famous writer. One can conclude, without being too judgmental, "Lord, what fools these mortals be!"
    What effect might such a voyage and encounter have had upon Fitzgerald's mind? It must have been difficult for him to write about the husband's and wife's flirtations. Probably Zelda Fitzgerald would not know about or recognize what he was experiencing, increasing each spouse's isolation. Moreover, this reincarnation of Ginevra King apparently did not respond to his coarse overtures; she apparently did

---

6. The diary is quoted with the permission of the Rare Book Division of the Buffalo and Erie County Public Library.

recognize Fitzgerald's public acclaim or notoriety, but nevertheless found him quite resistible. Seemingly, she was happy, wealthy, and (the cruelest revenge of ex-loves!) contented. Let each male reader imagine his own personality with a few extra, Fitzgeraldean additions, such as a tendency to romanticize or idealize and a sensitivity to hurts. Would a normal man's mind turn toward nostalgia—or speculate about what might have been? Would the meeting provoke memories and regrets? Would such a situation cause a keenly observant perceiver like Fitzgerald to be confused, ruthlessly self-analytical, partially self-deceiving? Would this situation speed up the writing of *Tender Is the Night* or contribute to the difficulty of creating the novel?

Indeed, this testing of the marriage involves sexual attractiveness in a conflict with generational implications. Adrian had been twenty-four and Eva had been nineteen when, contrary to her mother's wishes, she married him. When this fictional seven-year itch happens, Adrian is thirty-one, Eva is twenty-six years and one week old, their children's ages are not recorded, and Miss D'Amido is "not more than eighteen" (255). (Fitzgerald was thirty-one and his wife twenty-seven during this voyage. Lois Moran had been seventeen. Mrs. Porter, still a beauty, was forty-six but nevertheless shrewdly, harshly evaluative of Zelda Fitzgerald's appearance.) Yet Adrian addresses his seasick wife as "you poor baby" (259); each indulges the other's childishness, while both ignore their own children and their nurse through most of the horrible storm. Although Eva drunkenly gives "some woman an impassioned lecture upon babies" (264), the children do not seem to occupy much, if any, space in Adrian's mind. In the last scene, Estelle's extraordinary statement, "I like the boat better [than the train]," leads the parents to exchange "an infanticidal glance" (270), a sign, though perhaps only a temporary one, that the marital communicative bond of these characters, with their erratic mood swings, has been renewed.

Adrian, perhaps precociously ready for his "middle-aged crazies," or midlife crisis, has age-related feelings as he calls Miss D'Amido out of her stateroom for some hallway kissing:

"I had to see you," he said quickly.
"Careful," she whispered. "Mrs. Worden, who's supposed to be chaperoning me, is across the way. She's sick."

"I'm sick for you."

They kissed suddenly, clung close together in the narrow corridor, swaying to and fro with the motion of the ship.

"Don't go away," she murmured.

"I've got to. I've ——."

Her youth seemed to flow into him, bearing him up into a delicate, romantic ecstasy that transcended passion. He couldn't relinquish it; he had discovered something that he had thought was lost with his own youth forever. As he walked along the passage he knew that he had stopped thinking, no longer dared to think. (263–64)

Like many of Fitzgerald's remarkable scenes, this incident deserves commentary. Kisses given and taken in danger, while a "warden" is near, may well seem sweeter for the mutual commitment despite the danger of discovery. But Adrian's "I'm sick for you" has a faintly comic dimension; most modern women, when surrounded by seasickness, would not find that declaration to be an aphrodisiac! (Betsy will subsequently also fall victim to seasickness.) But the sense of "ecstasy," literally a *loss of sense of place,* and the reversal of coital flow into emotional resurgence, as her youth flows into him, could be psychologically stimulative.

As a close reader or a genetic critic might expect, Fitzgerald includes a noticeable amount of water or liquid imagery in "The Rough Crossing," from Adrian being "bathed in flash light by a photographer" (254) to an ironic, humorous postvoyage exchange as the temptress sees a reunited Adrian and Eva with their two children in the railroad compartment:

A pale and wan girl, passing along the corridor, recognized them and put her head through the doorway.

"How do you feel?"

"Awful."

"Me, too," agreed Miss D'Amido. "I'm vainly hoping my fiancé will recognize me at the Gare du Nord. Do you know two waves went over the wireless room?"

"So we heard," Adrian answered dryly.

She passed gracefully along the corridor and out of their life. (270)

Since both Eva and Adrian had, indeed, been there when the second wave washed over, drenching both, endangering both, Fitzgerald's " 'So we heard,' Adrian answered dryly" is both ironic and ambiguously arch, excluding Miss D'Amido by giving her only one meaning while Adrian's witticism could amuse Eva by referring to their shared experience. A genetic critic could note that Fitzgerald inserted "dryly" in the typescript. This handwritten revision signals both the superiority of wit and the author's and reader's triple knowledge. One hopes, in vain as it turns out, that the author figure would in the future make many witty remarks "dryly," but, as we know, the real Scott and Zelda Fitzgerald continued to drink in a complex, grotesque ballet of codependency, cooperating in the mutual assault and victimization of an alcohol-lubricated, dissolved marriage. The happy ending in this *Saturday Evening Post* story remains truly fictitious.

Fitzgerald's typescript includes a final evaluation ("it was all a dream"), which he manually revised to a more accurate, caustic assessment ("It was a nightmare—an incredibly awful nightmare" [270]). Indeed, much of the Fitzgeralds' life—even without ocean storms—must have felt like a nightmare. Yet in the newly tested fictional couple's words we can perhaps hear F. Scott Fitzgerald's desire for the isolation that would permit mutual devotion and some touching combination of lack of self-knowledge with self-renunciation:

> "Adrian, let's never get to know anyone else, but just stay together always—just we two."
> He tucked her arm under his and they sat close. "Who do you suppose those Adrian Smiths on the boat were?" he demanded. "It certainly wasn't me."
> "Nor me."
> "It was two other people," he said, nodding to himself. "There are so many Smiths in this world." (270)

Not many writers can capture a hopeful, bittersweet, self-denying, self-deceptive, and poignant moment as well as Fitzgerald can. One hopes that relatively few other writers have had to endure such personal tempests or such rough crossings while using the creative process to transform stressful life experiences into imaginative artistry.

"THE SWIMMERS": STROKES
AGAINST THE CURRENT

ROBERT ROULSTON

In an extraordinary paragraph midway through "The Swimmers," F. Scott Fitzgerald states that the protagonist seeks refuge from "insurmountable, inevitable" difficulties by swimming as another man might seek it in music or drink.[1] Then out comes a flood of images in which the waves off the Virginia coast become alternately symbols of oblivion and renewal. Struggling to attain "a point when he would resolutely stop thinking," Henry Marston swims far out "to wash his mind" in the sea and to view the "green-and-brown line of the Old Dominion with the pleasant impersonality of a porpoise." There the "burden of his wretched marriage" falls away with "the buoyant tumble of his body among the swells" as he moves in "a child's dream of space." After Marston recalls the "playmates of his youth," the metaphors expand to embrace all Americans who "should be born with fins," and the passage culminates with the conceit that "perhaps money was a form of fin" and that Americans, "restless and with shallow roots, needed fins and wings" (201).

Written at a time of crisis when life seemed to be tugging Fitzgerald in all directions, the story itself is a kind of equivalent of inebriation,

---

1. F. Scott Fitzgerald and Zelda Fitzgerald, *Bits of Paradise: 21 Uncollected Stories by F. Scott and Zelda Fitzgerald*, 201. All subsequent page references to "The Swimmers" are to this edition and will appear parenthetically in the text.

combining the incompatible and harmonizing the discordant. In the novel that would eventually incorporate passages from "The Swimmers," *Tender Is the Night,* Dick Diver's besotted friend, Abe North, after an especially destructive binge, experiences an almost mystical unitary state: "The drink made past happy things contemporary with the present, as if they were still going on, contemporary with the future as if they were about to happen again."[2] But just as the alcoholic's bliss soon fragments, so the unity in "The Swimmers" is constantly about to dissipate. Thus the contradictions throughout are not so much reconciled as they are in an uneasy equipoise, always about to collapse, much like the table full of glasses that Abe North nearly crashes into at the Ritz bar in Paris after his luminous moment.

The unstable mixture of genres and the clash between tone and structure make "The Swimmers" almost as difficult to assess as it was to write. After complaining that it was the hardest story he ever created, Fitzgerald wavered between regarding it as unsatisfactory and "not bad." Finally he consigned it to oblivion, first by excluding it from *Taps at Reveille,* and then by listing it among the works he wanted omitted from any posthumous collection.[3]

The divergent critical reactions reflect the problematical nature of the story. Robert Sklar, who admires its themes and its historical perspective, extols "The Swimmers" as the most important precursor to *Tender Is the Night* among the stories Fitzgerald wrote from 1927 to 1932. Matthew J. Bruccoli, though, while ranking "The Swimmers" as a "major story," objects to its trick plot and its overabundant material. Similar reservations are stated by Melvin J. Friedman in the most extended discussion thus far of "The Swimmers," an article examining analogues

---

2. F. Scott Fitzgerald, *Tender Is the Night,* 103.

3. Matthew J. Bruccoli, ed., *As Ever, Scott Fitz—: Letters between F. Scott Fitzgerald and His Literary Agent, Harold Ober—1919–1940,* 142. Writing to his editor Maxwell Perkins on March 26, 1935, Fitzgerald listed twenty-four hitherto uncollected stories to choose from and twenty-nine others to be "scrapped" (Matthew J. Bruccoli and Margaret M. Duggan, eds., *Correspondence of F. Scott Fitzgerald,* 406–7). "The Swimmers" is in the second list, perhaps in part because, like some others, it contains material that Fitzgerald cannibalized for *Tender Is the Night.* So, however, do some in the list of those to be reprinted. In fact, the very first paragraph of "The Rough Crossing" appears in the novel with only minor alterations. "The Swimmers" first appeared in book form in *Bits of Paradise.*

between the story and works by various French and American authors dealing with France and Virginia. Comprehensive studies of Fitzgerald's writings generally ignore "The Swimmers," comment on it casually, or dismiss it.[4]

"The Swimmers" does contain a great deal of material, but no more than "May Day" (1920), which has elicited far more admiration. In "May Day," Fitzgerald uses the loose structure and inclusiveness favored by his idol as a youth, H. L. Mencken, who published the work in his magazine *The Smart Set* in July 1920. In "The Swimmers," however, Fitzgerald crams a score of his favorite themes into the narrower confines of popular magazine fiction, using in the process narrative techniques that have not enjoyed great critical favor in this century. On certain levels, nevertheless, the story is completely successful, combining poignant lyricism with acute social observation and a high level of inventiveness. It also illuminates a wide range of problems besetting mankind in general and F. Scott Fitzgerald in particular in the summer of 1929.

For nearly half a decade his career had been foundering.[5] As if to prod himself out of his doldrums, Fitzgerald in March 1929 relinquished his lease on Ellerslie, his huge rented house outside Wilmington, Delaware, and set off for France. Following a similar move from Great Neck, New

4. Robert Sklar, *F. Scott Fitzgerald: The Last Laocoön*, 234–36; Fitzgerald and Fitzgerald, *Bits of Paradise*, 10; Matthew J. Bruccoli, *Some Sort of Epic Grandeur: The Life of F. Scott Fitzgerald*, 279; Melvin J. Friedman, " 'The Swimmers': Paris and Virginia Reconciled," 259–60. Scott Donaldson groups "The Swimmers" with "The Bridal Party" and "Babylon Revisited" as a demonstration of "the impotence of money to purchase either happiness or love" (*Fool for Love: F. Scott Fitzgerald*, 112). André Le Vot merely notes where and when Fitzgerald wrote the story and proceeds to discuss Fitzgerald's faltering progress that summer and fall in Cannes and Paris on the novel (*F. Scott Fitzgerald: A Biography*, 245). James R. Mellow lists it among Fitzgerald's writings for the summer without singling it out for special attention (*Invented Lives: F. Scott and Zelda Fitzgerald*, 339). Henry Dan Piper does little beyond noting how the story accepts the positive aspects of the American dream while condemning its excesses (*F. Scott Fitzgerald: A Critical Portrait*, 177). Kenneth Eble is similarly terse in his comments on the story as an examination of two dissimilar cultures (*F. Scott Fitzgerald*, 121). In his survey of Fitzgerald's short stories, John A. Higgins finds nothing to admire about "The Swimmers" beyond some effective passages and some good symbolism (*F. Scott Fitzgerald: A Study of the Stories*, 113–14).

5. Biographical details in this article come principally from Bruccoli (*Epic Grandeur*) but are supplemented with information from Donaldson, *Fool for Love;* Le Vot, *Fitzgerald: A Biography;* and Mellow, *Invented Lives.*

York, to the Riviera in 1924, he had completed *The Great Gatsby* in an intense burst of creativity. What had worked five years earlier did not work a second time. He arrived in Genoa after a bibulous voyage without having produced the chapters for his new novel that he had promised his editor, Maxwell Perkins. Fitzgerald did manage to dash off in March "The Rough Crossing," a story about shipboard shenanigans based upon a storm-tossed, westbound voyage the preceding year. But his sojourn that month in Nice, where he was jailed for disorderly conduct, presaged three months of debauchery in Paris, memorialized by Ernest Hemingway in *A Moveable Feast* and Morley Callaghan in *That Summer in Paris*.[6] In June, Fitzgerald rented a house in Cannes where he resumed work on his novel. Bruccoli believes that while there Fitzgerald produced no more than two extant chapters. The summer, though, was not a complete loss. In June he wrote "At Your Age" and in July and August "The Swimmers." With its partially resolved tensions and its premonitions of *Tender Is the Night,* the latter story could aptly be subtitled with a phrase from "The Rough Crossing," written a mere five months earlier: "no longer Here and not yet There."[7]

Even the barest summary of "The Swimmers" indicates both how autobiographical its material is as well as how the story incorporates many of Fitzgerald's favorite themes. Like so many of Fitzgerald's other stories, "The Swimmers" is built around a mésalliance, in this instance between an expatriate patrician Virginian, Henry Clay Marston, and his unfaithful bourgeois French wife, Choupette. The story also uses the formula of the victim who, through a sudden reversal, prevails over a victimizer, as in "Bernice Bobs Her Hair" (1920) and "Myra Meets His Family" (1920).

One day Marston returns early from his job at a bank to his apartment in Paris to discover Choupette with another man. After four weeks of delirium, Marston recuperates "at St Jean de Luz [*sic*]" with Choupette,

6. Although Callaghan and Hemingway provide portraits of Fitzgerald that are in general accord, Hemingway's is more jaundiced. In *Fitzgerald and Hemingway: A Dangerous Friendship,* Bruccoli sorts out the conflicting accounts of Callaghan's sparring match with Hemingway while Fitzgerald served as timekeeper.

7. Bruccoli, *Epic Grandeur,* 285; F. Scott Fitzgerald, *F. Scott Fitzgerald: A Selection of 28 Stories,* 129.

whom he still loves. There, one day, he spies a "perfect type of American" girl, a superb swimmer in her late teens, who suffers a cramp out in the water (192–93). Although he has never learned to swim, Marston attempts to rescue her, and she repays him by teaching him and his two sons how to swim properly. When the seaside idyll ends, Henry leaves with his family for a better-paying position at the bank's headquarters in Richmond, Virginia.

There three years later Choupette wishes to marry her new lover, a rich parvenu, Charles Wiese. Loath to give them custody of their sons, Marston sets off for a therapeutic trip to a beach near Norfolk where the young American girl who had taught him to swim in France unexpectedly materializes. Then Wiese appears and insists that Marston join him and Choupette on Wiese's motorboat for a discussion of the divorce. Wiese reveals that he has bribed a Paris psychiatrist to declare Marston mentally unfit to have custody of the children. The engine fails, and the boat begins drifting. Wiese and Choupette cannot swim, and Marston threatens to let the boat float out to sea unless Wiese signs a statement relinquishing all claims on the children. After stuffing the document and the psychiatrist's certificate into a waterproof tobacco pouch, Marston swims to a nearby lighthouse where he informs the keeper that he has known all along the boat would drift safely into harbor. At the end Marston accidentally meets his beautiful swimming instructor aboard a Europe-bound liner.

Henry Marston's difficulties with Choupette reflect Fitzgerald's own marital troubles. Zelda Fitzgerald, of course, was not French. But her command of the language, which Fitzgerald never mastered, may explain his identifying her with France. Then too her dalliance with the French aviator Edouard Jozan in Saint-Raphaël in the summer of 1924—under circumstances similar to those in Cannes in 1929—undoubtedly suggested a French predilection for adultery. Marston's more innocent involvement with an eighteen-year-old American girl resembles Fitzgerald's own flirtation with the young actress Lois Moran. Marston's physical and emotional breakdown in Paris combines Zelda Fitzgerald's health problems with Fitzgerald's own.

Yet this story, which includes so many of its creator's preoccupations, deals only obliquely with one of his most urgent personal problems: alcoholism. The hero seems not to drink at all. The only direct reference to liquor is to a gin fizz beside the wicker chair of the odious Charles Wiese. At the end of the ensuing confrontation between the two men, Choupette throws the unspecified contents of her glass into Marston's face.

Reticence on the subject was hardly Fitzgerald's norm. Heavy drinking is virtually central to the decline of the hero of his second novel, *The Beautiful and Damned*. Liquor flows destructively throughout early stories such as "May Day" and "The Camel's Back" (1920), as well as many later ones. It is also a major factor in the decline of Dick Diver in *Tender Is the Night*. Moreover, a mere three months after writing "The Swimmers," Fitzgerald created one of his more harrowing accounts of the subject in "Two Wrongs" (1930), in which the hero's deterioration anticipates Diver's. Alcohol, in fact, was very much on Fitzgerald's mind throughout 1929. In May his "A Short Autobiography" in the *New Yorker*—a year-by-year catalog of his own memorable drinking experiences—ends with a summation for 1929: "A feeling that all it [alcohol] has done for one has been experienced, and yet—*Garçon, un Chablis-Mouton 1902, et pour commencer, une petite carafe de vin rose. C'est ça, merci.*" His private reflections, however, had considerably less joie de vivre, his summation in his Ledger for the year being: "OMINOUS No Real Progress in ANY way *wrecked myself with dozens of people.*"[8] The wrecking ball had been his often boorish drunkenness.

As we have noted, though, in "The Swimmers" water serves as Marston's surrogate for alcohol, enabling him to maintain a patrician poise amid the swirl of most of his creator's favorite conflicts and themes. Choupette's affair with the millionaire parvenu Charles Wiese brings into the story the clash between the genteel and the vulgar that Fitzgerald had used so effectively in *The Great Gatsby*. The narrative line eventually carries Fitzgerald into subjects such as the decline of old values, the recurrence of past misfortunes, a yearning for a new beginning, the golden girl, sexual jealousy, the grand gesture, the insider versus the outsider, a longing for lost youth, the loss of illusions, the arrogance of the rich, Spenglerian pessimism, American optimism, motherhood, feminine freedom, masculine pride, French amorality, southern chivalry,

8. Matthew J. Bruccoli and Jackson R. Bryer, eds., *F. Scott Fitzgerald in His Own Time: A Miscellany*, 225; F. Scott Fitzgerald, *F. Scott Fitzgerald's Ledger: A Facsimile*, 183.

parvenu vulgarity, American technology, greed, a tug between the life force and the death wish.[9] Here too are important motifs in *Tender Is the Night* such as contrasts between Europe and America, the rich and the nonrich, work and indolence.

Fitzgerald complained to his agent, Harold Ober, about the story being "too big for its space." The initial readers of "The Swimmers," however, shared none of its author's doubts. Ober praised it as "the ablest and most thoughtful" story Fitzgerald had ever written. Thomas B. Costain, fiction editor of the *Saturday Evening Post*, which published "The Swimmers" on October 19, 1929, informed Ober that he thought the story "very fine." A staff member at a rival magazine, the *Woman's Home Companion*, wrote to Ober about her exceptionally high regard for the piece. Even the formidably conservative chief editor of the *Post*, George Horace Lorimer, liked "The Swimmers" so much, despite its risky subject matter, that he was willing to accept it "exactly as it stands" with "perhaps a change of one or two words."[10]

The editors of the *Post* probably admired the story for the very quality apt to make some critics uneasy: its narrative cleverness. "The Swimmers," in fact, has just the sort of story line that led reviewers and Hemingway to disparage Fitzgerald's *Post* fiction.[11] Serious writers throughout much of this century have shunned sudden reversals, elaborate hoaxes, timely encounters, missing documents, startling

9. Just when the influence of Oswald Spengler's *The Decline of the West* began and how extensive it was has been a topic of considerable controversy. For interesting discussions on the matter see Robert W. Stallman, "Gatsby and the Hole in Time," 14; Sklar, *Fitzgerald: Last Laocoön*, 134–36; Richard D. Lehan, *F. Scott Fitzgerald and the Craft of Fiction*, 30–36.

10. Bruccoli, ed., *As Ever*, 142, 143, 145, 154–55.

11. The reviewer in *The Nation*, September 18, 1920, complained that the stories in *Flappers and Philosophers* indicated that Fitzgerald had been producing "dross" in order to "sell it to *The Saturday Evening Post*" (Jackson R. Bryer, ed., *F. Scott Fitzgerald: The Critical Reception*, 36). William Rose Benét, reviewing *All the Sad Young Men* in the *Saturday Review of Literature*, April 3, 1926, asserted that the stories display "the pressure of living conditions rather than the demand of the spirit" (ibid., 268). A decade later T. S. Matthews, in the *New Republic*, called *Taps at Reveille* a "collection of potboilers" (ibid., 347). Even favorable reviewers sometimes objected to Fitzgerald's facility. When Fitzgerald suggested that Hemingway submit material to the *Post*, Hemingway replied: "Send Lorimer a story hell. I'm letting you send one for *both* of us" (Carlos Baker, ed., *Ernest Hemingway: Selected Letters—1917–1961*, 269).

coincidences, last-second rescues, surprising climaxes, and tidy denoue-
ments. Irving Howe's recent comments about the novel are applicable to
many modern short stories: "there is no 'once upon a time.' . . . In the
novel a complex of circumstances often emerges as a 'slice' of history,
since an illusion of historical stoppage is essential for that 'thickness'
of specification at which many novels aim."[12] That sense of giving a
"slice of history," though, is difficult to sustain when such traditional
artifices of plotting are used, a problem—as Howe notes—that was
virtually nonexistent for the creators of mythic figures such as Aeneas,
Tristan, and Faust. Indeed, Fitzgerald uses these devices sparingly in his
best fiction, albeit they abound in frivolous comedies such as "Head
and Shoulders" (1920) or "The Pusher-in-the-Face" (1925). But even
though some of the situations in "The Swimmers," such as the cuckold
catching his wife flagrante delicto and the use of elaborate stratagems
by all concerned, are the stuff of bedroom farce, where a large degree of
artificiality is essential, the prevailing tone of the story precludes laughter
as an appropriate response.

"The Swimmers," in fact, is closer to melodrama than to comedy.
George Steiner once defined melodrama as near tragedy.[13] More often,
perhaps, it is pseudotragedy. In either case, events seem moving toward
catastrophe only to veer off into a felicitous conclusion. In a sense, therefore, "The Swimmers" combines comic plotting with tragic grandiosity.
The story, however, is melodramatic on a deeper level. The moral rift
between the characters Fitzgerald favors and those he denigrates is much
wider than is usual in Fitzgerald's more earnest efforts. There the hero
is apt to be a flawed man whose troubles derive at least in part from his
own weaknesses. He may flee reality and be too enthralled by wealth like
Jay Gatsby, be too brash like Basil Duke Lee; he may vacillate between
emotional extremes like Amory Blaine, or drink too much like Anthony
Patch, Dick Diver, or the heroes of numerous short stories. In "The
Swimmers," though, Marston is the innocent victim of his unfaithful
wife and her ruthless lover. Throughout he is good, resourceful, indus-
trious, sober, and well mannered. The unnamed young woman whom he

12. Irving Howe, "History and the Novel," 29.
13. George Steiner, The Death of Tragedy, 133.

attempts to rescue is similarly prepossessing. She is beautiful, vigorous, competent, aristocratic, intelligent—and exhibits none of the cynicism of Marston's French wife.

Although he relentlessly denigrates Marston's foe, Wiese, Fitzgerald displays ambivalence toward the unfaithful wife. Despite her bad behavior, she has taste and perceptiveness: "Choupette, with something more than the rigid traditionalism of a French bourgeois taste, had made it [their Paris apartment] beautiful, and moved through gracefully with their children. She was a frail Latin blonde with fine large features and vividly sad French eyes" (189). Her comments on the fraudulence of the American dream reflect the author's own reservations about that glittering chimera. When Henry Marston contrasts his own values with hers, he concedes that hers have much to commend them: "For eight years, . . . he had lived her life, substituting for the moral confusion of his own country, the tradition, the wisdom, the sophistication of France" (196). Whatever her virtues, her actions invariably damn her. The plot, however, necessitates some blurring of Choupette's iniquity in order to make Marston's continued love for her plausible. On the other hand, Choupette's recurring infidelity certainly owes something to Fitzgerald's need to place the stigma for the divorce on someone other than the hero. This, after all, is a *Post* story at a time when divorce was all but unthinkable among a huge section of the reading public. Neither should one forget the apostate Catholic Fitzgerald's own disapproval of it.

Marston's chief antagonist is condemned the instant he makes his entrance: "[Marston] recognized and detested the type—the prosperous sweater, presumably evolved from a cross between carpet-bagger and poor white" (188). Thereafter Charles Wiese exhibits not one redeeming quality. A braggart and a bully, he bribes psychiatrists and hires expensive lawyers to achieve his nefarious ends. After Marston dares to resist, Wiese boasts: "On your side there's an obstinate prejudice; on mine there are forty million dollars. Don't fool yourself. . . . money is power." When the engine of his yacht fails, Wiese proves himself a coward. With a "shaking" voice he begs his enemy to rescue him and cravenly relinquishes claim on Marston's children (205, 207).

In his brutal treatment of Wiese, Fitzgerald reveals one of his own less attractive traits—snobbery. The same writer who could sympathize with once-poor outsiders such as Jay Gatsby and Monroe Stahr could lash out in certain contexts at upstarts, minority groups, or indeed anybody less patrician than the Maryland forebears of Fitzgerald's father. Let Fitzgerald select a hero from the upper orders such as Amory Blaine, Anthony Patch, Dick Diver, or Henry Marston, and out will come snipings at social climbers or less-favored groups. In fact, when Marston scoffs: "There's no time for humor" after Wiese has offered his "personal word of honor" (207), Marston seems disconcertingly like the well-connected Tom Buchanan scorning another rich parvenu, Jay Gatsby.

Even though "The Swimmers" does not contain anti-Semitic smudges like *The Beautiful and Damned* and almost no slurs at blacks, Asians, and Latins like *Tender Is the Night*, it makes an unpleasant linkage between Wiese's low-class ancestry and his contemptible behavior.[14] Marston, moreover, attributes the charm of his young girlfriend to her having "an Eastern Shore name, 'good as his own'" (202). He patently thinks that blood will tell, and Fitzgerald seems to agree more than is consistent with his affection for plebeians such as Gatsby and Stahr. It is as if in "The Swimmers" Fitzgerald wished to exorcise the part of his lineage that he identified in a letter to John O'Hara with his mother's family, the McQuillans: "I am half black Irish and half old American stock. . . . [The Irish half] looked down upon the Maryland side . . . who had . . . that sense of reticences and obligations that used to go under the word 'breeding.'"[15] Henry Marston seems unencumbered with embarrassing black Irish progenitors, but his family tree is adorned with an improbably romantic grandfather "who freed his slaves in '58, fought from Manassas to Appomattox, knew Huxley and Spencer as light reading, and believed in caste only when it expressed the best of race" (191).

But, as T. S. Eliot, Henry James, and Evelyn Waugh demonstrate, snobbery has its artistic uses, and the patriotic rhetoric that concludes the story comes more credibly from an old-line Virginian than from a more alienated figure. Marston sails past the Statue of Liberty in a burst

---

14. The passing reference to "nigger cooks" (197) would hardly have qualified as much of a racial slur in 1929.

15. Andrew Turnbull, ed., *The Letters of F. Scott Fitzgerald*, 103.

of prose at least as fervent as the verse of Fitzgerald's Maryland ancestor, Francis Scott Key. The passage, though, unlike "The Star Spangled Banner," flavors patriotism with a soupçon of criticism. Marston may have "a sense of overwhelming gratitude" that "America was there" and be glad that "in the heart of the leaderless people the old generosities and devotions" persist. But he cannot ignore the "ugly débris of industry," disregard "the tired, drawn, nervous faces of its great men," or forget the "country boys dying in the Argonne for a phrase that was empty before their bodies withered." Such discordant notes may not negate the organ-peal affirmation that the "best of America [is] the best of the world" (209–10), but they do keep the Europe-America contrast from being as stark as the one between Marston and Wiese.

A contrast between continents, however, does underlie the story. Fitzgerald begins with a nightmarish evocation of Paris permeated with gasoline fumes—"a terrible thing" promising no "rural escape" and suggesting only "roads choked with the same foul asthma." The opposition between America, with its "willingness of the heart" (187, 210), and Europe, with its stifling traditions and cynicism, is developed throughout with plot, characterization, dialogue, and description all contributing to the final effect with the professional proficiency that made Fitzgerald's agent and the editors of the *Post* admire the work.

But there is sometimes a dubious side to the kind of craftsmanship Fitzgerald displays in "The Swimmers." If at its best professionalism is a refusal to allow the quality of one's work to sink below a certain level, at its worst it is the cunning of the hack pretending to make something out of nothing. In Fitzgerald's case the weakest *Post* stories—especially those written under acute financial pressure in the mid-1920s and again in the mid-1930s—are formulaic and perfunctory. But in the best ones, such as "The Last of the Belles" (1929) and "Babylon Revisited" (1931), the merits seem the result of a fertile cross between Fitzgerald's deepest fears and hopes and the restraints under which he was working. Despite his complaints about having to write for the *Post*, Fitzgerald found the magazine a congenial home. Probably few writers with his artistic aspirations have been so immersed in popular fiction. He may have eventually found his way to Joyce, James, and Conrad; but he was weaned on Clarence E. Mulford, Horatio Alger, Anthony Hope,

Raffael Sabatini, and the anonymous author of Diamond Dick.[16] Then
too the kind of plotting favored by the popular magazines sometimes
provided a valuable corrective to the tendency to ramble that had marred
Fitzgerald's first novel and that is always a pitfall for writers with his
penchant for autobiography and for impressionistic mood building.

The very pattern of these stories, with their crises promising
disasters that are either averted or muted, accords with Fitzgerald's
manic-depressive personality. After all, for him unrealistic expectations
constantly led to inevitable disappointments followed by new anticipations. As a result, if no success ever satisfied him, no failure permanently
immobilized him. Fitzgerald belonged in the *Post* and its competitors
for another reason: His values and aspirations were close to those of the
ordinary American to a degree rare among writers of his stature. Any
man who could mope at forty over having failed to make the football
team at Princeton and who had aspired to be an undergraduate hero, to
be rich, to be universally admired, and to marry a campus-queen type,
could address a popular audience without the condescension James or
even Hemingway could have avoided only with the greatest difficulty.

The sentiments of the final section of "The Swimmers" would have
been as alien to those writers as the timeworn narrative methods in the
story. Yet those methods enable Fitzgerald to impose order upon and
provide valuable insights into almost intractable material. Fitzgerald's
penchant for the kinds of polarities he juggles with in "The Swimmers"
should have given him a Manichaean view of life, with the forces of
light arrayed in mortal combat against the forces of darkness. With
another kind of temperament, he might have been given to positing
vast political conspiracies and to joining movements to counter dia-
bolical plots. Instead, like Henry Marston, he usually veered between
pessimism and a Micawber-like expectation that something good would
turn up. As he would write at his spiritual and professional nadir in the

16. For discussions of the possible influence of some of these popular authors on *The
Great Gatsby,* see Taylor Alderman, "*The Great Gatsby* and *Hopalong Cassidy*" (Mulford);
Gary Scharnhorst, " 'Scribbling Upward': Fitzgerald's Debt of Honor to Horatio Alger, Jr."
(Alger); Daryl E. Jones, "Fitzgerald and Pulp Fiction: From Diamond Dick to Gatsby"
("Diamond Dick"); and Robert E. Morsberger, "The Romantic Ancestry of *The Great
Gatsby*" (Hope, Sabatini).

mid-1930s: "The test of a first-rate intelligence is the ability to hold two opposed ideas in the mind at the same time and still retain the ability to function."[17] The two ideas specified by way of illustration are that life is hopeless and that one must hope.

Such a vision is not the stuff of tragedy or realism, but of comedy and melodrama, where the engine on the yacht of one's antagonist will break down at the most opportune moment. It is also the vision of a manic-depressive who, in a down phase, yearns for the elation of being back up where all seems well, and youth and young love can be recaptured. Too often Fitzgerald himself tried floating up in a gin bottle. In "The Swimmers" he rides the crest in a paper skiff. As John Keats observes in the poem from which Fitzgerald derived the title of *Tender Is the Night*: "the fancy cannot cheat so well / As she is famed to do."[18] "The Swimmers" is so problematic because it sometimes seems on the verge of becoming what the hero accuses his wife and her lover of perpetrating, a "preposterous moral farrago" (208). The statement, significantly, is a paraphrase of one Edmund Wilson once applied to Fitzgerald's first novel. Wilson then went on to dismiss *This Side of Paradise* as being "not really about anything" and amounting to "little more than a gesture . . . of indefinite revolt."[19]

"The Swimmers," however, is about some very important things. It examines a man torn between past and present, old high hopes and new low realities—a man whose travails reflect those of Europe and America when the 1920s were about to come crashing to a close. The apparent disharmonies in "The Swimmers," as well as the poignancy of much of the writing, are appropriate to the subject matter and simultaneously mirror Fitzgerald's own predicament in the summer of 1929. The blend, too, of artificiality and very real problems may contribute to the effectiveness of the story. Some of Fitzgerald's very best fiction, including *The Great Gatsby*, combines a high degree of verisimilitude with the once-upon-a-time aura that Irving Howe finds alien to the modern novel. Howe also notes that works deeply embedded

17. Edmund Wilson, ed., *The Crack-Up*, 69.
18. John Keats, "Ode to a Nightingale," lines 73–74.
19. Edmund Wilson, *The Shores of Light: A Literary Chronicle of the Twenties and Thirties*, 28–29.

in the specifics of a certain time and place can lose their luster for later generations of readers, citing as a prime example Hemingway's *The Sun Also Rises*.[20] Fitzgerald's strange mixture of fantasy and realism, though, has thus far kept *The Great Gatsby* from fading. "The Swimmers" is no miniature *Great Gatsby* or even a small-scale *Tender Is the Night*, but it contains enough of the features of both to make it far more than just a *Saturday Evening Post* potboiler. If it is not, as Harold Ober contended, Fitzgerald's ablest and most thoughtful story, it is worthy of considerably more respectful attention than it has received.

20. Howe, "History and the Novel," 34.

"TWO WRONGS," OR ONE WRONG TOO MANY

SCOTT DONALDSON

"Two Wrongs" is "one of the best things you have ever done," agent Harold Ober wrote F. Scott Fitzgerald late in 1929. Fitzgerald was not sure about the story's commercial possibilities. It might be "too heavy" for the *Saturday Evening Post,* he warned Ober. It wasn't: Ober sold it to the *Post* for four thousand dollars, Fitzgerald's going rate (and the highest he achieved) with the magazine.[1] "Two Wrongs" ran in the January 18, 1930, issue, Fitzgerald included it in *Taps at Reveille,* Malcolm Cowley chose it for his twenty-eight-story selection, *The Stories of F. Scott Fitzgerald,* and, of course, it is reprinted in Matthew J. Bruccoli's comprehensive *Short Stories of F. Scott Fitzgerald.*

"Two Wrongs," in other words, has been readily available to scholars and readers throughout its sixty-five-year history, yet it has attracted scant critical attention. For the most part, those who have commented on the story have concentrated not so much on its merits as on its autobiographical content and its place in the genesis of *Tender Is the Night.* The most thoughtful reading is Alice Hall Petry's, but even she does not give "Two Wrongs" the thoroughgoing analysis it deserves.[2]

1. The correspondence between Ober and Fitzgerald is summarized by Matthew J. Bruccoli in a headnote to "Two Wrongs" (Matthew J. Bruccoli, ed., *The Short Stories of F. Scott Fitzgerald: A New Collection,* 513); F. Scott Fitzgerald, *F. Scott Fitzgerald's Ledger: A Facsimile,* 65.

2. Alice Hall Petry, *Fitzgerald's Craft of Short Fiction: The Collected Stories—1920–1935,* 147–48, 188–89. Petry rightly refers to "Two Wrongs" as "one of the least known stories of

About the story's autobiographical resonance, there can be no doubt. Fitzgerald wrote it in October and November 1929, as the stock market crashed, and the principal character of "Two Wrongs" follows a complementary boom-to-bust pattern. Bill McChesney, a brash young theatrical producer, has a series of hits on Broadway by the time he is twenty-six, when he meets—and later marries—a beautiful eighteen-year-old dancer from Delaney, South Carolina, named Emmy Pinkard. From the first, the grounds of Bill's eventual downfall are established. He is terribly egotistical, he foolishly yearns for acceptance by the social elite, and—most significantly—he drinks. These shortcomings undermine his work in New York, and in three years' time he moves to London, where he successfully produces two of his former Broadway hits for English audiences. The change in geography does not change Bill's behavior, however. In pursuit of the bottle and the British nobility—"He goes around with a lot of dukes and ladies," we learn—he drastically neglects Emmy, who is pregnant with their first child.[3]

McChesney reaches bottom when he leaves Emmy one night, crashes a dance given by Lady Sybil Combrinck (with whom, it is hinted, he has previously been intimate), and is summarily thrown out. He then tries to drink away this humiliation on an all-night bender replete with "arguments, and trying to cash a check, and suddenly proclaiming over and over that he was William McChesney, the producer, and convincing no one of the fact, not even himself" (524). When he drags himself home at dawn, he discovers that his wife has been at the hospital for hours, where their baby was delivered stillborn: "She had fallen down at the door of the hospital, trying to get out of the taxicab alone" (525). Emmy can forgive him, but she can never feel the same way about him.

Taps at Reveille." Others who have briefly considered the story, none at a length of more than a few pages, are Kenneth Eble, *F. Scott Fitzgerald*, 122–23; John A. Higgins, *F. Scott Fitzgerald: A Study of the Stories*, 114–15; John Kuehl, *F. Scott Fitzgerald: A Study of the Short Fiction*, 76, 78, 84–85; Richard D. Lehan, *F. Scott Fitzgerald and the Craft of Fiction*, 142–43; Bryant Mangum, *A Fortune Yet: Money in the Art of F. Scott Fitzgerald's Short Stories*, 90–91; Sergio Perosa, *The Art of F. Scott Fitzgerald*, 95–96; and Robert Sklar, *F. Scott Fitzgerald: The Last Laocoön*, 239–40, 256.

3. Bruccoli, ed., *Short Stories*, 520. All subsequent page references to "Two Wrongs" are to this edition and will appear parenthetically in the text.

The scene next shifts back to New York, and apparently five years have elapsed, for Emmy is now twenty-six. (The chronology seems somewhat confused.) To replace what Bill had once meant to her, she immerses herself in the dance: "four hours a day at bar exercises, attitudes, *sauts,* arabesques and pirouettes" (526). As she progresses in her art, her husband's career steadily declines. He had always worked in "great spurts," but these drain him as he grows older. In fact, he comes "to lean, in a way, on Emmy's fine health and vitality" (526). That she has become the dominant partner is illustrated on a November evening. She is now ready to dance in public, a jubilant Emmy tells Bill. In fact, "Paul Makova wants me to dance with him at the Metropolitan this season . . ." (527). Her husband has a piece of news for her as well. He has tuberculosis, and the doctor recommends that he go to Denver for the winter.

Emmy protests that "of course" she will go with him, but Bill will not hear of it. She must take her chance with the Metropolitan, he tells her; she has worked too hard to risk a postponement. In the end, she is persuaded to stay in New York to dance with Makova, while he travels to Colorado for convalescence, or for "a definite finish. He was sure that Emmy would come at the end, no matter what she was doing or how good an engagement she had" (530).

Such a bare plot summary does little justice to Fitzgerald's development of character and theme, but it does suggest how closely "Two Wrongs" mirrored his marital situation. Like Bill McChesney, Fitzgerald had enjoyed a remarkable early success, yet as he reached his thirties he found himself in the grip of alcoholism, with his energy level drifting downward. Zelda Fitzgerald, meanwhile, had thrown herself into her dancing with an obsession bordering on madness. (Six months after this story was written, she suffered a mental collapse.) Retrospectively, it is equally obvious that "Two Wrongs," like such other stories of this period as "The Rough Crossing" (1929) and "One Trip Abroad" (1930), functioned as a preliminary study for *Tender Is the Night.* The similarity is most striking in the pervasive theme of transference of vitality. Emmy takes on strength as Bill loses his, in precisely the same fashion as Nicole Diver in the novel gains strength while Dick dwindles into ineffectuality.

Moreover, much the same debilitating influences operate on both male principals. They begin with dangerously hard-to-achieve goals for themselves: to be the greatest in their field. They are harmed by acquiring too much money too easily; subsequently, they let idleness and dissipation erode their ambition. And in both fictions Europe itself has a corrupting effect. A case in point is the minor character of Lady Sybil Combrinck in "Two Wrongs," who, in her pursuit of "being bad," strongly resembles Lady Caroline Sibly-Biers, *Tender Is the Night*'s "wickedest woman in London." They are more than sisters, in fact, for in the original *Saturday Evening Post* story, the character is *called* Lady Caroline Sibley-Biers (notice that he altered the spelling from story to novel).[4] Fitzgerald changed her name to Lady Sybil Combrinck for the reprinted version of the story in *Taps at Reveille,* the year after *Tender Is the Night* was published.

Another obvious parallel is between "Two Wrongs" and "Babylon Revisited" (1931). As John Kuehl points out in his book on Fitzgerald's short fiction, Bill McChesney, Charlie Wales, and Dick Diver all trace the same pattern of "work, success, inaction, dissipation, illness," with the difference that in "Babylon Revisited" Charlie regains his health and prospers through hard work.[5] What Wales seems to possess that the other characters lack is a reservoir of character to draw upon. Fitzgerald insists on the importance of character in all three fictions. In "Two Wrongs," Emmy Pinkard is first described as "very young, with beautiful red hair, and more character in her face than her chatter would indicate . . ." (514). Later, Bill tells her that she is "always beautiful," perhaps because she has character in her face. "Character is the greatest thing in the world," he declares, and she's got more than anybody he knows (522).

The issue of character is central to the underlying message of "Two Wrongs." Like much of Fitzgerald's fiction, the story has a powerful ethical component, exemplified in the effort of the protagonist to atone for his sins. "Two Wrongs" is divided into four numbered sections, with the first three chronicling McChesney's fall from eminence and the last devoted to his presumed atonement. In writing his story this way,

4. F. Scott Fitzgerald, *Tender Is the Night,* 270; F. Scott Fitzgerald, "Two Wrongs," *Saturday Evening Post* 202 (January 18, 1930): 8–9, 107, 113, 199. The change in name is, I believe, the only revision made for the story's republication in *Taps at Reveille* and subsequent collections.
5. Kuehl, *Fitzgerald: Study of the Short Fiction,* 84–85.

Fitzgerald may have been catering to the expectations of the readers of the *Saturday Evening Post*. Whatever the motivation, the result is not convincing. For the first thirteen pages, "Two Wrongs" is a beautifully crafted tale of humiliation—a deeply felt emotion that Fitzgerald could communicate on the page with wrenching realism. Then, in the last five pages, the story turns into an unpersuasive saga of redemption and justification. After Dick Diver's dreadful night of debauchery in Rome, and his rescue by Baby Warren, he reflects that "No mature Aryan is able to profit by a humiliation. . . ."[6] Yet that is precisely what Bill McChesney supposedly does after *his* night of dishonor in London. The story's back is broken 70 percent of the way along.

II.

One way of isolating this problem is to consider how one feels about McChesney. His shortcomings are rendered so vividly in the first three sections that any subsequent attempt at reform is undercut in advance. The opening scene masterfully combines exposition with revelation of character. The first thing McChesney does is to call attention to his new shoes, and the "twenty-eight dollars" (513) he paid for them—at 1929 rates a stiff price indeed. From his fancy shoes, Bill goes on to boast of his college education and his manly appearance. Fellow producer Brancusi takes all this in and does what he can to deflate Bill's egotism. It isn't easy: Brancusi likes McChesney but is fully aware of his egotism.[7] So he responds with genial sarcasm to Bill's burst of bragging about his shoes:

> "Good-looking. Gentleman. Good shoes. Shot with luck."
> "You're wrong there," objected Bill. "Brains. Three years—nine shows— four big hits—only one flop. Where do you see any luck in that?" (513)

---

6. Fitzgerald, *Tender Is the Night*, 233.

7. Reliable as a source of information about McChesney, Brancusi is nonetheless unable—so the narrator tells us—to understand that Emmy Pinkard's combination of chatter and character derives from her upbringing in South Carolina. A New York City product, Brancusi is presumably incapable of grasping southern ways. Apparently no reference is intended to the sculptor Constantin Brancusi (1876–1957), who was living in Paris during Fitzgerald's time there.

Obviously, this "fresh-faced young Irishman exuding aggressiveness and self-confidence" (513) is riding for a fall, especially when his unwarranted pretentiousness is taken into account. For the usually brash McChesney has another mood or humor he sometimes adopts, that of a "quietly superior, sensitive . . . patron of the arts," working "hand in glove with Reinhardt for the artistic future of the theater" (513–14).

McChesney is something of a poseur, then, and never more so than in his attempts to infiltrate high society. As a Harvard undergraduate, Bill had been snubbed by the "Gold Coast boys" (as usual, Fitzgerald is accurate on questions of social snobbery; wealthy Harvard students of the time did in fact occupy expensive quarters known collectively as the "Gold Coast"), and now that he is the toast of Broadway he is determined to earn the acceptance of such "very fashionable people" (515). Still, he puts on a show of self-importance for almost everyone, including young Emmy Pinkard. At the restaurant where he takes her to lunch, he conspicuously says hello to heavyweight champion Jack Dempsey, tells Emmy he's made enough money in four years to "be comfortable" the rest of his life ("My!" she responds politely), and reveals that he's engaged to the famous actress Irene Rikker ("My!" Emmy repeats). Apparently, he makes an impression on her in an attempt to seduce her, but she is "a good girl" and he does not impose himself. Instead, he gives her a job in one of his productions, not only because she is the most beautiful person he has ever seen but also—the one touch that comes closest to redeeming him—because he has noticed that she has holes in her stockings: "Holes in stockings always moved him, softened him" (515–17).

Part 2 of "Two Wrongs" is seemingly designed to evoke a measure of admiration for McChesney, to go along with his sympathy for those who, like himself, started out poor and ambitious. Fitzgerald does not give one much to admire, however. At the end of this section, Bill and Emmy are married, but their courtship is not romanticized. Instead, the action focuses on the breakup of his engagement to Irene Rikker. Irene is cast as the female lead in McChesney's new play, with Frank Llewellen, a big, handsome actor, playing opposite her. Irene and Bill are not really in love to begin with. They have simply gravitated toward each other, the narrator explains, in the same way the two richest young people in a given town tend to be drawn together. Nonetheless, Bill succumbs to sexual jealousy during rehearsals, when it becomes apparent that an amour is developing between Irene and her leading man. At rehearsal, he provokes a quarrel with Llewellen in front of the entire company, including Emmy. The dispute ends in a one-punch fistfight, Llewellen knocking McChesney back across a row of seats. The play's author pulls Bill to his feet, and the stage manager offers to take a crack at Llewellen himself, but McChesney stops the trouble he has started by ordering everyone back to their places on stage: " 'Get back there!' Bill cried, holding a handkerchief to his face and teetering in the author's supporting arms. 'Everybody get back! Take that scene again, and no talk! Get back, Llewellen!' " (519).

By so acting, Bill "saved the show from his own folly," and after opening night it is clear that he "had a hit—they all had a hit." This incident draws Emmy to him as never before. It was "so brave of you not to let everything go to pieces" at rehearsal, she tells him. "You got control of everything so quick" (519). But control is precisely what he lacks, even at this stage. The show's success provokes him to drink: "After a good run [the play] closed just as he was drinking too much and needed someone on the gray days of reaction. [He and Emmy] were married suddenly in Connecticut, early in June" (520). It is patent that the McChesneys marry for different reasons. She loves him despite his faults and finds something positive to say even about his ridiculous provocation of Llewellen. He needs her to stroke his ego and to cheer him up when the cycle of drunkenness descends from exhilaration to remorse.

The third section, like the first, is first-rate. The scene is now London, with Brancusi once more on hand to provide an honest appraisal of Bill McChesney. Bill is basically "very nice," Brancusi maintains, "very handsome, very popular" (520). Still, Brancusi has journeyed to London to urge Bill to return to New York, to rescue him from his drinking and his infatuation with the nobility. When Bill arrives at the Savoy Grill to keep his appointment with Brancusi, he utters his version of a clipped, upper-class British greeting. "J'doo," he says, then goes on to confess that he would "like to be the Marquis of McChesney" (520). In conversation, it emerges that Bill left New York under a cloud, after a dispute with a business partner and two flops in a row. In London, however, his old plays are doing well, Lady Sybil Combrinck has "discovered" him, and he takes to the bottle in the afterglow of financial success and social recognition. He and Emmy have a child now, with another about to arrive, but he abandons her most evenings, including the climactic one when he presents himself at a formal dance to which Lady Sybil had, conspicuously, not invited him, for he has been unforgivably inattentive to *her* as well. At the dance she snubs him in his inappropriate tweeds and sees to it that he is "carried through a pantry . . . down a long hall, and pushed out . . . into the night" (524).

It is a comeuppance well deserved and makes an effective climax. Yet to compound the punishment and prepare for the ending, Fitzgerald adds the melodrama of Emmy's fall and her stillborn child. Bill has deeply wronged his wife. In the fourth and least satisfying section of the story, he undertakes to square the accounts.

As Petry points out, the "process of atonement" infuses much of Fitzgerald's late short fiction.[8] But the pattern of guilt and retribution that he carries Bill McChesney through fails to make a satisfactory ending to "Two Wrongs." There are two reasons. The first is that Fitzgerald does not lay a sufficient foundation for Bill's sudden acquisition of virtue. The second is that Fitzgerald is driven by the logic of the story's title to impute to Emmy much the same kind of a "wrong," or morally unjustifiable action, that Bill had been guilty of toward her.

Back in New York, Emmy devotes herself to her old dream of mastering the ballet: "She wanted to use herself on something she could believe in, and it seemed to her that the dance was woman's interpretation of music. . ." (525–26). Bill encourages her and imagines himself converting her passion into another production of his own—the first real American ballet. But he has trouble reestablishing himself in the theater. His history of drinking and fighting is against him, and he pays for his "irregular life" by suffering that lesion of vitality Fitzgerald wrote into several stories of this period, and later into "The Crack-Up" (1936). No longer cocksure, Bill clings to Emmy for support and hopes for better luck "next month, next season" (526).

At this point in their marriage, Emmy is proclaimed ready for the stage by her instructor, Donilof, and Bill learns that his "left lung is practically gone." His illness is a surprise to both of them; she has long since "ceased

8. Petry, *Fitzgerald's Craft*, 189.

to worry" about his "intermittent attacks of hypochondria" (527). The onset does, however, furnish him with what he regards as an opportunity for self-sacrifice. He insists that she dance with Paul Makova, and she insists that she go west with him for his cure, though she urgently wants to dance and he just as urgently wants her to accompany him. The matter is debated and drawn out between them with some degree of suspense, until his train finally leaves and he discovers that she has followed his instructions and that his compartment is empty.

"He knew then that he had lost her," Bill reflects, not without self-pity. He can see "the set-up without any illusions—this Paul Makova, and months of proximity, and loneliness—afterward nothing would ever be the same." Yet Emmy has given him little reason to suspect such a scenario. "She was a fine girl," he admits even at the end. "She had character." He recognizes that if she were to leave him, it would only be right, according to "some law of compensation." By taking himself out of her life, he reasons, "he had again become as good as she was; it was all evened up at last" (530).

Yet what has he done, exactly, except to follow doctor's orders and go to Colorado for his tuberculosis? And what has she done, except to fill her life with work instead of with the love he had betrayed? Even at that, Emmy can only bring herself to stay behind in New York by "think[ing] hard of London" (529). Her "wrong," in short, is hardly wrong at all. Just as he tries to present Emmy in a less-than-flattering light at the end, Fitzgerald also attempts to make a case for Bill. In fact, the narrator intervenes to proclaim Bill's essential goodness. When Bill tells Emmy that his disease is his problem, that he's brought it on himself, and that she must stay to dance, Bill speaks, we are told, "with that rough, generous justice that had first made her admire him, that made him rather tragic in his adversity, as he had always been bearable in his overweening success" (528). The difficulty is that no such "rough, generous justice" is previously illustrated in the story, while his braggadocio and "insecure bravado" (529) have been amply documented.

Still another difficulty is that Bill's conversion to morality is so immediate and complete as to ring false. It is as if his previous failings have all vanished in the aftermath of one disastrous night in London. If he ever takes another drink, it is not mentioned. He does not boast as before, nor pursue the approval of the upper classes. Such a total characterological change is not credible. In the first three sections of the story, Fitzgerald treats his principal male character with conspicuous critical objectivity. Then, suddenly, he turns advocate. As a result, Kenneth Eble has perceptively observed, "the reader is forced, probably unwillingly, to sympathize with McChesney at the end." Two other critics have addressed themselves to probable autobiographical influences on the ending. Those who read fiction as autobiography "may decide whether 'Two Wrongs' is self-condemnation or self-pity," Sklar writes. Petry proposes that "Two Wrongs" may be "too transparently a wallowing in self-pity or an exercise in self-justification." Indeed, the unsatisfactory ending may be traceable to Fitzgerald's confused feelings about himself and his wife as of the fall of 1929. For most of its length, "Two Wrongs" reads like a vivid exercise in self-condemnation. In part 4, the tone switches disastrously to self-pity.[9] The two wrongs Fitzgerald depicts do not make a right. And what is most wrong with "Two Wrongs" is its contrived conclusion, undermining what in other respects remains "one of the best things" Fitzgerald ever wrote.

9. Kenneth Eble, "Touches of Disaster: Alcoholism and Mental Illness in Fitzgerald's Short Stories," 44; Sklar, *Fitzgerald: Last Laocoön*, 240; Petry, *Fitzgerald's Craft*, 189.

FLAKES OF BLACK SNOW:
"ONE TRIP ABROAD" RECONSIDERED

J O H N   K U E H L

"One Trip Abroad" is among the seventeen short fictions F. Scott Fitz-gerald published in the *Saturday Evening Post* between March 14, 1925 ("Love in the Night"), and March 18, 1932 ("On Schedule"), that have come to be known as the *Tender Is the Night* cluster stories. Several were "stripped" for the novel, including superior pieces such as "Jacob's Ladder" (1927), "The Rough Crossing" (1929), and "The Swimmers" (1929), and thus did not appear in *Taps at Reveille,* the collection following *Tender Is the Night,* in 1935.

Published on October 11, 1930, "One Trip Abroad" stands between the "Kelly Version" (1929) and the "Dick Diver Version" (1932–1933) of the novel. Not only did Nicole Kelly give her name to Nicole Diver, but much specific material from the story resurfaced there as well: the storm that made the hotel crouch "amid tumult, chaos and darkness"; "the plague of locusts" that "the chauffeur explained" as "bumble-bees"; and T. F. Golding's yacht "bound upon a romantic voyage that was not dependent upon actual motion."[1]

Virtually all the motifs associated with *Tender Is the Night* are pre-figured by the cluster stories. European settings recur, often juxtaposed to American ones, and the novel's shifts back and forth between the

---

1. F. Scott Fitzgerald, *Tender Is the Night,* 155, 160, 265.

French Riviera and Zurich (with stops along the way) also characterize stories such as "A Penny Spent" (1925), where Corcoran escorts Mrs. Bushmill and her daughter from Paris to Brussels, Antwerp, Rotterdam, The Hague, and Capri.

The degenerate continental aristocracy and their wealthy American cohorts populating these settings become ubiquitous in stories such as "Majesty" (1929) and "The Hotel Child" (1931). During the first, heiress Emily Castleton, "one of America's perfect types," leaves Brevoort Blair at the altar. She turns up later with a "dissipated ne'er-do-well" named Prince Gabriel Petrocobesco, who "was invited by the police to leave Paris." Reminiscent of Henry James's ambassadors, her relatives pursue Emily and learn that "even the most outlying circles of international society were closed" to this "fat little fellow" of "obscure nationality," "an attractive leer and a quenchless thirst." Emily agrees to marry him only after he insists on being made king of Czjeck-Hansa, "a little country with two towns."[2]

Later, in *Tender Is the Night*, the continental aristocracy, after losing its power and prestige during World War I, has grown dissolute. Here we find Lady Caroline Sibly-Biers, a "fragile" and "tubercular" English-woman, bearing "aloft the pennon of decadence, the last ensign of the fading empire." Here, too, we find Tommy Barban, half French and "utterly aristocratic," who, as "the end product of an archaic world," has served the cause of nobility almost everywhere by killing Russian com-munists. Barban's efforts notwithstanding, the plight of the European elite is futile. Displaced and financially insolvent, it develops a penchant for wealthy Americans, a group only too glad for an opportunity to min-gle with it, a group typified by the Anglophile Baby Warren. McKisco's experience with people such as the rich Warrens—"an American ducal family without a title"—is that they have taken from the English "their uncertain and fumbling snobbery, their delight in ignorance and their deliberate rudeness."[3]

Tender Is the Night's nameless hotel in Lausanne, Switzerland, where "rich ruins, fugitives from justice, claimants to the thrones of mediatized

2. F. Scott Fitzgerald, *Taps at Reveille*, 233, 244, 245, 246.
3. Fitzgerald, *Tender Is the Night*, 268, 35, 157, 35.

principalities, lived on the derivatives of opium or barbital," was inspired
by the Hotel des Trois Mondes of "The Hotel Child." "People who are
no longer *persona gratis* in France or Italy" inhabit both.[4] Throughout
the short story, Fifi Schwartz, an eighteen-year-old "exquisitely, radiantly
beautiful [American] Jewess," encounters the decadent European elite.
Indigent thief Count Stanislas Borowsky of Transylvania, "wanted . . .
in Italy, France and Spain," courts her; the Marquis "Bopes" Kinkallow,
an alcoholic womanizer, propositions her; and Lady Capps-Karr, "the
tall Englishwoman with the long cigarette holder and the half-paralyzed
Pekingese," insults her. Contrasted to Fifi is "blond Miss Howard," whose
sponsors, the Taylors, "career people in the diplomatic service," consider
the Jewish girl "as much of a gratuitous outrage as a new stripe in the
flag." These "Europeanized Americans . . . could hardly be said to belong
to any nation at all."[5]

With the exception of Nicole Kelly, the cluster stories provide no firm
model for Nicole Diver. Her husband, Dick, is another matter. Both
he and Henry Marston of "The Swimmers" are southerners, Marston
having descended from "seven generations of Virginia ancestors." This
background resembles Diver's, for his great-grandfather had been gov-
ernor of North Carolina; he numbers Mad Anthony Wayne among his
predecessors; his father came north following the Civil War; he still
has cousins in Virginia and feels at home in Westmoreland County. If
Marston supplies the background, Dick Ragland of "A New Leaf" (1931)
supplies the foreground. Julia Ross, upon first seeing him at the Bois de
Boulogne, says, "He's without doubt the handsomest man I ever saw,"
but her date retorts that the "lazy, worthless" fellow has "got the worst
reputation of any American in Paris" because of "drink, women, jails,
scandals," and so "he's not received anywhere." A "Jekyll and Hyde"
figure, Ragland shares his successor's "old fatal pleasingness, the old
forceful charm."[6] The later Dick vanishes in the obscurity of upstate
New York, while the earlier one disappears at sea.

4. Ibid., 246. In "The Hotel Child," the third sentence reads "people who are no longer *persona grata* in Italy or France."
5. F. Scott Fitzgerald and Zelda Fitzgerald, *Bits of Paradise: 21 Uncollected Stories by F. Scott and Zelda Fitzgerald*, 274, 294, 276.
6. Ibid., 191, 292, 299; Fitzgerald, *Tender Is the Night*, 300.

Dick Ragland's attraction to Julia is not the only instance of an older man pursuing a younger woman in the cluster stories. Other relationships foreshadowing the Dick Diver–Rosemary Hoyt involvement include the pursuit of Rosemary Merriweather by Tommy McLane ("Indecision" [1931]), Helen Avery by George Hannaford ("Magnetism" [1928]), Annie Lorrie by Tom Squires ("At Your Age" [1929]), and Becky Snyder by René du Cary ("On Schedule" [1933]). Undoubtedly, the fullest and finest treatment of this motif occurs in "Jacob's Ladder," where thirty-three-year-old Jacob Booth views sixteen-year-old Jenny Delehanty as his Galatea. These childlike actresses represent youth and vitality to paternal males who consider them "Daddy's Girl[s]" and who have commenced the "process of deterioration," evidenced by Booth's worn-out vocal cords and Diver's avoidance of high diving.[7]

This process reflects "emotional bankruptcy," which Arthur Mizener called "the most pervasive idea [Fitzgerald] ever had." The author himself implies as much in his essay "Handle with Care" (1936), where he describes his own "crack-up" as "an over-extension of the flank, a burning of the candle at both ends; a call upon physical resources that I did not command, like a man over-drawing at his bank."[8] Fourteen years earlier, *The Beautiful and Damned*—in which the phrase "lesion of vitality" had first appeared—not only demonstrated how emotional bankruptcy resulted from personal relationships, hedonistic activities, and unsettled times (1920s prosperity, 1930s depression), but also presented its manifestations: drinking, brawling, infidelity, racial prejudice.

These manifestations recur throughout the cluster stories. In "Two Wrongs" (1930), twenty-six-year-old Bill McChesney marries eighteen-year-old Emmy Pinkard. She is an obscure dancer and he is a successful producer. The transfer of energy made famous by the Divers happens earlier between Bill and Emmy. Once married and a father, McChesney's plays begin to flop and his health to decline. Emotional bankruptcy climaxes when he drinks several highballs, then crashes the Mayfair party. Two footmen throw him out, and a nightmarish spree ensues.

7. Fitzgerald, *Tender Is the Night,* 11, 283.
8. Arthur Mizener, *The Far Side of Paradise: A Biography of F. Scott Fitzgerald,* 70; Edmund Wilson, ed., *The Crack-Up,* 77.

Meanwhile, Emmy has "fallen down at the door of the hospital, trying to get out of the taxicab alone."[9] She gives birth to their stillborn baby. Eventually, tubercular Bill, heading west toward death, must leave her behind alive and well. He has lost control through dissipation; she has acquired character through work.

The *Tender Is the Night* motifs scattered among the cluster stories converge in "One Trip Abroad," where Nelson and Nicole Kelly encounter many foreigners barely distinguishable from those at the Hotel des Trois Mondes. A cynical friend claims that their acquaintances have "shifted down through Europe like nails in a sack of wheat, till they stick out of it a little into the Mediterranean Sea." "International society," he continues, "is just about as hard to enter nowadays as the public rooms at the Casino."[10] One member, Count Chiki Sarolai, resembles Prince Gabriel Petrocobesco of "Majesty": "He was an attractive relic of the Austrian court, with no fortune or pretense to any, but with solid social and financial connections in France. . . . Count Chiki roved here and there, frankly sponging" (157). At a party aboard the Golding yacht, somebody remarks that the English are "doing a sort of dance of death" (152).

Such dissolute Europeans tend to corrupt more or less innocent American victims, as in the fiction of Henry James. Before Dick Diver married Nicole Warren and became an expatriate, "he wanted to be good, he wanted to be kind, he wanted to be brave and wise." This was the man Rosemary Hoyt, who admired his "layer of hardness . . . of self-control and of self-discipline," loved at first sight. Even so, between the time Dick discovered Nicole "flowering under a stone on the Zürichsee" and the time he met Rosemary, "the spear had been blunted." His emotional bankruptcy, "a lesion of enthusiasm," exhibits itself in the usual ways. There is a physical decline, as he loses his once superb strength and energy. There is a moral decline, too. He becomes sexually promiscuous, falling "in love with every pretty woman" he sees. An argument with a taxicab driver results in a brawl that lands him in jail. He drinks heavily and develops prejudices: "He would suddenly unroll

9. F. Scott Fitzgerald, *The Stories of F. Scott Fitzgerald: A Selection of 28 Stories*, 299.

10. F. Scott Fitzgerald, *Afternoon of an Author: A Selection of Uncollected Stories and Essays*, 151. All subsequent page references to "One Trip Abroad" are to this edition and will appear parenthetically in the text.

a long scroll of contempt for some person, race, class, way of life, way of thinking." Dr. Diver deteriorates from the serious, brilliant professional whose learned articles have been standard fare, whose ambition was "to be a good psychologist—maybe to be the greatest one that ever lived," to an absolute failure.[11]

Similarly, at the outset of "One Trip Abroad," Nelson and Nicole are among the well-adjusted, fortunate few—newlyweds who look forward to studying art and music in Europe:

> They were in their twenties, and there was still a pleasant touch of bride and groom upon them. A handsome couple; the man rather intense and sensitive, the girl arrestingly light of hue in eyes and hair, her face without shadows, its living freshness modulated by a lovely confident calm. Mr. and Mrs. Miles did not fail to notice their air of good breeding, of a specifically "swell" background, expressed both by their unsophistication and by their ingrained reticence that was not stiffness. If they held aloof, it was because they were sufficient to each other. (143)

However, these model young Americans, like other emotional bankrupts, will behave badly on their one trip abroad, as we shall see.

Money and marriage often touch off the degradation that European civilization exacerbates. Bill McChesney in "Two Wrongs" declines rapidly once he becomes successful, having produced nine shows in three years. A friend observes after another three years that Bill, now married and a father, consorts with dukes and ladies, but "had two flops in New York." When Nelson Kelly weds, then inherits five hundred thousand dollars, his corruption is guaranteed. Another Irishman, Dick Diver, "had never felt more sure of himself . . . than at the time of his marriage to Nicole. Yet he had been swallowed up like a gigolo, and somehow permitted his arsenal to be locked up in the Warren safety-deposit vaults."[12]

Among the cluster-story protagonists, only Charlie Wales of "Babylon Revisited" (1931) survives emotional bankruptcy unbroken. He follows the pattern developed by McChesney and Kelly and immortalized by

---

11. Fitzgerald, *Tender Is the Night*, 132, 18, 201, 208, 201, 265, 130–31.
12. Fitzgerald, *Stories of F. Scott Fitzgerald*, 294; Fitzgerald, *Tender Is the Night*, 201.

Tender Is the Night—vitality, success, inaction, dissipation, illness—but, unlike these fellow Irishmen, "he believed in character; he wanted to jump back a whole generation and trust in character again as the eternally valuable element. Everything else wore out." Wales ultimately wins the conflict that Fitzgerald added to the Jamesian international theme—work versus pleasure, responsibility versus irresponsibility, character versus dissipation—which may help to explain why "Babylon Revisited" has been called "Fitzgerald's one virtually flawless contribution to the canon of the American short story."[13] But while it has received considerable critical attention, "One Trip Abroad," its single qualitative rival among the cluster stories, remains neglected.

Although several critics have briefly discussed "One Trip Abroad"— Herbie Butterfield, Kenneth Eble, Bryant Mangum, James E. Miller Jr., Charles E. Shain, Robert Sklar, and others—this remarkable story has never before received an exclusive essay. Some commentators do not even like it. Sergio Perosa asserts, "Neither 'The Rough Crossing' nor 'One Trip Abroad' is worth much as a story from a strictly aesthetic point of view; their value lies in their open links with the subject matter of the novel." John A. Higgins argues, "Its chief weakness, as Perosa indicates, is inadequate motivation for the protagonists' decay. . . . There is also a lack of suspense concerning the Kellys' fate."[14]

Only Brian Way extols "One Trip Abroad" as an independently significant work of art: "As in all Fitzgerald's best short stories, the form of 'One Trip Abroad' is a particularly felicitous expression of the underlying structural necessities of its subject. Its episodes succeed each other like a series of moral tableaux—a kind of Jazz Age *Rake's Progress*— and within the broad canvas of each picture, there are striking vignettes, the excellent satirical sketches of minor expatriate types."[15] Surely Way is justified in implying that the artistic manipulation of *Tender Is the Night* motifs rather than their mere presence makes "One Trip Abroad" an exceptional short fiction. And surely this manipulation,

13. Fitzgerald, *Stories of F. Scott Fitzgerald*, 388; John A. Higgins, *F. Scott Fitzgerald: A Study of the Stories*, 121.
14. Sergio Perosa, *The Art of F. Scott Fitzgerald*, 100; Higgins, *Fitzgerald: Study of the Stories*, 120.
15. Brian Way, *F. Scott Fitzgerald and the Art of Social Fiction*, 90.

as he also suggests, involves the "felicitous expression of . . . structural necessities."

Like much of the author's finest work, the Kelly story utilizes the journey format announced by its title. Such journeys are frequently framed, here by a figurative storm at the beginning and a literal storm at the end.

"One Trip Abroad" opens in North Africa "on the edge of the Sahara" (142) near the Mediterranean Sea, as the Algerian place-names Bou Saada and Bir Rabalou establish. This setting, with its proximity to Egypt, is appropriate for the sort of turbulence that launches the action: "In the afternoon the air became black with locusts, and some of the women shrieked, sinking to the floor of the motorbus and covering their hair with traveling rugs. The locusts were coming north, eating everything in their path, which was not so much in that part of the world; they were flying silently and in straight lines, flakes of black snow" (142). Obviously, our attention is being drawn toward the Old Testament, where the ten plagues Moses brought on Pharoah and the Egyptians appear. Exodus 10:4 introduces the eighth: "Else, if thou refuse to let my people go, behold, tomorrow will I bring the locusts into thy coast." This plague later becomes the subject of Psalms 105:34, 35, which reads: "He spake, and the locusts came, and caterpillars, and that without number, / And did eat up all the herbs in their land, and devoured the fruit of their ground." Lest we miss the biblical context, Fitzgerald's young couple responds to the query posed by Mr. and Mrs. Liddell Miles, "Didn't catch any in your hair?" with the meaningful answer, "No. We survived the plague" (143).

Their interchange comes amid several travelers who have been paired off as American and European: the Smyrna-American and the British widow; the Wilmington family and the cockney airman; the New York nurse and the French chauffeur. They behave foolishly, the British widow "going down to Biskra to have one last fling with an as-yet-unencountered sheik" (142), and the New York nurse emitting "shriek after shriek of hysterical laughter" when the French chauffeur terms the locusts "bumblebees" (143). These people also survive *that* plague, though the international set (Fitzgerald's "ship of fools") will suffer retribution too, for public as well as private, European as well as American behavior comes under his scrutiny.

The literal storm or closing frame fulfills the augury posed by those ominous "flakes of black snow." During this storm, "the mountains and the lake disappeared completely" (163), its violence recalling the storm that climaxes "The Rough Crossing," designated "the wildest hurricane on the North Atlantic in ten years."[16] These upheavals reflect the expressionistic technique of objectifying internal states by external phenomena, a technique Fitzgerald had introduced in "The Ice Palace" (1920) and would perfect in "Babylon Revisited." Thus, the disorder germane to "stormy" marriages is dramatized through parallel storms, but whereas the husband and wife of "The Rough Crossing" emerge united from their hurricane, the Kellys' deluge leaves them all alone without "peace and love and health" (164).

When the storm subsides, Nicole finds herself "on the glass veranda" close to one member of "the couple, first seen in Algiers" (163), where the following exchange between the Kellys had transpired:

"I passed that couple in the hall just now."
"Who—the Mileses?"
"No, that young couple—about our age—the ones that were on the other motorbus, that we thought looked so nice, in Bir Rabalou after lunch, in the camel market."
"They did look nice."
"Charming," she said emphatically; "the girl and man, both. I'm almost sure I've met the girl somewhere before."
The couple referred to were sitting across the room at dinner, and Nicole found her eyes drawn irresistibly toward them. (144)

Always nameless, "that young couple" appears throughout the narrative as a déjà vu phenomenon. Both are "harder-looking," the husband "dissipated" in part 2; then, at the Café de Paris, they too experience "something strident and violent," for the wife's face is "pale now, and distorted with anger" (155, 156). Finally, during part 4, Nicole studies the girl:

It was an inquisitive face, she saw at once, possibly calculating; the eyes, intelligent enough, but with no peace in them, swept over people in a

16. Fitzgerald, *Stories of F. Scott Fitzgerald*, 267.

single quick glance as though estimating their value. "Terrible egoist," Nicole thought, with a certain distaste. For the rest, the cheeks were wan, and there were little pouches of ill health under the eyes; these combining with a certain flabbiness of arms and legs to give an impression of unwholesomeness. She was dressed expensively, but with a hint of slovenliness, as if she did not consider the people of the hotel important. (163)

Nelson did not like *him* either: "I ran into the man in the bar. . . . His face is so weak and self-indulgent that it's almost mean—the kind of face that needs half a dozen drinks really to open the eyes and stiffen the mouth up to normal" (163–64). Soon these "two dark forms" join the Kellys in "the dark garden" (164). With a shock of recognition, Nicole cries, "They're us! They're us! Don't you see?" (165), reversing the comical climax of "The Rough Crossing," where reconciled spouses deny their opposing selves.

Such repeated encounters with overt doubles reflect the Kellys' "process of deterioration." According to Robert Rogers, "one clinical counterpart of the manifest double in fiction is the visual hallucination of the physical self, an event known as 'autoscopy.'" He continues: "Hallucinations of seeing oneself . . . betray a morbid preoccupation of the individual with his own essence."[17] Not only does this explain why narcissistic Nicole regards the girl as an "egoist," but also why she and the man are usually by themselves, the proclivity of the Kellys, whose isolated early lives Nicole describes: "When I was young, my father had asthma and I had to live in the most depressing health resorts with him for years; and Nelson was in the fur business in Alaska and he loathed it" (145). After their marriage "on the Italian liner that had brought them to Gibraltar they had not joined the groups that leaned desperately on one another in the bar" (144). This aloofness at the beginning of the journey prepares us for Fitzgerald's concluding image: "Nelson and Nicole saw that they were alone together" (165). Loneliness, then, may well be a precondition for emotional bankrupts, and their charm, as instanced by Dick Ragland and Dick Diver, may well be a plea for love. And since both condition and symptom stem from profound psychic

17. Robert Rogers, *The Double in Literature,* 14, 18.

needs, neither marriage nor other human relationships can appease that hunger.

In an essay titled "The Significance of Fantasy in Fitzgerald's Short Fiction," Lawrence Buell comments, "The doubles in 'One Trip Abroad' represent another psychological law, a law of decay," demonstrating that the authorial "second manner" introduced by *Tales of the Jazz Age* can be successfully invoked in realistic works. But for those who agree with the contention that *manifest* "doubles are among the facile, and less reputable devices in fiction," Fitzgerald also created *latent* doubles.[18] Liddell and Cardine Miles embody what Nelson and Nicole Kelly might become. Although they are "bored with themselves" and are "somewhat worn away inside by fifteen years of a particular set in Paris," they exhibit "undeniable style, even charm" (143). These "formally sophisticated and frankly snobbish" (144) world travelers take the inexperienced Kellys to the Café of the Ouled Nails in Bou Saada, where the foursome watches wildly sensual belly dancing. When Nicole learns that the Berber girls will perform "Oriental style," or wearing only jewelry, she leaves despite Liddell's assertion, "After all, we're here to see the real customs and manners of the country; a little prudishness shouldn't stand in our way" (147). The Mileses, who appear at two separate parties later, adumbrate another dissipated American couple, Duncan Schaeffer and Lorraine Quarrles of "Babylon Revisited."

If Liddell and Cardine have survived emotional bankruptcy more or less intact, the nameless girl and man undergo that same process as they deteriorate from "charming" to "harder-looking" to unwholesome. This decline, which is motivated in ways already mentioned, involves incremental rather than dramatic action. Consequently, Fitzgerald chose, when writing "One Trip Abroad," the framed journey through alien territory, his most effective structural strategy. Reflecting their original progenitor, "May Day"'s Gordon Sterrett, who seems "to be sort of bankrupt—morally as well as financially," the Kellys go from place to place, though the earlier story requires twenty-four hours in Manhattan and the later story more than three married years in Europe. Such journeys may seem aimless yet they have inevitable destinations: for

18. Lawrence Buell, "The Significance of Fantasy in Fitzgerald's Fiction," 29.

Gordon Sterrett, "a small hotel just off Sixth Avenue"—the site of his suicide; and for Nelson and Nicole Kelly, "a country where very few things begin, but many things end" (161)—the site of her illumination.[19]

Fitzgerald is blatantly self-reflexive only once in the narrative: "This is the story of a trip abroad, and the geographical element must not be slighted" (161). His focusing our attention on geography should not surprise us, since he remains the greatest modern American exponent of psychic landscapes and their symbolic juxtapositions: North versus South, East versus West, America versus Europe. He even emphasizes the sequence of locations visited by the Kellys—"North Africa, Italy, the Riviera, Paris and points in between" (161)—no doubt hoping we will perceive, as they do not, the ever-diminishing distance from Switzerland, the journey's and the narrative's destination. Meanwhile, as Brian Way contends, the "episodes succeed each other like a series of moral tableaux."

The first significant episode transpires in Algeria. Dining with the Mileses at the Hotel Transatlantique, Nelson "reciprocated the bottle of champagne . . . and neither of them was accustomed to so much" (146). Afterwards, at the Café of the Ouled Nails, he expresses "evident reluctance" when Nicole follows her mirror image, "the attractive young wife," outside before the "Oriental style" dance commences. His "not coming" hurts Nicole and this leads to their initial fight. We are told "something was harmed, some precedent of possible nonagreement was set" (147).

In Sorrento a month later, the European setting begins to exact its toll: "Nicole and Nelson were at once too old and too young, and too American, to fall into immediate soft agreement with a strange land. Their vitality made them restless, for as yet his painting had no direction and her singing no immediate prospect of becoming serious. They said they were not 'getting anywhere'—the evenings were long, so they began to drink a lot of *vin de Capri* at dinner" (148). Their boredom produces the second significant episode, which occurs at an English-owned hotel. Here, an altercation with Gen. Sir Evelyne Fragelle and Lady Fragelle over a mechanical piano precipitates the Kellys' abrupt departure. Whereas

19. Fitzgerald, *Stories of F. Scott Fitzgerald*, 87, 126.

the Algerian sequence had ended with the author telling us, "they were finding [the world] in each other" (147), the Sorrento episode, which concludes part 1, ends with the declaration, "They were through with being alone" (150).

Nelson and Nicole are no longer alone during the second part, for two years later, after "hurried months in Paris or Biarritz," they have settled at Monte Carlo, where they enjoy a villa and "a large acquaintance among the spring and summer crowd" (150). Before Nicole lunches on T. F. Golding's yacht with "seven different nationalities" (152), we learn that she has "two men in love with her" and is meeting a third (150). Yet she shoves a glass vase containing flowers toward Nelson following this luncheon when overhearing him and her closest friend Noel Delauney exchange intimacies. Then wife attacks husband, who, out of self-defense, inadvertently blackens her eye. They eventually make up: "Nicole accepted his explanations, not because they were credible, but because she wanted passionately to believe them" (155). The story's third significant episode also illustrates how interconnected the Kellys and their overt doubles are, for it is bracketed by the nameless girl carrying "an armful of flowers" (151) and the violence she experiences opposite Nelson and Nicole at the Café de Paris. "His growing discontent" (152) and her vow, "we're getting out of it all soon, and we'll be serious and have a baby" (151), suggest that the Kellys belong among the "Americans . . . having a rotten time" (152).

Part 3 opens a month later in Paris, where "they made a conscientious list of the places they wouldn't visit any more and the people they didn't want to see again" (156). However, Nelson and Nicole merely change crowds from Americans "salted with Europeans" to Europeans "peppered with Americans." Both Kellys remain "handsome and intelligent," but though Nelson has begun painting again, "he was no longer willing to go out socially without the stimulus of liquor." Soon Nicole bears his son, hoping this will make him "serious and responsible" (157), a strategy that fails. Meanwhile, they meet Count Chiki Sarolai, who occupies their apartment during Nicole's hospitalization, then sticks Nelson for the twelve thousand dollars owed caterers from the canal-boat party on the Seine ostensibly given by the count's rich relatives, the de la Clos Hirondelles. While Nicole attends this party against doctor's orders, Chiki steals her jewel box and absconds. "I'm sick, sick!" she screams as the third part closes (161).

In the last part of the story, the Kellys, now married "a little more than four years," go "to Switzerland because they had to." There, where the waters are "sinister" beneath "postcard blue," "misery . . . from every corner of Europe" gathers (161–62). "Health had failed them both at the same time," with Nicole experiencing "two successive operations," and Nelson fighting "for life against jaundice." So they reside at the Lake Geneva of "sanatoriums and rest hotels" among "the obese, the wasted, the crippled and broken of all nationalities" (162).

The augury embodied by the locusts as "black flakes of snow" soon recurs through a catastrophic storm that produces "tumult and chaos and darkness." Retribution follows when Nicole, and perhaps even Nelson, recognizes that the "two new arrivals" (163) are actually themselves. Ironically, she therefore possesses all the distasteful qualities she has just attributed to the nameless girl—calculation, egoism, ill-health, slovenliness—while Nelson incorporates the "weak and self-indulgent" man (164). After these mirror images are assimilated and so made invisible, the Kellys stand "alone together in the tranquil moonlight" (165), "tranquil" because their ordeal is over, and "moonlight" because they are now enlightened.

The geographical journey in "One Trip Abroad," like those in "The Ice Palace," "The Diamond as Big as the Ritz" (1922), *The Great Gatsby,* and "Babylon Revisited," becomes a psychic quest for self-awareness. Such fine Fitzgerald fictions merge style and content "so that the thing you have to say and the way of saying it blend as one matter."[20] In "One Trip Abroad," Way's "felicitous expression of the underlying structural necessities" encompasses the storm framework, the biblical subtext, the manifest and latent doubles, and the incremental "process of deterioration"—a process that inevitably leads toward death-oriented Switzerland, "where very few things begin, but many things end" (161).

20. Wilson, ed., *The Crack-Up,* 304.

WHAT FITZGERALD THOUGHT OF THE JEWS: RESISTING TYPE IN "THE HOTEL CHILD"

BARRY GROSS AND ERIC FRETZ

"The Hotel Child" has been neglected by anthologists and critics alike. Since its publication in the *Saturday Evening Post* on January 31, 1931, it has been reprinted in *Bits of Paradise* and *The Short Stories of F. Scott Fitzgerald*. Relegated to the position of a "minor" work, it has consequently suffered from unhelpful comparisons to "major" productions by Fitzgerald and his predecessors. Matthew J. Bruccoli places "The Hotel Child" in the *Tender Is the Night* cluster stories, while Hilton Anderson is content to discuss the story as an unsuccessful parody of Henry James's *Daisy Miller*. The discussion of influences and prototypes is finally less than satisfying because, while the story does look backward and forward, it is good enough to stand on its own. "The Hotel Child" is certainly not Fitzgerald at his best, but its merits go beyond what the few critics who have written about it are willing to acknowledge.[1]

Perhaps the most interesting aspect of "The Hotel Child" is Fitzgerald's representation of the voluptuous and ambiguously clever American Jewess, Fifi Schwartz. One critic suggests that Fifi "is Jewish for no

---

1. Matthew J. Bruccoli, ed., *The Short Stories of F. Scott Fitzgerald: A New Collection*, xvii; Hilton Anderson, "*Daisy Miller* and 'The Hotel Child': A Jamesian Influence on F. Scott Fitzgerald"; Matthew J. Bruccoli, *The Composition of "Tender Is the Night": A Study of the Manuscripts*, 72; Robert Sklar, *F. Scott Fitzgerald: The Last Laocoön*, 243; John A. Higgins, *F. Scott Fitzgerald: A Study of the Stories*, 120–21.

apparent reason other than to allow her to have a domineering mother, who, it might be added, is not very successful in controlling either of her children." Despite the mild anti-Semitism of the comment (Jewish mothers as domineering?), it is a misreading of the story. It matters that Fifi is a Jew, and, furthermore, overlooking her Jewishness (her ethnicity) is one of the reasons critics have unanimously found the story "third-rate." "The Hotel Child" may be "cluttered, confused, melodramatic, and implausible," but it works today because it provides a representation of an "other" who resists the dominant order and undermines the outdated and outworn notion of an American melting pot.[2]

It is intriguing that Fitzgerald would deal with this subject in the 1930s, a period of the American experience when the threat to a homogeneous American culture was an unmistakable anxiety for the established white culture. Between 1880 and 1924, 24 million European immigrants (2.5 million of which were Jews), in addition to the economic and social instability that a burgeoning industrial order imposes, only served to exacerbate tensions between "native" Americans and the immigrants. Furthermore, Fitzgerald must have found the worldwide economic depression of the 1930s ironic in a personal manner. Zelda Fitzgerald experienced her first breakdown in April 1930, just six months after the American stock-market crash. In the midst of these two "crashes," then, one national and one emotional, Fitzgerald wrote "The Hotel Child."

In the 1930s, the threats of anti-Semitism in America and the memory of the Russian pogroms were palpable trepidations in the minds of Jewish Americans. The lynching of Leo Frank in 1914, the wildly anti-Semitic diatribes in Henry Ford's Dearborn *Independent*, the founding of the Ku Klux Klan in 1920, quotas in higher education, immigration restrictions (culminating in the National Origins Act of 1924), and, later, the anti-Semitic broadcasts of the Detroit radio priest Father Coughlin, did nothing to alleviate those fears. In short, it was a period in which Jews once again faced all-too-familiar discriminations and the accompanying anxieties.

2. Anderson, "*Daisy Miller* and 'The Hotel Child,'" 213; Sklar, *Fitzgerald: Last Laocoön*, 243; Higgins, *Fitzgerald: Study of the Stories*, 102.

It is no secret that in 1931, when the entire country was suffering from the deleterious effects of a worldwide depression, people were looking for scapegoats, and the Jews, as a result of their quick and visible assimilation, were easy targets. In the 1935 introduction to *Jews without Money*, Michael Gold directly addressed the virulent political anti-Semitism of the period: "Recently, groups of anti-Semitic demagogues have appeared in this country. They are like Hitler, telling the hungry American people that capitalism is Jewish, and that an attack on the Jews is the best way of restoring prosperity."[3]

The proponents of high culture were no less responsible for fomenting anti-Semitic rhetoric. The narrator of John Dos Passos's *Manhattan Transfer* (1925) tells us that Harry Goldweiser's "words press against [Ellen's] body, nudge in the hollows where her dress clings; she can barely breathe for fear of listening to him. . . . She feels very helpless, caught like a fly in his sticky trickling sentences. . . . his eyes are full of furtive spiderlike industry weaving a warm sweet choking net about her face and neck." Or consider the language of the narrators of T. S. Eliot's poems: "the rats . . . underneath the piles" and "the jew [*sic*] . . . underneath the lot." And Bleistein—"Chicago Semite Viennese"—staring "from the protozoic slime" and "the jew [*sic*] squat[ting] on the window sill, the owner," and "Rachel née Rabinovitch tear[ing] at the grapes with murderous paws." Eliot was no less xenophobic in his public addresses, as evidenced by a 1933 speech at the University of Virginia: "The population should be homogeneous; where two or more cultures exist in the same place they are likely either to be fiercely self conscious [*sic*] or both to become adulterate. What is still more important is unity of religious background; and reasons of race and religion combine to make any large number of freethinking Jews undesirable." Consequently, Jewish and non-Jewish readers of the 1920s and 1930s might have been surprised to read about Robert Cohn, the "tough Jew" of Hemingway's *The Sun Also Rises* (1926) who knocks out the aristocratic Mike Campbell in a fit of romantic despair, or about Joseph Bloeckman, the successful and

---

3. For a full discussion on the implications of ideological and economic anti-Semitism of the period, see John Higham, *Send These to Me*, especially chapters 8 and 9.

self-assured Jew of Fitzgerald's *The Beautiful and Damned* who punches Anthony Patch in the face, after Patch calls him a "Goddamn Jew."[4]

There is little evidence in his letters that Fitzgerald was concerned with the Jews, but his fiction reveals a man who sympathized and maybe even empathized with what it meant to be a Jew. Consider Meyer Wolfsheim of *The Great Gatsby*, a "small, flat-nosed Jew . . . with two fine growths of hair luxuriat[ing] in either nostril." Wolfsheim has an accent (he says "sid" instead of "said," "gonnegtion" instead of "connection," and "Oggsford" instead of "Oxford"), and his English is ungrammatical ("I like across the street better" and "Rosy had eat a lot all evening"). Nick observes that he eats "ferocious[ly]," and Wolfsheim shows Nick his cufflinks made "of human molars," both of which suggest the wolf, Wolfsheim as sinister and predatory. But this aspect of Wolfsheim is balanced, if not entirely dispelled, by Gatsby's obvious affection for him. It is not clear if he has invited Nick to lunch with Wolfsheim or if they run into Wolfsheim accidentally, but Gatsby does not attempt to avoid Wolfsheim or to shield Nick from Wolfsheim, even though he does not want Nick "to get a wrong idea of" him.[5]

On the morning of Gatsby's funeral, Nick goes to New York and finds Wolfsheim in an office marked "The Swastika Holding Company." (Did

---

4. John Dos Passos, *Manhattan Transfer*, 202, 244; T. S. Eliot, *Selected Poems*, 31, 34, 46; T. S. Eliot, *After Strange Gods*, 20; F. Scott Fitzgerald, *The Beautiful and Damned*, 437.

5. In a letter to John Lardner dated September 30, 1933, Fitzgerald writes the following about Gilbert Seldes: "When a Jew is interested he has the strong sense of the track that we other races don't even know the sprinting time of" (Andrew Turnbull, ed., *The Letters of F. Scott Fitzgerald*, 506). The following entry appears in *The Crack-Up*: "Jews lose clarity. They get to look like old melted candles, as if their bodies were preparing to waddle. Irish get slovenly and dirty. Anglo-Saxons get frayed and worn" (Edmund Wilson, ed., *The Crack-Up*, 151).

For critical discussions of Fitzgerald's representation of Jews see Milton Hindus, "F. Scott Fitzgerald and Literary Anti-Semitism"; William Goldhurst, *F. Scott Fitzgerald and His Contemporaries*, 176–87; William Goldhurst, "Literary Anti-Semitism of the 20s"; Barry Edward Gross, "Fitzgerald's Anti-Semitism—A Reply to William Goldhurst"; William Goldhurst, "An Answer to Barry Edward Gross"; Josephine Z. Kopf, "Meyer Wolfsheim and Robert Cohn: A Study of a Jewish Type and Stereotype." For more general discussions of Fitzgerald and ethnicity, see Mark Gidley, "Notes on F. Scott Fitzgerald and the Passing of the Great Race," and Peter Slater, "Ethnicity in *The Great Gatsby*."

F. Scott Fitzgerald, *The Great Gatsby*, 65, 69, 71, 73. All subsequent page references to *The Great Gatsby* are to this 1980 edition and will appear parenthetically in the text.

Fitzgerald know in 1925 that the *hakenkreuz* was in use in Germany and Austria as early as 1918 as the emblem of anti-Semitic, extremist nationalistic organizations? And if he did, why did he make it the name of Wolfsheim's company? Is that supposed to tell us something about Wolfsheim?) "A lovely Jewess . . . with black hostile eyes" (171) tells Nick that Wolfsheim is not in, but when he mentions Gatsby she goes into the inner office and Wolfsheim appears "solemnly in the doorway, holding out both hands" to Nick (171). He draws Nick into his office, "remarking in a reverent voice that it was a sad time for all of us" (172).

Wolfsheim recounts his first meeting with Gatsby, providing Nick and us with information that helps fill out the vague picture he and we have of Gatsby. Finding Gatsby in desperate need of clothes and food, Wolfsheim tells Nick he "made" Gatsby: " 'I raised him up out of nothing, right out of the gutter. . . . We were so thick like that in everything'—he held up two bulbous fingers—'always together' " (172). Since Wolfsheim was Gatsby's "closest friend," Nick knows he will come to the funeral, but Wolfsheim tells Nick he "can't get mixed up in it": "Let us learn to show our friendship for a man when he is alive and not after he is dead. After that my own rule is to let everything alone" (173). At lunch Nick took note of Wolfsheim's extreme caution: Wolfsheim's "eyes roved very slowly all around the room—he completed the arc by turning to inspect the people directly behind and I think that, except for my presence, he would have taken one short glance beneath our own table" (73). Here is a moral flaw, and his comment about showing friendship to the living sounds insincere and self-serving. Yet Fitzgerald has Nick notice that "the hair in his nostrils quivered slightly, and as he shook his head his eyes filled with tears" (173).

Wolfsheim is the last of Gatsby's three fathers. Gatsby's biological father, Henry C. Gatz, is, like Wolfsheim, "a solemn old man" (167) whose eyes also fill with "isolated and unpunctual tears" (168) and who also speaks ungrammatical English—"If he'd of lived, he'd of been a great man . . . he'd of helped build up the country" (169). He has shown the picture of Gatsby's house so often that it is "cracked in the corners and dirty with many hands" (173). Gatsby's first adopted father, Dan Cody, was also Gatsby's "best friend," who, like Wolfsheim, has pulled Gatsby out of hard times and given him a chance to succeed. Insofar as Wolfsheim is the last of Fitzgerald's three fathers (unless we go along

with Nick who says Gatsby was also a son of God: "The truth was that Jay
Gatsby of West Egg, Long Island, sprang from his Platonic conception
of himself. He was a son of God . . ." [99]), and the one under whose
patronage and tutelage Gatsby makes his fortune and embarks on his
pursuit of Daisy, Jay Gatsby is more Meyer Wolfsheim's son than Dan
Cody's. He is perhaps even more Wolfsheim's than Henry C. Gatz's, too
(Gatsby's "imagination had never really accepted [his parents] as his
parents at all" [99]), and though Mr. Gatz behaves more paternally now
(he "started right away" [168] as soon as he heard that Gatsby was dead),
it was Wolfsheim who fed Gatsby and "raised him up from nothing,"
and it was Gatz who "beat him" when Gatsby told him he "et like a hog."
Insofar as that is the case, Gatsby is, in effect, a Jew. He is, at least, the
novel's Jew, which may explain why Tom Buchanan, a xenophobe who
often sounds like Tom Eliot, so despises Gatsby.

Nevertheless, the lovely Fifi Schwartz represents both a departure
from and an amalgamation of previous representations of Jews in the
canon of Fitzgerald and modern American literature. Fifi becomes one
of Fitzgerald's "determined girl-woman" figures who controls the course
of her actions without being represented as an incorrigible shrew. Unlike
her male predecessors, who relentlessly pursue social position and, more
notoriously, the elusive shiksa, Fifi is assimilated at the beginning of the
story and gradually moves from the center of the decadent society. Amid
the debauched world of a fading European aristocracy whirls the sensual
yet naïve Fifi, who nearly yields to the temptations of the aristocracy but
finally uncovers the charade and redeems herself from the fitful gaze
of the European ladies and gentlemen. As an eroticized woman, Fifi
is initially the object of pursuit of admiring Gentile gentlemen, but,
through a series of revelations and unmaskings, she gradually becomes
the pursuer of the duplicitous impostors. Finally, it is the image of her
mother and the solidarity she feels for her that compel Fifi to reject the
offerings of the European aristocracy and find a sense of herself outside
of its trappings.

"The Hotel Child," set in a Swiss hotel, begins on the night of Fifi
Schwartz's eighteenth birthday party. As a beautiful young debutante,
Fifi has captured the imaginations of all the patrons of the Hotel des
Trois Mondes but especially that of the conniving Count Borowki, who
attempts to woo Fifi into a marriage and take control of her inheritance.

Included in the cast of deceitful European aristocrats is the dissipated Lady Capps-Karr and the Marquis "Bopes" Kinkallow. Accompanying Fifi is her mother and her brother, John, who drinks too much and gets mealymouthed over a dispossessed Russian countess. Midway through her party, Fifi is sent out by her mother to retrieve John who has snuck out with his Russian. When she returns, Mrs. Schwartz informs her that they will be returning to the United States shortly. Fifi resists, unwilling to go home where "everybody is so bigoted," and begins to think about marrying the Count in order to stay in Europe and live out her dream of becoming a titled aristocrat.[6] That night, a burglar steals two hundred dollars from Mrs. Schwartz's room, and in the morning she confirms her resolution to go home. Fifi, too, has made up her mind—she will accept the Count's proposal and elope with him that evening. Gliding down the stairs to give the Count her answer, she overhears something that causes her to change her mind, but a break in the narrative keeps the reader unaware of her revelation.

That evening, Mr. Weicker, the assistant manager of the Trois Mondes who blames Fifi for all the problems of the hotel, sees Borowki leaving the hotel under the pretense of going to visit his mother. Later, a fire breaks out in the bar, and, as Weicker rushes around, he receives a call from the police informing him that they are bringing Borowki and an unidentified woman back to the hotel for identification. When the entourage enters the hotel, Weicker discovers that Borowki is wanted in three countries. He is more interested in Borowki's companion, though, because, thinking it is Fifi, he imagines he has found the culprit of the fire and the burglary. To his surprise, Borowki's companion is the English debutante and very proper Miss Howard. Fifi, it turns out, has been out helping her "stumbling and reluctant" (614) brother back to the hotel and is absolved from participation in the scandals of the Trois Mondes. The story closes with Borowki incarcerated for his crimes and Lady Capps-Karr and the Marquis Kinkallow evicted from the Trois Mondes for their part in starting the fire after a drunken attempt to cook potato chips in alcohol. In a final image, a triumphant Fifi explains

6. Bruccoli, ed., *Short Stories*, 605. All subsequent page references to "The Hotel Child" are to this edition and will appear parenthetically in the text.

to a Parisian bartender why she declined Borowki's hand in marriage and how she uncovered the mystery of the hotel burglar.

In the Hotel des Trois Mondes (literally, the Hotel of the Three Worlds), Fitzgerald has created a literary topos that suggests the larger issues of the story. More than a mere parody of James's Trois Couronnes in *Daisy Miller,* the hotel neatly works within the context of the story itself.[7] The reader might pause to wonder about the "three worlds" Fitzgerald has in mind. Our reading of the story, which focuses on Fifi's ethnicity, seems to suggest that the three worlds might be the three competing spheres of the American, the European, and the Jew. The Trois Mondes, "a place where one's instinct is to give a reason for being there" (598), occupies a middling, marginal, and shady position in an unfashionable "corner" of Europe. It is a transitory place where "routes cross" (as opposed to a place where people establish roots) and where damaged reputations ("people who are no longer *persona grata* in Italy or France" [598]) come to flex their wounded egos. It is a world of masks and disguises where travelers literally "pass" through, but figuratively "make" themselves up in order to "pass" as other than who they are.

The patrons of the hotel engage in a dubious charade of concealed selves. "On a gala night at the Hotel des Trois Mondes a new arrival would scarcely detect the current beneath the surface" (599), and the hotel is "full of people who were actually rich and noble," people who display "fine embroidery" in public but take "cocaine in closed apartments" (601). The English and American women of the hotel herd themselves together in "galler[ies]" and appear as plastic apparitions: They are all "of a certain age," and the English women have "dyed hair and faces powdered pinkish gray," while the American women seem to have undergone "snowy-white transformations" as they appear in their "black dresses and lips of cherry red" (599). Count Borowki, the scheming and insolvent Romanian (Fifi has it wrong when she says he is from Hungary), acts out his social deceptions as he attempts to cajole Fifi into marriage. The Count, whose "shining brown eyes of a stuffed deer" (600) make him as false as the assembly of synthetic women, temptingly offers to place Fifi among the gallery of pretenders when he draws her

---

7. Anderson, "*Daisy Miller* and 'The Hotel Child,'" 215.

aside and whispers, "My American dream girl, we must have you painted in Budapest the way you are tonight. You will hang with the portraits of my ancestors in my castle in Transylvania" (601). Objectifying her beauty, the Count threatens to transform Fifi into an aesthetic image by destroying the living and breathing original.

Fifi is, indeed, already a work of art who might have stepped out of a Hopper painting. An "exquisitely, radiantly beautiful Jewess," Fifi has a "fine, high forehead" and "waves and curlicues of soft dark red" hair. Where the other women are passive and costumed, Fifi is alive with energy: Her eyes are "bright, big, clear, wet and shining," her lips are "real," and the "strong young pump of her heart" beats "close to the surface." Fitzgerald eroticizes Fifi, describing her "body as so assertively adequate that one cynic had been heard to remark that she always looked as if she had nothing on underneath her dresses" (599), and when she enters the ballroom "at a sort of little run" on the evening of her eighteenth birthday, she "swayed her lovely hips and tossed her lovely head" as she "bumpily" led a procession of admiring gentlemen through the scene (600).

Furthermore, Mrs. Schwartz is contrasted with the self-conscious pseudo-aristocrats who surround her. While the gazes of the English and American women of the hotel nervously swing back and forth from Fifi to the dancing, Mrs. Schwartz sits "apart" (599) from the gallery with a friend, thinking of her family. Fitzgerald has not made Mrs. Schwartz fat, has not inlaid her with diamonds, and has not given her a Yiddish accent out of burlesque. Instead, she is demure and self-possessed as she quietly thinks about "Fifi and Fifi's brother, and about her other daughters, now married, whom she considered to have been even prettier than Fifi" (599). In her "effortless indifference" to "what was said by the groups around the room," Mrs. Schwartz becomes the real aristocrat of the story—she is a "plain woman" who "had been a Jewess a long time" (599) and who has a "clear grip on the past (606)— and she replaces the decadent aristocrats who surround her. Ultimately, it is the story's direction and intent for eighteen-year-old Fifi to attain the maturity and detachment of her mother, to learn the lessons of pride and independence that being "a Jewess for a long time" can teach.

However, the Schwartzes are not beyond "passing" as others. Highly assimilated Jews, the Schwartzes do indeed seem Jewish by surname only; Fifi's brother's name is John, and her sisters are Amy and Gladys, and of course "Fifi" does not suggest centuries of diaspora. Indeed, Fifi's name is closely, yet ambiguously, associated with the ubiquitous Pekinese that Miss Howard carries throughout the story. An obvious symbol of conspicuous consumption, Fitzgerald's association of Fifi with the Pekinese seems to be a subtle gibe at the young Jewess. Strangely, Fitzgerald endows Fifi with canine characteristics: In addition to her name, she "yelp[s]" in annoyance (603) and "wrinkl[es] her brow" (602). The observant reader of "The Hotel Child" might pause at this associa- tion to consider Fitzgerald's disturbing comment in "Echoes of the Jazz Age" where immigrants are compared to common (and uncommon) animals:

> With each new shipment of Americans spewed up by the boom the quality fell off, until toward the end there was something sinister about the crazy boatloads. . . . I remember a fat Jewess, inlaid with diamonds, who sat behind us at the Russian ballet and said as the curtain rose, "Thad's luffly, dey ought to baint a bicture of it." . . . There were citizens travelling in luxury in 1928 and 1929 who, in the distortion of their new condition, had the human value of Pekinese, bivalves, cretins, goats.[8]

Yet Fitzgerald is obviously having fun with the animal metaphors when he has Fifi scream in frustration, "I think it would be a good thing if the hotel caught fire and burned down with all the nasty cats in it" (607) and "Oh, I'm so furious! I never saw so many old cats!" (608).

As wealthy and visible Jewish Americans, the Schwartzes occupy a tenuous position in the hotel society. The Taylors, a family of "very Europeanized Americans" who "could hardly be said to belong to any nation at all" except "to a sort of Balkanlike state composed of people like themselves," consider Fifi "as much of a gratuitous outrage as a new stripe in the flag" (600). Mr. Weicker is predisposed to blame the Schwartzes for simply being in his hotel, and he looks to them whenever there is trouble brewing.[9] There are three major threats against the

8. Wilson, ed., *The Crack-Up*, 20–21.
9. In a 1938 letter to his daughter, Fitzgerald wrote, "I am known as a left-wing sympathizer and would be proud if you were. In any case, I should feel outraged if you

hotel in the story—unrespectable clientele, crime, and fire—and Weicker initially looks to the Schwartzes as the probable cause for all of them. He does not blame Count Borowki, who has not paid his bill in three weeks but has told Weicker that "his mother . . . would arrange everything" (601). Nor does he reproach Lady Capps-Karr, whose "night-going phonograph" has caused a large family to leave the hotel but who is "a *grande cliente;* one could count three bottles of whisky a day for herself and entourage, and her father in London was good for every drop of it" (601). When we first meet the hotel manager, he is looking into the bar where "Fifi's phonograph roared new German tangoes into the smoke and clatter" (600). Unlike the hoards of adoring men, Weicker "had not come to admire Fifi" but to inquire "as to why matters were not going well at the Hotel des Trois Mondes this summer" (600). In addition to the "sagging American Stock Exchange" (601), the presumed thief in the hotel, and the "finicky" (601) nature of the customers, Weicker's gaze is obviously directed toward the problem that the Schwartzes pose to the respectability of his establishment.

Later, after he is informed that Mrs. Schwartz had two hundred dollars stolen from her chiffonier, Weicker suspects Borowki (who is the actual criminal), but, finding him "hooked firmly on to the end of a line older than the crown of St. Stephen," he turns his fitful gaze to the victims, blaming them for their presence: "On the other hand, there was no doubt as to who had been robbed, and Mr. Weicker's indignation began to concentrate on Fifi and her family, who might have saved him this trouble by taking themselves off some time ago. It was even conceivable that the dissipated son, John, had nipped the money" (606). Finally, when a late night fire blazes in the hotel bar, Weicker's first thought is to blame Fifi, who, earlier, raging after being dismissed from the bar, screamed at Weicker (expressing a defiance that no Gentile author had previously given to a Jewish character): "I never saw such a narrow-minded bunch of people in my life; always criticizing everybody and making up terrible things about them, no matter what they do

---

identified yourself with Nazism or Red-baiting in any form" (Turnbull, ed., *Letters,* 37). But by giving Weicker a German name in 1930, was he somehow aware of the German hostility for Jews in 1930?

themselves. I think it would be a good thing if the hotel caught fire and burned down with all the nasty cats in it" (607). Of course, it is the titled European aristocrats and not the American Jews who are the real cause of all the hotel's problems. Borowki is revealed as the burglar, and his and Miss Howard's aborted elopement precludes Miss Howard from being introduced in English society. Fifi's indignant words might have been good enough cause to implicate her in the fire, but it is eventually discovered that the blame resides with the dissipated Marquis Kinkallow and Lady Capps-Karr.

There is no attempt on Fifi's part to mask her Jewishness, and "The Hotel Child" would have been quite a different story had Fitzgerald represented Fifi and Mrs. Schwartz as concealing their ethnicity. When Count Borowki begs for her hand in marriage and declares, "There is no flaw or fault in you," Fifi "modestly" retorts, "Oh, yes. . . . I got a sort of big nose. Would you know I was Jewish?" (608). But the Count, himself thoroughly immersed in self-sustaining social disguises, thinks nothing of her aside and, "with a touch of impatience," returns to flattering Fifi into a union (608).

Fitzgerald cleverly uses mirrors as literary tropes for Fifi to become the agent of revelation and to amplify her own self-discovery. As reflecting devices, mirrors represent reality only as it appears; they mirror external-ities, and the world of the Trois Mondes is a place where superficialities dominate the field of vision. However, mirrors serve a double, seemingly disparate, function in "The Hotel Child." On one hand, they provide the vision to reflect Fifi's exquisite yet narcissistic self, and on the other hand, they serve as devices for her to uncover the deceptions of Count Borowki. The first time we notice the mirror in the story occurs while Borowki intently tries to convince Fifi to elope. Lady Capps-Karr approaches their table, insulting Fifi ("I've noticed Miss Schwartz. . . . And of course I've noticed Miss Schwartz's clothes" [609]) and then continues on her way. Borowki continues his seduction and "half an hour later Fifi got up with indecision on her face" and nods when Borowki asks her to give her answer by seven. But after he escorts her across the room, he sees "her vanish into a dark hall mirror in the direction of the lift" (609). The next time she will see Borowki, it will be as a reflection in that very mirror, but the image she receives turns the tide of the story and sets Fifi on the road to self-discovery.

After Mrs. Schwartz informs Fifi that they will be returning to the United States, it appears she will enter into a union with the Count by default. Resolved to marry and become part of European aristocracy, Fifi sets off to accept the Count's offer to elope that very evening. However, as she descends the stairs of the hotel, she remembers "halfway that in her distraction she had omitted an official glance in the mirror," and, in a wonderful moment where vanity meets revelation, she stops in front of the mirror outside of the grand salon to learn two things: First, Fifi "learned . . . once more" that she was "beautiful," but then, just before the narrative break between parts 2 and 3, "a sudden sound broke the stillness of the gloomy hall and Fifi stood suddenly breathless and motionless" (611). We do not learn the details of Fifi's epiphany until the end of the story when, sitting on a barstool and sipping a lemonade, Fifi relates the story to an interested bartender. Fifi's rapport and easiness with the bartenders of the story (she tells a good part of her own story to them) and her inclination to sit at the bar sipping ginger ale or lemonade is a charming touch in "The Hotel Child." Standing in front of the hall mirror, Fifi says she heard the Count telling Lady Capps-Karr ("the one who set the hotel on fire") that his "one nightmare is that she'll [Fifi] turn out to look like her mother" (615). Realizing "there was something the matter with him" (615), she becomes the detective who solves the theft of her mother's money when she goes to the store and discovers the cigarette case he had given her as an "engagement" present was purchased with the very same one-hundred-dollar bill stolen from her mother's room.

Fifi's self-realization occurs when she uncovers the deception of Borowki, and it is the image of her mother that saves her from his seductions. As she moves through "The Hotel Child," Fifi gains experiences that allow her ultimately to reject the order to which she aspires. Early in the story, Fitzgerald describes her as an innocent: "Fifi was not critical, nor was she aware of being criticized herself" (599), and later she mistakes Count Borowki's declarations of false love as heartfelt sentiments. The narrator observes that "one would suppose that a normal American girl, who had been to an average number of moving pictures, would have detected a vague ring of familiarity in Count Borowki's persistent wooing" (601), but Fifi is flattered and agrees to an engagement. Furthermore, unable to see the bigotry that surrounds her in the Trois Mondes, Fifi protests against returning to the United States, complaining that "everybody is so bigoted there. A girl hasn't the chance to meet the same sort of men, even if there were any. Everybody just watches everything you do" (605). Mrs. Schwartz has to remind Fifi that the same circumstances apply in the Trois Mondes, but, at this point in the story, Fifi is still unable to see beyond the charade of deception. Yet, in a touching moment, Fifi "put her arms around her mother's waist, realizing that it was she and not her mother, with her mother's clear grip on the past, who was completely lost in the universe" (604–5). But the innocent, vain, and narcissistic young girl matures in the course of the story so that, by the end, she has solved the mystery of the hotel burglar, uncovered the deception of Borowki's intentions, defeated the Furies, and found a new sense of herself.

Fifi's pride and solidarity with her mother preclude her from yielding to the temptations of the Count and result in her acquiring a new sense of herself outside of the artificial and restricted world of the Hotel des Trois Mondes. Throughout the story, she is clearly lost in an elusive fantasy of aristocratic dreams: "But for Fifi all the romance of life was rolled up into the last three impressionable years in Europe . . . and [she remembered] the feeling that she had sometimes, when she danced with Borowki, that he was dressed in gleaming boots and a white-furred dolman" (610). However, though she is immersed in and infatuated with high society, her mother and all she stands for is Fifi's foremost influence and model. "Lost in the universe" (606) throughout the story, Fifi naïvely whirls around a social order that can gawk at her but ultimately will never allow her within its realm. She imagines herself married to the Count and, consequently, exchanging insults with Lady Capps-Karr: "It was Borowki, then, and the chance of living fully and adventurously. He could go into the diplomatic service, and then one day when they encountered Lady Capps-Karr and Miss Howard at a legation ball, she could make audible the observation that for the moment seemed so necessary to her: 'I hate people who always look as if they were going to or from a funeral'" (610–11). It will never happen, of course, but it is not until she overhears the insult against her mother that she saves herself from falling prey to the duplicity of Borowki and all he represents.

It is interesting that this quirky story, which challenges many of the ideological notions about Jews of the period, would be published in the

Saturday Evening Post, a publication with a white, middle-class, family-values audience. One might wonder if the lack of attention paid to the story might be a result of its undermining of the expectations of its original readers. Nevertheless, Fifi is interesting to us today because she does not assimilate into the larger society of the Hotel des Trois Mondes; she both retains and attains a sense of herself outside of the homogeneous social world of confidence men and painted women. Fifi's character is anomalous to other Jewish representations by Gentile authors who, when they are not comparing the Jew to pests and scavengers, tend to use them as embodiments of the socially fluid melting pot of American society. These Jewish representations confirm American values when they are introduced as members of the gauche nouveau riche but gradually acquire an "improved" sensibility and style and assimilate into the dominant culture.

Consider Simon Rosedale of Edith Wharton's *The House of Mirth.*[10] Wharton introduces Rosedale as a "plump, rosy man of the blond Jewish type." But, despite his "smart London clothes fitting him like upholstery," his prospects of being accepted into New York society are slim—one socialite "declared that he was the same little Jew who had been served up and rejected at the social board a dozen times within her memory." Yet Rosedale "advanc[es] in social experiences," and midway through the narrative his position has significantly changed. "Making his way through the dense mass of social antagonisms," Rosedale has gained an "enviable prominence in the world of affairs"; he acquires public positions, is invited to banquets, becomes a candidate at one of the fashionable clubs, and has been invited to a dinner at the Trenors. He even becomes a candidate for the hand of Lily Bart but declines the opportunity when Lily becomes entangled in sordid affairs.[11]

Fitzgerald similarly represents Joseph Bloeckman in *The Beautiful and Damned* as an upwardly mobile Jew who assimilates and even, like Rosedale, has the opportunity of revenging prejudices that were previously held against him. Bloeckman, a "stoutening, ruddy Jew" with

---

10. In a letter to Fitzgerald on June 8, 1925, Wharton praised *The Great Gatsby,* noting (among other things) that "it's enough to make this reader happy to have met your *perfect* Jew . . ." (R. W. B. Lewis and Nancy Lewis, eds., *The Letters of Edith Wharton,* 482).

11. Edith Wharton, *The House of Mirth,* 16, 19, 249, 310.

"overwide" nostrils, seems, to Anthony Patch, "underdone, boiled looking." At the beginning of the narrative, Bloeckman introduces himself to Patch "with a little too evident assurance" for Patch's taste, but a year later, Bloeckman has

> grown tremendously in dignity. The boiled look was gone, he seemed "done" at last. In addition, he was no longer overdressed. The inappropriate facetiousness he had affected in ties had given way to a sturdy dark pattern. . . . This dignity appeared also in his personality. . . . Having been fawned financially, he had attained aloofness; having been snubbed socially, he had acquired reticence. Whatever had given him weight instead of bulk, Anthony no longer felt a correct superiority in his presence.[12]

Fifi, however, begins the narrative squarely in the center of the decadent, aristocratic world of European manners (recall the promenade in the beginning of the narrative) and, through a series of self-revelations, rejects the homogeneous order and sets out to "pierce" the "alien sky" and "find her own way through envy and corruption" (606). By the end of the story, Fifi has turned the assimilation process inside out. Bloeckman and Rosedale negotiate their "selves" until they have assimilated into the larger society; as their narratives progress they transform themselves into the image of their peers. Fifi, however, triumphs over her social peers. Fitzgerald sets this up by making her into a "tough" Jew like her predecessors, Cohn and Bloeckman. She gets to scream and scratch her way through the antagonisms that the European aristocrats present to her. Indeed, Fifi's chance at Jewish revenge occurs when she digs into the Marquis Kinkallow's face after he makes unwanted advances: "Fifteen minutes later the car stopped at a point several blocks beyond the café and Fifi stepped out. The marquis' face was now decorated by a long, irregular finger-nail scratch that ran diagonally across his cheek, traversed his nose in a few sketchy lines and finished in a sort of grand terminal of tracks upon his lower jaw" (604).

In her triumph, however, Fifi moves beyond the petty concerns of the hotel's patrons and toward a new understanding of herself. Near the end of the story, Fitzgerald notes that the beleaguered Fifi has staved

---

12. Fitzgerald, *The Beautiful and Damned,* 93, 94, 207.

off the attacks of the hostile and jealous European aristocratic women (the Furies): "They had not got her—not yet. The Furies had withdrawn a little and stood in the background with a certain gnashing of teeth," and after Fifi's exit the story ends with "a certain doubt among the eldest and most experienced of the Furies if they would get her, after all" (615). Fitzgerald's language resonates with Wharton's *The House of Mirth* when Lily Bart struggles to evade the Furies of New York society: "More and more, with every fresh mischance befalling her, did the pursuing Furies seem to take the shape of Bertha Dorset; and close at hand, safely locked among her papers, lay the means of ending their pursuit."[13] By the end of the story, Fifi's points of reference have been turned around. No longer the pursuer of that elusive place within European aristocracy, Fifi becomes the investigator who uncovers their duplicity and recovers a sense of herself outside of their world. Unlike her Jewish predecessors who gradually move to the center of their societies, Fifi finds a sense of herself by ambiguously withdrawing from the middle. With "her face gentle with new hopes," she "tottered" out of the bar (drunk, no doubt from too much lemonade!) "looking for completion under the impression that she was going to the *couturier*" (615).

We can only speculate on the focus of Fifi's "new hopes"; however, Fitzgerald's characterization and use of literary tropes suggests that it is Mrs. Schwartz, the "real" aristocrat of the story and the model for Fifi's gradual development, who has provided her daughter with the necessary vision to see beyond the duplicity of Borowki and friends. Finally, it matters that Fifi is a Jew in the same way that the Jewishness of Cohn, Bloeckman, Rosedale, Wolfsheim, et al. is integral to the texts in which they appear. In the late twentieth century, though, Fifi's removal at the end of her story presents an interesting challenge to the idea of an American melting pot that assimilated "others" into a homogeneous culture. Unlike her predecessors, Fifi resists, albeit ambiguously, casting her gaze away from the center and toward the example of her mother who has "been a Jewess a long time" (599).

13. Wharton, *The House of Mirth*, 305.

AN UNSENTIMENTAL EDUCATION:
"THE RUBBER CHECK"

RUTH PRIGOZY

Five years have rolled away from me and I can't decide
exactly who I am, if anyone.
—Letter from F. Scott Fitzgerald to
Maxwell Perkins, May 1932

Sometimes he was able to forget that he really wasn't
anybody at all.
—Fitzgerald, "The Rubber Check"

Fitzgerald wrote "The Rubber Check" in May 1932, probably at the Hotel Rennert in Baltimore, Maryland, during one of the bleakest periods of his life.[1] After the Fitzgeralds' return to the United States in September 1931, following Zelda Fitzgerald's release from Prangins Clinic in Switzerland, they took a six-month lease on a house in Montgomery, Alabama, where Fitzgerald continued to produce short stories to reduce the enormous debt that had resulted from his wife's illness. (He had written eight in 1930 and the same number by September 1931.) He then spent several months in Hollywood but had to return quickly when Zelda

---

1. Matthew J. Bruccoli, ed., *The Price Was High: The Last Uncollected Stories of F. Scott Fitzgerald,* 425. All subsequent page references to "The Rubber Check" are to this edition and will appear parenthetically in the text.

Fitzgerald suffered a relapse. In February of 1932, she entered the Phipps Clinic of Johns Hopkins University Hospital. While there, she wrote her autobiographical novel, *Save Me the Waltz*, and sent it off to Maxwell Perkins without showing it to her husband. Fitzgerald was angered by her action, in particular by her transparent and unflattering portrait of him. "My God," he wrote to her doctor, "my book made her a legend and her single intention in this somewhat thin portrait is to make me a non-entity."[2]

In March of 1932, Fitzgerald noted in his *Ledger,* "Scotty sick, me sick, Mrs. Sayre playing the fool . . . everything worser and worser, Zelda's novel arrives, neurosis, strained situation." Determined to leave Montgomery and to be closer to his wife, Fitzgerald moved into the Hotel Rennert in Baltimore after their lease expired in April. "The Rubber Check" was the third story he wrote during this unsettled period; in April he completed "Family in the Wind" and "What a Handsome Pair!" "The Rubber Check" was published in the August 6, 1932, *Saturday Evening Post,* but Fitzgerald received less than his usual fee—three thousand dollars, down from the four thousand dollars to which he had recently been accustomed. The story was among those Fitzgerald described as "Stripped and Permanently Buried"—stories that he mined for lines and phrases for possible use in his novels, and it was not collected until 1979, when Matthew J. Bruccoli included it in *The Price Was High.*[3]

Much of the scant critical attention "The Rubber Check" has received has been dismissive or disparaging. Robert Sklar describes it as "a conventional genteel story, with overtones of bitterness, that was his poorest story in half a decade." John A. Higgins calls it "a preposterous story despite being based on an actual experience," and Scott Donaldson, admitting that "it has its moments," concludes that "it fails for lack of feeling." Bryant Mangum finds it "much less entertaining than many other Fitzgerald stories dealing with the corrosive influence of wealth," its main character so unsympathetic that the story is often irritating. A few critics have responded more positively to the story. Matthew J.

2. Matthew J. Bruccoli, *Some Sort of Epic Grandeur: The Life of F. Scott Fitzgerald,* 325.

3. F. Scott Fitzgerald, *F. Scott Fitzgerald's Ledger: A Facsimile,* 186. In Matthew J. Bruccoli, ed., *The Notebooks of F. Scott Fitzgerald,* there are twelve passages culled from "The Rubber Check": numbers 112, 430, 480, 597, 907, 908, 1164–67, 1401, 1435.

Bruccoli, in his introduction to the story, calls it "underrated," and Henry Dan Piper, without commenting on its overall merits, calls it a "vigorous defense of a poor but capable young man who has been cruelly humiliated by some rich boys because he inadvertently cashed a bad check—as Fitzgerald himself had once done." Kenneth Eble, in the same autobiographical vein, sees the story as coming "closest to revealing Fitzgerald's own feeling of occupying a social position to which he was not really entitled" and notes that the list-making of a character in the story is reflective of Fitzgerald's "own compulsions" for making up lists during the period of his crack-up.[4]

Two other critics discuss the story at greater length and in each case suggest that it is a richer, more complex work than others have suggested. Although Brian Harding finds that it "rehearses the old story of the poor boy in search of the rich girl," it does so "in a new mode, restating, in hyperbolic terms, many of the ideas that had been part of all the stories." For Harding, the "crude reduction of the success story and the emptying of character . . . can hardly be unintentional." He thus concludes that in "The Rubber Check," Fitzgerald wrote a parody of the love story as a form of social aspiration, exposing "the conventions on which that story depended and created radical tales of alienation—stories of men without countries and without selves." Harding's analysis is intriguing, but the problems in shifting authorial distance throughout the story make his case for intentional parody less than persuasive. Finally, as I indicate in an overview of Fitzgerald's stories written during the depression, " 'The Rubber Check,' in many ways a very interesting work, suffers from Fitzgerald's over-identification with Val, the protagonist. . . . Val himself has no distinction, strength, or solidity. Were it not for such an important lapse, the ending, wry, ironic, and honest, would prove more effective than it does. . . ."[5] Although I still

4. Robert Sklar, *F. Scott Fitzgerald: The Last Laocoön*, 248; John A. Higgins, *F. Scott Fitzgerald: A Study of the Stories*, 154; Scott Donaldson, "Money and Marriage in Fitzgerald's Stories," 81; Bryant Mangum, *A Fortune Yet: Money in the Art of F. Scott Fitzgerald's Short Stories*, 125; Bruccoli, ed., *Price Was High*, 417; Henry Dan Piper, *F. Scott Fitzgerald: A Critical Portrait*, 176; Kenneth Eble, *F. Scott Fitzgerald*, 121, 122.

5. Brian Harding, " 'Made for—or against—the Trade': The Radicalism of Fitzgerald's *Saturday Evening Post* Love Stories," 128–29; Ruth Prigozy, "Fitzgerald's Short Stories and

believe that Fitzgerald's shifting distance from Val weakens the story, I would qualify my earlier remarks considerably. Upon reconsideration, I conclude that "The Rubber Check" has been undervalued in the past by every commentator and that it deserves the full discussion that follows. I hope to demonstrate that, despite its flaws (and few of Fitzgerald's stories are flawless), it belongs among the most complex and important stories he ever wrote.

The incident upon which the central complication of "The Rubber Check" was based occurred in 1920 when Fitzgerald cashed a check for more money than he had in his account (Perkins usually deposited money directly to his bank account). He soon discovered that because the next day was Saturday, Scribner's would not be able to cover the overdrawn check in time. "The result was that he spent the interim in a cold sweat, momentarily expecting the police to arrive and carry him off to jail," Piper observes.[6] That Fitzgerald not only remembered the incident but also was able to recreate all the tension and anxiety associated with it twelve years later suggests how strong its impact was on his psyche.

For his fictionalized treatment, Fitzgerald used the incident as a catalyst for a new exploration of subjects and themes that had always figured prominently in his work: money, social class and class distinctions, manners, clothes and their symbolic value to personal identity, loss of romantic illusions, love (real or illusory), the past and the golden moment, and finally, the quest for personal freedom. Like *This Side of Paradise,* and so many of his stories of sad young men, "The Rubber Check" is about the education of its protagonist. By 1932, however, Fitzgerald had learned so many lessons about his own life and his society that, while generally belonging to the category Scott Donaldson so ably describes as "tales of rejection and disappointment" with the author's "disturbing sense that pursuit and capture of the golden girl was not really worth the trouble and heartache," the story transcends that genre.[7] "The Rubber Check," like *The Great Gatsby, Tender Is the Night,* "Winter

---

the Depression: An Artistic Crisis," 121. This essay discusses all the short stories Fitzgerald wrote during the depression, and the impact of the depression on his art.

6. Piper, *Fitzgerald: Critical Portrait,* 85.

7. Donaldson, "Money and Marriage," 82.

Dreams" (1922), "Babylon Revisited" (1931), and other major Fitzgerald works, approaches its subjects with a sophisticated clarity that results in a highly ambiguous and original treatment of familiar material.

The plot is simple: Val Schuyler, a middle-class boy who has pushed his way into the social world of the rich, is embarrassed into picking up the lunch bill for a group of friends of Ellen Mortmain, the beautiful rich girl he has been pursuing for years. He writes a check assuming that his mother will cover the overdraft, and Mr. Templeton, at whose home he has been staying, provides him a reference. His mother refuses to cover it, the check bounces (later she relents and pays it), and the damage to his name and reputation has been done. From that moment on, Val suffers cruel snubs, rejections, and abject humiliation by those at whose social functions he had previously been a welcome attendant. In a few quick plot twists, Val rises socially when he inherits money, falls financial victim to the depression, and ends up on a farm, cultivating Mr. Templeton's cabbages, while contemplating without enthusiasm the prospect of marrying wealthy Mercia Templeton and an assured future, save for the beauty and romantic love he had always craved.

The story spans nine years, including a three-year flashback, taking Val from eighteen to twenty-seven, the years from 1922 to 1931. Like so many other Fitzgerald stories written during this period, the style is spare, but imagistic, without the lavish rhetoric of earlier stories of this type. Indeed, the images carry the weight of the narrative, providing a firm symbolic matrix that reinforces the major themes.

At the outset, the circular pattern of the story is revealed in Val's discussion with his mother about her impending marriage (her fourth) and his memories of his first encounter with the very rich. Val's thoughts are always centered on money; he offers no objections to his mother's marriage, providing the new husband "doesn't get what's left of your money" (417). When his mother informs him that if Val should die during her trip abroad, she will keep his remains in cold storage until she returns—to save the money of an extra trip—Val accepts his being kept "on ice" good-humoredly, but refuses to accept another name change. His name, originally Jones, had, after the second husband, become Schuyler, an aristocratic name that provided him with an identity that could open doors to the world of his dreams. Like Gatsby, the new name emboldens him; as in a tale of fantasy, he walks through a stone gate opening into the Mortmain mansion's "heavenlike lawn with driveways curling on it" (417) and a landscape dotted with a conservatory, tennis courts, a circular ring for ponies, and an empty pool. Even the roses are "proud, lucky" and the dust "aristocratic." Val knows at once, "This is where I belong" (418), and his pursuit begins. Fitzgerald thus links money, identity, death, and romantic illusion at the outset; the rest of the story chronicles the slow erosion of Val's youthful dream. The circularity of the driveway symbolizes the pattern of Val's quest: He ends without achieving the freedom that he assumes money will ensure. He tells Ellen, "I don't want to be owned" (420) without realizing the price he, like so many of Fitzgerald's aspiring young men, are forced to pay.

Val is self-educated in the manners of the rich. He has cultivated his voice and his social skills; perhaps his most important virtue to the Mortmains, he knows his place, accepts his lower social status, and is thus allowed to attend the family throughout "the years of his real education." (419). He has cheerfulness, wit, good manners; "he was invariably correct and dignified, he never drank too much, he had tried to make no enemies, he had been involved in no scandal" (426). Yet his real education has not begun. Val's new identity is linked inseparably with appearance—particularly clothes. Just as Gatsby's shirts symbolize his self-delusory social status, Val's knowledge of clothes indicates his own awareness of social acceptability. Thus, he does not manipulate Ellen's fascination with him, never taking advantage of "the romantic contrast between his shining manners and his shiny suits" (420). Later, however, he succumbs to his own masquerade; indeed, as his clothes improve, he becomes intoxicated with his new identity. Sadly, after the incident of the rubber check has tarred his reputation, he learns that the clothes masked only the emptiness of his own self: "His role took possession of him. He became suddenly a new figure, 'Val Schuyler of New York'" (420).

But what is his identity? Unfortunately, like Gatsby, he never allows himself to admit a self other than the inventions of his romantic imagination.[8] But Val lacks Gatsby's passion and drive; his work (in a

---

8. Ward McAllister is one of Val's models. McAllister (1827–1895) was introduced as a young man to New York society by a relative. Years later he returned to that city and carved

brokerage house) is boring, and his muted passions are spent only on play. Whatever cachet he assumes he has acquired is illusory. The author assures us that "What stamped him as an adventurer was that he just could not make any money" (419). After a season of Mrs. Templeton's gossip has irrevocably branded him a dishonest climber, Val is barred from the "rich and scintillant" (427) world he has grown to love. His clothes can no longer conceal the emptiness at the core of his soul: "No longer did the preview of himself in the mirror—with gloves, opera hat and stick—furnish him his mead of our common vanity. He was a man without a country—and for a crime as vain, casual and innocuous as his look at himself in the glass" (427).

After his inheritance, Val still assumes that perfect attire assures social identity. Fitzgerald now distances himself from Val, perhaps because he has not learned from his painful rejections: "Regard him on a spring morning in London in the year 1930. Tall, even stately, he treads down Pall Mall as if it were his personal pasture. He meets an American friend and shakes hands, and the friend notices how his shirt sleeve fits his wrist, and his coat sleeve incases his shirt sleeve like a sleeve valve; how his collar and tie are molded plastically to his neck" (432). Val's obsession with clothes becomes farcical when, unable to pay his London hotel bill, he dons as many layers of clothing as his body can bear, lurches clumsily out the door and pulls himself, sweating profusely, onto a bus. Ironically, when we last see Val he is wearing work clothes, digging among the cabbages.

For all his education, Val had never really learned the lesson of the very rich: Money is not enough. His background, his social class, would forever bar him from full participation in their world. The rubber check itself proved a convenient symbol of Val's social unacceptability: "The check had been seized upon to give him a questionable reputation that would match his questionable background" (429). The painful rejections after the incident constitute Val's true education. The story is memorable for the searing documentation of those rejections. Fitzgerald's

---

out a position as a leading social lion. It was McAllister who named the best New York families "the Patriarchs" and widened the social hierarchy to include the "Four Hundred," a phrase that achieved more lasting fame than its creator.

recollection of his own pain twelve years earlier undoubtedly translated into Val's, and the reader is caught up in the drama of carefully timed, destructively skillful social snobbery.

Val's first snub occurs, ironically, when he is attired in "full evening dress," cutting such an impressive figure that "sometimes he was able to forget that he really wasn't anybody at all" (425). A debutante dancing partner excuses herself, confessing that her mother did not want her to dance with Val. Another similar snub leads him to confront Mercia Templeton who he knows does not like him (she seems to see through his facade whenever they meet). Unable to elicit an explanation from her, he confronts her mother, who he suspects had spread ugly gossip about his rubber check some months earlier. Feeling "helpless rage" as he looks at the "calm dowagers" (426) on the balcony, he tells Mrs. Templeton how unfair it is to hold against him what college boys do all the time. She brushes him off, and he continues to attend similar parties. But the unfortunate incident does not go away, and Val continues to meet suspicion and mistrust in his social forays.

When Ellen Mortmain, back from Europe, asks him to accompany her to a weekend party at the Halbirds', Val accepts, and learns thoroughly and painfully that *they* will never forget. Here Fitzgerald uses clothing as a metaphor for rejection. When Val enters a room, "the conversation faded off . . . giving him the impression of continually shaking hands with a glove from which the hand had been withdrawn" (428). For Mrs. Halbird's "soft brutality," Fitzgerald again invokes the glove: "there was a rough nap on the velvet gloves with which she prepared to handle Val" (429). After a series of probing questions about his background, she suggests that Val is too old (at twenty-three) for these parties and that he associate with people who are in the working world. This, his most searing lesson, and the continued rejections now pierce his "protective shell." His anxieties are reflected in a dream, where "many fashionable men and women sat at a heaped table and offered him champagne, but the glass was always withdrawn before it reached his lips" (430).

Finally, Val is forced to face the reality of his social existence when he overhears some of the Halbirds' young guests discussing him. He learns that, indeed, he is regarded by their parents as an adventurer, that Mrs. Templeton has used him as "part of her New York conversation" (430), that Mercia's defense of him is unavailing, and, perhaps most hurtful, that rich boys leave rubber checks all over New York without exacting any social penalty. Val leaves the Halbirds' quietly, at night, and in another circular driveway, sees Ellen Mortmain emerge from a car where he glimpses "a small, satisfied mustache above a lighting cigarette" (431). The gates of paradise are firmly closed to him. But Val's education in the anguish of social snobbery is not complete; believing that money is the social leveler, after he gains his inheritance (ironically, it is his mother, not he, who dies, and he does become the beneficiary), he abandons those who had rejected him and becomes a man of the world. He knows that "his apprenticeship had been hard, but he had served it faithfully, and now he walked sure-footed through the dangerous labyrinths of snobbery" (431).

No longer a victim, and just as mistaken about his status and identity as in the past, Val dabbles as an art dealer while continuing his self-education: "His drift was toward the sophisticated section of society, and he picked up some knowledge of the arts, which he blended grace-fully with his social education" (431). It is at this point that the story falters, for Fitzgerald's identification with Val, so strong when he was an innocent victim, now weakens as Val becomes a snobbish arriviste, thus giving some weight to the opinions of his detractors. I have noted elsewhere that a weakness in Fitzgerald's stories "is related to point of view and distance, particularly in relation to the protagonists. Fitzgerald is most successful when his central character is both a participant and an observer of the action, weakest when the protagonist is simply a member of the upper class or an outsider."[9] At the same time, Fitzgerald resorts to a mechanical plot trick, the too-neat reversal, as the financial tides of the depression sweep away Val's small inheritance, and he once again faces the specter of poverty.

In this story of a social climber, romantic love is a casualty of changing fortunes, as it is so often in Fitzgerald's fiction. As Scott Donaldson notes, "As he grew older, he could no longer care very much whether his young man won the golden girl."[10] In "The Rubber Check," although Val's pursuit of Ellen Mortmain is one of the narrative strands, it is subsidiary

9. Ruth Prigozy, "F. Scott Fitzgerald," 107.
10. Donaldson, "Money and Marriage," 81.

to the protagonist's search for self-definition in the cold fortress of the very rich.

Although Ellen Mortmain is the obvious symbol of his youthful dreams, Fitzgerald does not invest her with the same magnetism characteristic of such other femmes fatales as Judy Jones ("Winter Dreams"), Edith Braden ("May Day" [1920]), or Jonquil Cary (" 'The Sensible Thing' " [1924]); singularly absent is the charged romantic rhetoric that customarily accompanied descriptions of the protagonist's love interest. Instead, Fitzgerald uses striking, almost parodistic images that seem to mock as well as describe Ellen: "The face of young Ellen Mortmain regarded him with the contagious enthusiasm that later launched a famous cold cream. Her childish beauty was wistful and sad about being so rich and sixteen" (418). We are never certain, as we are in other Fitzgerald stories, that Val really desires the young woman of his dreams; their brief romance seems more an accident of propinquity than genuine love. Val's role in Ellen's world had led inevitably to his being cast as suitor, indeed as a well-regarded suitor. Living that role intensely, "suddenly he really was in love with her" (420). Val's narcissistic appreciation of his own performance and his love for Ellen are inextricably connected. As his identity gradually melts away during the incident of the rubber check, so too does his love: "He felt a sudden indifference toward her" (423) as he tries to salvage his reputation. After the incident has been resolved, "in his relief at being spared the more immediate agony, he hardly realized that he had lost her" (425).

Years later, he has come to London to see Ellen or "attempt to recapture something in his past" (432). She is engaged to someone else, like herself impoverished by the depression, but the rubber check still darkens Val's name and clouds his identity. Ellen asks (reminiscent of Tom Buchanan's words to Gatsby at the Plaza Hotel), "Who are you, Val? I mean, aren't you a sort of a questionable character? Didn't you cheat a lot of people out of a whole lot of money with a forged check or something?" Realizing that he has lost her, he feels only "a sentimental regret"; the stronger sensation is the sense that his own identity has been eroded by the Mortmain's bankruptcy, that "all around her he could feel the vast Mortmain fortune melting down, seeping back into the matrix whence it had come, and taking with it a little of Val Schuyler" (433). Money, whether his mother's or Ellen's, is indissolubly linked with love;

yet paradoxically, for Fitzgerald, money is inevitably the barrier between lovers, and, as Donaldson notes, "too much money militates against true love."[11] In this story, Fitzgerald questions the nature of love and the possibility of authentic feeling in a society so thick with social striations, but he leaves the matter unresolved.

As in so many of Fitzgerald's later stories, the protagonist lacks passion and vitality. Val's passivity (indeed his good manners) fails to ignite the tension normally inherent in the quest for the romantic dream. The authenticity of romantic love in the story is further clouded by the intermittent presence of Mercia Templeton, who is not conventionally beautiful, but is intelligent, perceptive, and, as we later discover, deeply in love with Val. Val's cynicism at the end—he will marry Mercia for her money—is ambiguous. Mercia is clearly superior to Ellen and has no illusions about Val, who at last has no illusions about himself. He clearly finds her attractive, if too aggressive, but he will marry her. It is unclear whether his sadness at the end is for the loss of his illusions, for being forced by need to marry a woman he doesn't love, for the loss of his self-image, or most likely, for the loss of what had always been the object of his strivings: "His precious freedom—not to be owned" (436). The casualty in "The Rubber Check" is romantic love as it is associated with youthful illusion, but money—and a lot of it—is the undeniable necessity for life.

At the end, Val is "sophisticated . . . he had that, at least, from his expensive education" (436). His most valuable lesson is that, for him, there was never a remedy; money alone could never have won him the freedom he craved. Fitzgerald, writing in the depths of the depression, understood that the kind of freedom Val seeks is given at birth: "He knew in his sadness that the only way he could have gotten what he really wanted was to have been born to it" (436). "Not to be owned" assumes an assured selfhood, an unsought entitlement that those born into great wealth accept as their privilege. Fitzgerald weaves the depression itself into this fable of lost illusions. When Ellen Mortmain loses her fortune, she is not impoverished. Wrapped in the calm security of her class, "she had survived the passing of her wealth; the warm rich current of

---

11. Ibid., 85.

well-being still flowed from her" (433). Like Gatsby, Val has become the victim of his own illusions. No amount of money can purchase the automatic self-assurance of those born into great wealth and social status. Thus his sadness at the end may be less at having to marry a girl he does not love than at knowing that for him, genuine freedom had been lost before his quest had ever begun.

"The Rubber Check," although reminiscent of other Fitzgerald stories and novels, is memorable as a mature exploration of the meaning of money, social class, and the romantic illusions of an aspiring young man. It is particularly notable for its style, for what Jay McInerney describes as "the conversational intimacy of his narrative voice," and for the complexity of its ideas.[12] Because Fitzgerald relies upon the brief but sharp image rather than extended rhetoric, because so much is suggested rather than delineated, because the structure so clearly reveals the underlying thematic pattern, "The Rubber Check" takes on the quality of a fable, tracing an archetypal American struggle for success. Val's circular journey takes him from rags to riches to rags, with the possibility of new riches waiting. But the roses at the beginning of the tale have metamorphosed into the cabbages at the end; regardless of what Val achieves in the future, the final image of this once-elegant social climber cultivating a rich man's garden is Fitzgerald's wry commentary on the American myth of success. As in several other stories of this period, Fitzgerald takes a mature, backward look at the subjects of his youthful fictional successes. The results were often stale and contrived, but here the author's reassessment of many familiar subjects results in a subtle, artistically rich work.[13]

Why is this an underrated, neglected story? Undoubtedly the central flaw is the character of Val and Fitzgerald's inability to maintain a consistent distance from him. Unfortunately, Mercia's reproach that Val seems superficial is close to the mark, as Fitzgerald's sharp narrative

12. Jay McInerney, "Fitzgerald Revisited," 23. McInerney notes that, unlike the modernist works of his contemporaries, "Fitzgerald's third-person narratives always sound as if they are verging into the first person, as indeed they sometimes do. . . . F. Scott Fitzgerald never disappeared from his stories. They were entirely personal, intimate, and confidential."
13. "Indecision" (1931) and "A Change of Class" (1931) are two of these less than successful stories.

stroke indicates: "Actually he cared deeply about things, but the things he cared about were generally considered trivial" (422). But if Val is superficial, why do we feel so keenly the rebuffs and rebukes directed at him? Fitzgerald, as I have elsewhere suggested, was unable to find the narrative stance from which to observe Val Schuyler, and, as a result, the reader is left in doubt as to the seriousness of his search.[14] That the issues Fitzgerald raises are important, that he treats them with sophisticated assurance, is never in question. But the characterization of Val is so thin throughout that, although the story should be read as a fable, it needs a more consistent figure to carry the weight of meaning Fitzgerald attaches to his protagonist.

Admirers of Fitzgerald should not, however, overlook "The Rubber Check." Fitzgerald's writing, in the new, sparer style he was cultivating in his later years, is close to the level of his more celebrated depression-era stories such as "Crazy Sunday" and "Babylon Revisited." His treatment of romantic love and illusion, identity, caste and class, and the dream of success is as complex as in many of his past works. It illuminates *This Side of Paradise, The Great Gatsby,* the early stories, and his own uncertainties during the depression. "The Rubber Check," finally, is quintessential Fitzgerald. In the story of his life and his art, it deserves if not a chapter, then at least a secure place of its own.

14. Prigozy, "Fitzgerald's Short Stories and the Depression," 120–21.

"WHAT A HANDSOME PAIR!"
AND THE INSTITUTION OF MARRIAGE

JAMES L. W. WEST III

F. Scott Fitzgerald wrote "What a Handsome Pair!" in April 1932, not long after he and his family had moved into La Paix, the large Victorian house on the Turnbull estate near Baltimore in which they would live until December 1933. Fitzgerald was gathering himself for an extended effort to finish *Tender Is the Night*; "What a Handsome Pair!" was one of three stories he produced that spring in order to earn money with which to finance a stretch of uninterrupted work on the novel. The story was written during a difficult period in the Fitzgeralds' marriage. They were in the midst of a complex dispute over Zelda Fitzgerald's novel *Save Me the Waltz*—specifically over her use of the common material of their lives in her book. Fitzgerald was also beginning to realize that his wife would never be entirely well or whole again and that their marriage had probably been irreparably damaged by internal competitiveness.

"What a Handsome Pair!" was published that summer in the *Saturday Evening Post* (in the issue for August 27), but Fitzgerald did not include it in *Taps at Reveille*, his last short story collection, published by Scribner's in the spring of 1935. The story lay uncollected until 1973, when it was reprinted in *Bits of Paradise*. Virtually no criticism has been written about it; one finds the odd paragraph here and there, but no one has done much more than note the obvious autobiographical elements in the narrative.[1] "What a Handsome Pair!" is not one of Fitzgerald's very best stories, but it is still of considerable interest, partly because it anticipates certain characters and themes in *Tender Is the Night* and partly because it presents a thoughtful meditation on the institution of marriage.

The narrative is conventional in form and language. It is related by an omniscient voice that does not intrude or editorialize; the reader has access, from time to time, to the thinking of all the major characters, but there is no real attempt to probe for motives or to analyze behavior. Characterization is instead created by action and dialogue. The story is episodic in structure, beginning in the spring of 1902 and ending in the fall of 1915, with a brief glimpse forward to 1918. Fitzgerald presents a series of scenes from a marriage and is careful to let us know, in each new scene, just where we are situated in time and what has happened to the characters since we last saw them.

"What a Handsome Pair!" is the story of Stuart and Helen Oldhorne, a good-looking, beautifully matched couple who begin their married life with much optimism and a good deal of physical and financial capital, but who, through a combination of bad luck and mutual competitiveness, see their relationship deteriorate and eventually fail. At the beginning of the story, Helen is engaged to her cousin, Teddy Van Beck, a talented young pianist and composer. Helen realizes, though, that she and Teddy have little in common. He is devoted to his piano, but she has a tin ear and middlebrow tastes in music. She prefers riding and outdoor sports, but he is terrified of horses and is uncomfortable outside his studio. While engaged to Teddy, Helen meets and falls in love with Stuart Oldhorne, a handsome young bachelor whose looks and interests suit her perfectly. "He had been a star athlete at Yale and a Rough Rider in Cuba," we learn, "and was the best young horseman on Long Island."[2]

---

1. John A. Higgins, *F. Scott Fitzgerald: A Study of the Stories,* 154; Kenneth Eble, *F. Scott Fitzgerald,* 121; Matthew J. Bruccoli, *Some Sort of Epic Grandeur: The Life of F. Scott Fitzgerald,* 330–31; Ruth Prigozy, "Fitzgerald's Short Stories and the Depression: An Artistic Crisis," 115.

2. F. Scott Fitzgerald and Zelda Fitzgerald, *Bits of Paradise: 21 Uncollected Stories by F. Scott and Zelda Fitzgerald,* 343. All subsequent page references to "What a Handsome Pair!" are to this edition and will appear parenthetically in the text.

Helen breaks her engagement with Teddy in the spring of 1902 and marries Stuart in the late summer of 1903. Teddy is greatly hurt by Helen's defection but takes care not to show it; he marries on the rebound, even before Helen and Stuart are wed, choosing as his wife a woman as different from Helen in looks and social class as he can find. She is an Irish waitress named Betty, rather older than he; her face is plain and her accent plebeian, but her devotion is certain. Teddy remains a peripheral figure in Helen's life, and we sense that he uses her (or, rather, his idealized image of her) as an inspiration for much of the music he writes over the next decade.

The Oldhorne marriage flourishes during its first few years. Stuart and Helen are an athletic version of the Fitzgeralds, moving in fashionable circles where they are much admired. Often they compete in polo, golf, and tennis matches. "They liked to feel fit and cool together," the narrator tells us. "They thought of themselves as a team, and it was often remarked how well mated they were" (345). Both are from families of moderate wealth and can live initially on their investments, but Stuart makes a mistake on the stock market during the Panic of 1907 and is left insolvent. Thereafter the couple gets by on Helen's income and on what Stuart can bring in by working, first as a manager of a horse-racing operation and later as a golf teacher and professional. Fitzgerald has deliberately introduced adversity into their nearly perfect lives. They are wonderfully gifted and beautifully matched, but they have not yet had to confront much in the way of deprivation or frustration. How well (Fitzgerald seems to ask) will their marriage stand these strains?

Helen continues to compete in her various sports as an amateur but is not satisfied with that role. Fitzgerald presents her as a protofeminist, not much interested in rearing her children and irritated by the attitudes of her class toward women who engage in athletics. She reaches a peak of frustration during a women's polo match in which one member of her team is almost forced to ride sidesaddle because her husband will not have her seen in public wearing breeches. When Helen and her fellow competitors are chased off the polo field so that the men can begin their match on time, she explodes in anger to Stuart: "How can women ever expect to be any good if they have to quit every time the men want the field? All the men want is for the women to come up to them in the evening and tell them what a beautiful game they played!" (350). Stuart, in the meantime, has his own frustrations. His need for employment has forced him to associate with men of new money who are crass and condescending. Helen wins the trophies now, while Stuart must spend his time giving golf lessons to rich dubs.

The Oldhornes eventually become "visiting people"—professional guests who move from estate to estate, living rent-free in cottages on the grounds and giving instruction in tennis and golf to their wealthy benefactors. Living on the margins of upper-class Long Island society puts new strains on their relationship. One of Stuart's duties, for example, is to pay attention to the pampered wives of wealthy men, and this angers Helen. "My gallantry is simply a matter of business," he explains to her. "Lessons have brought in three hundred a month all summer" (357). Helen is also vulnerable in this way, and Stuart is keenly jealous: "He was aware, too, that there was always some man in their life now—some man of power and money who paid court to Helen and gave her the sense of solidity which he failed to provide" (357). Fitzgerald does not say so (the story was appearing in the *Post*, after all), but the Oldhornes are moving in a fast, monied set, and there must be a good deal of casual infidelity in evidence. It is in this atmosphere that their marriage must survive.

Weary with this style of living and motivated, one senses, by an irrational desire to hurt her husband, Helen begins to see Teddy Van Beck, who has drifted back into her life. Teddy has been enormously successful with his music. Famous now, he gives concerts at Carnegie Hall and has become petted and lionized. He has also become a philanderer, but Betty, to whom he is still married, does not scold him. She is presented to us as a creature of considerable humor and folk wisdom: "So long as he doesn't take too much to drink and knows where his home is," she explains, "I don't bother about where he wanders" (353). She provides Teddy with what he needs as an artist—a stable home life against which to rebel and a forgiving, maternal figure to whom he can return. The marriage of these two, while hardly conventional or ideal, is at least productive. Betty has borne a child, for whom she cares attentively—in contrast to Helen, whose children attend boarding schools during the year and are farmed out to grandparents during summers and vacations. And Teddy has composed wonderful music, for which he is famous—in contrast to

Stuart, who has created nothing. All that the Oldhornes really have to show for their years together is a collection of loving cups, which they display (ironically enough) in a trophy case that the prescient Teddy gave them as a wedding gift.

Helen's flirtation with Teddy fizzles out. "She loves her husband," Teddy explains in chastened tones to the patient Betty. "She follows me a certain distance just like she always has, and then—" (355). We sense, though, that Teddy is secretly glad to avoid an affair with Helen. It is really her image that fascinates him, not her actual self; he knows that physical intimacy with her would probably destroy an essential source of his creativity. Indeed, for all his weakness in character Teddy is presented to us as a consummate professional, aware of the sources of his inspiration, able to shut out the distractions of his personal life, and ruthless about translating his pain into art. Music is both his vocation and his refuge; in this way he enjoys an advantage over a man like Stuart, who must express himself in physical action.

World War I begins in 1914, however, and offers a reprieve to Stuart. "He was a warrior; for him, peace was only the interval between wars," the narrator explains. "Here was the game of games beckoning him"— a chance to recapture his identity and manhood on the field of battle (359). It is therefore a great disappointment to Stuart when he is rejected by the Royal Canadian Air Force because of an old eye injury that (again ironically) he received from a brassie swung by an inept golf pupil. Helen, as it turns out, is the one who manages to go to the war. She organizes a Red Cross unit from among her women friends and sails to Europe in the autumn of 1915, leaving Stuart behind on the dock, confused and abandoned:

> For the first time in twelve years he was alone, and the feeling came over him that he was alone for good; knowing Helen and knowing war, he could guess at the experiences she would go through, and he could not form any picture of a renewed life together afterward. He was discarded; she had proved the stronger at last. It seemed very strange and sad that his marriage should have such an ending. (360)

This should also be the end of Stuart's life; like Dick Diver he should enter a period of decline, perhaps living out his years as a drifter on the edges of Long Island society. But "What a Handsome Pair!" was a work of popular fiction, written for the *Saturday Evening Post,* and Fitzgerald could not permit such a bleak conclusion. He therefore rescued Stuart with two sentences near the end of the story that gave the reader a quick glimpse into the future. Stuart, we learn, fights in the war after all, apparently in the American forces: "He could not know that his life was not destined to be a failure. He could not read the fine story that three years later would be carved proud above his soldier's grave, or know that his restless body, which never spared itself in sport or danger, was destined to give him one last proud gallop at the end" (362). This hinted-at rescue through a gallant battlefield death, though plausible, is not especially convincing. It reads like an afterthought, something added to make the story a little more palatable. Fitzgerald does not make his readers face up to the true implications of this narrative: that Stuart is drained and defeated beyond hope of recovery and that Helen has emerged the victor. Stuart's real end, we sense, comes as he watches her ship pull away from the pier in New York, leaving him alone and in contemplation of his failed life.

It is worthwhile to speculate a little about who might have stood as models for the characters in "What a Handsome Pair!" Two names come to mind: Theodore Chanler and Tommy Hitchcock. Chanler was a talented American pianist and composer with whom Fitzgerald became friendly during the late 1920s in Europe. Fitzgerald was introduced to him by Gerald and Sara Murphy, who had taken Chanler into their circle. Born in 1902 and thus a little younger than Fitzgerald, Chanler was a member of a prominent New England family. As a youth he had showed much talent in music, both as a performer and as a composer, and had studied in America with Hans Ebell, Arthur Shepherd, and Percy Goetschius. He continued his training in England and France and produced some promising work in 1919 and 1920. His specialty, then and later, was setting poetry to music; two of his best early songs were set to poems by William Blake and Archibald MacLeish. During the period in which Fitzgerald knew him, Chanler was still largely unknown and was writing very little. Eventually, in the late 1930s, he would gain much notice for a cycle of songs for voice and piano titled *Eight Epitaphs,* which were based on poems by Walter de la Mare. Later Chanler wrote highly praised music for children's voices; he also produced the score for a George Balanchine ballet and wrote a chamber opera based on one of the Grimms' fairy tales.[3]

Chanler provided Fitzgerald with an approximate starting point in *Tender Is the Night* for Abe North, a composer of youthful promise who has become blocked and is wasting himself with alcohol and other dissipations. Chanler, however, was unlike Abe in that he managed to cut loose from the idle expatriate crowd. Chanler went so far as openly to break with the Murphys over what he felt was their aimless self-indulgence, and he returned to the United States where he married in 1931 and began to produce the work that would earn him a substantial reputation before he died in 1961. Abe, in the novel, tries to change his ways but is unsuccessful. Like Chanler he returns to the United States with the intention of resurrecting his career, but he fails and eventually is beaten to death outside a speakeasy in New York.

It is impossible to say how much Fitzgerald knew or could intuit about Theodore Chanler in April 1932, when he was writing "What a Handsome Pair!" The points of correspondence between Chanler and Teddy Van Beck, though, are close enough to be intriguing and suggest some links between and among Abe North, Ring Lardner, Teddy Van Beck, Theodore Chanler, and Fitzgerald himself, who, like Dick Diver, feared that his early promise was not being fulfilled—a major theme in *Tender Is the Night*.

Similar connections can be drawn between Tommy Hitchcock and Stuart Oldhorne. Hitchcock, born into a well-to-do northeastern family, entered World War I early, while still a teenager, and flew for the Lafayette Escadrille, shooting down two Boche aircraft before being downed and captured himself. He managed to escape from a guard during a train trip from one prison to another; he then made his way to Switzerland and eventually to Paris, where he was hailed as a hero. After the war he attended Harvard, became an investor in New York, and made himself into the best American polo player of his generation. These details are mirrored in Stuart Oldhorne, who rode with the Rough Riders,

3. For information about Chanler's career, see David Ewen, *American Composers: A Biographical Dictionary;* David Mason Greene, *Greene's Biographical Encyclopedia of Composers;* and Robert Tageman, "The Songs of Theodore Chanler."

worked on Wall Street, was an excellent horseman, and played top-level polo.[4]

Fitzgerald met Hitchcock on Long Island in the early 1920s and was intrigued enough by him to base two of his best-known characters on him. Scholars and biographers have frequently pointed to Hitchcock as the model for Tom Buchanan in *The Great Gatsby* and for Tommy Barban in *Tender Is the Night*. The connections are certainly valid. Like both of Fitzgerald's characters, Hitchcock was an uncomplicated man of action and a focused competitor. Fitzgerald, however, must have seen another side to Hitchcock, a side reflected in Stuart Oldhorne, who is gentle, kind, and thoughtful. Here, as with Theodore Chanler, Fitzgerald took Hitchcock as a beginning point for a character but added much else to the portrayal. Specifically he added the internal struggles from his own marriage and the necessity for a man to become a professional so that his wife can enjoy the freedoms of an amateur.

The point of these speculations is that Teddy Van Beck and Stuart Oldhorne in "What a Handsome Pair!" belong to a group of characters from Fitzgerald's short stories who stand in a line of progression leading to *Tender Is the Night*. The line includes Jacob Booth of "Jacob's Ladder" (1927), Adrian Smith of "The Rough Crossing" (1929), Henry Marston of "The Swimmers" (1929), Bill McChesney of "Two Wrongs" (1930), Charlie Wales of "Babylon Revisited" (1931), and Joel Coles of "Crazy Sunday" (1932). All these men (and others in different stories) are trial sketches for major characters in *Tender Is the Night*. Bits of all of them can be found in the novel. In the case of "What a Handsome Pair!" the two male leads were broken up and redistributed. Parts of Teddy Van Beck are present in Abe North; parts of Stuart Oldhorne can be identified in Tommy Barban; parts of both, mixed with much of Fitzgerald himself, can be discerned in Dick Diver. One can also see Helen Oldhorne as a preliminary study for both Nicole Diver and Rosemary Hoyt.

"What a Handsome Pair!" can be read as an exercise in autobiographical musing. Like Stuart and Helen, F. Scott and Zelda Fitzgerald began their marriage as a glamorous team but saw their partnership

---

4. For a good biography of Hitchcock, see Nelson W. Aldrich Jr., *Tommy Hitchcock: An American Hero.*

damaged badly by competitiveness. Like the Oldhornes, the Fitzgeralds were injured by "the conflict that had grown out of their wanting the same excellences, the same prizes from life" (358). The man, in each case, has had to be a professional so that the woman could develop herself as an amateur. One thinks here of Fitzgerald's support of his wife's efforts to become successful in the ballet and in other art forms. The man then resents it when the woman begins to compete with him, as Zelda Fitzgerald was doing by writing *Save Me the Waltz*. "Just try to remember I'm your best friend," Stuart reminds Helen near the end of the story. "Sometimes you act as if we were rivals" (358).

Stuart, in fact, supports Helen's move toward independence, though he must realize subconsciously that he will be discarded when she is ready to strike out on her own. This sacrifice of self seems to be related to a guilt-ridden desire that Fitzgerald himself harbored during this period of his life, a curious wish that his wife might somehow draw sanity and wholeness from him, leaving him empty but morally redeemed—a theme that one also finds in two stories from a little earlier in Fitzgerald's career, "Jacob's Ladder" and "Two Wrongs."[5] One sees this theme portrayed quite powerfully in *Tender Is the Night* in Dick's psychological suckling of Nicole until her health is restored and she is strong enough to cast him off.

There is more than a little authorial bitterness running through "What a Handsome Pair!" Helen, like Nicole Diver and like Zelda Fitzgerald (earlier in the marriage), possesses an essential selfishness that allows her to be coldhearted about draining her husband so that she can develop herself as she wishes. But this bitterness, as always in Fitzgerald's work, is balanced by an admiration for anyone clearheaded enough to put emotion aside and pursue self-interest as an end in itself. Marriage is an alliance, to be sure, but it is also a competition—however veiled that aspect might be to outside eyes. The winner is always the one who has seized the greater share of the resources, the energy and momentum of the marriage, and used them for his or her own purposes.

---

5. "Jacob's Ladder" appeared first in the *Post* in August 1927; "Two Wrongs" was published there in January 1930. The first story was collected in *Bits of Paradise*, the second in *Taps at Reveille.*

"What a Handsome Pair!" can in fact be read as a meditation on marriage. Fitzgerald presents us with a series of questions about the institution: Should one marry a partner of the same tastes and talents? Must husbands and wives have similar social backgrounds? Should an artist marry the woman of his dreams? Is infidelity always destructive to a relationship? Must one partner in a marriage necessarily be subordinate to the other? Must one partner become a professional if the other is to shine as an amateur? Can a marriage endure intense internal competitiveness?

Fitzgerald does not attempt to answer these questions. Instead he poses them as a series of implied dialectics, no one of which is finally resolved. Perhaps men and women of similar tastes and talents should marry— that is certainly the conventional wisdom—but if they do, they will have to learn strategies for avoiding the kinds of internal argument and competitiveness that can destroy a marriage. Stuart and Helen do not develop such strategies; thus they find themselves still very much in love but watching in dismay as the forces of internal competition pull them farther and farther apart.

Should husbands and wives have similar social backgrounds? Perhaps so, but the matrimonial alliance of the aristocrat Teddy Van Beck and his Irish Betty is the strongest in the story. Like the Oldhornes, they have competed within their marriage, but owing to their different social roots they have pursued different prizes and have both been able to win. Betty wants home and security and the means to raise her child well; to have these things she is willing to excuse Teddy's infidelities. Teddy, for his part, requires time and solitude in which to create his music, and he needs the adoration of an audience. To have these necessities he is willing to tolerate Betty's plainness, her inappropriate behavior at restaurants and parties, and her lack of interest in his music. These two have struck a bargain, probably unconsciously, which ensures the longevity of their marriage and the ultimate achievement of their separate goals.

It would be a mistake, however, to assume that Fitzgerald wanted this kind of marriage for himself. He might have thought wistfully from time to time of having a dowdy wife who would look after the home fires while he won the applause of admirers, but he must have known on a deeper level that the eccentric, talented, and unconventionally beautiful woman whom he had married had been the source for much of his fiction and that without her he might never have achieved much beyond the youthful promise he showed in *This Side of Paradise*. Unlike Teddy Van Beck, Fitzgerald *had* married the woman of his dreams, and he had had a marvelous run with her during the early years of their marriage. Now, however, he was watching her weaken and disintegrate—partly as a result of her erratic nature but partly as a consequence of his own bad judgment. Teddy Van Beck, we sense, will never face such a dilemma.

Fitzgerald's view of marriage in "What a Handsome Pair!" is bleak, but one must read the story attentively and probe beneath its surface to see the pessimism. This was a story written for the *Post,* after all, and Fitzgerald knew that he could not question the institution of marriage too openly in the pages of that magazine. There is some suggestion toward the end of the narrative that Europeans—especially the British—have more sophisticated attitudes toward the internal politics of marriage than do Americans, but Fitzgerald does not develop that line of thought. If he had pursued it, he might have said that marriage ought to be more a pragmatic alliance or working partnership than a love duet. Yet Fitzgerald, in the spring of 1932, probably still believed a little in the ideals of romantic love and hoped somehow to salvage a portion of the magic that his marriage had once held.

Fitzgerald seems to suggest in the story that the Van Beck marriage is more sensible and healthy than the Oldhorne marriage, but it is hard to believe that he saw much liveliness or promise in the Van Beck alliance. Although outwardly placid, it is dull; it endures, but probably in the long run Betty's tolerance will not be good for Teddy because it will encourage his self-indulgence and vanity. The Oldhorne marriage is the one that should have blossomed and flourished, but the pressures of society, money, and competitiveness have destroyed it, and Fitzgerald seems to believe that this outcome was inevitable. Certainly he does not appear to be sanguine about marriage as an institution; neither union in this story is entirely satisfactory, and both are finally limiting and harmful to the men and women involved in them.

"What a Handsome Pair!" also shows us Fitzgerald in the role of social historian. The story is told retrospectively, with its action carefully arranged to reach a climax during the early part of World War I, the event that would change the game so thoroughly for people of Fitzgerald's generation. Helen's athleticism and independence are advanced for her time; she will be much more at home in the postwar world than she was in prewar society. Stuart's redemption, by contrast, can only be accomplished by a tried-and-true nineteenth-century plot device—a hero's death on the field of honor. It is better, one feels, that Stuart does not live past 1918.

The clearest element in the story is Fitzgerald's admiration for Teddy Van Beck's professionalism. Teddy is an artist very much in Fitzgerald's mold. He is a skilled craftsman who writes for a sophisticated audience, but he also infuses his work with great emotion and personal feeling, taking dangerous chances as he walks the tightrope between artistic respectability and popular appeal. Teddy's capacity and willingness to create beauty from his own unhappiness separate him from the crowd and protect him in the end from the upheavals of love and war. At work in his studio, he is insulated and safe.

One scene, early in the story, makes this clear. The scene occurs on a bright Sunday morning early in September 1903, when Helen drops by Teddy's apartment to tell him about the plans for her wedding to Stuart. This is a difficult moment for Teddy: Helen has just met his dumpy Irish wife, whom she has mistaken for the cleaning woman. Obviously Helen is happy herself and is keenly anticipating her upcoming marriage and the consummation that will come during her honeymoon. When she asks Teddy whether he is happy too, he gives a revealing answer: "Sure, I'm happy," he says. "I'm working" (346). After she leaves he turns immediately to his music:

> He sat at the piano, a pencil behind his ear. Already his face was resolved, composed, but his eyes grew more intense minute by minute, until there was a glaze in them, behind which they seemed to have joined his ears in counting and hearing. Presently there was no more indication in his face that anything had occurred to disturb the tranquillity of his Sunday morning. (347–48)

Fitzgerald knew about this kind of creative detachment; he was practicing it, in fact, while writing "What a Handsome Pair!" He was taking an immediate, hurtful experience—his and his wife's disagreement over who had the rights to fictionalize their marriage—and transforming it into a saleable short story. In doing so he was distancing himself from his immediate personal pain and from his ambivalence over his treatment of his wife, who was ill. Fitzgerald knew that he would require even more of this kind of artistic detachment for the job that faced him in the months to come. He would need to take the brilliant beginnings of a novel, reimagine them, and draw heavily on his and his wife's recent personal tragedies for the emotional underpinnings of his novel. Then he would have to objectify those emotions and write the book that would rescue his career and make him famous again. It was not Teddy Van Beck's Griselda-like wife whom he wanted. Instead it was Teddy's cool artistic vision—his ability to shut out the world, draw on his past, and create—that Fitzgerald needed for the task that lay ahead.

BETTE WEAVER, R.N.: "HER LAST CASE"

GEORGE MONTEIRO

From May through August 1934 Fitzgerald wrote "No Flowers," "New Types," and "Her Last Case." The three stories were bought by the *Saturday Evening Post* for three thousand dollars each, though the *Post* warned Fitzgerald's agent, Harold Ober, that "these stories were not what was expected from F. Scott Fitzgerald."[1]

"Her Last Case" appeared in the *Post* on November 3, 1934. The story was not reprinted during its author's lifetime, even though Fitzgerald once thought he might include it in *Taps at Reveille*. At the last moment he dropped it in favor of "The Fiend" (1935) and "The Night of Chancellorsville" (1935). "Fitzgerald was attempting to expand his market and increase his artistic options, including the option of writing brief, experimental pieces," explains Alice Hall Petry, and the substitution of these stories "in lieu of 'Her Last Case' reflects this." Excluded from the last of the collections put together during its author's lifetime, "Her Last Case" did not surface again until 1979 when it was reprinted in *The Price Was High*.[2]

---

1. Matthew J. Bruccoli, *Some Sort of Epic Grandeur: The Life of F. Scott Fitzgerald,* 389.

2. Alice Hall Petry, *Fitzgerald's Craft of Short Fiction: The Collected Stories—1920–1935,* 149. Notably, Fitzgerald did not intend to scrap "Her Last Case" entirely (as he did some other stories). See Fitzgerald's letter to his editor Maxwell Perkins dated March 26, 1935, in which he chooses among his stories those that he will admit to a new collection and ones that might be published "only in case" of the author's "sudden death" (Matthew J.

For the most part, only Fitzgerald's biographers show interest in "Her Last Case," and then not much. Arthur Mizener sees it as the result of a "love affair" that eventually gave him a setting and some feeling about this very tentative relation, while Scott Donaldson treats the notion of an "affair" gingerly even as he identifies the locale of the story. Matthew J. Bruccoli calls it simply "a *Post* story about alcoholism," set at Welbourne, the home of Elizabeth Lemmon, a close friend of Maxwell Perkins, Fitzgerald's editor at Scribner's.[3]

Critics have been largely silent on "Her Last Case." Bryant Mangum calls it the "most successful" of Fitzgerald's "four stories about young people in the medical profession" that he published in the *Saturday Evening Post,* but he devotes only two short paragraphs to it. In what might well be the longest published commentary on the story (twenty-three lines), John A. Higgins admits that the "story holds together better than any since 'Crazy Sunday,' " but he complains that Fitzgerald mars it by making a "fatal last-minute switch to the happy ending." Kenneth Eble makes a brief passing reference in his book about Fitzgerald to "Her Last Case," and in a later essay finds it "contrived" though "full of hints about Fitzgerald's feelings toward his past and present condition."[4]

Fitzgerald's own explanation of why he dropped "Her Last Case" from *Taps at Reveille* is instructive. He claimed that in rereading a Thomas Wolfe story he was turned against his own work, writing to Perkins:

> The real thing that decided me about "Her Last Case" was that it was a *place* story and just before seeing it in *published form* I ran across Thomas Wolfe's "The House of the Far and Lost" and I thought there

---

Bruccoli and Margaret M. Duggan, eds., *Correspondence of F. Scott Fitzgerald,* 406–7). Matthew J. Bruccoli, ed., *The Price Was High: The Last Uncollected Stories of F. Scott Fitzgerald.* All subsequent page references to "Her Last Case" are to this edition and will appear parenthetically in the text.

3. Arthur Mizener, *The Far Side of Paradise: A Biography of F. Scott Fitzgerald,* 253; Scott Donaldson, *Fool for Love: F. Scott Fitzgerald,* 127–28; Bruccoli, *Epic Grandeur,* 393.

4. Bryant Mangum, *A Fortune Yet: Money in the Art of F. Scott Fitzgerald's Short Stories,* 134–35; John A. Higgins, *F. Scott Fitzgerald: A Study of the Stories,* 159; Kenneth Eble, *F. Scott Fitzgerald,* 122; Kenneth Eble "Touches of Disaster: Alcoholism and Mental Illness in Fitzgerald's Short Stories," 47.

was no chance of competing with him on the same subject, when he had
brought off such a triumph. There would inevitably have been invidious
comparisons. If my story had anything to redeem it, except atmosphere,
I would not hesitate to include it but most of it depends on a mixture of
hysteria and sentiment—anyhow, I did not decide without some thought.[5]

Fitzgerald persisted in seeing "Her Last Case" as a story "about Welbourne," an antebellum house in Virginia, where Perkins had taken
Fitzgerald to visit Elizabeth Lemmon, Perkins's cousin and close friend,
in July 1934, a month before Fitzgerald wrote the story.[6] Fitzgerald's letter
to Perkins, dated July 30, reported on his weekend stays at Welbourne,
which continued after Perkins had left. Just how directly "Her Last Case"
draws on those experiences is revealed in the following excerpt from that
same letter:

The bottom sort of fell out of things after you left. We sat around for a
few hours and talked a lot about you. The only flaw in the evening was the
fact that afterwards I didn't seem to be able to sleep any better in Virginia
than I did in Maryland, so after reading an old account of Stuart's battles
for an hour or so, I got dressed in despair and spent the small hours
of the morning prowling around the place, finally snatching two hours
of sleep between seven and nine. The next day . . . I decided to take the
three o'clock bus back to Washington. . . . By the way, I had never ridden
in a bus before and thought it was rather a horrible experience after the
spacious grace of that house.[7]

Into the story Fitzgerald would weave this alcoholism, this insomnia,
and this house-prowling, plus references to Stuart's cavalry and his
Washington bus ride (though he reverses the direction of the trip).[8]
    Interestingly enough, it is in the same letter to Perkins that Fitzgerald
first mentions Thomas Wolfe's story "The House of the Far and Lost":

    5. John Kuehl and Jackson R. Bryer, eds., *Dear Scott/Dear Max: The Fitzgerald–Perkins
Correspondence*, 213.
    6. Ibid., 209.
    7. Ibid., 203.
    8. On Fitzgerald's perhaps typical behavior toward his nurses, see William Katterjohn,
"An Interview with Theodora Gager, Fitzgerald's Private Nurse."

This morning before breakfast I read Tom Wolfe's story in *Scribner's*. I thought it was perfectly beautiful and it had a subtlety often absent from his work, an intense poetry rather akin to Ernest [Hemingway] (though naturally you won't tell Tom that because he wouldn't take it as a compliment.) What family resemblance there is between we three as writers is the attempt that crops up in our fiction from time to time to recapture the exact feel of a moment in time and space exemplified by people rather than by things—that is, an attempt at what Wordsworth was trying to do rather than what Keats did with such magnificent ease, an attempt at a mature memory of a deep experience.[9]

Not then but only later, as we have seen, did Fitzgerald decide that both "Her Last Case" and Wolfe's "The House of the Far and Lost" were "place" stories and that as a place story Wolfe's was superior to his own. Fitzgerald could not have helped admiring, for instance, Wolfe's opening description of the English house set back from the road, a mile out of town, which sets his story: "It was a magnificent house of the weathered gray stone they have in that country, as if in the very quality of the wet heavy air there is the soft thick gray of time itself, sternly yet beautifully soaking down forever on you—and enriching everything it touches— grass, foliage, brick, ivy, the fresh moist color of people's faces, and old gray stone with the incomparable weathering of time."[10]

There was also an intriguing description of an alcoholic, though Wolfe's story, unlike Fitzgerald's, only incidentally mentions alcoholism:

He was a stocky well-set man with iron-gray hair, bushy eyebrows, and the red weathered face which wore the open color of the country on it, but also had the hard dull flush of the steady heavy drinker.

I never saw him drunk, and yet I think that he was never sober: he was one of those men who have drunk themselves past any hope of drunkenness, who are soaked through to the bone with alcohol, saturated, tanned, weathered in it so completely that it could never be distilled out of their blood again. Yet even in this terrible excess one felt a kind of grim control—the control of a man who is enslaved by the very thing that he controls, the control of the opium eater who cannot leave his drug but

9. Kuehl and Bryer, eds., *Dear Scott/Dear Max*, 203–4.
10. Francis E. Skipp, ed., *The Complete Short Stories of Thomas Wolfe*, 147.

measures out his dose with a cold calculation, and finds the limit of his capacity, and stops there, day by day.[11]

Perhaps because it hit rather close to home, this little bit of description had something to do with Fitzgerald's decision against his own story. Yet, understandably, he put the matter more broadly. In the face of Wolfe's superior performance, he found nothing to "redeem" his story other than "atmosphere," and "atmosphere," he claimed, was not enough. Besides, he added, the atmosphere itself depends upon "a mixture of hysteria and sentiment."[12]

Fitzgerald came down too hard on this story. If it does not rival his best half-dozen or so stories, it is nevertheless far better than its burial in the pages of the *Saturday Evening Post* would seem to indicate. After all, it is not really about "place," nor are its salient emotional qualities describable as those of "hysteria and sentiment." To see the story as primarily the former or to look too narrowly for evidence of the latter will preclude all possibility of the attentive reader's hearing the essential story (or stories) that "Her Last Case" tells.

First of all, despite its (already identified) strongly autobiographical elements and besides its portrait of a Fitzgerald-like alcoholic, "Her Last Case" does not tell, except in the most superficial way, the story of Fitzgerald's visits to Welbourne in July 1934. He said as much to his hostess, Elizabeth Lemmon: "The story is so detached from any reality I am sure it won't cause you or [your] family any annoyance."[13] Consider that bus ride, moreover, a bus ride that Fitzgerald claims was his first ever. In the story, that bus ride is taken not by Ben Dragonet, the alcoholic in his midthirties in need of private-duty nursing (obviously the Fitzgerald figure), but by Miss Bette Weaver, the twenty-four-year-old nurse who has come out from Washington to take on this "last" case before retiring from the profession to become the wife of a young physician who will practice in New York.

In fact, in this story, powered by a major reversal in which the nurse, fully contrary to her initial expectations, will be seduced into falling

11. Ibid., 157–58.
12. Kuehl and Bryer, eds., *Dear Scott/Dear Max,* 213.
13. Bruccoli and Duggan, eds., *Correspondence,* 383.

in love with her patient and at the last decide to stay with him at the expense of her "safe" marriage, the author brilliantly uses her bus-ride experience to foreshadow that structuring reversal. "Washington had been stifling," he writes in the opening paragraph, "and, insulated by the artificially cooled bus, she was unprepared for the sharp drop in temperature; it was not what she expected from Virginia in July" (571). Enclosed within the temperature-regulated air of an air-conditioned bus, she leaves behind a "stifling" Washington to emerge into a "sharp[ly]" cooler Warrenburg, Virginia. The air in the bus that initially and up to a point in the journey kept her cool later served (though she did not know it) to keep her warm. So, too, do her emotional climate and affective temperatures change (barely perceived, if perceived at all) during the course of her days at the Dragonet mansion.

In trying to use his autobiographical material but not wanting to use it autobiographically, Fitzgerald decided to make his principal story not about the alcoholic patient but about his latest nurse. Fitzgerald, of course, never had qualms about centering stories and major portions of his novels in the psyches, personalities, character, and behavior of women. He insisted that there was a part of himself, as an artist, that was female. And whether or not we are convinced that it was in some way so, it is incumbent upon the critic to grant him the possibility that the author's belief that it was so enabled him to write a story like "Her Last Case." To this conviction he was able to add considerable observation in the 1930s of a certain group of women who were clearly identified, both professionally and socially. Because of his own sicknesses and the absence of an illness-ridden Zelda Fitzgerald, who in those years was already in and out of asylums and sanitariums, it was with various private nurses (and secretaries) that, seriatim, he lived most intensely during periods lasting weeks and months.

Descriptive details and the very character of the fictional Bette Weaver are drawn, it is safe to assume, from those nurses who actually attended Fitzgerald over the years. Here is the background the author gives her:

Born and bred in a desolate little streak of wind and rain on the Pennsylvania border of Maryland, her days as probationer, "blue nurse," graduate nurse, had opened a new world to her. They had been happy years—she had had good cases; almost always nice men and women, who lived or died with respect and liking for her, because she was lovely to look at and considered a fine young nurse. She had taken every kind of case in her three graduate years—except infantile paralysis, which she avoided because she had three little nephews in Baltimore. (572)

On this, her "last" case, she will feel all the poignancy of being "off then for the last time with the starched white uniforms, the sense of adventure, of being used for some purpose larger than herself, some need greater than her own. The last time—because in one month she would become housewife and handmaiden to young Dr. Howard Carney, of the Mercy Hospital in New York" (573).

Miss Weaver, who has been trained in a hospital program, is not particularly well educated. Yet Fitzgerald, who had a penchant for casting young women as his Pygmalions—to the examples of his daughter Scottie and Sheilah Graham can be added his nurses—does not make Miss Weaver's poor education the reason for her rather shaky sense of history. Encountering signs that speak chauvinistically of Stuart's Cavalry but not bothering to read the writing on them beyond the first few words, she is revealed as having an interest in such matters that is "as faint as that of most women in the record of old wars" (571). Indeed, her sense of history appears to be nourished only by movies she has seen: "She thought of Marion Davies in a hoop skirt dancing the lancers with handsome Confederate officers, and of books about gallant, fierce times, and gracious houses and Negro 'ha'nts.' It was all a lovely blur— she was pretty sure that George Washington wasn't in the Civil War, and also that Château-Thierry came a little later, but she was sure of little more" (572). Carrying around such fuzzy information, she is nakedly vulnerable, it is no wonder to learn, to this "handsome man with very dark deep-set eyes" (574). He not only speaks in "the sort of voice that can 'do anything with anybody,' a voice that could beg, command, wheedle, storm or condemn" (574), but talks to her winningly about the romantic history of his house as well:

"Do you see that windowpane with the name scratched on it? Well, that was made by a diamond ring belonging to the Gallant Pelham— made on the morning of the day he was killed. You can see the year— 1864. You know who the Gallant Pelham was? He commanded Stuart's

horse artillery at twenty-three. He was my hero when I was a boy."
(576)[14]

It is only a matter of time, one decides, before she will sit herself down
to read that "dusty volume of Pollard's *War between the States* from the
stacks" (583).

What happens to the nurse's professionalism complements thematically this history-love nexus. That professionalism breaks down, of
course, when she falls in love with her patient. She, whose most obvious
sign of control comes when she takes up her patient's wrist, wondering
if his pulse indicates (a hallmark for Fitzgerald) "any lesion of vitality"
(580), now discovers that the tables are turned when she goes out
horseback riding and it is "his fingers" that rearrange "her reins this
afternoon instead of her fingers taking his pulse" (581). We read that
"she realized with a sort of surprise that he was no longer her patient—
it was he who dominated the days" (581). And there is more: "With the
change a sense of disloyalty to Howard [her fiancé] lodged itself in her
mind—or was it rather a sense that she should have felt disloyal?" (581).
Of course, when this happens, and when similar breakdowns in her
professional demeanor occur, she is always out of uniform, that white-
starched "shield" (581), as the author calls it (and as the heroine seems
to perceive it). After all, "she would feel much better in her uniform, far
more in armor, more able to cope with any situation" (574).

And that "shield" brings us to another matter. There are hints of
certain literary mythologies that give Fitzgerald's otherwise realistic
narrative its romantic cachet. With its reversals and displacements, that
"romance" runs to a narrative of this sort: A maiden capable of wearing
white comes to "a new lonely place with," romantically, "a storm in the
air" (572). In this mysterious place lives a "wounded" being whose very
surname suggests that within himself can be found the "dragon" that

---

14. In 1936 Fitzgerald drew up a list of Modern Library titles for his nurse at Asheville,
North Carolina ("The Education of Dorothy Richardson," 227–28). He drew up other, more
extended lists for Sheilah Graham (Sheilah Graham, *College of One*, 81–131, 203–19).

As Fitzgerald acknowledged to Elizabeth Lemmon, "Of course the detail about the
initials of the 'Gallant Pelham' will identify the place to such neighbors of yours who read
the *Saturday Evening Post*" (Bruccoli and Duggan, eds., *Correspondence*, 383).

threatens him and that must be defeated or "killed." (That Fitzgerald's mind ran to such "mythy" suggestions—alcohol/"dragons"/knights—is further evidenced by the bottle of "Sir Galahad" gin that surfaces in the texture of "An Alcoholic Case" (1937), another story from this period.)

Some of the displacements, then, are that the pure white knight is a woman, and the man who is "wounded" is himself the dragon that must be slain by the knight who brings him a new "regime." But rather than slaying the dragon, the maiden/knight decides not to bring her last case (read: quest) to a conclusion, but to extend its duration so that it will "last forever" (590).

But Fitzgerald has crossed this quest story with at least two other literary paradigms, for the young private nurse—Miss Bette Weaver—is cast by her author as (1) a Sue Barton–type (named obviously for Clara) or a Cherry Ames–type from the cheap popular fiction aimed at adolescent females in Fitzgerald's time and well into ours, and (2) a modern literary counterpart of the nineteenth-century novel's convention of the governess (which also stands behind the nurse depicted in popular fiction, especially of the 1930s and 1940s). Bette Weaver is very much like a Jane Eyre who comes to care for children and "discovers" Rochester, that ogre who captures her love and her loyalty, or, better still, the unnamed governess who sees as her duty the consuming need to save Flora and Miles, her young charges. At the Dragonet estate we are in a world much like that of the governess at Bly, one in which it is revealed that the "master" has a daughter who must be cared for because her mother wishes to bargain her away to the father (an odd situation for a twentieth-century nurse assigned to what is possibly an adult "psychiatric" case but totally natural and common to the situation of a nineteenth-century governess).

The lord of the manor even treats the nurse as he might a governess. "Miss Weaver," he says, "I didn't expect you till six o'clock. It's now half-past five. After six o'clock I'm your patient; until then—the veranda" (575–76). And it is in such a governess's world that we find houses that, having "floated up suddenly through the twilight of the rain," can be described: "It was all there—the stocky central box fronted by tall pillars, the graceful one-story wings, the intimate gardens only half seen from the front, the hint of other more secret verandas to face the long southern outdoors" (573). But there is no Quint here, as there is in *The Turn of the Screw,* no Miss Jessel. All the wandering through the halls at 3 A.M. in this antebellum mansion is done by the master himself, even if at the end of that first night of walking through the house, seeming "ghosts" do make an appearance:

> In the hall, dusky now with the real dawn, she [the nurse] felt an electric silence. And suddenly, as he [the patient] said Listen! again and raised his finger, she felt the little hairs on her neck stand out from it, felt a tingling along her spine. In a split second it all happened. The great front door swung back slowly on its hinges and the hall was suddenly full of young faces and voices. Ben Dragonet sprang to his feet, his voice clear over the young voices, over the many voices:
> "Can't you see it now? These were my people, bred to the sword, perished by the sword! Can't you hear?"
> Even as she cried out frantically, clinging to the last shreds of reality. "You must go to *bed!* I'm going to give you more sedative!" she saw that the big front door was still open. (578)

These "ghosts," who appear to signify something like the "dead weight of the past" (587), do not reappear as such. The function of their one appearance seems to be to prepare us for the sudden appearance of other "ghosts" from Ben Dragonet's past, his divorced wife and young daughter. The former was also "kin" before she was wife, as we learn from the shadowy Scotswoman, Jean Keith, who also forms part of the Dragonet household:

> "His cousin, his wife that was. She's back again. She's there with him. She's breaking him all over again like she always did. I heard them laughing together—laughing awful, like they laughed when they were children and she first got hold of him. Listen! Can't you hear them laughing, as if they hated each other?
> ". . . . It was she that did it [caused him his injury]; it wasn't the bullets in the war. I've seen it—I've seen her come and go. Six months past she came here, and six months he walked the floor in the night and turned for the liquor bottle." (584)

When the nurse counters accurately with the observation, "But they're divorced. The little girl said—," the quick answer from the Scotswoman is "What's that to her, or to him. She owned him in her black heart when he was no higher than my shoulder, and she comes back to feed on his goodness, like a vampire feeding on his blood to live by" (585).

Now, of course, we have been shifted temporarily to the literary world of Emily Brontë. We have a reincarnation of Cathy and Heathcliff out of that other Victorian novel *Wuthering Heights*, though we are not far from the world of Scott and Zelda Fitzgerald either—a world without hope. As Fitzgerald put it, "I left my capacity for hoping on the little roads that led to Zelda's sanatorium." One can see how the author has used for his own purposes the notion that the twin specters of Zelda Fitzgerald and his daughter Scottie would perforce intrude in any new relationship that he might have. In "Her Last Case," however, he imagines a new and different ending for this impasse, though it is one, it should be noted, that is not particularly hopeful or promissory in any specific way. After all, the nurse's last case, it is threatened (as Fitzgerald sometimes felt about his own last case), will last forever. The enhanced portent that the phrase has taken on, between its use in the title of the story and its appearance in the concluding sentence, turns the ending into something quite the opposite of what the casual reader of the *Saturday Evening Post,* looking for a "marriage-will-solve-all" happy finale, might think he has found. It is an ending that rivals in ironic effect those rare unhappy happy-marriage endings of nineteenth-century American novels such as Henry James's *The Bostonians* or William Dean Howells's *April Hopes.*[15]

It is, of course, the nurse's perception that her patient needs her that makes her decide finally to stay on with him when the time comes to go away. It is his need, and possibly his sorrow, that seduces her into staying. As Fitzgerald put it in his notebooks, in a discrete item not tied to this or any other story, "Do you know what your affair was founded

---

15. Matthew J. Bruccoli, ed., *The Notebooks of F. Scott Fitzgerald,* 204.

The Bostonians (1886) and *April Hopes* (1887) conclude, in order: "But though she was glad, he presently discovered that, beneath her hood, she was in tears. It is to be feared that with the union, so far from brilliant, into which she was about to enter, these were not the last she was destined to shed" (Henry James, *Novels 1881–1886,* 1218–19); and "If he had been different she would not have asked him to be frank and open; if she had been different he might have been frank and open. This was the beginning of their married life" (W. D. Howells, *April Hopes,* 354).

on? On sorrow. You got sorry for each other."[16] Sorrow and need seem to be the combination that binds Heathcliff and Cathy, Jane Eyre and Rochester, the dragon-slayer and the dragon-victim, this young nurse and her patient-lover.

16. Bruccoli, ed., *Notebooks*, 190.

THE CARTOONIST, THE NURSE, AND
THE WRITER: "AN ALCOHOLIC CASE"

ARTHUR WALDHORN

> Then I was drunk for many years, and then I died.
> —Fitzgerald, *The Crack-Up*

With expertise born of experience, F. Scott Fitzgerald began writing fictional accounts of alcoholics as early as 1915. Once sketched as genial, harmless drunks, as in "The Camel's Back" (1920), the portraits darkened as he shadowed in the lineaments of his ill-fated protagonists, as in "A New Leaf" (1931) and "Crazy Sunday" (1932). He wrote "An Alcoholic Case" in December 1936, and, by the time it was published in the February 1937 issue of *Esquire*, Fitzgerald had already explored the subject in more than a dozen tales and essays—and had himself been arrested or hospitalized for alcoholism eight times. All the stories about drunkenness mirror to some extent Fitzgerald's own inward torment, though frequently the image is distorted, reflecting his and his protagonists' twisted posturings as they try to reconcile living well and cracking up.

Despite its relevance to an understanding of Fitzgerald's life and art, "An Alcoholic Case" long lay unnoticed and, until 1951, was not reprinted. Citing it as a story that suggests Fitzgerald's "own dilemma, unforgettably," Malcolm Cowley included it (along with seven other previously unpublished stories) in *The Stories of F. Scott Fitzgerald.*

Since then, the story has been reprinted four times.[1] Even after its reappearance, "An Alcoholic Case" drew sparse critical response. Sergio Perosa and John A. Higgins were the only critics to notice the story before the 1980s, and each of them devoted merely a paragraph or less to an aesthetic appreciation.[2]

Subsequent critical interest in "An Alcoholic Case" (as with many of Fitzgerald's tales of drunkenness) has been more biographical than literary, a specimen illustrative of the process and progress of a disease, alcoholism. The clinical impetus toward such analysis began in 1970, its source extraliterary, in an essay by Donald W. Goodwin, a physician. Goodwin's "The Alcoholism of F. Scott Fitzgerald" explores possible sources of Fitzgerald's alcoholism: heredity, desires and failures, and relationships (within the family, between writing and alcoholism, and, finally, between alcoholism and mental illness). Goodwin's study centers on Fitzgerald's disease rather than on his fiction, and he concludes inconclusively about both: "The origin of his alcoholism is as inscrutable as the mystery of his writing talent."[3] Goodwin's benchmark essay inspired several later studies.

Increasingly aware of alcoholism as a disease rather than as a social aberration, critics began to reexamine the relationship between Fitzgerald's alcoholism and his writing. Several include in their essays brief reference to "An Alcoholic Case." Kenneth E. Eble's study pursues linkages between alcoholism and mental illness. Eble treats "An Alcoholic Case" cursorily, but he groups it with "A New Leaf" among stories that "directly confront alcoholism by name" and detail "an alcoholic's unsuccessful attempt to reform or be cured." Julie M. Irwin also makes but passing reference to "An Alcoholic Case," citing it as another instance of her thesis that Fitzgerald's short stories, studied chronologically, "read like the progressive case history of a classic alcoholic."[4]

---

1. F. Scott Fitzgerald, *The Stories of F. Scott Fitzgerald: A Selection of 28 Stories*, 384. "An Alcoholic Case" has been reprinted in *The Bodley Head Scott Fitzgerald*, vols. 2 (1959 and 1961 editions only) and 6; and in "*The Diamond as Big as the Ritz*" *and Other Stories*, vol. 1 of *The Stories of F. Scott Fitzgerald*.

2. Sergio Perosa, *The Art of F. Scott Fitzgerald*, 143; John A. Higgins, *F. Scott Fitzgerald: A Study of the Stories*, 166.

3. Donald W. Goodwin, "The Alcoholism of F. Scott Fitzgerald," 90.

4. Kenneth Eble, "Touches of Disaster: Alcoholism and Mental Illness in Fitzgerald's Short Stories," 45; Julie M. Irwin, "F. Scott Fitzgerald's Little Drinking Problem," 418.

Thomas B. Gilmore and George Monteiro have each written useful essays about "An Alcoholic Case," fusing literary analysis with scientific knowledge of alcoholism. Gilmore argues that what really matters is how Fitzgerald's "experience of alcoholism or his attitudes toward it appear in or shape his work." His treatment of "An Alcoholic Case" is sketchy but not uncritical, dismissive of its aesthetic achievement but admiring of its "discerning study of alcoholic psychology." Monteiro's reading—the most comprehensive and extended analysis to date—is far more tolerant of the story's shortcomings and overly generous in assessing its artistic worth. His essay nevertheless deserves credit as a conscientious and detailed attempt to muster factual and aesthetic evidence in defense of Fitzgerald's craft and, above all, as the first to apportion more than two paragraphs of analysis in the fifty years following the publication of "An Alcoholic Case."[5]

For Fitzgerald, 1936 was a punishing year. His wife was institutionalized in Asheville; his mother died as did his close friend Ring Lardner; and he broke his clavicle while diving, making it necessary to write by dictation. He was also nearly broke and heavily in debt, owing twenty thousand dollars to Scribner's and his agent, Harold Ober. And he was drinking more and more heavily. On one occasion, after he fired a revolver and threatened suicide, a nurse (one among many during these years) was assigned to stay with him to help control his drinking.[6] It is hopeless to attempt a precise statement about why he was drinking so much. Multiple possibilities exist, among them that, as Goodwin notes, alcohol briefly "emancipates the writer from the tyranny of mind and memory."[7] What is clinically undeniable, however, is that alcoholism affords its victim—and often those closest to him—endless opportunities for self-deception, denial, and evasion.

5. Thomas B. Gilmore, *Equivocal Spirits: Alcoholism and Drinking in 20th-Century Literature*, 96, 105. Gilmore's basic premise is that Fitzgerald's perceptions of his alcoholic characters were most penetrating before he became an alcoholic himself. As a drinker and sometimes a drunk, but not yet an alcoholic, he maintained an objectivity he would later lose. Gilmore's insight has been most helpful to me in shaping my own reading of "An Alcoholic Case." George Monteiro, "Fitzgerald vs. Fitzgerald: 'An Alcoholic Case.' "
6. See Matthew J. Bruccoli, *Some Sort of Epic Grandeur: The Life of F. Scott Fitzgerald*, 414; William Katterjohn, "An Interview with Theodora Gager, Fitzgerald's Private Nurse."
7. Goodwin, "Alcoholism," 90.

In the months just prior to his writing "An Alcoholic Case," Fitzgerald would endure yet more demeaning experiences, any of them likely to stagger a frail psyche. Together, they were powerful enough to short-circuit an emotional overload and trigger alcoholism, a disease temporarily enabling escape from the horror of reality. Following the appearance of "The Crack-Up" in *Esquire* early in 1936, Fitzgerald suffered in quick succession Hemingway's nasty reference in "The Snows of Kilimanjaro" to "poor Scott Fitzgerald and his romantic awe" of the rich; Dos Passos's snide letter urging him to stop grinding out "little pieces" for *Esquire* and get busy with a "first-rate novel"; and a devastating journalistic portrait by Michel Mok, published in the *New York Evening Post* as a fortieth birthday interview and describing him as a drunk with the "pitiful expression of a cruelly beaten child."[8] Before the interview appeared, Fitzgerald again attempted suicide, this time by swallowing a bottle of morphine.

Almost desperately, he needed comforting, that dependency the alcoholic often relies on to abet his denials and evasions. He begged it from Hemingway but got none. Marjorie Kinnan Rawlings wrote a mothering note, assuring him that "when you're sore through and through . . . it has to heal in its own way. . . ." Despite his groans and complaints, however, Fitzgerald did not wholly surrender to despair. By December, he was able to write to C. O. Kalman, an old friend from St. Paul, that though he had been too ill "to do any decent work" for the past six months, "I am up and around to the extent that I am finishing a story this week."[9] That story was "An Alcoholic Case," one of nine he wrote for *Esquire* during 1936, for each of which he was paid $250.

Theoretically, the technical apparatus of "An Alcoholic Case" provides Fitzgerald an excellent opportunity to explore the recesses of an alcoholic's underworld. A compact narrative of about three thousand words, it is divided into two sections and two days. Using both external and

8. Matthew J. Bruccoli and Jackson R. Bryer, eds., *F. Scott Fitzgerald in His Own Time: A Miscellany*, 299. The succeeding reference to Fitzgerald's suicide attempt is in Matthew J. Bruccoli, ed., *As Ever, Scott Fitz—: Letters between F. Scott Fitzgerald and His Literary Agent, Harold Ober—1919–1940*, 282.

9. Matthew J. Bruccoli and Margaret M. Duggan, eds., *Correspondence of F. Scott Fitzgerald*, 459–60, 464.

internal narrative, the story thrusts its two central and nameless (archety-pal?) characters at once into hand-to-hand struggle for possession of a bottle of SIR GALAHAD'S DISTILLED LOUISVILLE GIN. The hotel suite to which the alcoholic cartoonist has been confined becomes a plausible arena in which to observe not only the combat between him and his nurse but also the alcoholic's ritual practice of dependency, denial, and self-destructiveness.

Those flashes into the darkness of alcoholism provide the best writing in "An Alcoholic Case," and they are all recorded auctorially, from outside the action. At least part of the horror limned resides in glimpsed rem-nants of the cartoonist's charm and considerateness. He draws cartoons as gifts for the nurse and seems genuinely concerned that she may step on broken glass from the shattered gin bottle or that he has hurt her wrists and elbow during their struggles. What makes these humane gestures ironically unreliable is that their motives are suspect. For they are also the gestures of someone whose only purpose—whether by charm or by force—is to get what he wants, a drink. Worse, the cartoonist's seemingly genteel intentions cannot disguise the reality that he hurls and smashes a bottle when his demands are not met and that he does twist and hurt the nurse's wrist. The auctorial observer leaves no doubt that the cartoonist is destructive, a threat to others as well as to himself.

The cartoonist's denial and dependency are also precisely observed. He glibly turns aside at the outset any need for help or support (" 'Don't you believe in anything?' she demanded. 'Nothing you believe in. . . .' ") and warns the nurse that if she refuses him his drink, he'll not only smash the bottle but step on the glass as well.[10] He greets the nurse's return from her agency "casually" with a "genial, indifferent smile" (441), and stands before her deceptively self-assured "in dinner clothes even to a derby hat—but minus his studs and tie" (440). Recorded externally as dramatic dialogue, the scene projects the cartoonist's vain effort to deny what reader and nurse cannot ignore: "the pallor and the fever on his face and . . . the mixed peppermint and gin on his breath" (441).

The cartoonist is psychically as well as sartorially incomplete since he cannot acknowledge much less confront what he is. Like a helpless child,

10. Fitzgerald, *Stories of F. Scott Fitzgerald*, 436. All subsequent page references to "An Alcoholic Case" are to this 1951 edition and will appear parenthetically in the text.

he needs the nurse to find his studs and tie his tie. And though he says that he wants to change his rumpled shirt himself, he sits passively on the toilet seat and lets her remove his clothes. Every gesture Fitzgerald records illustrates the cartoonist's denial and dependency. Thus, his insistence that he is on his way to see the president's secretary is a transparent ploy to solicit a glass of sherry from the nurse. Thrusting a lit cigarette against the copper plate on his rib, he tries to substitute the image of war hero for that of barfly, deflecting attention from his alcohol-soaked psyche and wooing sympathy for his war-wounded body and mind.

Fitzgerald's most successful rendering of the cartoonist's destructiveness, denial, and dependency follows the failure of the alcoholic's gambit for pity as a war hero. When the nurse, though sympathetic, tells him that the copper plate is "no excuse for what you're doing to yourself" (442), he bends his "great brown eyes on her, shrewd—aloof, confused" and signals to her his "Will to Die" (446). Fitzgerald's adjectives—"shrewd," "aloof," "confused"—are marvels of discernment. "Shrewd" stands alone, the crucial word of the three, suggesting the cartoonist's determination to weaken the nurse's resolve through his charisma and her indiscriminate pity. "Aloof" and "confused," paired but incompatible, imply respectively his remoteness and indifference to others except as they serve his needs and his muddied perception of his actual situation.

With incisive fragments such as these, Fitzgerald demonstrates why, as he once said, no story of his can ever be a complete failure. But the same climactic scene evidences Fitzgerald's unwillingness or inability to maintain artistic control and demonstrates why, as a result, the story fails. Thomas Gilmore has written of *Tender Is the Night*: "To give a full, convincing picture of Dick Diver's alcoholism might have been as intolerably painful to Fitzgerald as accepting his own."[11] The same is true of Fitzgerald's portrait of his cartoonist in "An Alcoholic Case." To avoid a relentless objectivity that might reveal the cartoonist (and himself) whole, Fitzgerald allows the consciousness of the nurse to enfeeble both narrative and characterization.

Every telling example of the alcoholic's destructiveness, denial, and dependency cited thus far has been presented from an objective point of view, through external rather than internal narration. It is the nurse's

---

11. Gilmore, *Equivocal Spirits*, 103.

fevered consciousness, however, that registers the sepulchral signal of the cartoonist's "Will to Die." She then elaborates with a morbid, purpled passage wedding sight, sound, and smell into a romantic belief that "death was in that corner where he was looking" (442). The nurse's consciousness transforms what should have been poignant drama to pathos and melodrama.

Several commentators have noted that Fitzgerald chose the nurse to gain necessary distance from what came frighteningly close to self-portraiture. Perosa and Higgins argue that the nurse provides "an effective detachment of vision" and that, as a central intelligence, she is a credible "objective observer." George Monteiro's argument is more subtle and ingenious. Fitzgerald, he notes, hoped to tell a "double story" (that of the alcoholic and his nurse) by retaining the narrative voice but filtering all events through the consciousness of the nurse. Thus, on one hand, Fitzgerald enlists the reader's belief in his objective portrait of "an alcoholic case" while stretching distance between his character and himself. On the other hand, he is also able to move the story to an entirely different plane—the story of "the nurse's professionalism and the breakdown of that professionalism."[12]

These arguments have some merit yet fail for two reasons. First, they endow the nurse with more credibility as a witness than she deserves, certainly more than Fitzgerald gives her. And second, they ignore several awkward and unresolved ambiguities raised by Fitzgerald's peculiar use of the nurse as a central consciousness. Analyzing the character of the nurse poses no serious difficulties. She is gentle, affectionate, warm-hearted, and weak—a surrogate wife or lover figure more sympathetic than objective. Her failure is not, as Monteiro suggests, that she loses her objectivity, but that she has a scant store to begin with. Little about her suggests the kind of disciplined observation a nurse (private or otherwise) should possess. She stays on a case primarily because she *likes* the patient (436), and, consequently, adjusts her insights to her affections.[13] At the end of her first involuntary wrestling match with the cartoonist,

---

12. Perosa, *Art of F. Scott Fitzgerald,* 143; Higgins, *Fitzgerald: Study of the Stories,* 166–67; Monteiro, "Fitzgerald vs. Fitzgerald," 112–13.

13. Gilmore dismisses the nurse as "a character of minimal intelligence and no intrinsic interest" (*Equivocal Spirits,* 105).

she turns for respite to her novel—*Gone with the Wind*—"about things so lovely that happened long ago" (436). Given her pliability, it is little surprise that she alters her report to excuse the cartoonist from his actual responsibility for breaking the gin bottle (437).

Even when her perception is sound, as it occasionally is, she fails to act on it. Determined at the end of the first section that "she would never take an alcoholic case again" (438), she defends him against the other nurses, rejects offers of easier assignments, and asks to return to care for him: "The nurse's brown eyes were alight with a mixture of thoughts—the movie she had just seen about Pasteur and the book they had all read about Florence Nightingale when they were student nurses" (440).

A curious counterpart to the nurse is her employer, Mrs. Hixson. Once, like the young nurse, "proud, idealistic, overworked" (439), Mrs. Hixson has become efficient, tough-minded, insightful, her vision of an alcoholic harsh and unrelenting: "Some alcoholics are pleasant and some of them are not, but all of them can be rotten" (440). Mrs. Hixson's voice is closest to the auctorial voice that speaks plain and gruff words about the cartoonist. But it is neither the voice nor the consciousness that meets Fitzgerald's necessity.

What Fitzgerald needed when he was down was someone to comfort him, to help him deny or at least disguise his problem. In "An Alcoholic Case," the nurse fulfills that need. Whether consciously or not, Fitzgerald burdens the nurse with a myopic view of reality. Thus, as she sweeps up the shards of the broken gin bottle, she ponders sadly but irrelevantly that the "glass, in its fragments, was less than a window through which they had seen each other for a moment" (438).[14] The cartoonist, she regrets, knew nothing of her family or the man she had almost married. She did not know about his wife and young sons or "what had brought him to this pitch," what had happened to him, "all trim and handsome as he must have been five years ago" (438). The nurse ignores data that might enable her to see her patient clearly and clinically, and instead

14. Fitzgerald intrudes an incomprehensible "parallel" to the smashed bottle by referring twice to cracked and broken windows in the bus the nurse uses on her way to and from her agency.

rhapsodizes about what might have been. Her dodgings screen her from reality and, because they cushion her patient's dependency and abet his resistance to admitting his illness, diminish her value as nurse. More important in terms of the technique of fiction, as her credibility as nurse diminishes, so too does her reliability as a central consciousness. Indeed, she manages to displace sympathy from herself to the cartoonist.

Why does Fitzgerald allow the nurse's perceptions and his story to drift into such errant disarray? Possibly to satisfy his own unspoken and unacknowledged psychological needs. No matter that the proportions and focus of his story suffer. Fitzgerald seems to have a higher purpose: "When she came up to the suite and found him all helpless and distraught she would despise him and be sorry for him" (440). As long as the nurse is sorry for the cartoonist, the alcoholic's path to self-pity and denial stays open, an admission of illness postponed. That path Fitzgerald chose for both his cartoonist and himself. If the nurse is a little bit in love with the idea of her patient's helplessness and hopelessness, Fitzgerald seems to ask, what harm? By introducing a malleable internal consciousness who relaxes and undermines auctorial rigor and dissipates narrative coherence, Fitzgerald indulges the nurse's needs, comforts the cartoonist and, perhaps, himself. Unable to separate the cartoonist from his creator, Fitzgerald does them both a disservice and his nurse and his reader as well. Ambiguity is admirable in fiction, chaos not. Fitzgerald flounders, unable to decide whether he wants his cartoonist to be sympathetic or repulsive, victim of society, self, or disease. He scapegoats his nurse by instilling in her thoughts and actions nearer his own need than her literary function.

Despite its faults, "An Alcoholic Case" aspires to, even if it falls short of, didactic cogency and aesthetic resolution. "Despise him *and* be sorry for him" (440; emphasis mine), the nurse reflects, suggesting that whatever Fitzgerald's ambivalence about his cartoonist, he believes at last that his fictional character, like himself, deserves both censure and compassion. What Fitzgerald could not acknowledge was that an alcoholic's first step toward recovery is to admit his alcoholism. His inability to do so lends a sad irony to the nurse's final, misguided insight: "It's just that you can't really help them and it's so discouraging—it's all for nothing" (442).

RECOVERING "THE LOST DECADE"

ALICE HALL PETRY

As I have argued elsewhere, F. Scott Fitzgerald's achievement as a writer of short fiction—his choice of subject matter, his style, his technique—was intimately related to events in his own personal life: "With the possible exception of Emily Dickinson, whose poetic achievement is largely meaningless without some awareness of her personal feelings for the Rev. Charles Wadsworth, Fitzgerald is arguably the most dramatic example in American literary history of an author whose private life is reflected, consciously or otherwise, in virtually everything he wrote." Further, even Fitzgerald himself recognized that his personal life eerily paralleled historical events in the United States, with his own young manhood coinciding with America's emergence as an international power in World War I, with his career—and excesses—peaking with the dynamic but self-indulgent 1920s, and with his troubled early middle age coexisting with the miserable 1930s: "Fitzgerald's *Ledger* summary of his thirty-third year—'*The Crash! Zelda + America*'—reveals how he identified the events of his life with the history of his time."[1] This was a man, in other words, for whom his personal life, his writings, and the historical moment constituted a kind of trinity—a trinity that must be borne in mind if one is to respond correctly to his writings.

1. Alice Hall Petry, *Fitzgerald's Craft of Short Fiction: The Collected Stories—1920–1935*, 4; Matthew J. Bruccoli, *Some Sort of Epic Grandeur: The Life of F. Scott Fitzgerald*, 307.

A case in point is "The Lost Decade," which was written in July 1939 and appeared in *Esquire* in December of that year. It remained uncollected until its inclusion in the 1951 Cowley edition of Fitzgerald's stories, and what little commentary it has generated has focused on the sources and impact of the brevity of this eleven-hundred-word "short short" story. Perosa sees "the extreme of stylistic compression and essentiality" of "The Lost Decade" and other stories of the period as reflecting how Fitzgerald "had learned and absorbed the lesson of economy and precision inherent in Hemingway's stories and in most of his writings." Mizener notes that Fitzgerald's later stories were made shorter due primarily to the requirements of *Esquire*. One result of this imposed brevity is that Fitzgerald's "quiet, humorous acceptance of suffering and disaster" becomes disentangled from plot—"and the brilliant, subtle movement of his final prose gets its full effect. We do not need to be told what to feel about Mr. Trimble of 'The Lost Decade'; knowing him is enough." Indeed, continues Mizener, these later stories, "in spite of their brevity—perhaps even because of it—are purer in motive and more directly and delicately written than any of Fitzgerald's earlier stories."[2]

Similarly, Mangum observes astutely that "the starkness of the description" in "The Lost Decade" contributes dramatically to the impression of Trimble's "disorientation in a world that he is really seeing for the first time in a decade." And Higgins praises the story for its "pithiness without barrenness," but then identifies as a "small flaw" Fitzgerald's handling of setting: "Setting is adequately, but not really effectively, conveyed by suggestion through a minimum of descriptive phrases." In point of fact, however, we know as much about the story's setting as is necessary for an appreciation of Trimble—and in particular for an appreciation of the ways in which Trimble reflects Fitzgerald. Kreuter and Kreuter deem the story "a hyperbolic treatment of [Fitzgerald's own] sense of non-fulfillment and of remorse about the immediate circumstances of his own life."[3] But that negative response

2. Sergio Perosa, *The Art of F. Scott Fitzgerald*, 146; Arthur Mizener, *The Far Side of Paradise: A Biography of F. Scott Fitzgerald*, 322.

3. Bryant Mangum, *A Fortune Yet: Money in the Art of F. Scott Fitzgerald's Short Stories*, 162; John A. Higgins, *F. Scott Fitzgerald: A Study of the Stories*, 170; Kent Kreuter and Gretchen Kreuter, "The Moralism of the Later Fitzgerald," 72.

to Trimble/Fitzgerald reveals only half the picture. To understand the story fully, one must acknowledge that it simultaneously presents a *positive* image, one affirming the joy of recovery from the disease of alcoholism and offering the promise of a life, a career, and a nation regaining the stability and productivity they somehow had "lost" in the 1930s.

The story is quickly told, and it draws upon an incident from Fitzgerald's own life. In November 1938 Fitzgerald was hired to collaborate with Budd Schulberg on a screenplay about Dartmouth College's annual Winter Carnival. According to James L. W. West III, "When young Schulberg was told that he would be working with Fitzgerald, he said, 'My God, isn't Scott Fitzgerald dead?' Fitzgerald did not hear the remark, but obviously he sensed Schulberg's attitude toward him and restated it fictionally in 'The Lost Decade.' "[4]

In the story, Schulberg is thinly veiled as young Dartmouth graduate Orrison Brown. A subeditor-cum-"gofer" at an unnamed New York–based news magazine, Brown is asked to squire around town one Louis Trimble. Trimble's name "evoked some vague memory," but Brown cannot place it.[5] His attempts to determine Trimble's identity and his whereabouts for the previous ten years form the bulk of the plot, rendering "The Lost Decade" a kind of mystery story. As such, it may owe less to Hemingway than to Arthur Conan Doyle, from whom, according to Owen Dudley Edwards, Fitzgerald received "his first lessons in literary economy, in the structure of the short story deployed with scientific precision, and in the use of the commonplace for the creation of haunting atmosphere."[6] Eventually, Brown learns that Trimble was the architect who designed the Armistead Building—and that after the completion of this Manhattan landmark, Trimble "was taken drunk . . . every-which-way drunk" (472). Suddenly, Brown realizes the truth about Trimble's decade-long absence from "civilization" (471): " 'Jesus,' he said to himself. 'Drunk for ten years' " (473).

4. James L. W. West III, "Fitzgerald and *Esquire*," 161.

5. F. Scott Fitzgerald, *The Stories of F. Scott Fitzgerald: A Selection of 28 Stories*, 470. All subsequent page references to "The Lost Decade" are to this edition and will appear parenthetically in the text.

6. Owen Dudley Edwards, "The Lost Teigueen: F. Scott Fitzgerald's Ethics and Ethnicity," 187.

More than anything else, the power of "The Lost Decade" is derived from its premise. Few prospects are more pitiful than that of a talented individual self-destructing through substance abuse, and Fitzgerald's refusal to explain how or why Trimble—evidently a dynamic architect and a graduate of the prestigious "Massachusetts Tech" (471)—came to be drunk for ten years makes his case all the more terrifying. Perhaps there was no discernible trigger for his descent into alcoholism; or what is worse, perhaps the trigger was his very talent, his good looks, his intelligence, his first-rate education—and his public success. This possibility gains credence from Fitzgerald's taking care to specify that Trimble's ten-year drunk began the same year the Armistead Building was erected: 1928. Had the drinking problem begun in 1929, readers would assume Trimble had simply been responding to the national problem of the collapse of the stock market and the ensuing depression. Instead, his difficulties began at a golden time in the national economy—and a golden time in his own career. It was when the beautiful and original skyscraper was finally *completed*—"Erected 1928" (472)—that Trimble went downhill, in that infamous Fitzgeraldian paradigm (seen most familiarly in the case of Dick Diver and Nicole Warren) of transference of vitality.

The trigger was not difficulties with the design, problems with construction, or loss of financial backing. The trigger was success, with the "erected" building causing the collapse of its creator. It was a scenario that could be appreciated fully by F. Scott Fitzgerald, the handsome Princetonian responsible for designing and for seeing through to successful completion yet another beautiful and original creation, his masterpiece *The Great Gatsby*. It was a novel so remarkable that even Fitzgerald himself, its "architect," stumbled for years as he sought to create a worthy successor in his fourth novel. And during that period of false starts and painful rewrites—indeed, throughout the 1930s—Fitzgerald was burdened with personal crises so relentless and overwhelming that he would have agreed completely with Orrison Brown's boss that "Some people would consider themselves lucky to've missed the last decade" (470).

The most apparent crisis, as noted, was his inability to write a new novel; and by the time *Tender Is the Night* finally appeared in 1934, a depression-weary nation evinced little interest in what it perceived as a chronicle of the rich and famous on the Riviera. It garnered only polite critical applause and disappointing sales. Also during this period, Fitzgerald saw his formerly lucrative and reliable *Saturday Evening Post* story market essentially dry up, for reasons both financial and editorial. Further, he had witnessed his wife descend into mental illness: Her first breakdown occurred in Paris in April 1930, the second came in February 1932, and the last was in January 1934. Thereafter, Zelda Fitzgerald spent most of her life in expensive private psychiatric hospitals. With his wife incapacitated, Fitzgerald attempted to raise their daughter Scottie virtually alone. For years he shunted his little family from hotel to apartment to rented house, unable to locate an emotionally secure home base. In addition, he had run up shockingly high personal debts, particularly with his agent, Harold Ober; by 1937 the sum was approximately forty thousand dollars.[7] Not surprisingly, he had taken up serious drinking during these years—not the tippling of the teenager or the undergraduate, and not the too-heavy "social" drinking characteristic of the Prohibition era, but the kind of elbow-bending distinctive of a bona fide alcoholic.

Indeed, Julie M. Irwin has argued that one may trace in Fitzgerald's short fiction the three phases of alcoholism, culminating in the third-stage level of the disease that is characterized by "blackouts" of increasing duration. Trimble thus would be in that final stage noted for "malnutrition, decreased tolerance [for alcohol], morning drinking, and estrangement from friends and family, evolving in many instances to the classic Skid Row disaster and ending in death."[8] In other words, Trimble is doomed.

Or is he?

If it is true that Trimble is in the final and most severe stage of alcoholism, then we should see him "plagued by physical and psychological problems"; we should see him drinking "constantly," and "if ethyl alcohol cannot be found, he will drink cough syrup, shaving lotion, rubbing alcohol, anything with alcohol that he can get his hands on"; further, "suicide is common at this stage. Be it suicide, illness, or accident, by one means or another the [third-stage] alcoholic stands a good chance

7. Bruccoli, *Epic Grandeur*, 423.
8. Julie M. Irwin, "F. Scott Fitzgerald's Little Drinking Problem," 418.

of dying soon."[9] This hardly sounds like Louis Trimble. As a man with an almost morbid interest in illness, Fitzgerald must have known well that his depiction of Trimble runs counter to the clinical portrait of the third-stage alcoholic. Trimble is a man, after all, who passes up the infamous "21" Club and Moriarity's in order to find some place noted for food rather than drink; and when he finally walks away from Brown at the end of the story, the young man observes that "there was nothing about him that suggested or ever had suggested drink" (473). Further, far from looking haggard, unkempt, or hollow-eyed, Trimble is described as "a pale, tall man of forty with blond statuesque hair" (470). Instead of being loud or antisocial, he has a mild, subdued manner "that was neither shy nor timid, nor otherworldly like a monk, but something of all three" (470). Indeed, Trimble is clearly obsequious with young Brown ("Let's eat somewhere along here . . . —you choose" [471]) and is said repeatedly to be "obedient," whether to traffic lights (471) or to Brown's directives:

> It was all kind of nutsy, Orrison decided—and changed himself suddenly into a guide.
> "From here you get a good candid focus on Rockefeller Center," he pointed out with spirit "—and the Chrysler Building and the Armistead Building, the daddy of all the new ones."
> "The Armistead Building," Trimble rubber-necked obediently. "Yes—I designed it." (472)

Getting "a good candid focus" on his surroundings is likewise not what one would expect of a third-stage alcoholic, a class that is notorious for bleary eyes and an incapacity to concentrate. The central metaphor of "The Lost Decade" is eyesight, and in Trimble's case good vision—and in particular a sensitivity to detail—are of paramount importance. He yearns to immerse himself in sensations of which teetotalers are generally unaware, such as "the back of people's heads" and "how their heads are joined to their bodies" (471). His desire to study detail is expanded to include sound: "I'd like to hear what those two little girls are saying to their father. Not exactly what they're saying but whether the words float

9. Ibid., 423.

or submerge, how their mouths shut when they've finished speaking" (471–72). This almost surreal receptivity to sensory detail even includes tactile impressions: " 'The weight of spoons,' said Trimble, 'so light. A little bowl with a stick attached' " (472). This heightened sensitivity to reality proves infectious: As the story closes, Brown himself "felt suddenly of the texture of his own coat and then he reached out and pressed his thumb against the granite of the building by his side" (473). As Le Vot points out, this keen attention to "the lowly but fundamental details of daily life" is reminiscent of Fitzgerald's description of his bus ride in "Afternoon of an Author" (1936): "He loved life terribly for a minute, not wanting to give it up at all."[10]

But what is more to the point—and what seems too readily lost in these moving evidences of Trimble's newfound responsiveness to reality—is that they are symptoms of his own personal and professional rebirth. Trimble has already decided that he will "take a look at"—not "visit"— his alma mater the following week (471), evidently a pilgrimage to a place from his happy, pre-binge past, and one associated with the moment in his personal history when he was launched into a brilliant career. The return to "Tech" would be a way of confirming visually his psychological readiness to begin that brilliant career a second time.

Further, let us remember that "The Lost Decade" revolves around his visit to the New York office of a "news-weekly" (470). The implication is that Louis Trimble is "news" once again. He is back in the world of architecture—and Fitzgerald leaves us with no doubt that he will indeed make that four o'clock appointment with the magazine's chief editor. To be sure, the ten-year drunk has left him subdued, with a childlike curiosity about his environment and in temporary need of a reverse-Charon to guide him back to the world of the living. And yes, as his surname suggests, he still may be inclined to "tremble," to be a bit shaky in his transition from the liquid of alcohol to the granite of skyscrapers and daily living. But Trimble is emphatically a man for whom the worst is over; and if there is a psychological distancing that prevents him from seeking contact with the edifice he himself designed—"I've been in it— lots of times. But I've never seen it. And now it isn't what I want to see.

10. André Le Vot, *F. Scott Fitzgerald: A Biography,* 291.

I wouldn't ever be able to see it now" (472)—he nonetheless can derive some satisfaction from knowing he is responsible for "the daddy of all the new" buildings in Manhattan (472).

One may argue that Fitzgerald's depiction of Trimble on the threshold of a second brilliant career and virtually recovered from alcoholism reflects wishful thinking on his part. It is questionable that one could regain preeminence a second time in a high-powered, rapidly changing field such as architecture after a ten-year absence, and it is a donnée of health science that one can never recover fully from alcoholism; keeping the disease under control on a daily basis is the most for which one can hope. But it still seems clear that Fitzgerald has faith in the future of Louis Trimble—and that faith seems to reflect Fitzgerald's own situation at the moment of the story's composition. As of July 1939, World War II was still essentially a European problem. What Fitzgerald could see was a nation at peace and an economy enjoying a definite, if modest, upswing. For a man who identified so insistently with his country and historical moments, all this could only bode well.

Even more to the point, by the time he came to write "The Lost Decade," Fitzgerald had for two years been working rather steadily as a screenwriter in Hollywood, earning at times up to $1250 per week, in addition to collecting fees (usually $250 per story) from *Esquire*. His money woes seemed finally under control: "I've paid off 99/100 of my debts," he wrote with pride and relief to *Esquire* editor Arnold Gingrich in the letter that accompanied the manuscript of "The Lost Decade."[11] Further, his experiences in Hollywood and the promise of financial stability had led him to begin work excitedly on what probably would have been a fine novel, *The Last Tycoon*.

11. West ("Fitzgerald and *Esquire*") discusses Fitzgerald's *Esquire* earnings. As for the Hollywood income, Dardis (*Some Time in the Sun: The Hollywood Years of F. Scott Fitzgerald, William Faulkner, Nathanael West, Aldous Huxley, and James Agee*) records that Fitzgerald "earned a weekly salary of $1,000 at MGM for the last six months of 1937 and $1,250 per week for all of 1938." Since Fitzgerald worked forty-five weeks in 1938, the studio paid him approximately $68,000; and Dardis calculates that by the standards of the 1970s, this sum was roughly equivalent to $200,000—"all this at a time when income taxes were either tiny or nonexistent" (29); Matthew J. Bruccoli and Margaret M. Duggan, eds., *Correspondence of F. Scott Fitzgerald*, 535.

True, Zelda Fitzgerald would never recover fully from her schizophrenia, but she did have periods of lucidity, and Fitzgerald was able to secure outstanding medical care for her both here and abroad. Daughter Scottie had proved to be an intelligent, attractive, responsible young woman, who had matriculated at Vassar College in September 1938. He had found a measure of peace and love, plus a semipermanent home, with writer Sheilah Graham. And he was able to look back at *The Great Gatsby* with a degree of calm pride: That novel was "the daddy of all the new ones," and no one could ever gainsay that he had left a permanent mark on the landscape of literature.

In short, after the public confessional of "The Crack-Up" (1936) and the penance of debts, of guilt over his wife, even of eating out of tin cans in North Carolina in November 1935, Fitzgerald by July 1939 apparently felt that he had made his separate peace.[12] He was still a bit fragile emotionally and physically—surely the cracked-plate metaphor in the *Esquire* essay "Pasting It Together" (March 1936) relates on some level to the tremble/Trimble pun of "The Lost Decade"—but in general this was a man who, like Trimble, felt that the past was behind him and that the new decade of the 1940s held the promise of good things to come. As he wrote Scottie in June 1940, about six months after the publication of "The Lost Decade," "What little I've accomplished has been by the most laborious and uphill work, and I wish now I'd *never* relaxed or looked back—but said at the end of *The Great Gatsby:* 'I've found my line—from now on this comes first. This is my immediate duty—without this I am nothing.'" Those words, plus the textual evidence of "The Lost Decade," betoken not what Perosa characterizes as "a straw man" for whom "there seems to be no possible escape or redemption," but rather a man who has recovered his sense of vocation—and his sense of self.[13] In short,

---

12. Bruccoli, *Epic Grandeur,* 404.

13. Andrew Turnbull, ed., *The Letters of F. Scott Fitzgerald,* 79; Perosa, *Art of F. Scott Fitzgerald,* 145. Perosa's appraisal would apply more accurately to Don Birnam, the dipsomaniac antihero of Charles Jackson's 1944 novel *The Lost Weekend.* Birnam loves Fitzgerald's work and expresses dismay over the impact of alcoholism on the writer's career. Ponders Birnam, "Why were drunks, almost always, persons of talent, personality, lovable qualities, gifts, brains, assets of all kinds (else why would anyone care?); why were

once the context in which it was created is recovered and understood, one sees that ultimately "The Lost Decade" is Janus-faced: It does look, with much remorse, at an unfortunate past—but it looks just as clearly, with quiet hope, to a promising future.

---

so many brilliant men alcoholic?" (Charles Jackson, *The Lost Weekend*, 221). That Jackson may have written the echoically titled *The Lost Weekend* in response to "The Lost Decade" is lent credence by entry 1576 in Fitzgerald's *Notebooks:* Jackson once turned up drunk at Fitzgerald's doorstep, announcing, " 'I feel I owe you more than I can say. I feel you formed my life,' " (Matthew J. Bruccoli, ed., *The Notebooks of F. Scott Fitzgerald*, 252).

PART II

STUDIES OF
STORY GROUPS

INITIATION AND INTERTEXTUALITY IN
THE BASIL AND JOSEPHINE STORIES

JAMES NAGEL

F. Scott Fitzgerald's stories about Basil Duke Lee and Josephine Perry do not constitute his finest efforts in fiction. Indeed, in subject, theme, and style, as well as in the general subtlety of his artistic methods, it is difficult to imagine that these stories were composed *after* his brilliant success with *The Great Gatsby* in 1925. Their inception followed Fitzgerald's return to the United States from France in 1926, when he took writing assignments in Hollywood before moving to Delaware. It was there, early in 1928, that he reached back to childhood material for a series of stories, all but one of which was published in the *Saturday Evening Post,* then paying him over thirty-five hundred dollars for each story. He produced nine Basil stories in just over a year, beginning in February of 1928, and they were published almost immediately after composition. He wrote "The Scandal Detectives" in March, for example, and it appeared in the *Post* on April 28. The last of these stories, "Basil and Cleopatra," was finished in February of 1929 and published on April 27, thus completing the Basil sequence. After the fallow period following *The Great Gatsby,* it was a productive return, creatively and financially. He did not begin the corresponding Josephine stories until after he had returned to Europe in 1929. He wrote the initial piece in the Josephine series, "First Blood," in January of 1930, and it appeared in the *Post* on April 5. Zelda Fitzgerald had her celebrated emotional breakdown that month, and she went to a clinic in Switzerland for therapy. He worked on these five stories intermittently over the following year, finishing the sequence with "Emotional Bankruptcy" in June of 1931, and its publication in the *Post* on August 15 marked the end of the series. The following month he returned to America, resumed his work in Hollywood, and never completed these stories, which he intended to end with a concluding episode that brought Basil and Josephine together.[1]

Unlike *The Great Gatsby,* these stories contain predictable events, expository intrusions, abrupt shifts of time into the future as well as the past, unconvincing changes in the attitudes of the characters, and plots that hang on the breathless possibilities of a look, a dance, a kiss. Even Fitzgerald seems to have had mixed feelings about them: In 1934 he proposed a volume of the stories to Maxwell Perkins, suggesting that he would add a final story that united the two characters. He included many of these stories in *Taps at Reveille* in 1935, including "The Scandal Detectives," "The Freshest Boy," "He Thinks He's Wonderful," "The Captured Shadow," and "The Perfect Life," all of which are about Basil, as well as "First Blood," "A Nice Quiet Place," and "A Woman with a Past" in the Josephine series. He listed "Emotional Bankruptcy," which concludes the Josephine sequence, among those stories he felt worthy of publication in a new collection in the event of his sudden death.[2] On the other hand, he included four of the stories in a list of works that should be permanently "scrapped," including one of the best of them, "Basil and Cleopatra." Over the last six decades, notwithstanding the comment by Kenneth Eble that the Basil stories "are as excellent in craftsmanship as any . . . Fitzgerald ever wrote," some scholars have, in acts of omission and neglect, tended to side with the more negative of Fitzgerald's assessments.[3]

1. All references to the Basil and Josephine stories refer to F. Scott Fitzgerald, *The Basil and Josephine Stories.* All subsequent citations are to this edition and will appear parenthetically in the text.

2. See Fitzgerald, *Basil and Josephine,* 8–9; Matthew J. Bruccoli and Margaret M. Duggan, eds., *Correspondence of F. Scott Fitzgerald,* 406.

3. The four stories listed were "A Night at the Fair," "Forging Ahead," "Basil and Cleopatra," and "A Snobbish Story." Fitzgerald's letter to Maxwell Perkins, dated March 26, 1935, is printed in Bruccoli and Duggan, eds., *Correspondence,* 406–7; Kenneth Eble, *F. Scott Fitzgerald,* 23.

Although criticism on the Basil and Josephine stories has not been voluminous, it has maintained, from the beginning, a generally sophisticated level. The stories have received passing reference in numerous books and articles, and the major critical documents demonstrate what has become the common assessment of Fitzgerald readers—that these stories do not compare, artistically or thematically, with the best of the novels and short fiction but that nonetheless they reward close reading and contemplation. The early scholarship on the stories came indirectly, in comments relating the stories to biographical events or to more important works. In his 1963 study of the composition of *Tender Is the Night*, Matthew J. Bruccoli provided passing comment on the stories, calling them an "episodic autobiographical novelette" that contains some "excellent writing." His other comments on the stories relate to the exploration of the theme of emotional bankruptcy, given greater depth in the novel. In 1966 Richard D. Lehan ignored the Basil stories completely and mentioned the Josephine stories only as a gloss on *Tender Is the Night;* his most valuable observation is that "A Nice Quiet Place" was published in *Taps at Reveille* and the Josephine character is called "Rosemary" at one point, suggesting a conceptual link between the novel and the story. His other comments link the biographical Ginevra King with the fictional Josephine, emphasizing on both levels the idea that emotional involvements have moral implications. Lehan, however, did not give the stories any direct analysis.[4]

Two years later, Sergio Perosa provided brief but excellent commentary on the two series. His approach is to analyze Basil in his role as a "philosopher" passing through his formal and social education toward an inner maturity he does not possess in the early stories. Josephine, on the other hand, is discussed as the quintessential "flapper" even though the term had not yet been invented at the time her stories take place. Perosa acknowledges that there are "childish and naive" aspects to these stories, but he finds much of value in them, including the awareness that "the principle of evil is already active in the idyll of youth; boys and girls act out of malice or spite, and the suffering that they cause

---

4. Matthew J. Bruccoli, *The Composition of "Tender Is the Night": A Study of the Manuscripts,* 56, 69; Richard D. Lehan, *F. Scott Fitzgerald and the Craft of Fiction,* 57, 92, 127.

may in itself become a maturing experience." His assessment of the Basil sequence suggests a pattern of progressive growth culminating in "Basil and Cleopatra" and the rejection of "sentimental love," the establishment of a new psychic balance, and an optimistic look to the future. Josephine, in Perosa's view, does not experience comparable growth, despite some elements of self-recognition, and her stories end with her feeling more bitterness than regret. What unites the two groups of stories, from this perspective, is the underlying theme that "the principle of evil and conflict is present everywhere, even in the golden years of youth and adolescence."[5]

Constance Drake in 1969 devoted her attention exclusively to the Josephine stories, arguing that the theme of emotional bankruptcy unites all five. In a persuasive development of this idea, she explores the theme of the "gradual emotional destruction of a character" to its culmination in the concluding story, which dramatically portrays that "a romantic sensibility coupled with self-indulgence will lead to wasted emotions until there are no more to waste." In 1971 John A. Higgins discussed each of the Basil stories as focusing on a stage in his development toward a more mature understanding of himself. Higgins devotes but a single paragraph to each story, but he is insightful about the painful but necessary conflicts at the heart of each work, particularly in his observation that the stories all have a duplicate structure that exposes Basil to the same situation twice in each story. Higgins casts the Josephine stories in counterpoint to Basil's progressive development: "Josephine does undergo a series of maturing and disillusioning experiences like Basil, but whereas his maturing was an ascent toward his 'unknown destiny' and his eyes at the end are still fixed on the stars, Josephine's movement is actually a decline from the freshness of innocence into jadedness." In a series of brief analyses, Higgins demonstrates the wisdom of this observation, concluding with the comment about "Emotional Bankruptcy" that "no piece of Fitzgerald's short fiction conveys more intensely the horror of the realization that one's emotional resources are exhausted."[6]

One of the most extensive and informed discussions of the two groups of stories is the introduction by Jackson R. Bryer and John Kuehl

5. Sergio Perosa, *The Art of F. Scott Fitzgerald*, 88, 93.
6. Constance Drake, "Josephine and Emotional Bankruptcy," 6, 12; John A. Higgins, *F. Scott Fitzgerald: A Study of the Stories*, 108, 115, 117.

to *The Basil and Josephine Stories* in 1971. They present a detailed account of the composition and publication history of the stories along with a discussion of their historical and biographical context. Their assessment builds on the work of previous scholars, particularly Higgins and Bruccoli, and their judgment is consistently sound, particularly their balanced conclusion that "these are not uniformly excellent short stories, especially those in the Josephine series, but they benefit enormously from being read as two series and as ironically juxtaposed sequences."[7]

Kenneth Eble ignored that advice in 1977 in the revised edition of his 1963 study *F. Scott Fitzgerald,* separating his discussions of the two groups of stories and ignoring the thematic counterpoint between them. Indeed, though Eble presents some interesting biographical parallels between Fitzgerald and Basil (including the fact that Fitzgerald wrote a play titled "The Captured Shadow" in 1912, the same year Basil does), he has little to offer by way of analysis. Eble considers the stories to be "excellent in craftsmanship," written at the "peak of Fitzgerald's skill." He concludes that the opening of "The Freshest Boy" "could not be improved upon." He misreads the painful episode in "He Thinks He's Wonderful" in which Basil, attempting to impress the father of Ermine Bibble, talks too much and loses his chance to go on vacation with his beloved. Eble thinks that this incident constitutes an "excellent comic scene." His final position is that these stories portray Basil's deepening awareness of himself and that, by the end, he has developed a more mature judgment, a commonplace assessment by 1977. He is harder on the Josephine stories, finding them slight, and his biographical judgment here is often suspect: Eble does not say how he knows that Josephine represents "Fitzgerald's vision of an ideal woman." It seems unlikely that Fitzgerald would regard someone so superficial, manipulative, and immature as the epitome of femininity. Nor does Eble demonstrate that Josephine's thoughts "are more Fitzgerald's than the character's." Part of Eble's problem may have been that he seems not to have been aware of the previous scholarship on the stories.[8]

Joseph Mancini Jr. offered a much more sophisticated essay on the Basil stories in "To Be Both Light and Dark." Mancini does not so

---

7. Fitzgerald, *Basil and Josephine,* 26.
8. Eble, *F. Scott Fitzgerald,* 23, 26, 28, 115–19.

much present new information on or insights into these stories as cast
the prevailing insights into the arcane rhetoric of Jungian psychology,
reading Basil's mother as "anima," a feminine mirror of his inner self.
In the process, Mancini also relates the inner turmoil in these stories to
that in Fitzgerald's best work, particularly *The Great Gatsby* and *Tender
Is the Night*. Mancini's work is insightful, detailed, and imaginative, but
he does not explore the stories artistically, nor does he relate them to
the countering Josephine sequence.[9]

That work remained to be done by Alice Hall Petry in *Fitzgerald's Craft
of Short Fiction,* in some ways the best of the discussions of Basil and
Josephine, though she deals exclusively with the stories included in *Taps
at Reveille.* Petry explores not only the biographical and composition
history of the stories but gives them a close reading in context as well.
She reiterates Fitzgerald's monetary motivation in writing the stories,
giving the price per story as four thousand dollars. She is the first scholar
to suggest that the "emotional bankruptcy" theme pervades and unifies
the entire volume of *Taps at Reveille* and is not restricted to the stories
involving Josephine. Petry is finally almost as enthusiastic about these
stories as Eble, for she concludes that "with their generally uncluttered
styles, simplified plots, restrained dialogue, subtle metaphors, and gentle
humor, these stories show not the petrifaction of a talent, but its final
blooming." Her discussion of the interrelationship of the two sequences
is excellent, and she explores the success and disillusionment that invests
each of the stories, drawing the distinction that Basil seeks social success
while Josephine pursues her dream of love. In all, Petry's book is an
excellent contribution to the scholarly study of these two groups of
stories.[10]

Also in 1989 Brian Harding offered a brief discussion of the economic
theme of "Forging Ahead," stressing the "boy gets rich, boy gets girl" plot
and the sudden rescue of Basil's family from financial ruin. Harding's
conclusion is that "the Alger myths are exploded, only to be replaced
by the '20s version: a real-estate windfall." John Kuehl's treatment of

9. Joseph Mancini Jr., "To Be Both Light and Dark: The Jungian Process of Individuation
in Fitzgerald's Basil Duke Lee Stories," 89–110.

10. Alice Hall Petry, *Fitzgerald's Craft of Short Fiction: The Collected Stories—1920–1935,*
154, 161.

the stories in his *F. Scott Fitzgerald* is a slightly revised version of the introduction he had done with Jackson R. Bryer for *The Basil and Josephine Stories*. Although it is useful to have it available in a new format, one perhaps more accessible for undergraduates, Kuehl adds nothing of substance to his earlier discussion.[11]

Of much greater interest is Bryant Mangum's *A Fortune Yet*, which contains a substantial discussion of the Basil and Josephine sequence. Mangum argues convincingly that the Basil stories trace a progression from adolescence to maturity, with the protagonist fighting romantic illusions all the way but learning to function in an adult world. Basil is appealing because he is sensitive, ambitious, and eager to learn from experience, whereas Josephine is rebellious, insensitive, and snobbish, and her self-absorption leads her into emotional bankruptcy. Mangum is also persuasive in arguing that Fitzgerald's motivation for developing the two sets of stories was monetary, not artistic, and that during their publication his fee increased to four thousand dollars for each story, the highest payment he was ever to receive.[12]

What is evident from the history of scholarship is that the Basil and Josephine stories are a fascinating component of the Fitzgerald canon. Biographically, the Basil stories relate closely to elements of Fitzgerald's own life just as those about Josephine resonate with parallels to his thwarted adolescent romance with Ginevra King.[13] More broadly, the two sequences of stories show him still exploring the rich social texture of Buffalo, St. Paul, and his Minnesota origins, especially in terms of the bitter comedy of youth. Their greater importance in the canon, however, is in form, genre, and artistry, for they collectively relate to two important literary traditions growing in popularity at the time the stories were composed, interests largely ignored in previous Fitzgerald criticism: the bildungsroman, a form at the heart of the development of the novel, and the short story cycle, a tradition older than the novel, not nearly as

11. Brian Harding, " 'Made for—or against—the Trade': The Radicalism of Fitzgerald's *Saturday Evening Post* Love Stories," 124–25; John Kuehl, *F. Scott Fitzgerald: A Study of the Short Fiction*, 93–101.

12. Bryant Mangum, *A Fortune Yet: Money in the Art of F. Scott Fitzgerald's Short Stories*, 106–17.

13. Fitzgerald, *Basil and Josephine*, 21–24.

well understood, yet equally as vibrant a genre in American literature. Indeed, in 1919 Sherwood Anderson had united the two conventions in *Winesburg, Ohio* with great success, and before the Jazz Age had ended Ernest Hemingway had made his contribution to this generic synthesis in *In Our Time,* as had Jean Toomer in *Cane* and William Faulkner in *Go Down, Moses,* to mention only a few examples from the period. Although Fitzgerald never completed his sequence tracing the development of Basil and Josephine, and never wrote the concluding story that was to bring them together, the two groups of stories do constitute an intertextual "cycle" in that each of the stories is greatly enriched and deepened when placed in the context of the related group, and each sequence is further enriched when seen in thematic counterpoint to the other, as a review of the individual stories makes clear.

"That Kind of Party" can be discussed as a Basil story only on a provisional basis: Although Fitzgerald called the protagonist Basil in the manuscript, the published story changes the name to Terrence R. Tipton. The story is often discussed with the Basil group, however, not only because Terrence displays all the personality traits possessed by Basil in the subsequent narratives but also because it constitutes the beginning of a line of development that is enriched through stories that trace seven years of his development. "That Kind of Party" establishes the still point from which to measure Basil's growth and development as he struggles with egomania and manipulation, as he explores his attraction to girls, his successes and failures in school, his relationships to parents and authorities, and as he matures in his understanding of himself and the limits of his personal magnetism. The stories in the sequence each focus on dramatic moments of internal conflict that mark stages in his development regardless of whether they depict his ignominious defeat or gratifying success. Using "That Kind of Party" as a Basil story provides a group of three stories that deal with him prior to his departure for boarding school, a group further unified by its focus on his earliest romantic stirrings and defeats and introducing the central motifs that inform the entire sequence. This interpretative convenience does not change the name of the protagonist to "Basil," however, nor does it change the fact that Fitzgerald never completed his work on the stories to resolve this and other difficulties in constructing a fully unified story sequence.[14]

Although the Basil stories conclude with his collegiate experiences at Yale, they begin when he is only about ten (his friends are all ten and eleven) and a student at Mrs. Cary's Academy. The scion of a family that values private education and expects academic success and proper decorum, young Terrence Tipton is engaged in struggles outside the motivational concerns of his mother. The emotional fact that impels everything in this story is his infatuation with Dolly Bartlett and his hope of creating another opportunity to play kissing games with her. Toward this end, he is willing to manipulate and abuse his closest friends, to deceive adults who trust him, to punch a handicapped boy who mocks him, to sacrifice all and everyone for the gratification of his aims. Having once experienced the thrills of embracing Dolly, he is thwarted in his attempt to convince his mother to allow a party (she suspects his true motivation). Undaunted, he cons the innocent Joe Schoonover into seeking permission from his more permissive mother, and she acquiesces. Fearing that even she will forbid the playing of "clap-in-and-clap-out," he forges a telegram designed to lure her out of the house during the party, a plan that goes awry when the telegram is delivered to his own home by mistake. Nonetheless, despite numerous emotional twists and childish recriminations, Terrence succeeds in his desires and ultimately embraces Dolly, leading to an expository denouement: "In one day he had committed insolence and forgery and assaulted both the crippled and the blind. His punishment obviously was to be in this life. But for the moment it did not seem important—anything might happen in one blessed hour" (42). The story thus concludes with Terrence gratified in his success and having evaded the kinds of humiliations and internal struggles that come in subsequent stories. In the process of his initiation into manhood, this story marks not a significant advance but a starting point in which he reveals a rampant egomania and a

---

14. Previous scholars of the story have also considered "That Kind of Party" in the Basil sequence and cast it as the starting point for the protagonist's growth (Kuehl, *Fitzgerald: Study of the Short Fiction*, 96; Eble, *F. Scott Fitzgerald*, 23–24).

penchant for deceit and manipulation. Unlike the best stories in the sequence, in this opening narrative the protagonist learns little about himself and grows imperceptibly, if at all. In context, however, "That Kind of Party" is important in that it introduces the character traits that are at issue in the subsequent eight stories along with the unifying motifs of romance and school, manipulation and defeat, success and gratification.

These issues are central to the first of the "true" stories involving Basil Duke Lee, "The Scandal Detectives," a complex and unconvincing story that takes place during his last few months in St. Paul before he goes off to boarding school to prepare for Yale. The titular matter involves a book, written in invisible ink, that contains the indiscretions of other children. The point of the enterprise, however, is not the literary value such a narrative might contain, nor the simple pleasure Basil and his cohorts might derive from knowing and recording embarrassing information about others; rather, it is intended as a weapon to be employed at some indeterminate moment: "It was treasured against the time when its protagonists should 'do something' to Basil and Riply. Its possession gave them a sense of power" (45). The implications of such a document are rather different, however, notwithstanding the fact that Basil is but fourteen. A record of social indiscretions may indeed denote an advantage against other children, but it is also an artifact of insecurity and ineffectuality, strongly suggesting that Basil lacks the assurance that he can deal fairly with his rivals, compete openly with any hope of success, and muster the substance to face open conflict. Although he is described as being "bright and lazy at school" (45), his moral education has only just begun.

The central lesson for Basil in this story derives from his most heartfelt objective: to secure a kiss from Imogene Bissell, a divine creature of thirteen, in exchange for his school ring. The factor that unites the romantic quest with the scandal detectives is the appearance of a rival, Hubert Blair, who not only possesses a "virtuosic athletic ability" but also has the assurance Basil lacks: "He [Hubert] was confident; he had personality, uninhibited by doubts or moods" (51). He has no need for a book of scandal. Young girls are fascinated by him, and young boys understandably dislike him. Against Hubert's athletic and social prowess, Basil can display only a genteel priggishness, decked out for a party in his "white duck knickerbockers, pepper-and-salt Norfolk jacket, a Belmont collar and a gray knitted tie" (49). It is clear that Basil is no match for his rival, and Hubert wins the affections of Imogene and the opportunity to take her home from the party.

This development inspires in Basil not an impulse for direct confrontation nor open competition but an attempt to intimidate anonymously through his scandal group, and they send warning notes to Hubert's house and plan to tie him up and stuff him in a garbage can. This narrative line is replete with poetic justice, as Basil, disguised as a southern planter, confronts Hubert in the alley without benefit of a supportive gang, and he "made a startling discovery. He discovered he liked Hubert Blair—liked him as well as any boy he knew" (57). This transformation has more to do with Basil's fear and insecurity than with any transcendent revelation of Hubert's character, and it precipitates the first of Basil's humiliations when he runs, leaving Hubert free to concoct stories of his victory. The second ignominious development is when Hubert receives the coveted kiss from Imogene. In terms of his manifest objectives, Basil has lost on all fronts. The expository assertions of the omniscient narrator in the denouement that Basil has somehow grown from this experience, renouncing his desire to be a gentleman burglar and learning to function within the law, are singularly unconvincing: "All he knew was that the vague and restless yearnings of three long spring months were somehow satisfied" (63).

These concluding remarks are important as a stage in Basil's growth over the sequence of stories, but they also point to some of the problems with the narrative. For one thing, whatever growth is purported for Basil is not dramatized as a logical outgrowth of the action, somehow inherent in the conflict and resolution, but merely asserted in exposition by a superior narrative intelligence, relating the events two decades after they take place, able to foretell the future as well as the past. The suggestion that these events were satisfying, or even edifying, for Basil is problematic, for he seems to glean the wrong lessons from his actions. Rather than learning something about the dangers of infatuation, or the weakness of his attempts at intimidation, he simply decides he no longer cares for Imogene. It is difficult to conclude with Kenneth Eble that the story depicts Basil's triumph of imagination and development of scruples.[15] In a sense, he fails to transcend his need for a book of scandal or to grow internally in any meaningful degree, and the concluding assertion of the story seems dramatically unearned: "His face was turned without regret toward the boundless possibilities of summer" (63).

The key story for internal growth is "A Night at the Fair," the last of the stories to take place prior to Basil's departure for prep school. Indeed, this story is central to his development through the rites of passage of his disjointed bildungsroman and an excellent illustration of the intertextuality of the narrative line. No one of the first three stories is as important as is their interrelationship, for the motifs of romantic longings and social aspirations set amid the conflicts between Basil's insecurity and egomania, introduced in the first two stories, are resolved in the third. And it is not until this story that Basil demonstrates any significant internal development.

The plot of "A Night at the Fair" is not as important as its character transformations. The central conflict derives from the simple fact that Basil's close friend Riply Buckner has been given long trousers while Basil is still in short pants, a fact Riply uses to decided advantage in the courtship of young ladies at the Minnesota State Fair. In due course, Basil also gets his trousers, using his imminent departure for school in the East as the justification, and he kisses a girl at the fair, albeit under less than romantic circumstances and with a significance that could not have been anticipated. That the story concludes with his apparent victory in winning the attentions of Gladys Van Schellinger, only to have her reveal that her true affections are for Hubert Blair, is a characteristic deflation of ego for Basil, a development that is becoming common in his developmental stages. If there is nothing remarkable about this narrative line, what it all means for Basil, and what it reveals about the person he is becoming, is actually quite important.

That much of the action of the story takes place at the fair is thematically significant, for the fair is the locus of both stability and transition. It is, in one sense, a celebration of the agrarian values of the past,

---

15. Higgins, *Fitzgerald: Study of the Stories*, 106. The narrator asserts that a janitor found the book of scandal "years later" (45) and also that Imogene would, in "a few years," become the "belle of many proms" (47); Eble, *F. Scott Fitzgerald*, 25.

with exhibits of farm produce and animals that suggest the simple and homely values of rural life in the Midwest. On the other hand, also in evidence are the automobiles and airplanes of the technological world, the "hoochie-coochie shows" of a new age, and the courtship rituals that distinguish Basil's generation from the previous one. What these details indicate is that young Basil Duke Lee, of Holly Avenue in St. Paul, growing up without benefit of a father to guide him, is in the process of entering the new world. Before him is not only Speed Paxton in his Blatz Wildcat but also Elwood Leaming, who drinks, smokes, and is rumored to frequent burlesque shows. It is no place for a boy still in short pants, and Basil is humiliated to display such a graphic emblem of his immaturity in the context of the fast society of the fair. Because of his clothes, Basil loses the interest of a girl on the Old Mill ride, who much prefers the more mature Riply.

The key development in the story is not so much that Basil secures his long trousers, itself a transitional moment for him, but that his blind date for the evening proves to be unattractive in every sense. Nevertheless, Basil finds it within himself to behave as a proper escort. He not only takes her on the ferris wheel, but he kisses her at the appointed moment as well, motivated not by the desire for conquest so evident in the first two stories but by a sense of obligation and decency. It is his first unselfish act in the sequence of stories, and it is significant. As the narrator explains, even though Basil has no interest in the girl and would prefer to be alone, "he was unable to hurt anyone whom he thought of as an inferior" (77–78). Although Basil does seize an opportunity to escape his group when they encounter the dazzling Hubert Blair, he has done so with delicacy. Despite his humiliation at the end of the story, when his infatuation is deflated by the revelation of Gladys's interest in Hubert, Basil moves through his first significant rite of passage, manifest externally by the acquisition of long trousers and internally by an act of gratuitous kindness on his part when he acts graciously to an unattractive young girl. It is the first indication of an incipient generosity of spirit, but it will not be his last.

"The Freshest Boy" and "He Thinks He's Wonderful" provide episodes in thematic counterpoint surrounding Basil's first year of prep school at St. Regis. The central concerns of his developing identity and sense of himself, his relationships with his peers, his forays into romantic dramas, his realizations about the effects of his unbridled ego on the people around him resonate throughout both stories and are of greater moment when taken as intertextual contrast rather than as isolated stories.

It is significant that train trips begin both stories, the journey east to school in the first instance, the trek home in June in the second. "The Freshest Boy" shows Basil at fifteen dreaming of his heroic conquests in the East, first as a romantic figure, "The Shadow," in a Broadway restaurant with a woman dancing on the table. In his fantasy, he is in charge of the situation, sophisticated, capable. The second daydream has similar motifs, as Basil imagines himself being sent into a football game to save the day for St. Regis. These dreams present in fantasy what the narrator formulates directly in "He Thinks He's Wonderful," that "he wanted to be a great athlete, popular, brilliant and always happy" (107). The harsh reality that intrudes between these two dream episodes is of a differing tone, however, for Basil reflects that he talked too much in St. Paul at the Country Day School and became very unpopular. It is this issue, not romantic heroism, that dominates the story.

But Basil has not changed when he arrives at St. Regis, and he quickly becomes the most detested and unpopular student at the school, mocked and ridiculed by the other boys, observed with dismay by the faculty. The best that can be said for him is that he is aware of the vehicle of his fate: "He saw now that in certain ways he had erred at the outset—he had boasted, he had been considered yellow at football, he had pointed out people's mistakes to them, he had shown off his rather extraordinary fund of general information in class" (90). Basil's roommate moves out, and the other children call him "Bossy," important in that Fitzgerald uses nicknames as a motif in his works and the inception of a new name for him, "Lee-y," will mark his first stride toward acceptance at St. Regis.

At the heart of the story, however, is an opportunity to escape his unpopularity in the world he has made for himself by fleeing to Europe and school in Grenoble or Montreux, a prospect that initially emboldens him and looms as the perfect resolution to his dilemma. He learns of the opportunity, significantly, on a trip to New York to the theater, in which context he observes Ted Fay, the Yale football captain, having problems of his own: His girlfriend is obligated to marry her theatrical benefactor, Mr. Beltzman. The resolution of this issue comes in another story, but the Ted Fay incident is important in that it reveals to Basil the fact that even the most celebrated person he has observed faces personal difficulties, as does the hapless Mr. Rooney, who gets drunk and makes a fool of himself in public. Basil decides to stay at St. Regis and face up to his problems. As John A. Higgins points out, in so doing, "Basil takes a long step on the road to maturity, realizing that he must overcome his unpopularity rather than run from it." Ironically, on the social level, he is less successful in the world he has yearned for in the East than he was in St. Paul; psychologically, however, he has come to see that he must understand his unpopularity and change his character if he is to be accepted, and this realization establishes a foundation for much of his subsequent growth in the following stories.[16] His minor success in gaining some respect from the other boys, and being called Lee-y in basketball at the end of the story, suggest the promise of future development.

"He Thinks He's Wonderful," which takes place in June of 1912, the end of Basil's first year at St. Regis, suggests that his incremental gains toward maturity have been minor, however. On the train ride back to St. Paul, Basil sits with Margaret Torrence, who observes that he has lost some of the "ultraconfident" tone of the previous summer (108). Indeed, his initial return to St. Paul is a triumph, as several girls choose him as their favorite beau (111). Basil is sufficiently emboldened to give advice on popularity to another boy, Joe Gorman, who is offended. Soon, the girls lose interest in him, and Basil has a reputation for being "stuck up" (112). All of this concludes with an opportunity to go with Minnie Bibble and her family to Glacier National Park, which Basil desperately desires. Attempting to impress Mr. Bibble, he becomes loquacious in the extreme and loses the chance. Again, he is forced to the realization that he has made an error, offended people in an attempt to ingratiate himself with them, and that his fate is of his own making. It is an important realization for him parallel to that in the previous story, though his behavior continues to display more recapitulation of immature egomania than transformation to a more mature balance.

In "The Captured Shadow," Basil is fifteen and still a student at St. Regis School. What is fascinating about this story is how Fitzgerald

---

16. Higgins, *Fitzgerald: Study of the Stories*, 107; Eble, *F. Scott Fitzgerald*, 27.

uses Basil's aspirations as a playwright to reveal aspects of his developing personality. His aborted musical comedy "Mr. Washington Square"
displays his continuing obsession with the world of the millionaire club
with its attendant dashing young gentlemen and their debutantes. "Hic!
Hic! Hic!" is a farce in a fashionable apartment near Broadway in New
York that rests on the lame joke of hiccups being interpreted for Latin
phrases. Most pointedly, however, since it has intertextual reference to
earlier stories, is the melodrama "The Captured Shadow," which again
is set in a fashionable home in New York. In this play Basil draws on his
own childhood fantasies in "The Scandal Detectives" about becoming a
gentleman burglar (45) and in "The Freshest Boy," in which he introduces himself on the train taking him east to prep school as "Basil Lee,
better known as the Shadow" (83). Perhaps because it is to some extent
an exercise in self-exploration, Basil throws himself into the writing of
this play, staying up all night, absorbing himself completely into the
transformation of his experience into art.

This enthusiasm inspires new dimensions of personal growth for Basil,
as when he suppresses his personal feelings and casts his old rival Hubert
Blair as the lead in the play, only to have Hubert quit shortly thereafter
(141). On the other hand, in the matter of the female lead, Basil once
again resorts to his characteristic manipulation: He needs Evelyn Beebe
for the role, but she is going with her family to the seashore for the
summer. With considerable calculation, Basil then arranges for her
younger brother to visit a boy who has the mumps. The brother gets the
mumps, the family cancels the trip, and Basil has his leading lady, "fully
aware that it was the worst thing he had ever done in his life" (143). That
he considers the moral consequences of his manipulation suggests the
beginning of an ethical conscience, something not previously discernible
in Basil, and a significant, if painful, triumph. That this matter is the
most important issue in the story is suggested structurally by the fact
that the story ends with Basil tormenting himself with what he has done
to little Ham (150). On this level, as Alice Hall Petry has indicated, the
story depicts "a good boy, moral and above all imaginative, coming to
grips with a world that does not always cherish such qualities."[17] His

17. Petry, *Fitzgerald's Craft*, 159.

developing conscience in this story outstrips the fact that he devotes himself to writing and staging the play and that it is a smash success even though he must stop the play in Act 2 and begin a scene over again when the players skip a major section. What is ultimately of moment is that, for the first time in his life, Basil has seriously considered the well-being of another person.

In "The Perfect Life," Fitzgerald takes this motif, a developing moral conscience, in an unexpected direction as Basil, obsessed with improving himself, becomes an insufferable prig. Basil is still at St. Regis at age sixteen and is becoming something of a football hero, running sixty yards for a touchdown. Beneath the surface, he is fatherless, ostracized by the older boys at school, and somewhat adrift in his formation of himself. When he meets John Granby, a student at Princeton, he is impressed by Granby's high ideals for him and his suggestion that Basil should concentrate on his "power of influencing all these boys to lead clean, upright, decent lives" (153). Predictably, this concept brings out the worst in Basil, and he resolves to be "perfect," to become "wonderful inside and out," and he soon fantasizes himself as president of the United States: "He would face the nation from the inaugural platform on the Capitol steps, and all around him his people would lift up their faces in admiration and love . . ." (154–55).

Within a month, Basil has become a self-righteous bore, lecturing other boys on the perfect life, commenting on their behavior. Rather than exploring these matters in depth, however, the story turns back to romantic interests. The transformation for Basil comes not out of some inner sense of self but from his relationship with a new girl, Jobena Dorsey, a flapper whose Jazz Age values conflict directly with his moral posturing. Attempting to impress her with his righteousness, he offends her with his proselytizing; he says to her, "It grieved me a lot this afternoon to see you smoking nicotine and dancing modern suggestive dances that are simply savagery" (165). Understandably, she flees from Basil into an engagement with the wild Skiddy De Vinci. When he later hears Jobena refer to him as a "nasty little prig" (166), he is at last inspired to reexamine his new values, for "deep in his heart he believed that what she had said was true" (167). As in "The Captured Shadow," Basil finds self-knowledge in a painful realization, and he relents by getting Skiddy drunk to prevent his elopement with Jobena. As Higgins has observed, "Basil realizes with horror that his priggish righteousness is only driving into 'sin' the girl he is trying to reform. With fine comic irony, Fitzgerald has the instrument of sin, drink, become the instrument of redemption."[18] This transformation impresses Jobena, and the story ends with their kiss and Basil's realization that flagrant righteousness is not an avenue to the perfect life.

"Forging Ahead" is the last of the Basil stories prior to his enrollment at Yale, and in this story he is sixteen, about to turn seventeen in September, and very much in a quandary about his college education. The external circumstances are that the family has lost a great deal of money in unwise investments, and Basil's mother can no longer afford to send him to an Ivy League university. Looming in Basil's imagination is the ignominious fate of attending a state university, bereft of the "incomparable girl" (178), devoid of the elite cachet Yale could give him. Basil is so terrified by the prospect that he volunteers to work for the summer at common labor, inspired by the sure and certain example of Horatio Alger's *Bound to Rise.*

His first effort is a job on the railroad, which does not suddenly and gratuitously metamorphose into a vice presidency, to Basil's disappointment, and he is instead summarily fired from his position. Presuming on rather distant family ties, he begs a job of his great-uncle, Benjamin Reilly, and secures a tenuous appointment that includes escorting his cousin Rhoda to parties all summer. This arrangement proceeds tolerably enough until Ermine Bibble unexpectedly appears and creates the inevitable conflict, as Basil finds himself with two dates to different parties on a single Saturday night. The best humor in the story comes from Basil's attempt to finesse the situation by hiring Eddie Parmelee to go to Rhoda's party, only to have Eddie pass the obligation on to a Japanese student with impossible English and no sense of American customs. The resolution of the conflict is decidedly deus ex machina, as Basil discovers his family has sold some real estate holdings for $400,000 and there is no longer any financial restriction on his enrollment at Yale. This news is combined with the sudden revelation that Basil has become engaged to Ermine. The principal gains for Basil in this story

18. Higgins, *Fitzgerald: Study of the Stories,* 107.

derive from his brief experience at hard labor and his resorting once again to imagination and deception, and merciful good luck, to achieve his desires.[19]

The concluding, and most important, story in the Basil sequence is "Basil and Cleopatra," which has Basil at Yale still in love with Ermine Bibble, who is now at a prep school in Connecticut. The central conflicts involve his academic failures and their interference with his eligibility for football set against the inconstancy of the erstwhile Ermine, whose heart has been won over by a Princeton rogue named Littleboy Le Moyne, with whom she has a romance on a train. Failing a trigonometry examination, Basil is temporarily suspended from football but passes a special test just in time to triumph over Princeton and become the hero of the game. His satisfaction is compromised, however, by the discovery that Ermine has rejected Le Moyne for yet another lover, which causes Basil to confess that he still loves her but regards her as a kind of Cleopatra. Although he sees Ermine again, he rejects the idea of resuming their courtship, exhibiting, for the first time, some measure of emotional maturity. He ends the story an athletic hero at Yale, a marginal student, and a failure at love.

Although it is perhaps too much to conclude, as does Sergio Perosa, that "Basil turns his back on the world of youthful emotion and enters a new, virile world, free from his many prejudices and weaknesses," it is clear that Basil has grown substantially in the course of the nine stories about him. He has here enjoyed his moment of revenge in his triumph over Le Moyne, the kind of satisfaction that obsessed him in the early stories in St. Paul, only to discover the hollow satisfactions of retribution. He has transcended the petty need for advantage that invested "The Scandal Detectives" even as he finally has his moment of victory over a rival. He has won and lost at love and found within himself the knowledge that he has been enamored with love itself, a theme that begins in "That Kind of Party" and "The Scandal Detectives" and forms a major motif throughout all the stories. His principal area of satisfaction has come from athletics, an issue from "The Scandal Detectives" to "Basil

19. Perosa sees a growing maturity in Basil in his capacity to be faithful to Ermine in this story (*Art of F. Scott Fitzgerald,* 90).

and Cleopatra," and he experiences the just rewards of his hard work and abilities. Whereas in the early stories he was "socially inept and, hence, spiritually and socially isolated," now his football exploits have won the admiration of students who formerly despised him.[20] Where once he was arrogant and self-aggrandizing, as in "He Thinks He's Wonderful," now he is humble in his acceptance of praise, knowing in his moment of success. These stories thus trace Basil's movement from insecure adolescence to a more mature formation of self, a triumph over egomania and insecurity that comes at the end of a long series of personal deflations.

Coordinate with the nine stories about Basil Duke Lee are five about the winsome ingenue Josephine Perry, Fitzgerald's embodiment of that "national historical phenomenon," the flapper.[21] As individual works, only the concluding "Emotional Bankruptcy" has attracted critical attention, and that primarily as a gloss on *The Great Gatsby* and *Tender Is the Night,* novels that overpower these slender tales of adolescent romance. However, as an interrelated series, the Josephine stories constitute an abbreviated feminine bildungsroman, with a psychological depth approaching that of the more famous novels, one that provides thematic counterpoint to the more fully developed saga of Basil. As a sequence of stories, as opposed to individual units, they explore a deeper and more complex emotional matrix as sixteen-year-old Josephine progresses through her coquettish exhilarations and emotional manipulations to a final romantic exhaustion at age eighteen.

It is clear that the Josephine stories are essentially independent works and that though Fitzgerald developed a plan to merge these stories with the Basil sequence, he never revised them to accommodate this arrangement. Each story introduces the characters by full name (even though they may have already been introduced in previous stories), establishes again the relationships among family members, and describes the settings. As in the Basil stories, each narrative depicts a transitional moment in adolescence, and the central issue revolves around Josephine's success or failure in attempting to manipulate those around her for

20. Ibid.; Petry, *Fitzgerald's Craft,* 189.
21. Petry, *Fitzgerald's Craft,* 183.

romantic conquest. Her goal seems not so much to find someone she can always *have* but to win a trophy for temporary display, and each story offers an installment on this central theme.

"First Blood" takes place in Chicago in 1914, the year Josephine turns sixteen, and the plot rests on her emergence as an ingenue and a rival for her sister, Constance. The title implies much of the theme, referring less to the inception of the World War in Europe, kept very much in the background, than to the romantic war Josephine has just begun at home—and she approaches romance as a form of combat. As she exhibits no respect for her parents in the opening of the story (217), she will show none for her sister, none for the young men she attracts, and ultimately none for herself. She is initially drawn to Travis de Coppet, a dandy who carries a "gold-headed cane" (219), and she anticipates a kissing date with him in an automobile, a modern emblem of changing technology and morality that sets this generation apart from their parents. But these plans are replaced by the appearance of Anthony Harker, who, at age twenty-two, is dating Josephine's older sister. That Josephine shows no hesitation in pursuing her sister's beau reveals something about her in this first story that will add resonance to the last: She functions within a solipsistic world of romantic mystery in which other people count only as players in her emotional drama.

She begins her manipulations by flirting with Anthony when he comes to call on Constance, continues her attentions at a dance with a lingering smile of "tender melancholy" (225), and finishes him off with a breathless kiss in the car and a confession of her love for him (227). The victory is momentary, however, and Anthony quickly loses interest when she writes to him, for her letters reveal less the woman than the child. The only expressions of emotion she can manage are those she has gleaned from popular songs, "as if they expressed the writer's state of mind more fully than verbal struggles of her own" (228). Anthony's break with her, his abrupt assertion that he has never loved her, leads to both a night of crying for her and an immediate remorseful letter from him professing desperate love, an epistle, once having been received, she immediately discards. As Kenneth Eble has observed, "Josephine has what she wants: not Harker himself but the satisfaction of knowing she could have him if she wished." The story ends with her aborted attempt to marry Travis, he of the golden cane, a plan that fails for want of a willing minister.

Throughout, the story reveals her as "determined, conceited, rebellious, indiscreet, and yet very young and innocent."[22] She has a superficial beauty that attracts virtually any young gentleman she wishes, but it is undermined by the egoistic immaturity of her desires, for she displays no substance whatever on which to base a mutually enriching relationship.

"A Nice Quiet Place" introduces a number of thematic modulations on the idea of pursuit and conquest as Josephine becomes involved with three young men in 1914. Although the Perry family normally summers in Lake Forest, a town of social elegance and romance away from the heat of Chicago, Josephine's mother, at the urging of Constance, decides to send Josephine to Island Farms, a rustic and isolated family enclave free of the romantic temptations that so enslave her younger daughter. Despite these restrictions, Josephine manages to develop three romantic relationships. In the first, she encourages Ridgeway Saunders, wins his attention, then loses him when he succumbs to the charms of one Evangeline Ticknor. It is a telling moment for her: "For the first time in her life she had been thrown over . . ." (241). The next battle is at Island Farms, where she attempts to interest the dashing Sonny Dorrance, who tells her he is married to a black woman, and she is crushed for a second time (249). These two incidents do not deepen her understanding of emotional vulnerability so much as they embolden her resolve and make her even more ruthless than before.

Her revenge is particularly insidious. At a dance in Lake Forest, Josephine flirts with and then kisses Ridge in a car, humiliating poor Miss Ticknor, who makes a hasty retreat back East; then she makes advances toward her sister's fiancé, Malcolm Libby, wins his affections, and causes great consternation when the two of them are discovered in compromising circumstances on his wedding day. Feeling socially but not morally embarrassed, Josephine leaves immediately for Island Farms to attempt to recoup in the matter of Sonny Dorrance, having discovered his ruse of an imaginary wife. In all, Josephine has felt the sting of rejection twice, recovered to turn one defeat into victory, and gone on to another conquest. In the process she has hurt both Evangeline and Constance, and she has evened the score for being banished to

---

22. Eble, *F. Scott Fitzgerald*, 116.

Island Farms at the beginning of the story. If these events are clichés of mundane adolescent romance, the moral stakes inherent in them are not, for they touch on issues of integrity and respect and idealistic longings, themes that invest the most mature of Fitzgerald's works.

In the next story, "A Woman with a Past," Josephine is seventeen and attending Miss Brereton's School in New Haven. Although there are assertions by the narrator to the effect that she has grown blasé and wants to find someone she "would love more than he loved her" (258), her behavior repeats the familiar pattern. Once again the story begins with her romantic domination of a young man, Ridgeway Saunders, who squires her to the prom at Yale, and the dissatisfaction in victory that leads her almost immediately to pursue Dudley Knowleton. Attacking on another front, she kisses Book Chaffee to have the experience of romancing a southerner, gets locked in a bedroom with him in a prank, and escapes, rather resourcefully, by jumping out a window into the snow below. Although she soon thereafter is expelled from school in an incident involving another boy, the key incident in the story is her pursuit of Dudley and his rejection of her for another young lady. The narrator's assertion in this case that "for the first time in her life she had tried for a man and failed" (277) is true within the confines of the story but false intertextually, for she was rejected a year earlier by both Ridgeway and Sonny Dorrance in "A Nice Quiet Place." Despite this point, the story introduces the motif of thwarted desires on two levels, the pursuit of an individual boy and the quest for an idealized true love. In time it will become apparent that her commitment to the second objective almost certainly precludes the attainment of the first.

The most curious plot in the sequence, that of "A Snobbish Story," reveals how Josephine is herself manipulated by someone even more unprincipled than she. The story is set in Lake Forest during the summer of 1916. Eschewing her traditional dance with Travis de Coppet in the local vaudeville show, she succumbs to the charms of John Boynton Bailey, a writer who casts her in the leading role in his play "Race Riot." In due course it becomes clear that he is married and pursues Josephine only to get funding for his production from her father, the wealthy Herbert T. Perry. In the midst of her own intrigue, she sees her father at lunch in a hotel with a peroxide blonde and misinterprets the encounter, assuming that her father is engaged in an affair. In fact, he is paying off the woman on behalf of his brother-in-law, a detail Josephine does not discover until later. What is equally important at this juncture is the revelation of Josephine's view of her father as "the cherished ideal of her life" (286) and her reflections on the warm relationship between her parents, her mother often holding her father's head in her lap. When Bailey's wife attempts suicide as a result of his attentions to Josephine, the theme of romantic "play" reveals a dark underside as the story "shows the increasingly serious consequences of Josephine's philosophy." Although there is justice in the observation by Higgins that all of this constitutes "a terrible mélange of mixed tones, superfluous and disproportioned scenes, and confused handling of themes, especially the titular theme of snobbishness," it is also true that the serious undercurrents of this penultimate escapade foreshadow an even more tragic development in the concluding story, "Emotional Bankruptcy."[23]

In this tale Josephine turns eighteen while attending Miss Truby's Finishing School, her education apparently having taken a social turn after the failure of her academic ambitions in New Haven. Josephine has become even more beautiful and still longs to love someone completely, a minor point at the beginning but the central issue in the conclusion, and she is once again accused of being blasé, this time by her friend Lillian. On the surface the story is about the Princeton prom and Josephine's simultaneous flirtation with Louie Randall, Martin Munn (who brings another young lady at Josephine's suggestion), and Paul Dempster, who is deeply in love with her. Predictably, she is attracted to yet another gentleman, the dashing Captain Edward Dicer, home on leave from the French Aviation. When the machinations of her strategy are at last successful, and he kisses her and tells her of his love, she can only confess that she feels nothing. To his shock, she says that "when you kissed me I wanted to laugh." When he asks again if she loves him, she replies: "I've got nothing to give you. I don't feel anything at all" (319). When he leaves in dismay, she has time for reflection: " 'Oh, what have I done to myself?' she wailed. 'What have I done? What have I done?' " (320). Significantly, this question concludes the Josephine stories, suggesting structurally that the answer resides in the entire sequence of events.

---

23. Higgins, *Fitzgerald: Study of the Stories,* 117, 118.

The answer to that question is of a deeper thematic resonance than these adolescent romantic plots would at first suggest, for "no piece of Fitzgerald's short fiction conveys more intensely the horror of the realization that one's emotional resources are exhausted."[24] The full significance of this story, however, rests in the intertextual thematic development throughout the five stories. Josephine's genuine love for Dicer is best revealed, for example, not in what she says to him but in the narrator's projection that she "wanted to take his head in her lap" (311), an allusion to the moment in "A Snobbish Story" when she remembers how her mother used to caress her father in precisely this way (286). The reference suggests that Josephine's longings have moved to a more mature level, to a desire to give as well as receive, to a desire for the genuine caring and tenderness her parents exhibit toward one another. Having attained this awareness, it is all the more tragic that she finds herself emotionally exhausted.

Indeed, as a group the stories are often enriched by intertextual references, as when in the first story Josephine says to Travis, "I've decided not to kiss any more boys, because I won't have anything left to give the man I really love" (221). Set against the concluding lines of the last story, this remark perfectly foreshadows her progressive affective desensitivity. As Constance Drake formulates it, "a romantic sensibility coupled with self-indulgence will lead to wasted emotions until there are no more to waste."[25] The comments in "A Woman with a Past" that Josephine has grown blasé suggest a charming affectation in New Haven that deepens in the final story to leave her emotionally dead. Josephine's attempt to marry Travis in "First Blood" resonates throughout all the other stories whenever the issue of marriages arises, as do her manipulations and rejections and self-delusions.

As individual units, the Josephine stories thus focus on isolated dramas of romantic pursuit, most often resolved with a minor conquest or failure. As a short story cycle, however, they constitute a tragic sequence of Josephine's progressive debasement of emotions to the ultimate epiphany at the end that she is dead inside. This progression runs in direct

---

24. Ibid., 117.
25. Drake, "Josephine and Emotional Bankruptcy," 12.

counterpoint to the stories involving Basil, since his transformations are toward greater emotional sensitivity, a more mature self-awareness, and a more humble social integration. These two sequences are rich in ironic contrast, but it would not have been easy to synthesize the two lines of action, despite the fact that they are united by "the motifs of emotional bankruptcy, the corruption of innocence, and the destructive power of charm. . . ." Basil is brought through painful recognitions to develop some regard for the integrity of other people; in contrast, Josephine is left with nowhere to turn, her psychic resources depleted, the tragic consequences of her romantic extravagance having finally been made apparent. As Alice Hall Petry has said, "The Josephine stories are bitter; it is emotionally draining to read about an attractive, intelligent girl whose life Fitzgerald so carefully depicts as purposeless, hopeless."[26] From this point of view, it is not surprising that F. Scott Fitzgerald never wrote the concluding story to the Basil and Josephine series that was to bring them together. But even without the projected concluding story, the stories of Basil and Josephine constitute a short story cycle that deserves renewed attention as a work of psychological subtlety and intensity, if not of polished artistry, and they should be considered worthy components of the Fitzgerald canon.

26. Higgins, *Fitzgerald: Study of the Stories*, 118; Petry, *Fitzgerald's Craft*, 183.

PHILIPPE, "COUNT OF DARKNESS," AND F. SCOTT FITZGERALD, FEMINIST?

PETER L. HAYS

In April 1934 Fitzgerald began a series of four linked stories set in ninth-century France, the nucleus of a historical novel he never finished.[1] Known as the Philippe or Count of Darkness stories, they were rejected by the *Saturday Evening Post* and purchased somewhat grudgingly by *Redbook*, as a favor to Fitzgerald, and published by *Redbook* in October 1934 and June and August 1935; the fourth and final story was not released until after Fitzgerald's death, in November 1941.[2] For a time, Fitzgerald considered extending the four stories rather than writing *The Last Tycoon*. He projected taking Philippe from the age of twenty, when the stories open, to the age of seventy, with eight stories or chapters dealing with his youth (with only four of the eight ever written), three

---

1. Historical romances were not new to Fitzgerald: He did an impressive job at Princeton in a little-considered short story, "Tarquin of Cheapside" (1917), that pictures Shakespeare as a rapist who used that experience to write "The Rape of Lucrece." It is published as such in *Tales of the Jazz Age*, though Fitzgerald spelled the title's last word "Cheepside," and it is under that title that John Kuehl reprints it in *The Apprentice Fiction of F. Scott Fitzgerald: 1909–1917*. There are also, as Janet Lewis points out, "The Night at Chancellorsville" (1935) and "The Fiend" (1935) ("Fitzgerald's 'Philippe, Count of Darkness,'" 30).

2. Matthew J. Bruccoli and Margaret M. Duggan, eds., *Correspondence of F. Scott Fitzgerald*, 590. Bryant Mangum reports that Fitzgerald got $1,250 for the first story, $1,500 for each of the next two, but does not say what *Redbook* paid for the final posthumously run story (*A Fortune Yet: Money in the Art of F. Scott Fitzgerald's Stories*, 144, 145).

chapters with his maturity, and two "great episodes" with his old age.[3] He entertained the notion for two years, but finally, and wisely, abandoned it, for the Count of Darkness stories are seriously flawed by Fitzgerald's weakness in writing about unexperienced, completely imagined scenes and by laughable dialogue, a movie version of imagined medieval slang. Fitzgerald's daughter, Scottie, thought the stories so inferior that they should not be collected or reprinted, but Fitzgerald himself had thought otherwise, writing in 1935 to Maxwell Perkins, his editor at Scribner's, listing stories to be collected and printed in the case of his (Fitzgerald's) sudden death, including consideration of all four Philippe stories.[4] However, the stories, with one exception, have never been reprinted, never collected, making scholars work from microfilm of *Redbook* or poor photocopies of microfilm.[5] This situation is regrettable, for the stories, despite their failings, reveal much about Fitzgerald, his mode of composition, his aims, both novelistic and human—Mangum talks of Fitzgerald's attempt to write salable popular fiction—and Fitzgerald's sympathy for feminism not yet adequately analyzed.[6]

To dispense with many of the weaknesses first, the stories are poorly put together. Bruccoli says that the stories were written on alcohol, and sometimes it shows, along with *Redbook*'s poor editing.[7] The first story begins in 872, but the second story, which takes place the next day, is

3. Sergio Perosa, *The Art of F. Scott Fitzgerald,* 133. Since Perosa gives no other bibliographic information in his text, he is evidently working from Fitzgerald's manuscript notes; judging from his account of the stories, there are significant differences between the manuscript versions and their published form. Also, Perosa has only six stories dealing with Philippe's youth, whereas Bruccoli, also using the Princeton manuscript and quoting from Fitzgerald's notes, details the themes of the next four stories, or eight in all (*Some Sort of Epic Grandeur: The Life of F. Scott Fitzgerald,* 388). Janet Lewis confirms the scheme of eight stories of youth, ages twenty to twenty-five, three of maturity—thirty, thirty-eight, forty-five—and two final episodes at ages fifty-five and seventy; she publishes Fitzgerald's typed "General Plan of Philippe" from the Princeton manuscript ("Fitzgerald's 'Philippe, Count of Darkness,'" 10–11, 28).

4. Bruccoli, ed., *The Price Was High: The Last Uncollected Stories of F. Scott Fitzgerald,* 513; Bruccoli and Duggan, eds., *Correspondence,* 407.

5. The exception is the first story, "In the Darkest Hour," reprinted in Bruccoli's *Price Was High,* 512–29, but Bruccoli has appended the wrong date to the story: it was published in October 1934, not 1935 as his headnote indicates.

6. Mangum, *Fortune Yet,* 143–44.

7. Bruccoli, *Epic Grandeur,* 388.

headlined as occurring in 879. In the first story, Charles is Philippe's father; in the third story, his father is Bertram. Fitzgerald has Louis the Stammerer as king, saying that Charles the Bald had died five years before, in 867; Charles, however, died in 877. Moreover, Fitzgerald makes Charles Charlemagne's son, not the grandson he was.[8] Louis's men are armed with crossbows ("Kingdom," 60), not likely in ninth-century France. In the first story, Philippe's domain is fifty miles west of Tours; in the third story it seems east. Nor is the text sure whether Philippe's fortification is on the north bank of the Loire or the south; the third story has conflicting evidence for either interpretation. There are five Norse prisoners in the first story, reduced inexplicably to two in the second. Philippe's right-hand man is "Jacques" in the first two stories, "Jaques" in the last two; and, unfortunately, Fitzgerald evidently did not know the pun on "Jaques" as "jakes," a privy (see, for example, *As You Like It*), provoking some unintentional humor, especially when he calls the peasant "Sir Jaques" ("Kingdom," 60), and when Philippe calls the people on his land "these jakes" ("Hour," 522).

Fitzgerald's attempt to write dialogue for the peasants and for Philippe as tough guy produced some ludicrous results. In the first story, Philippe eats "flapjacks" (514) and the Moors are "yeller devils" (515); he asks a Norseman, "No speak Lingua Franca?" (514); he greets two peasants with "Howdy," and they respond to his question as to how many live in the region, which they interpret as his intention to steal from all, by saying, "Used to be a right smart lot of them. . . . You mought as well move along" (516). This is Hollywood's notion of how Ozark hillbillies talk; equally from a Hollywood western is Philippe's saying, "Answer me like that once more, and I'll let daylight through you" (518). In the second story we have such anachronisms as a "sugar daddy" (22), a sandwich (23), "pipe down" (68), "bunk," "oke"—presumably short for "okay"—and "pup-tent" (69). Equally laughable, as several critics

---

8. F. Scott Fitzgerald, "The Kingdom in the Dark," 59, 62. For reference within the text of my article, I will refer to the stories by abbreviated title: "In the Darkest Hour" as "Hour"; "The Count of Darkness" as "Count"; "The Kingdom in the Dark" as "Kingdom"; and "Gods of Darkness" as "Gods"—and then by page number. For the last three, I will supply the page number from the *Redbook* issue in which the stories appear, their only source; for the first, "Hour," I will use the page numbers from *Price Was High*.

have pointed out, is Philippe's macho pose and language. To a French girl he has acquired by killing the Norsemen who had captured her, he commands, "Come here and see what you taste like." When she calls him "darling," he interrupts: "Call me 'Sire!' . . . And re*mem*ber; there's no bedroom talk floating around this precinct!" ("Count," 21; ellipsis and emphasis Fitzgerald's). Typical of Fitzgerald's general unawareness is the fact that he intended to call the completed novel *The Castle,* but then Kafka does not seem to be an author he read.[9]

There are other historical blunders. Philippe wears a gold-embroidered cloak and a moorish helmet in a country with good reason to loathe Moors, both items inviting attack and robbery; Fitzgerald's very story reveals, accurately, how bloodthirsty and rapacious were the people of the period, whether high- or lowborn. Few would take the time to ask Philippe his identity but would ambush him for his possessions, including the white Arab stallion he rides, but he is not attacked, not even by a Viking. The lone stranger on the white horse, defending the poor squatters against invading marauders, also suggests popular culture's influence on Fitzgerald in shaping his hero, as much or more than Fitzgerald's statement in his Notebooks that Hemingway was his model for Philippe.[10] And here we get to Fitzgerald's concept of the hero. In his mature novels, his protagonists' misfortunes are always larger than themselves; that is, his protagonists are paradigmatic individuals. Thus "the foul dust" that preys on Gatsby is indicative of the corruption inherent in American capitalist society, especially during the immoral Roaring Twenties. Dick Diver's collapse echoes that of both the depression and Western civilization. Monroe Stahr embodies both America's love of illusion and the struggle of the individual artist working in a collaborative and commercial environment. It is apparent from the text that Fitzgerald wants Philippe to be more than an individual adventurer. His very surname, Villefranche, suggests how Fitzgerald associates Philippe with France. So do thoughts that Fitzgerald attributes to him: "Philippe's idea was a prefiguration of an age already beginning. . . ." ("Hour," 524).

Thus, Fitzgerald casts Philippe as a Renaissance man, centuries before the event, or describes him, "Embodying in himself alone the future of

9. Bruccoli, *Epic Grandeur,* 387.
10. Ibid.; Bruccoli's source is Edmund Wilson, ed., *The Crack-Up,* 177.

his race, he walked to and fro in the starry darkness" ("Hour," 529), a combination of Stephen Dedalus and Jay Gatsby. Equally pretentious and didactic:

> This was an epoch of disturbance and change; all over Europe men were thinking exactly like Philippe, taking direction from the arrows of history that seemed to float dimly overhead. Each of those men thought himself to be alone, but really each was an instrument of response to a great human need. Each knew that the spirit of man was at low tide; each one felt in himself the necessity of seizing power by force and cunning. ("Hour," 522–23)

In short, Philippe as Machiavelli, six centuries in advance.[11]

Each of the four stories has some form of the word "dark" in its title, a way of insisting on the tales as stories of the Dark Ages, perhaps reflecting on the Great Depression and perhaps on Fitzgerald's own state of depression in 1934 when *Tender Is the Night* did not do as well as he had expected.[12] What Philippe, in fact, brings to Touraine is the notion of vigorous feudalism, an organizing principle that has been missing since the destruction of the Roman empire and the subsequent raids by Moors and Vikings. Philippe will collect tolls from merchants crossing the ford of the Loire beneath his fortification and protect the peasants in return for a share of their produce on their tenant farms and their labor on his rough-hewn castle and their service to him. He, in turn, owes loyalty and service to the king. Yet the sentiments that Fitzgerald ascribes to Philippe are anachronistically democratic. (Beyond that, Fitzgerald hoped to include Marxist elements as well in the full novel.)[13]

Fitzgerald is accurate in portraying the squalor, misery, and lawlessness of the period, but his depiction of Philippe as democrat is either that of a most unusual hero, who has nothing in common with the

11. Or, as Lehan sees it, Faustian man, the paradigmatic medieval man as described in Oswald Spengler's *The Decline of the West*. See Richard D. Lehan, *F. Scott Fitzgerald and the Craft of Fiction*, 152; and Richard D. Lehan, "F. Scott Fitzgerald and Romantic Destiny," 150–51.

12. Perosa, *Art of F. Scott Fitzgerald*, 132; "Fitzgerald took refuge unconsciously among the specters and puppets of an age in which the fabric of history and society offered an 'objective correlative' to the conditions of chaos and darkness of his soul."

13. Bruccoli and Duggan, eds., *Correspondence*, 590.

class-conscious age the author seeks to represent, or Philippe is out of his time, a wished-for egalitarian in an undemocratic age. He is Philippe Count Villefranche, owner of twenty miles along the Loire (in one story, twenty square miles in another), and stepson of the Vizier of Cordova, at a time when class distinctions were impenetrable. His men are mocked for their poor weapons by the king's bodyguard ("Kingdom," 62); the king refuses his hospitality, looking at "the flock of chickens and the litter of pigs that roamed the courtyard" ("Kingdom," 64); the king's sentries refuse to wake a man of importance when Philippe brings warning of Vikings, summoning only a squire, whom Philippe must bribe to see a knight, and so up the social ladder to duke and then king ("Kingdom," 64). In the fourth story, the Duke of Maine takes the ill-dressed Philippe for a messenger, calling him a clown and asking to see his master ("Gods," 88). Yet Philippe advances the poor peasant Jacques to be his right-hand man, his assistant and counselor, and Fitzgerald knights the peasant, calling him Sir ("Kingdom," 60), as Philippe himself does later ("Gods," 88). Elsewhere, Brian, a monk, addresses Philippe impertinently,

> "Pardon me master—or sire—or whatever you call yourself today—"
> "Watch your tongue, you unfrocked devil!" said Philippe goodhumoredly.
> "I'll call you Philippe, like it or not, my boy." ("Kingdom," 60)

A nobleman of the era would not have liked it; Philippe would have been punished calling a duke or the king by his given name. Similarly, when Griselda, former mistress to King Louis, now Philippe's lover and fiancée, complains of his equal distribution of toll taken from merchants with "those monkeys in the valley" ("monkeys" as epithet is probably another anachronism), Philippe reacts most nobly: "They're not monkeys; and if you can't get over that kind of talk, then you're no fit wife for a chieftain. They're *us*. I'm *them*—it's hard to explain—" ("Gods," 32; emphasis Fitzgerald's). Social equality would indeed have been hard to explain in ninth-century France, and while Fitzgerald's intentions are commendable for his hero, their inappropriateness undermines the validity of the Count of Darkness stories.

On the other hand, under whatever circumstances Fitzgerald wrote the stories, they do show evidence of effort and foresight as to the integration of early details with later plot lines. In addition to the narrative description setting the stories in the Middle Ages, Fitzgerald lards his text with atmospheric terms: "pantler," "slinger," "abattis," and "pennon," to mention a few.[14] In the first story, he is careful to provide Le Poire with a daughter (though not careful enough to provide "Poire" with the article of the proper gender in French), for Le Poire's daughter figures prominently in the fourth story, not written until seven months later, when the first story was already in print.[15] Fitzgerald specifically notes the presence of caves in the area close to Jacques's hut, again an element that is important in the fourth story, as is Jacques's ability to rally a group of men to him quickly, seemingly without question or dispute, in spite of the fact that he is a lowly peasant and not the head man of the community. In all these details, Fitzgerald is providing material to build upon in the climactic fourth story, just as his line in the fourth story that the Duke of Maine was a man "with whom Philippe was to have much to do in later life" ("Gods," 88), prepares us for later plot complications never written.

Most criticism of the stories, where there has been any, has been negative, including my own up to this point. Sergio Perosa, whose comments go beyond the biographical and are more extensive than most, thoroughly damns the stories thus: "There is no possible unity of vision or an informing idea."[16] Perosa is wrong. Although the idea is present only in embryonic form, its outline is readily apparent. Philippe is the wise fool, the type of rash, headstrong young man of courage but little sense who must learn through experience to control his impetuous impulses, the type from Parzival through Tom Jones, and thus the Count of Darkness stories begin a bildungsroman or *Entwicklungsroman*, as well as an epic. Griselda asks Philippe, "Don't you think you have any faults *ever*? Do you always think you're so perfect?" He replies, "I guess

---

14. Janet Lewis mentions the "two pages of books and articles he used or intended to use in researching the novel. He consulted books on French and European history, the fifth volume of Gibbon, Belloc's *Europe and the Faith*, and Jessie Weston's *From Ritual to Romance*." She also reprints the two-page list of *Encyclopaedia Britannica* articles Fitzgerald consulted ("Fitzgerald's 'Philippe, Count of Darkness,'" 9, 18–19).

15. Mangum, *Fortune Yet*, 180–81.

16. Perosa, *Art of F. Scott Fitzgerald*, 136.

I do" ("Gods," 33; Fitzgerald's emphasis). Pride goeth before a fall, and
Philippe literally takes a fall. In an attempt to impress the Duke of Maine
at their meeting, Philippe rides up quickly, jumps his horse over a row
of stakes, and the horse lands badly, throwing Philippe. It is then that
the Duke says:

> "Catch your breath! I'm in no hurry! I want to see your master."
> Panting and dazed by his fall, Philippe could not articulate.
> The Duke turned and said to an attendant: "Here, give this fellow a jolt
> of wine—maybe he's the local clown and we can use him." ("Gods," 88)

Acting rashly and unable to speak when he should is something Philippe
shares with Parzival at the Grail Ceremony, an attribute Eliot used in
The Waste Land, lines 38–39: "I could not / Speak"—and Fitzgerald's
admiration for Eliot's poem and his use of it in *The Great Gatsby* are
well known. Philippe even plays Fisher King, teaching his peasants to
spear eels at night by lantern light as a way to provide food for their
barren wasteland.[17] And if Fitzgerald extended his reading of source
material beyond Weston, he would have found that Chrétien de Troyes's
patron, for whom he wrote *Li Conte del Graal,* was Count Philip of
Flanders.

Something else Philippe shares with Percival/Parzival is the sobriquet
of clown. Heretofore Philippe has acted hastily, taking no one's advice
but his own, frequently making mistakes. The most usual realm for him
to err in is in his dealings with women. With them, Philippe is as inept as
Parzival was with the damsel of the tent, Jeschute. And here, Fitzgerald's
efforts to make Philippe an egalitarian, while out of place historically,
are brilliantly integrated, for Philippe matures as he recognizes women
as equals in thought, feelings, rights, and even power.

Fitzgerald begins the process in the second story. Philippe has acquired
Letgarde, a seventeen-year-old girl, from the Vikings who had captured
her, Vikings whom Philippe kills. He makes her his possession, servant,

---

17. Lewis ("Fitzgerald's 'Philippe, Count of Darkness,' " 9) and Perosa (*Art of F. Scott
Fitzgerald,* 133) acknowledge that Fitzgerald read Jessie Weston's *From Ritual to Romance* in
preparation, and Fitzgerald would have found a discussion of Perceval/Parzival in Weston's
book.

lover-to-be, while telling his men to acquire wives, in an approximation of the Rape of the Sabine Women. To supervise the construction of his fort, Philippe wants to ride his stallion to the top of a nearby hill:

> Catching the beast and saddling him, he pulled Letgarde up with him after he had mounted. The force of his pull almost wrenched her arm from her socket.
>
> Smarting with sudden rage at the indignity, she waited in fright as, guiding the animal with his legs only, he next swung her about from a position facing him, to one that would later be called postilion. Furious and uncomfortable, she rode off behind him toward a destination of which she knew nothing.
>
> . . . On the summit, he . . . slung her to the ground with almost a reverse of the gesture with which he had taken her up. She stood shaken, injured, terrified. . . . ("Count," 21–22)

Letgarde deserts him that very day, hides, starves, and drowns trying to ford the Loire. Philippe mourns for her, recognizing that he is responsible for her death, "just because I used her rough on the horse when I was in a hurry" ("Count," 70). In an attempt to atone, he adopts an orphan peasant girl (whom we never see in the next two stories), but he has learned a lesson, one made apparent in the fourth story.

Philippe has taken in Griselda, a mistress of King Louis who has escaped the king. Louis suspects Philippe of sheltering her but cannot prove it and sends men to burn Philippe's fort. Soon Philippe and Griselda become lovers, and Philippe visits the local abbot to have the banns announced for their marriage; while there, the abbot warns Philippe to beware a pagan cult flourishing in the area, one turning the inhabitants against Christ. Immediately thereafter, the Duke of Maine appears on the scene, hunting, with an enormous troop of five hundred men, far more than Philippe and his peasants could withstand. Griselda tries to persuade Philippe to accept her counsel: " 'You wouldn't take advice from a mere woman, would you? . . . Don't take our men down there to meet them,' she said emphatically. 'A woman telling me how I should do!' " ("Gods," 33). But Philippe is persuaded and accedes, a step in his maturation, meeting the Duke with only his personal bodyguard of ten. Then Griselda tells him to accept the advice of Jacques also. Confused, Philippe wonders what the peasant can do. Griselda then introduces herself to Jacques as a member of a witch cult by chanting a simple charm, thereby gaining his cooperation: *"Esta es buena parati. Esta parati lo toma"* ("Gods," 88). She has somehow recognized Jacques as a member of a witch cult (I hesitate to call either one a "witch" because of current connotations), realizing that it is his position of authority in the cult that enabled him to rally men to Philippe's cause in the first story and to cement his own authority over them. She also knows that there are many cult members among the Duke of Maine's men who, if they could be appealed to, would be loathe to attack fellow religionists. Convincing Jacques that she is also a cult member, she says to Philippe, "Darling, we can fix these men. . . . All you got to do is soft-soap the leader . . . [another anachronistic expression]. Jaques and I will fix the men" ("Gods," 88).

After falling from his horse, recovering, and sizing up the situation, Philippe takes the Duke hostage, but he is still under possible siege by the Duke's five hundred men. That night, Griselda and Jacques take him to the *esbat* of the witch cult, presided over by Le Poire's daughter, Becquette, the local priestess. When Becquette, blaming Philippe for her father's death at Viking hands, demands Philippe's death at the hands of both coven members and those of the Duke's men attending the ritual, Griselda reveals herself to be high priestess of the witches of Touraine and countermands Becquette's demand, saying that Philippe is one of them and that she and he will be married according to the rites of the cult.

Although we see little of the witch cult, Fitzgerald was at pains to make it a pagan fertility cult, Wiccan in today's terms, rather than something Satanic and anti-Christian. Becquette, as priestess, presides on a stone couch before a waterfall; "other women carrying torches were posted at her head and feet, and piled about the sides of the stone couch were products of the harvest—grapes and apples, bundles of rye and wheat" ("Gods," 90). The *esbat* takes place in a cave, the womb of mother earth, a frequent location for witch cult gatherings. Fitzgerald's sources were meager—they still are—for pagan rituals in the Middle Ages. Most sources of information about such cults come from witch trials of the fifteenth and later centuries, when Inquisitors and prosecutors saw anything pagan as specifically Satanic. Fitzgerald, though he mentions Satan in his manuscript, deletes any such reference from the published story.[18] The cult is an alternative to Christianity, not a dedicated opponent. However, as implied by the etymology of "pagan" (country dweller) and "heathen" (one who lives on a heath), pagans and heathens were not city dwellers but country folk, farmers, people for whom fertility was a necessity for survival. They lived on the land and persisted in their worship of ancient nature deities, hence the cult's oft-used name, the Old Religion. The Catholic Church, on the other hand, was associated with royalty and nobility, established first in cities, and, as numerous reformation attempts made obvious, was often swollen with land and wealth. Thus, there was a political and economic opposition between pagan worshippers and the established Church, intuited by Fitzgerald, and it is this opposition that the abbot in the fourth story fears at least as much as he does the blasphemous acts of his parishioners, for whom he has shown no other concern in the stories.[19] It is this same political power against the nobility that Griselda enlists for Philippe (a count, but hardly rich) against the Duke of Maine.

18. Perosa (*Art of F. Scott Fitzgerald,* 133) and Lewis ("Fitzgerald's 'Philippe, Count of Darkness,'" 9) cite Fitzgerald's sources, in addition to Weston, as the *Encyclopaedia Britannica,* for which Margaret Murray wrote the entry on witchcraft for the 14th edition (1929; Murray's article was the Britannica's explanation until the 1974 edition), and Murray's *The Witch Cult in Western Europe.* Fitzgerald did get the charm by which Griselda identifies herself to Jacques from Murray, as well as the ritual marriage to Satan (*Witch Cult,* 179). Murray found the charm—*Esta es buena parati / Esta parati lo toma*—in Pierre de Lancre's tome, an account of fourteenth-century French witch trials (273). De Lancre misprints the Spanish: *para* is one word, a preposition, *ti* its object. They were spoken at ritual marriages, and can be translated as "This one is good for you / She is there for you. Do you accept?" Philippe, growing up in Spain, would have understood these words as Griselda spoke them, and he would not have called them a "secret lingo" ("Gods," 88), nor would the celebrants at the *esbat* use them as a salutation to the priestess.

Perosa says from the manuscript sources that Griselda admits to having been deflowered by Satan and must marry fellow cult member Jacques, not Philippe (*Art of F. Scott Fitzgerald,* 135). Lewis confirms this, quoting from Fitzgerald's text the ritual whereby Griselda and Jacques would separate witch cult followers from nonpagans among the Duke of Maine's men ("Fitzgerald's 'Philippe, Count of Darkness,'" 16–17).

19. Murray cites no examples other than that of Joan of Arc and the antifertility charms of witches to hurt their enemies. But there were no sources available to Fitzgerald to document such class opposition in ninth-century France, and his putting it there is his own artistic creation. Similarly, the emerald that Griselda wears to identify her as chief priestess is Fitzgerald's invention (and an appropriately visual one for a Hollywood-influenced version of the ritual).

Thus Philippe's life is saved from Becquette's followers, as are his men and wood fort from attack by the forces of the Duke of Maine, both through Griselda's intercession. Philippe has listened to her advice and that of the peasant Jacques; he has curtailed his natural impetuosity, somewhat controlled his rashness, and benefited. He has, uncommonly so for a ninth-century leader (male, here, being understood), listened to a woman and a low-born peasant and discovered that they could help a count of France. Although he has considered himself a devout Christian—Fitzgerald has shown him praying throughout the stories and acknowledging fealty to Church and God—he is more pragmatist than Christian: "I haven't got any conscience except for my country, and for those who live in it. . . . All right—I'll use this cult—and maybe burn in hell forever after" ("Gods," 91). The noble, altruistic, idealistic attitude is not typically ninth century, nor is the nationalism, and the willingness to burn in Hell echoes *Huckleberry Finn*. But Philippe concludes, "But if these witches know better, then I'll be one of *them!*" ("Gods," 91). Fitzgerald ends the story with Griselda mocking both her own cult's fertility images and Philippe by suggesting that they carve a totemic beast on the gate of the fort that is half lion, half pig, "half for fighting, half for farming" ("Gods," 91).[20]

Perosa is wrong in stating that Fitzgerald had no "unity of vision or informing idea." In the six months that the stories cover, we see twenty-year-old Philippe begin to mature and come to his majority, marked in part by his treatment of Griselda, a growth paralleled by the development of feudalism in ninth-century France. Philippe embodies what Wolfram von Eschenbach, the *Parzival* poet, says that he is recounting, an account of "a brave man slowly wise."[21] How far Fitzgerald would have taken intertwined ideas, it is impossible to say. To what extent the later stories would have continued to involve pagan witch cults is also impossible to say. But it is apparent, even in the four brief stories, that Philippe's

20. Lehan sees Griselda and her witch cult as evil (*Craft of Fiction*, 152), as does Mangum, who sees her power as evil and her as a corrupting force (*Fortune Yet*, 145–46). I do not agree, and certainly the humor of her remark, plus the fact that she has saved Philippe's life, argue against such a reading. However, we don't have any subsequent stories to see how the relationship between the characters and religion would have been developed.

21. Perosa, *Art of F. Scott Fitzgerald*, 136; Wolfram von Eschenbach, *Parzival*, 5.

maturity is marked by his growing self-control and growing willingness to recognize the rights of those the ninth century would have regarded as inferiors: peasants and women—especially women.

There is very little detailed critical analysis of Fitzgerald's treatment of women characters, the three main pieces being by Judith Fetterley, Mary A. McKay, and Sarah Beebe Fryer. Fetterley sees no distance whatsoever between author and narrator of *The Great Gatsby*, interpreting the novel as "centered in hostility to women," with Daisy as the novel's scapegoat; *The Great Gatsby* is the only work of Fitzgerald's that she considers. Both Mary A. McKay and Sarah Beebe Fryer see a progression in Fitzgerald's works, from the vamps in *This Side of Paradise* to the self-supporting women of *The Last Tycoon*. Fryer considers the novels only, but she praises Fitzgerald for his accurate depiction of women's roles in the 1920s, and she traces a development of greater independence and self-sufficiency in the women characters over time; moreover, she sees the condescending behavior of the men toward women as an indictment of the male characters—particularly of Dick Diver—and not of the author. Fryer quotes Frances Kroll Ring, writing about Fitzgerald's attitude toward his daughter: "She must be prepared to have an independent life. . . . He was keenly aware of a changing world for women and he wanted his daughter to be ready for that world with education, goals, self esteem."[22]

McKay also sees a continuum of development from Fitzgerald's early work to the last, unfinished novel, a development that she, like Fryer, links first to his desire for his daughter, Scottie, to make the most of her opportunities for education and so be prepared for a career, and then to his relationship with self-sufficient career woman Sheilah Graham. The letters to Scottie stress her need to do well in math and science, the very subjects Fitzgerald himself did poorly in, and they go from 1933 (the year before the Philippe stories were written) until his death in 1940. McKay examines only one short story, "The Cut-Glass Bowl" (1920); she does not, for example, consider the early story "Diamond Dick and the First

22. Judith Fetterley, *The Resisting Reader: A Feminist Approach to American Fiction*, 72; Sarah Beebe Fryer, *Fitzgerald's New Women: Harbingers of Change*, 96; Frances Kroll Ring, *Against the Current: As I Remember F. Scott Fitzgerald*, 82.

Law of Woman" (1924), which has a forceful, nonworking female heroine and, like the Philippe stories, uses stilted, stereotypical dialogue.[23] No feminist critic has yet considered such strong women characters as Myra in "Myra Meets His Family" (1920), Daisy Cary in "The Bowl" (1928), or Nell Margery in "I Got Shoes" (1933); Daisy and Nell work to support themselves, Myra does not. Nor have they considered Caroline Dandy in "The Bridal Party" (1930), strong, but in rather conventional, old-fashioned ways.

There is a paucity of attention to Fitzgerald's treatment of women in both the novels *and* the short fiction, especially in the less-studied short stories. We do not know how he would have revised *The Last Tycoon* had he lived, nor how he would have developed his view of women or their treatment by men as a way to characterize the men; it is, however, a novel with a woman narrator. As a social chronicler, it would have been impossible for Fitzgerald to ignore the added responsibilities of women during World War II. But it is fascinating that Fitzgerald, writing in Christian Baltimore in 1934, when women were given only slightly more power and credence than in ninth-century France, should have matched his hero with a heroine out of Wicca, the pagan old religion in which divinity was feminine.

23. Mary A. McKay, "Fitzgerald's Women: Beyond Winter Dreams," 311–24.

WILL THE REAL PAT HOBBY PLEASE STAND UP?

MILTON R. STERN

In the critical activity of rediscovering, reviving, or redressing, there always is at least the faint effluvium of crusade that permeates the proceedings. In the spirit of the campaign, critical affirmations tend to become overstated, and the phenomenon of mild overheating is true of responses to the Pat Hobby stories. The reaction is occasioned by the relative neglect of these vignettes (compared to the attention paid to Fitzgerald's novels and the more familiar short stories) and by the negative responses in many of the reviews that greeted the edition collected in 1962 by Arnold Gingrich from the pages of *Esquire*, where the Hobby stories had appeared in an unbroken monthly series from January 1940 through May 1941.[1]

They "could just have well remained in whatever mellowing archives old Esquire magazines are kept in," wrote one reviewer. The stories are "wearying," asserted another. "There's more life and poignancy in the Fitzgerald-Gingrich correspondence that makes up the introduction than in the whole Pat Hobby saga." And a third concluded that the stories are "stiff" and "tiresome. The fact that 21 years have passed before anyone thought it necessary or desirable to collect them is the tipoff."[2]

1. F. Scott Fitzgerald, *The Pat Hobby Stories.* All subsequent page references to the Pat Hobby stories are to this edition and will appear parenthetically in the text.
2. Ray Lewis White, "The Pat Hobby Stories: A File of Reviews," 178–79.

As everyone knows by now, the Pat Hobby stories are a series of short fictions bordering on sketches, featuring an ignorant, unintelligent, unprincipled, desperate, seedy, little gray has-been of a screenwriter whose life and values illustrate, both sadly and comically, the grubbily materialistic debasement of the human spirit in the gross vulgarity of Hollywood. Pat is a plagiarist and thief. He is an opportunistic blackmailer. He is a parasitic scrounger. He is a rummy and a liar. He is a fumbling womanizer. He is a witless gambler. He is obtuse, unimaginative, stupid, talentless, and abysmally fatuous. In a letter to Gingrich, Fitzgerald called him "a complete rat." He is that. But his wobbly life is such a soup of failure that in its bathetic and sometimes hilarious trickle from soggy misadventure to soggy misadventure, it also evokes disdainful sympathy for poor Pat—one wants to call him "poor Pat."

When Gingrich's edition appeared, with knowing certainty most of the reviewers treated the Pat Hobby series as disguised but transparent versions of Fitzgeraldana, autobiography at one remove. Presumably, the episodes provided a glimpse not only into the oxymoron of Hollywood as a comic Greek tragedy, an Attic abasement of morons, but also of the real Pat Hobby as a Mr. Hyde persona of Francis Scott Key Fitzgerald's worst fears and guilts about himself.

The crusading counterattack is represented fiercely by an essay from a French academic, Elizabeth M. Varet-Ali. It offers the voice of the avenging critic-angel finally, by God, setting things right so that "*The Pat Hobby Stories* will at last be allowed to take the place they deserve. . . ." Varet-Ali sees in the series a coherent thematic center in which the real Pat Hobby is something quite other than an alter-ego for Fitzgerald, and Hollywood is something much more than materials for local color vulgarity. The real Pat Hobby is a metaphor for the tenuousness of American identities; Hollywood is a metaphor for the national fatuities of a culture that determines and dissolves human identity; and the stories are a chronicle of the connection between the culture and the tenuousness of identity: "As a genuine product of the studios . . . [Pat] is at once base agent, pale imitator, and true victim of the system. . . . His outrageous blunders, his incompetence, are the replica of what takes place every day around him." Varet-Ali continues:

> In terms of human appeal, the absence of commentary makes the portrait at times unbearable in its harsh detachment. . . . What the ruthless

portrait suggests is that Hollywood, the nation's most popular symbol of Art and Success, perhaps soon its main access to anything like culture, in fact relies on the tritest themes, the grossest illiteracy, and the basest motives and make-believe illusions imaginable. No wonder it can breed (with a few exceptions) such a race of "ignoramuses," "mental cadavers," and "sub-microscopic protozoa" . . . and rats as Pat Hobby belongs to.[3]

In these observations, Varet-Ali comes at the center of the stories, though there still remains the question of the extent to which a discoverable central theme is a guarantee of literary quality. Among the commentators, both the attackers and the redeemers have some justice on their side.

The sparse reprinting of the Pat Hobby stories reflects Fitzgerald's mixed legacy of art and fluff and the relative worth of the stories. If we add Bruccoli's 1989 collection of Fitzgerald's short stories to Bryer's meticulous 1982 bibliography of collections, we find that the many compilations of Fitzgerald's selected stories reprint only six of the seventeen Hobby pieces—and this tally does not account for the collections that include *no* Pat Hobby stories.[4] "A Patriotic Short," which Fitzgerald thought too "confused" and among "the less interesting," has been reprinted five times; "Two Old-Timers," which Fitzgerald considered among the "weakest" of the pieces, has been reprinted six times; " 'Boil Some Water—Lots of It' " four times; "Teamed with Genius" three times; and "No Harm Trying," which Fitzgerald judged "not up to" the good ones, twice.[5]

However, frequency of reprints, oddly enough, by no means reflects the amount of attention Gingrich's collection attracted when it first

3. Elizabeth M. Varet-Ali, "The Unfortunate Fate of Seventeen Fitzgerald 'Originals': Toward a Reading of *The Pat Hobby Stories* 'On Their Own Merits Completely,' " 87, 98–99, 105, 107–8. The French journal in which this essay appears contains sentences that demand some study and repunctuation before they make clear sense. (I have quietly made a few minor corrections in the material I quote.) Also, the article contains errors in reference and citation. Nevertheless, it is a lively and intelligent attempt to destroy the myth that Fitzgerald was *manqué* and *épuisé* as a writer by the time he wrote the Pat Hobby stories.
4. Matthew J. Bruccoli, ed., *The Short Stories of F. Scott Fitzgerald: A New Collection;* Jackson R. Bryer, ed., *The Short Stories of F. Scott Fitzgerald: New Approaches in Criticism,* 304–7.
5. For reprintings of the Pat Hobby stories through 1982, see Jackson R. Bryer, "The Short Stories of F. Scott Fitzgerald: A Checklist of Criticism," especially part 1 (304–7) and part 7 (348–77). Since 1982, " 'Boil Some Water—Lots of It' " has been reprinted in Bruccoli, ed., *Short Stories.*

appeared. Bryer provides a comprehensive list of reviews of Fitzgerald story collections up to 1982, and they reveal the moment of revival interest in Fitzgerald rather than the literary merit of the fiction. Bryer lists thirty-nine reviews of *Flappers and Philosophers* from 1920 through 1921. Reflecting Fitzgerald's meteoric arrival with *This Side of Paradise* and the impetus of *The Beautiful and Damned,* there were fifty-six reviews of *Tales of the Jazz Age* from 1922 through 1923. Bryer finds forty-two reviews of *All the Sad Young Men* during 1926; and—by the time *Tender Is the Night* was published the falling off had become noticeable—*Taps at Reveille* was greeted with twenty-six reviews in 1935. Thereafter, the number of reviews Bryer found traces a clear pattern of neglect and rediscovery. For 1945, the year that Edmund Wilson began the Fitzgerald revival with his edition of *The Crack-Up,* Bryer lists *two* reviews of Dorothy Parker's *Portable F. Scott Fitzgerald;* and for 1951, the year that Arthur Mizener and Malcolm Cowley firmly established the revival, Bryer finds only twelve notices for Cowley's epochal *Stories of F. Scott Fitzgerald.* But with the revival, the short prose pieces began to acquire greater prominence. Mizener's *Afternoon of an Author* garnered fifty-two reviews in 1957 and 1958 according to Bryer and then a glut on the market at the turn of the decade diminished reviewer interest in new Fitzgerald titles. The reissue of *Flappers and Philosophers* received thirty-two notices in 1959, and in 1960 new reprints of *Taps at Reveille* and *Tales of the Jazz Age* were given only thirty and twenty-eight reviews respectively.[6]

Exactly here is where Pat Hobby lifts his stolen hat and bows. In 1962, after a two-year breathing space in the revivalistic glut, reviewers were again interested, for Bryer found *sixty-three* of them paying heed to Gingrich's edition of the stories, producing the second highest number of notices for any collection of Fitzgerald's short fiction.[7] And across the spectrum, the reviews revealed the representative nature of the Hobby

6. Bryer, ed., *Short Stories of F. Scott Fitzgerald,* 323–47.
7. Bryer lists only Matthew J. Bruccoli, ed., *The Price Was High: The Last Uncollected Stories of F. Scott Fitzgerald,* as receiving more reviews (sixty-seven in 1978–1979) during this period of revival and literary housekeeping. John Kuehl, ed., *The Apprentice Fiction of F. Scott Fitzgerald: 1909–1917,* received twenty-three notices in 1965–1966; and Bryer finds thirty-eight notices for *The Basil and Josephine Stories,* by F. Scott Fitzgerald, in 1973–

pieces. As in the 1950s the essence of critical response fractured into three clear categories.

There were those who said, "Oh dear, not again. Let Fitzgerald rest. Is there no end to the same old stuff? He doesn't hold up, his stuff is dated, its interest is for addicts only." There were those who read admiringly, moved that Fitzgerald remained undimmed by time, shining as freshly and brightly as ever. Those readers concluded that as the years go by Fitzgerald emerges more and more compellingly as one of the classics. A third group felt that in retrospect Fitzgerald's short pieces are a mixed bag, the newly republished stuff not as good as his well-known best stories, but many of them quite good indeed. For all readers, however, there was agreement about the forceful substantive presence of nostalgia, dolor, spree, waste, horror, and regret—of disintegration—in Fitzgerald's good and very good stories. Evocative of so much reviewer response, in this, as in all ways, the Pat Hobby stories remain paradigms not of the best, but of the general average of Fitzgerald's short fiction.

Like the ironic contradictions between Fitzgerald's confused legacy of self-evaluation and the editorial selection of Pat Hobby stories, the stories are in no way more representative of the fate of Fitzgerald's short fiction than in the contradiction between popular notice and critical neglect. Gingrich's edition might have generated sixty-three reviews, but, except for a small handful of essays on the Pat Hobby stories, there has been very little notice taken of these pieces, even in books whose central subject matter is that of the Pat Hobby stories: Fitzgerald and Hollywood. One entire book on Fitzgerald's fiction in films and his work in films offers only three short paragraphs on the Pat Hobby stories. John Kuehl's recent book on Fitzgerald's short fiction allows five pages for all seventeen stories, but devotes those pages to a summary of representative plot and characterization and to the point that the style of the stories is that of Fitzgerald the leaver-outer. Bryant Mangum's 1991 book devotes six pages to the Pat Hobby stories, providing intelligent précis and the observation that they share a triangular structure connected by three variously related points: failure, hope of success, and failure. In his

---

1974, when *Bits of Paradise: 21 Uncollected Stories by F. Scott and Zelda Fitzgerald* received twenty-seven.

study of Fitzgerald in Hollywood, Aaron Latham makes only fleeting
mention of two Pat Hobby stories, "Teamed with Genius" and "Mightier
Than the Sword," which Fitzgerald thought was one of the two weakest
of all the Hobby episodes.[8]

This lukewarm critical response was first articulated by Cowley in
his 1951 introduction: "Most of the Hobby stories weren't very good by
[Fitzgerald's] own standards, but they caught the Hollywood atmosphere
and they also made fun of the author's weaknesses, thereby proving that
Fitzgerald hadn't lost his ironic attitude toward himself or his gift of
double vision." Perhaps the coexisting tugs toward praise and denial are
summed up in two pieces of scholarship of the 1970s. In a periodical
piece, John O. Rees argued that Fitzgerald's "fine, under-valued comic
gift relaxes occasionally, among too many easy targets here, but it has
not deserted him; we see his grotesques in the glaring sunshine of the
working day." Fitzgerald's fine touches give us the nuances of authority:
"Like Pat himself, his Hollywood has its bizarre authenticity, its small but
undeniable share of felt life." And as for style, the "prose is tempered to
the *macho* requirements of the old *Esquire,* but it is not without charm;
it bespeaks a departure, as much as a falling-off, from Fitzgerald's earlier
lyricism. This style is as supple as ever, and its wry, spare cadences are
well suited to the gimcrack world it portrays." And if memory is a theme
in all of Fitzgerald's fiction, it is centrally and especially so in the Pat
Hobby stories.[9]

Rees's essay sums up the arguments of the defenders as Walter Wells's
does those of the detractors:

> The Pat Hobby Stories . . . remain the hastily written ephemera of . . .
> [a still-gifted] craftsman. Few of the stories possess any plot complexity,

---

8. Gene D. Phillips, S.J., *Fiction, Film, and F. Scott Fitzgerald,* 146–47; John Kuehl, *F. Scott Fitzgerald: A Study of the Short Fiction,* 117–22; Bryant Mangum, *A Fortune Yet: Money in the Art of F. Scott Fitzgerald's Short Stories,* 163–71; Aaron Latham, *Crazy Sundays: F. Scott Fitzgerald in Hollywood,* 66, 184–85. In addition to the essays on Fitzgerald and the movies in Bryer, ed., *Short Stories of F. Scott Fitzgerald* (especially Robert A. Martin, "Hollywood in Fitzgerald: After Paradise"), see also DeWitt Bodeen, "F. Scott Fitzgerald and Films."

9. F. Scott Fitzgerald, *The Stories of F. Scott Fitzgerald,* xxiv; John O. Rees, "Fitzgerald's Pat Hobby Stories," 555, 556, 558.

or demonstrate any compensating subtleties of character, theme, or technique. On the contrary, their narrative technique is occasionally quite clumsy, and their exposition, as in "Putative Father," embarrassingly stilted. Their irony, sole *raison d'être* for a number of the stories, is often heavy-handed; plot structures are forced; and circumstances contrived. . . . The *Stories* are, in short, hurried fictions which bear the scars of deadline.

While grinding out his monthly Pat Hobby submissions to *Esquire*, Fitzgerald was giving artistic priority—and the last of his real talent—to his own Hollywood novel.

Yet, Wells concludes, in their limitations, the Pat Hobby stories reflect essential topics in Fitzgerald's fiction: breakdown of identities, appearance versus reality, and disintegration as the central theme.[10]

Perhaps the Hobby stories might be summed up in an observation that Bruccoli made in the introduction to *The Price Was High* about the stories he collected in that volume: "It is becoming fashionable to claim that Fitzgerald was better as a short story writer than as a novelist. This [is a] truly eccentric notion. . . . Certainly it would be preferable for Fitzgerald to have written another novel instead of the stories collected here."[11]

The zephyrs of controversy still stir occasionally around the matter of literary quality. Is the real Pat Hobby a product of hasty hackwork put together for the money, or is he in fact the vehicle for carefully revised fictions that deserve greater recognition? Here, too, the truth seems to be both. The unhappy facts of the Gingrich–Fitzgerald correspondence make it clear that in their initial composition the stories *were* rushed piecework hastily written for the money. For much of the time that Fitzgerald was writing them he was freelancing at Universal Studios during weekdays. On weekends he wrote stories. Note the proximities of the dates. On September 16, 1939, the first story, "A Man in the Way," came in to *Esquire*. On September 21 Fitzgerald submitted not only a revision of the story but also a second episode, " 'Boil Some Water— Lots of It.' " On September 27 he sent the revisions of the second piece,

10. Walter Wells, *Tycoons and Locusts: A Regional Look at Hollywood Fiction of the 1930s*, 104, 121, and passim.

11. Bruccoli, ed., *Price Was High*, xx.

and on October 2 Gingrich received the third Hobby, "Teamed with Genius." On October 6 the revision of "Teamed with Genius" arrived together with a second revision of " 'Boil Some Water—Lots of It.' " On October 14 Fitzgerald gave the magazine the fourth and fifth Hobbys, "Pat Hobby's Christmas Wish" (published first, in the January 1, 1940, issue, which appeared in the last week of December as the Christmas issue) and "Pat Hobby's Preview." On October 27 "No Harm Trying" arrived, followed by "Pat Hobby's College Days" on November 8. Five days later, Gingrich received "Pat Hobby's Young Visitor" (published as "Pat Hobby, Putative Father"), and then there was a period of silence during which, Fitzgerald explained, he had "been sick in bed again and gotten way behind."[12] On December 19 he sent in "Two Old-Timers," and on Christmas Day he dispatched "Mightier Than the Sword."

Thereafter, in the new year, there were longer intervals between appearances of the "scenario hack" to whom Fitzgerald was "getting rather attached." On January 8 Fitzgerald sent "A Patriotic Short." On February 6 "Pat Hobby and Orson Welles" arrived, and on Valentine's Day "On the Trail of Pat Hobby." On March 9 Gingrich became privy to "Pat Hobby's Secret," which was followed by "Pat Hobby Does His Bit" on March 18. On March 28 *Esquire* enjoyed a view of "Homes of the Stars," and in early summer, on June 25, Gingrich had "Fun in an Artist's Studio," the last of Pat Hobby's sad flings.[13]

When one empathetically contemplates this composition schedule and considers that not only was Fitzgerald giving most of his time to Hollywood during the regular workweek but also that he was working as much as he could on *The Last Tycoon*, and that for much of the period his working time was diminished by ill health, the evidence becomes quite clear. Despite somewhat longer interruptions between pieces in 1940, and despite the most affectionate pro-Fitzgerald crusading spirit, one has to conclude that the Pat Hobby stories *were* a job of quick piecework ground out for money.

On the other hand, when one considers that these rushed creations were subjected to revisions and rerevisions and that Fitzgerald tinkered

12. Arnold Gingrich, "Introduction," xv.
13. Gingrich, "Introduction," xi. All dates are furnished by Gingrich.

with their arrangement and worried Gingrich about the order of the sequence; when one considers how intensely and nimbly Fitzgerald was able to work when he was writing well; and when one considers Fitzgerald's many heartfelt and verifiable statements in his correspondence about his pride in his professional expertise and his care with his short fiction, it seems equally mandatory to conclude that though the Pat Hobby stories were in fact hastily thrown off, at least in first draft, they were not necessarily therefore all junk.[14]

Fitzgerald was not a double-talker, but he left a double legacy when he evaluated his work as a short-story writer. By the end of the 1930s—he created Pat Hobby in 1939—he was humbled, uncertain, and financially desperate, yet heartbreakingly tenacious about his own sense of his literary worth. That combination brought his judgments to very different conclusions from one day to the next. In his introduction to *The Pat Hobby Stories*, Arnold Gingrich provides material that allows us to reconstruct some of Fitzgerald's fluctuating judgments.

In October 1939 Fitzgerald considered the sixth Hobby story he wrote—published tenth in the series—"No Harm Trying," "not up to the last story ['Pat Hobby's Preview']." He followed "No Harm Trying" with "Pat Hobby's College Days," of which he said, "This is an in and outer, but," justifying its quality, "I think certainly *as good* as the last" (emphasis mine). On Valentine's Day of 1940, Fitzgerald wrote that "Pat Hobby's College Days" "seems the weakest of all to me." Yet in January he had written to Gingrich, "The weakest of the Hobby stories seems to me to have been 'Two Old-Timers' and 'Mightier Than the Sword.' If you could hold those out of type for a while I might be able either to improve them later or else send others in their place." Commenting on "On the Trail of Pat Hobby," Fitzgerald wrote, "This is a short, but it seems to me one of the very funniest of all. . . . I think this really has a couple of belly laughs." But in a letter of March 15, Fitzgerald ranked "On the Trail of Pat Hobby" along with "Two Old-Timers," "Pat Hobby's Preview," "Pat Hobby's College Days," "A Patriotic Short," and "Mightier

14. Although neither the manuscripts nor the revised typescripts of the Pat Hobby stories are available, the nine pages of Fitzgerald's notes on them reproduced by Matthew J. Bruccoli, ed., in *F. Scott Fitzgerald: Manuscripts, Vol. VI, Part 3*, 451–59, indicate Fitzgerald's usual plotting, planning, and rethinking.

Than the Sword" as "the less interesting of the series." In March he again designated the group as "the least good of the stories."[15]

When he mailed in "Pat Hobby's Secret" (March 1940), he told Gingrich,

> I think this one should go in as early as possible (that is if you agree with me that it is one of the best). The strongest should come first in comedy because once a character is really established as funny everything he does becomes funny. At least it's that way in life.
>
> If you agree then, I hope you have this substituted for any of the earlier stories except . . . ["Pat Hobby and Orson Welles," "No Harm Trying," or "Pat Hobby, Putative Father"]. It is better than any of the others I feel sure.

Fitzgerald's desire to move stories toward the beginning of the series was a reflection of his rankings. He wanted to put the ones he thought best in early. "Don't you think it's one of the best?" he asked Gingrich when he submitted "Homes of the Stars." He asserted that "this is good enough to be shoved ahead of . . . the least good of the stories. This could come after 'Pat Hobby Does His Bit.' "[16]

With "Fun in an Artist's Studio," he sent Gingrich a request to "put it ahead of those I have designated in other letters as being mediocre"; and when he sent in a revision of "A Patriotic Short," he asked Gingrich to "insert it before any others as far as possible." But in July 1940 Fitzgerald wanted to move the previously denigrated "No Harm Trying" to appear immediately after "Pat Hobby Does His Bit" as "next in order of merit." And then, on October 15, he wired Gingrich that his previously highly rated "PATRIOTIC SHORT SO CONFUSED IT WILL STOP INTEREST IN SERIES. . . . CANT YOU SET IT UP AGAIN. . . . YOUR LETTER PROMISED TO HOLD IT OUT." His uneven, oscillating judgments reflected the rush of his production. Fitzgerald worried about the arrangement of the series, but he also became confused about that arrangement and in any event he necessarily was compelled to bow to Gingrich's order of publication. Gingrich, after

15. Matthew J. Bruccoli and Margaret M. Duggan, eds., *Correspondence of F. Scott Fitzgerald*, 589–90; Gingrich, "Introduction," xiv, xvi, xvii, xviii.

16. Gingrich, "Introduction," xvii–xviii; Bruccoli and Duggan, eds., *Correspondence*, 593.

all, had to plan issues ahead of time with the materials he was certain he had on hand. In the fate of the arrangement, in Fitzgerald's judgments about worth, and in the connection between publication and Fitzgerald's frenzy about money, the Pat Hobby stories are a paradigm of the history of much of Fitzgerald's short fiction.[17]

There is another critical doubleness that makes one conclude "both . . . and" rather than "either . . . or" in considering the quality of the Pat Hobby stories. An absolutely essential yet overlooked critical point is that it makes all the difference in the world if one is reading the Pat Hobby stories as a book or if one is reading any one of the stories as an individual piece.

In the enthusiasm of his introduction to the Pat Hobby stories, Arnold Gingrich exulted in the collection as the first edition of a new Fitzgerald book. He insisted that people would have to recognize that in revising and fussing about the stories, Fitzgerald had created another *book,* one that he thought of as a book and that should be designated a book. Fitzgerald "began thinking of them, after the first three were written, as a collective entity," reconsidering their order and relationship for "the over-all delineation of the character of Pat Hobby." Although the stories do not constitute a novel, Gingrich admitted, they are, nevertheless, a "full-length portrait" that Fitzgerald "thought of . . . as a comedy." At the lowest ebb of Fitzgerald's fame and reputation, except "for the then current Pat Hobby stories, none of his work was any longer in the public eye," and Fitzgerald cared about their quality: "I can't calm down after a story till I know if it's good or bad."[18]

But the stories are a collection. They are not a fully organized single fiction. They do not maintain the evolutionary development of form or narrative that arises from the organic arrangement of parts in a book. If they are to be seen as what amount to chapters in a book, the Pat Hobby stories, in their relation to each other, offer a series of similar episodes rather than developmental, cumulative organization of shape in one unified incremental structure. For all that he foresaw the possibilities of a book in Pat Hobby, Fitzgerald much more immediately saw his own

17. Bruccoli and Duggan, eds., *Correspondence,* 593, 602–9; Gingrich, "Introduction," xx.
18. Gingrich, "Introduction," ix, x, xi.

financial desperation. *Esquire* policy allowed for advances on stories, for the advances cemented a hold on an author, in effect guaranteeing first option on future output. And as his correspondence with Gingrich makes sadly clear, Fitzgerald wanted payment for each story on or before delivery, sometimes even before he wrote it. All he could do was wring his hands and lament the fact that the monthly installments did not appear in an order devoutly to be wished. As he wrote to Gingrich, "It was too bad to begin the Pat Hobby series with that story ['Pat Hobby's Christmas Wish'] because it characterizes him in a rather less sympathetic way than most of the others. Of course he's a complete rat, but it seems to make him a little sinister which he essentially is not. Do you intend to use the other stories in approximately the order in which they were written?"[19]

If they are read as a book, the stories suffer badly from too much repetition in too brief a space (the Gingrich edition contains 158 small pages of large type). In the inescapable need to reintroduce Pat Hobby with each new story, according to the demands of that story as a freestanding individual entity in a monthly magazine that the reader might not have seen before and might not see again, Fitzgerald had to repeat many basic details. Most of the instances in which Pat's identity is created—the fact that, though sadly fallen in the 1930s, in his former estate in the 1920s he had been married three times, had made two to three thousand dollars a week during the heyday of silent films, and had had a uniformed chauffeur; the fact that he is both schlemiel and schlimozzle, a conscienceless but wistful hanger-on at the studios and a fervent worshipper at the Santa Anita track—would have been deleted or revised if Fitzgerald truly had been writing the stories as a book. But when read together in one volume the stories provide justification for commentators who complained of stiffness and tiresomeness in the prose. Just as the calendar of submissions speaks with sad eloquence about the Pat Hobby stories as pieces rushed for the money, so the wearisome repetitiousness, when traced out, becomes undeniably clear. It would be wearisomely repetitious to trace all the wearisome repetitiousness; a brief and incomplete demonstration of only

---

19. Gingrich, "Introduction," xv.

three central details—Pat's age, his salary, and his Hollywood longevity—
illustrate the point.

Pat is first introduced as "a man of forty-nine" on page 10. Thereafter,
as we proceed through the series we are told that "Pat was forty-nine"
(13); that "now he was forty-nine" (21); that Pat's strength was that
"of his forty-nine years" (27); that Pat is admonished, "Don't give up at
forty-nine" (30); that Pat is a "venerable script-stooge of forty-nine" (52)
with "old eyes" (53) and, in fact, "red old eyes" (54); that he sees out of
eyes "not so very bloodshot" (62); that Pat has "red-rimmed" eyes (72);
that Pat was "a dolorous and precarious forty-nine" (82) and "tightened"
his "red-rimmed eyes" (83). " 'I'm in my forties,' said Pat, who was forty-
nine" and who had "dismal, red-streaked eyes" (93). We are told that
Pat's date "would never let those red-rimmed eyes come close" (100);
that Pat is "only a writer—at forty-nine" (103) and that the director
"glanced into Pat's red-rimmed eyes" (104); that "Pat was forty-nine with
red-rimmed eyes" (128); that he was "Pat Hobby, a man of forty-nine"
(136), and that "we perceive . . . through the red-rimmed eyes of Pat
Hobby" (142) that "a man forty-nine is not considered human" (152).

Similarly, Pat's longevity in Hollywood and the facts of his diminished
salary (now $250 to $350 a week) are given again and again by Fitzgerald,
and not always consistently from story to story. On page 1 we are told
that as a scenarist Pat has "twenty years' experience," and on page 4 he
complains about "three-fifty a week, when I used to get two thousand."
Thereafter, the reader is informed that Pat "had thirty [screen] credits;
he had been in the business, publicity and script-writing, for twenty
years" (15). Jack Berners, the producer, will give Pat "two weeks . . . at
two-fifty" (19).

" 'Two-fifty!' objected Pat. 'Say there was one time you paid me ten
times that!' " (19). Fitzgerald continues the point with the information
that "Pat had been in Hollywood since he was thirty—now he was forty-
nine" (21); that Pat had been "flung" a "timely bone of three weeks at
three-fifty" (22); that Pat whines, "I been in the industry fifteen years,
Jack. I've got more screen credits than a dog has got fleas" but that
nevertheless he will be paid "just what Republic paid you last month—
three-fifty a week" (29). Had Orson Welles, "like Pat, been in Hollywood
over twenty years? Did he have credits that would knock your eye
out? . . ." (41). We are informed that, credits and all, poor Pat is "lucky

to get a few weeks at three-fifty" (42); that "ten years ago he had camped beatifically in the range of . . . [three thousand dollars a week]—now he was lucky to get a few weeks at $250" (53); that a producer offers him "four weeks at two-fifty" (59), and that Pat "had collaborated in over two dozen moving picture scripts, most of them, it must be admitted, prior to 1929" (62); that Pat could only hope to be put on a picture "at three-fifty a week" (63), and at work could only complain about "this miserable, uncertain two-fifty a week" (66); that Jack Berners will pay Pat his "last writing price, two-fifty for the week" (87); that, challenged, Pat insists, "I been in this business twenty years" (93), and again, "I been here twenty years" (95); that Pat "was an old timer in pictures; he had once known sumptuous living, but for the past ten years jobs had been hard to hold" (102–3). "You're on the payroll," he's told, "at two-fifty a week for three weeks" (104). He's good for a "small chore . . . one week at two-fifty" (115), even though the studio "had been home to him for twenty years" (121). "Pat Hobby, who was an old-timer," explains that "I been in this business, publicity and script, for twenty years" (143) and that "I got credits going all the way back to 1920" (144), but "I only get three-fifty now" (145). And, as is always the case, "Pat's four weeks at two-fifty would be up tomorrow" (151).

It would be critically stupid to fault Fitzgerald for the reiterations caused by the necessities of writing individual stories as individual stories. But unfortunately, the repetition has a precisely definable cumulative effect concerning the stories as a book. It causes the reader to begin to skim, to skip the familiar background details, and to look for events that make one story's worth of essential background different from another's. That is, the book form nudges readers into a desire for fiction that turns upon event, either in inventiveness of episode or intricacy or twist of plot. And that is the single most unfair demand to level against these stories. They were not written primarily for twist or complexity of plot. Approximately one-third of them ("Pat Hobby's Christmas Wish," "A Man in the Way," " 'Boil Some Water—Lots of It,' " "Teamed with Genius," "Pat Hobby's Secret," and "No Harm Trying") depend conventionally on plot, but for the most part the Pat Hobby stories are deliberately free from concoction and commentary; they are episodes, satiric revelations of exactly the subject matter Varet-Ali (and several others) have identified. Approximately one-third of them ("Pat

Hobby Does His Bit," "Pat Hobby's Preview," "A Patriotic Short," "Fun in an Artist's Studio," "Two Old-Timers," and "Mightier Than the Sword") seem deceptively plotless, almost like sketches, but they too, like all the stories, are episodes in satiric revelation. Even the O. Henry–like endings that Fitzgerald seems to employ in some of them are reversals not only for exploitation of a popular market (they are, partly, that), but also and—primarily—for the ironic upsetting of Hobby's hopes as a metaphor for the squandering and debasement of human desires in stupidity, bad luck, and vulgar trivialization.

The "plotless" style of these stories is a foreshadowing of what came to be the norm in popular magazines of literary sophistication such as the *New Yorker* and was a culmination of literary battles that influenced Fitzgerald's style. Fitzgerald had been intrigued by the clever plotting of O. Henry; moreover, he grew up in and was swayed by the traditional chronological development of story by serious artists he admired and respected, Henry James and Edith Wharton. On the other hand, he was enormously impressed and educated by experiments in narrative voice and chronology by those who had learned from and gone beyond James, especially Conrad and Joyce. No history of literary style need be recounted here. The barest outline will suffice to locate the Pat Hobby stories in the context of Fitzgerald as short-story writer.

As coercive, commonly held, unifying beliefs and value systems disintegrated throughout the postmedieval Western world in the more liberal diversities of modern pluralism and secularism, the source of reality shifted for artists from external depiction to internal experience. The merger of mimesis and oneiros gave primacy to setting, action, dialogue, and form itself as signs of interior meaning. Those denominated naturalists insisted on unvitiated, objectively unadorned presentation of everything external to human will and fate as forces meaningless in themselves but totally identifying and deciding human will and fate. The symbolists insisted on uncensored presentation of interior perspective as the determinant of the meaning of the externals. In the modernist merger of realist and romantic, these otherwise opposing parties of metonymy and metaphor met in an insistence on style as truth—dialogue, event, sentence structure, and characterization pared down to and symbolic of the essentials of experience. These essentials are organized not according to conventional and chronological development of narrative progress in the artificially arranged plotting of beginning, middle, and end, of rising action, climax, and falling action, but according to the episodic and epiphanic nature of experience. Probability (within the nature of the experience presented) and irony (in America after the disillusion of the Civil War and increasingly after World War I) replaced coincidence, contrived twist, and dramatic convenience.

The experimental modernists led to the disappearance of the commenting narrator and an entire style of storytelling and form in the triumph of epiphany over traditional plotting of event. In style and narrative event, Flaubert and Chekhov "replaced" Dumas and de Maupassant as progenitors and models. In the American extension in which Fitzgerald was active, Sherwood Anderson and Ernest Hemingway replaced O. Henry and Booth Tarkington. The conquest was completed in the 1920s, and by 1939, when Fitzgerald began composing the Pat Hobby stories, magazines such as *Esquire* indicated the extent to which the effects of the modernist revolution had established the mode of the literary marketplace. Not only because of its marketing attempt at male sophistication but also because of its attempt at *modern* sophistication, *Esquire* cultivated a macho, cosmopolitan, ironic style whose terseness bespoke both aims. With the stripped-down, realistically presented externals in his fiction creating the unstated internals, Hemingway, of course, was *Esquire*'s prize stable horse, and his influence on Fitzgerald should be reckoned as part of the magazine's demands in the dynamics of development in Fitzgerald's style. The Runyonesque and Lardneresque nuances of the prose in the Pat Hobby stories are not exclusively attributable to the success enjoyed by Runyon and Lardner in the literary marketplace. Nor are those nuances by any means exclusively attributable to Fitzgerald's deep affection and respect for Ring Lardner. Rather, they must be seen in their fullest context; for Fitzgerald, Hemingway summed up the import of artistic nuances in all the intellectual, experiential—and victorious—reverberations of the serious literary marketplace.

Fitzgerald's letters reveal hard-guy attitudes as well as what their author saw as an invaluable "female" sensibility within himself. In overall tone, however, the letters clearly come from a man who can be tough but not macho, who is romantic but not sentimental, who is vulnerable but courageously perseverant even when cynical. Yet, Fitzgerald's voice tends to change tonally in his letters to Hemingway. It becomes marginally harder, more smart-guy and macho; deeply and subtly Fitzgerald felt a need, conscious or otherwise, to pander to Hemingway. The variation of voice is a revelation of Fitzgerald's sense of subordination to Hemingway, who was a threatening presence in the problematical relationship between the two men. It is sufficient to say that for Fitzgerald, widely and profoundly, consciously and unconsciously, Hemingway summed up an entire chapter of history in the development of Western literature. On a smaller, more conscious, and more immediate level for Fitzgerald, Hemingway summed up success in the modernist modes of the serious literary marketplace; and, on the smallest, most conscious, and most immediate level, Hemingway summed up the stylistic contexts of *Esquire* magazine. The style of the Pat Hobby stories, at the point Fitzgerald's life had reached in 1939, is an eloquent and profound statement of Fitzgerald's sense of place within the history of the literary marketplace.

But the *individual* genius of F. Scott Fitzgerald requires that one define it by historical contexts only very cautiously. In his own prodigious talent Fitzgerald hardly played the sedulous ape. He retained to the end his own distinctive style. It has become a commonplace to assert that *The Great Gatsby* represents Fitzgerald's breakthrough into mastery of modernist economy and dense organization, that *Tender Is the Night* is a relapse into lyricism, and that with *The Last Tycoon* Fitzgerald was regaining the true path that, as he said in his letters, he had found and wished he had stuck to after *The Great Gatsby*. However, Fitzgerald himself felt that *The Great Gatsby* was held together in part by overlapping blankets of prose, and no reader with any sensibility can be unaware of its lyricism. Furthermore, the incredible history of versions and revisions and hopes for further revisions of *Tender Is the Night* invites examinations and explications that reveal the novel to be as fully economical and densely organized as anything Fitzgerald ever wrote. And the prose of *The Last Tycoon* fragment contains passages as lyrically evocative as anything in either *The Great Gatsby* or *Tender Is the Night*. In all three masterpieces there is romantic lyricism as well as the ethic of modernist literary economies.

In sum, the Pat Hobby stories do not mark a "new" style in Fitzgerald. Along with others of his 1930s prose pieces *as well as several stories of the 1920s* they signal the marketplace dominance of Hemingwayesque modernism that always had been *a part* of Fitzgerald's own style. The Pat Hobby stories are a stripping away of evocative lyricism, largely in a diminution of descriptive passages. In the consequent relative bareness of the style lies the reason that as a book *The Pat Hobby Stories* do not quite match the evocative power of the best of the Hollywood novels, Nathanael West's *The Day of the Locust*. From the descriptive full development of several characters to the description of houses, furniture, and the "neon piping" around the Los Angeles canyon rims at sunset, West creates an intensely evocative sense of Southern California *place* as national mortuary of the soul. In the Pat Hobby stories, Fitzgerald limited himself to one *aspect* of his stylistic capacities, not because the subject was Hollywood but because the context was *Esquire*. As *The Last Tycoon* indicates, to the end Fitzgerald remained unbeatable at evocative description and characterization when he created it for a book; had that book been finished it would have been *the* great American Hollywood novel. Fitzgerald set aside his heaviest artillery in writing the Pat Hobby stories because he was writing not a book but one brief short story at a time with *Esquire*'s space restrictions and narrative preferences. Fitzgerald's aim, after all, was to focus each time on one character and one occupation and one constantly ironic fate. It would be unfair and wrong to fault *Esquire*. It did not hurt Fitzgerald's talent and it provided him both a living and an exercise in the current idiom of respected style.

The success of the style depends upon Fitzgerald's control of the bareness. Most of the stories are essentially even in quality, so one may select at random. The very first, "Pat Hobby's Christmas Wish," becomes as good an example as any for a glimpse of the effects of stylistic strength and weakness.

There are moments in this story when the satiric quotidian style of a character's dialogue becomes that of the invisible narrator, and at that instant the writing seems merely cheap and rushed: Pat "had been hired to script an old-fashioned horse-opera and the boys who were 'writing behind him'—that is working over his stuff—said that all of it was old . . ." (2). Given what one expects about the mind of Hopper, a coworker from whom this information extends, "horse-opera" and "boys" are perfectly appropriate. They are working parts of the modernist trick of implying that the reader, without receiving commentary, is at once objectively observing a moment of experience, and yet is also aware of a perception in which the experience exists within the character's texture of sensibility. "Horse-opera" and "boys who were 'writing behind him'" work the difficult trick exactly. But the material within the dashes ("—that is working over his stuff—") belongs entirely to Fitzgerald, who is explaining to the reader, and who, in his persona of totally removed, satiric, olympian narrator, has a very different mode. Given the distancing occasioned by the style's unadorned, uninterpretive terseness of statement, even the echo of a hint of an intruding narrator is obtrusive, and disconcertingly so when suddenly that narrator's idiom is indistinguishable from the patois of the character. The momentary merger unnecessarily raises disruptive questions about the problem of the omniscient narrator as persona.

Yet, in the same passage in which he falters, Fitzgerald also displays superb control over the bare, episodic quality of the story, whose experientially realistic nonsequiturs turn out not to be nonsequiturs at all, but the introduction of a beautifully crafted development of relation between character and event. While waiting for his new secretary, Pat reminisces with Hopper:

> He broke off as the sight of a woman, pad in hand, entering his office down the hall recalled him to the sorry present.
>
> "Gooddorf has me working over the holiday," . . . [Pat] complained bitterly.
>
> "I wouldn't do it."
>
> "I wouldn't either except my four weeks are up next Friday, and if I bucked him he wouldn't extend me."
>
> As he turned away Hopper knew that Pat was not being extended anyhow. He had been hired to script an old-fashioned horse-opera and the boys who were "writing behind him"—that is working over his stuff—said that all of it was old and some didn't make sense.
>
> "I'm Miss Kagle," said Pat's new secretary.
>
> She was about thirty-six, handsome, faded, tired, efficient. She went to the typewriter, examined it, sat down and burst into sobs. (2)

Abjuring embellishment or explanation, Fitzgerald works the very cadences of the sentences to create tone. The intonation of series in the last two sentences suggests the impersonality of a shopping list, reverberating against the impersonality of the situation: the loneliness of those few who have to work on Christmas Eve in the large institution that is indifferent enough about their feelings to require their holiday presence in the first place. Miss Kagle's bursting into sobs is given force by the unexpected connotational difference between the act and the style of its presentation. Except for a very few moments, that kind of swift and sophisticated stylistics characterizes Fitzgerald's expert control of economical bareness throughout the prose in all the Pat Hobby episodes.

In the first seven short sentences of the story, Fitzgerald has managed to convey all of the following: (1) a hard-boiled, satiric tone ("It was Christmas Eve in the studio. By eleven o'clock in the morning, Santa Claus had called on most of the huge population according to each one's deserts. . . . And tips of fifties, tens and fives from producers, directors and writers fell like manna upon the white collar class" [1]); (2) the fact that Pat Hobby is cheap, broke, penurious, or all three (he had gotten rid of his secretary the day before in order to avoid buying her a Christmas present); (3) the fact that there is an intense caste system in the Hollywood studios, and those who *have* get more than those who haven't; (4) the fact that Hobby knew that the new secretary whose momentary arrival he awaited would not expect a Christmas gift on her first day on the job; (5) the knowledge that Pat Hobby would be self-seeking and unscrupulous; and (6) the knowledge that he is a very low man in the caste system. Moreover, most of the reader's knowledge is implanted by implication in a few selected facts rather than by direct statement from narrator to reader.

Fitzgerald catches the exact gesture in swift strokes. This is the selection of details to signal the end of Miss Kagle's sobbing:

> "Nothing's as bad as it seems," . . . [Pat] assured her unconvincingly.
> "What's it, anyhow? They going to lay you off?"
> She shook her head, did a sniffle to end sniffles, and opened her note book. (3)

The sureness of that last sentence provides the concrete visibility of the entire scene. In a similar manner, with three quick half-lines Fitzgerald completes the foundation for the rest of the story:

> "Who you been working for?"
> She answered between suddenly gritted teeth.
> "Mr. Harry Gooddorf." (3)

The skillfully highlighted sobbing and the gritted teeth lay to rest any doubts the reader might have about the conspiracy formed by these two newly met strangers to blackmail Mr. Harry Gooddorf, Pat for a sinecure at the studio, Miss Kagle for revenge against a lover whose mistress and secretary she had been until he noticed that she had begun to age. And, of course, the blackmail "evidence" being mistakenly construed as proof of murder, the conspiracy comes, like all of Pat's shabby hopes, to nothing.

As plot and characterization join through economical sureness of detail, in one hilarious and inventive word Fitzgerald can characterize the pretentiousness and abysmal ignorance of Pat Hobby as Hobby dictates a scene to Miss Kagle:

> "Ext. Long Shot of the Plains," he decreed. "Buck and Mexicans ap-
> proaching the hyacenda."
> "The what?"
> "The hyacenda—the ranch house." (4)

Had Fitzgerald not been impelled by financial desperation to hurry the job, his revision practices would have maintained all the Hobby tales at that same level of sweet control and invention. But the rush shows occasionally. In "Pat Hobby's Christmas Wish," the word *put* creates just the right touch as Pat says, " . . . if I put 'you rat' the scene won't have any force" (4). But when the same word becomes the author's, there is an instant of stylistic jarring in which Fitzgerald did not yet realize that he had not quite come back up out of the mind of the character into his own: "He substituted the word 'Scram!' for 'Get out of my sight!', he *put* 'Behind the eight-ball' instead of 'In trouble' . . ." (36; emphasis mine).

There are several indications of haste or carelessness here and there. In "Pat Hobby's Christmas Wish," Fitzgerald has Miss Kagle buy Pat a linen handkerchief—on Christmas morning. In "Pat Hobby's Preview," Pat starts out with twelve dollars. Fitzgerald then has Pat buy "a two-dollar shirt changing into it in the shop and a four-dollar Alpine hat—thus halving his bank account which, since the Bank Holiday of 1933, he carried cautiously in his pocket" (97). Within a few paragraphs Fitzgerald has Pat make "a further inroad on his bank account to pay for his six whiskeys"—and then Pat takes his date "into the restaurant for dinner" (98). Even at Great Depression prices and with all his magic, Fitzgerald can't bring that one off. It is also highly improbable that because the star broke his leg an entire crew would leave the location ("Pat Hobby Does His Bit") and unwittingly abandon the unconscious Pat Hobby to lie interminably in the road in the protective casement of iron that the director locked him in as protection in a stunt shot. It is mildly annoying that Fitzgerald's arithmetic is off in figuring the amount that Eric, the script boy, has left after Pat has taken his extortionist cut ("No Harm Trying"). But *most* of these occasional signs of carelessness are minor enough that neither the firmness nor the patina of the stories is destroyed.

What is not salvageable is a regression into the kind of story idea that once might have sold to the *Saturday Evening Post* or *Redbook* or the *Woman's Home Companion* in the happier finances and lighthearted receptivity of an earlier day. Neither the romantically far-fetched nor the absurd in plot material married well with the realistic style of the stripped-down Fitzgerald in the grimmer ambience and marketplace of the late 1930s. Within the irony-seeking modernist insistence on the probabilities of the kind of experience presented, "Pat Hobby, Putative Father" seems silly because of the unlikelihood that any woman who would have married Pat would have gone off to become a great and sacred lady of India, making Hobby's unknown son a Rajah princeling. Similarly, "Pat Hobby's College Days" falls apart because it hinges unbelievably on the inability of Pat's secretary to dispose of his empty booze bottles in any buildings of the studios or in any of the canyons or coastline around Los Angeles. These two tales and the moments in which control of style slips lend an air of shallowness to the stories as a book. Yet, except for those two stories and despite the scarce moments of disrepair, the Pat Hobby series, read as individual pieces at separate sittings, are successful and even glowing works of real craftsmanship whose style and theme meaningfully reflect significant literary and cultural history as well as the development of a component part of Fitzgerald's style.

The one strength of the book format is its intensification of theme. No observer of style and theme in the Pat Hobby stories can fail to see that the theme is as consistently and coherently organized as the style. In these episodes Fitzgerald continues one of the purposes that is at the center of his better-known and highly admired stories as well as of *The Great Gatsby, Tender Is the Night,* and *The Last Tycoon:* an exploration of belonging, of the precariousness of personality in a world in which one's very identity is dependent upon modes of behavior and appearance most shallowly conceived. For Pat, *being* is money, cars, women, recognition; without the kind of success that Hollywood spotlights, one is just one of "them," the dead: the faceless, nameless, envious, worshipful, nonentities jostling restlessly in the darkness beyond the brilliance of the roped-off walkway down which the fluorescent insiders prance on their way to the exclusive preview. From Pat's perspective in a Great Depression world where there were either no jobs or, if one were lucky, wages of eighteen dollars or so for a forty-eight-hour workweek, to work at an ordinary job for ordinary pay in the ordinary world of ordinary days is the obscure and sullen dusk of death. In this urgent sense of being or not being, the frantically unprincipled Pat will do anything to hang on in any way to any scintilla of existence. Every aspect of existence in Hollywood confirms Pat's desperate definition of life and death. And the house of life is the studio.

In "Pat Hobby's Preview," Pat and his date are not allowed into the theater, which is showing a new film whose screen credits, for a rare and blessed change, exhibit Pat's name as one of the writers. Inside are the living luminaries. Outside are the nonexistent. Fitzgerald, without a word of comment, creates the situation and the setting, the watching crowd, as the total source of identity. When the doorkeeper consigns Pat to the oblivion of insignificance by refusing him admittance, Pat's date immediately dissociates herself from him: "Nothing in her face indicated that he was anything but what he thought he was—all alone" (99). Among the insignificant there is neither vivifying solidarity nor solacing identity:

> Though the preview crowd had begun to drift away, with that vague American wonder as to why they had come at all, one little cluster found something arresting and poignant in the faces of Pat and Eleanor. They were obviously gate-crashers, outsiders like themselves, but the crowd resented the temerity of their effort to get in—a temerity which the crowd did not share. Little jeering jests were audible. (100)

But then, because the movie is so rotten that his cowriter doesn't want his name on it, his collaborator strides out of the theater and in angry, condescending disgust gives Pat his tickets. In the obtuse and callous gracelessness that characterizes Hollywood and for which Pat is the paradigm, Hobby is perfectly happy to enter, even this way, into the region of the blessed:

> He seized Eleanor's elbow in a firm grasp and steered her triumphantly towards the door:
> "Cheer up, baby. That's the way it is. You see?" (101)

As one of the best and funniest of the stories, "Pat Hobby and Orson Welles" brilliantly exploits every detail of a slapstick situation to indicate why the real Pat Hobby, ineffectively predatory, totally insensitive, and graceless Pat Hobby, is also poor Pat Hobby. The archetypal has-been, Pat forlornly clings to a bygone identity from the days of the silents, using his cachet from other days to buy a bit of time and space among the living. As long as he was still recognized by the guards and allowed to enter the studios (admission and exclusion are constant motifs in these stories), he *belonged,* even if only as a shadowy scrounger. But a new ukase from the gods has wiped out what is left of Pat's capital. Again and again the Pat Hobby stories become translations into a breezy American idiom and Hollywood locale of Kafka's *The Castle.* New guards are posted at all the studio gates to remedy lax admissions practices. Everyone will need a valid pass.

The guards humiliate Pat and condemn him by denying his craved identity: no pass, no membership. Hysterically he tries to use his contacts in the studio hierarchy to secure a pass for readmission, but Pat remains in the commoner's outer darkness: "On the third day he was frantic with gloom. He had sent note after note to Jack Berners [a sympathetic producer] and even asked Louie [the studio bookie] to intercede—now word came that Jack had left town. There were so few friends left. Desolate, he stood in front of the automobile gate with a crowd of staring children, feeling that he had reached the end at last" (44).

Through a lucky near-accident at the gate, Pat shares a ride with Mr. Marcus in his limousine. Mr. Marcus, God (the ultimate financial power) in the studio, recognizes Pat from the old days and the two men reveal a mutual fear of change, both of them reactionaries who find their security in very different levels of the status quo. Pat has felt a displacing threat in the looming of newness associated with the advent of l'enfant terrible, Orson Welles:

"Who's this Welles?" Pat [had] asked of Louie, the studio bookie. "Every time I pick up a paper they got about this Welles."

"You know, he's that beard," explained Louie. (41)

In the Welles-less security of the limousine and the old times, Pat and Marcus sentimentalize about the superiority of the simple life: " 'That's what I'd like,' said Mr. Marcus gloomily. 'A farm—with chickens. Maybe a little nine-hole course. Not even a stock ticker' " (46). But Pat is not talking nine-hole pastoralism. In his elemental need for a pass that will readmit him to the heavenly castle and permit him to live, he feels his very life threatened by the inexorable march of progress. Whatever function the likes of Pat Hobby might pretend to in the industry, the likes of Orson Welles would find no place for it:

"Mr. Marcus," he said so sincerely that his voice trembled, "I wouldn't be surprised if Orson Welles is the biggest menace that's come to Holly-wood for years. He gets a hundred and fifty grand a picture and I wouldn't be surprised if he was so radical that you had to have all new equipment and start all over again like you did with sound in 1928."

"Oh my God!" groaned Mr. Marcus.

"And me," said Pat, "all I want is a pass and no money—to leave things as they are."

Mr. Marcus reached for his card case. (47)

Orson Welles never enters the story in person. He is a menacing background presence in Pat's preposterously reactionary sense of things:

At this studio . . . [Pat] never felt unemployed—in recent times of stress he had eaten property food on its stages—half a cold lobster during a scene from *The Divine Miss Carstairs;* he had often slept on the sets and last winter made use of a Chesterfield overcoat from the costume department. Orson Welles had no business edging him out of this. Orson Welles belonged with the rest of the snobs back in New York. (44)

Quickly Pat becomes a butt of jokes. With winks and nudges among themselves, the lower castes within the gates begin to call Pat "Orson," a development in which "for the first time in his life . . . [Pat] began to feel a loss of identity" (47). Fitzgerald makes the issue focal: "Now to lose one's identity is a careless thing in any case. But to lose it to an enemy, or at least to one who has become scapegoat for our misfortunes— that is a hardship" (47–48). In the ultimate practical joke, Jeff Boldoni, the makeup man, convinces Pat that he really does look like Orson Welles, and to prove it, if Pat will allow Boldoni to fashion a Wellesian "muff" on Pat's face, Boldoni will lend him the "ten smackers" (49) for which seedy, needy Pat yearns. Pat does not suspect that the beard can be removed only with a thorough soaking. Jeff offers to drive Pat to a shooting set where bearded men are needed and slyly places a sign reading ORSON WELLES in the windshield as Pat rides in the back seat. Jeff then proceeds to drive Pat all over the lot as people gawk. Perceiving the slowly oncoming automobile, an elderly man in an obviously important group falls to the sidewalk:

> "My God, did you see that?" exclaimed Jeff. "That was Mr. Marcus."
> He came to a stop. An excited man ran up and put his head in the car window.
> "Mr. Welles, our Mr. Marcus has had a heart attack. Can we use your car to get him to the infirmary?" (51)

In the spacious pecking order of Hollywood success, "those few who decide things are happy in their work and sure that they are worthy of their hire—the rest live in a mist of doubt as to when their vast inadequacy will be disclosed" (47). Confronted with merely himself as *the* New World identity on the golden throne, the poor real Pat Hobby breaks under the burden. The mighty Orson can fell both high and low, but Pat bolts from the car, rushes from the lot, flees *out* through the gates, and throws himself into Mario's bar, where "three extras with beards stood at the rail" and where Pat can exercise his belonging and his "simple life" at the only level he can manage any longer:

> With a trembling hand he took the hard-earned ten dollar bill from his pocket.
> "Set 'em up," he cried hoarsely. "Every muff has a drink on me." (51)

Taken together, the stories are compounded of hints about the problematic, unstable, and platitudinous nature of identity precariously based upon the fatuous surfaces that debase all possibilities of being to showbiz clichés. In "Pat Hobby, Putative Father," when Pat bids goodbye to his son, about whom he really feels and knows nothing except that the young man might be a source of income, "he turned away—feeling like—like Stella Dallas" (69). As in "Pat Hobby Does His Bit," he cannot be said to have profound feelings, and his sense of self arises from the vulgar sentimentality factory: " . . . working or not Pat liked to pass his days in or near a studio. He had reached a dolorous and precarious forty-nine with nothing else to do" (82). His pride, any essential independent self, is gone; in "Pat Hobby's Preview," Pat eats insults with neither resentment nor regret just as long as for a moment it can "be like old times walking with a cute little blonde past the staring crowds on the sidewalk" (96). All he needs is the artificial inflation, no matter how temporary, that a job at a studio gives him. In "No Harm Trying," even the "prospect of a job. . . . anesthetized the crumbled, struggling remnants of his manhood, and inoculated him instead with a bland, easy-going confidence. The set speeches and attitudes of success returned to him" (103).

His criterion for being remains one of belonging to the charmed circle of those who lunched with the president and who had swimming pools. In "A Patriotic Short," what he remembers as the sign of his own humanity was "how he had arrived at the studio in his car driven by a Filipino in uniform; the deferential bow of the guard at the gate which had admitted car and all to the lot, his ascent to that long lost office which had a room for the secretary and was really a director's office . . ." (116–17). We find, when "On the Trail of Pat Hobby," that, shallow to the core, the real Pat Hobby in his decay has nothing but unreality. All that's left as his "destination, his refuge, was the studio, where he was not employed but which had been home to him for twenty years" (121). Poor Pat Hobby because the residual precipitate of the phony *is* the real Pat Hobby, and that, for Fitzgerald, is the pity and the terror. Americans have lost America by identifying it with everything that Hollywood is and spawns, and thereby have lost themselves.

Consequently, neither Fitzgerald nor the Pat Hobby stories conveniently single out the executives as villains. Some are crass and vulgar and stupid, but then so is low-man Pat and so are the crowds beyond the velvet ropes. The moving picture is not one in which greedy manipulators exploit the long-suffering, resistant, producing masses, but one in which manipulator, mass, and all are joined in a national, symbiotic, and ugly dissolution of humanly meaningful culture. In fact, some of those on top are people of superior sensibility. If, as in "Pat Hobby's Secret," "perversely Pat Hobby's sense of justice was with the producer, not the writer" (53), F. Scott Fitzgerald also found that often the Monroe Stahrs were superior to the people who worked for them. And on a lower level in the Pat Hobby stories, producers Harry Gooddorf, Jack Berners, and Carl Le Vigne are characters endowed by their sympathetic creator with patience, forgiveness, sympathy, and intelligence.

Like Fitzgerald's problematic sympathies, an evaluation of the Hobby stories requires a divided allegiance. "Pat Hobby, Putative Father" and "Pat Hobby's College Days" would be best removed, and there is residual foolishness in the idea that anyone vaguely resembling Pat Hobby, even at the height of his career, would have been chosen by the moguls to represent the writers and take the place of "Doug" Fairbanks at a luncheon with the president of the United States ("A Patriotic Short")—unless one sees this story as a paradigmatic condensation of the collective theme of all of them. But gems such as "Two Old-Timers," "Pat Hobby's Christmas Wish," "No Harm Trying," "Fun in an Artist's Studio," and "On the Trail of Pat Hobby" survive the collateral irritations of some of the book around them. The more the Pat Hobby stories are reread, the more professionally effective their hard-boiled style becomes.

Whatever the mixture of ingredients that produced Fitzgerald's evaluation at any given time, since his death his pronouncements about his work have left a double critical heritage to all commentators, among whom the unwise choose one legacy over another. The complexity and changefulness of his assessments of his self and his short stories were expressed in letters and essays; they have been cited so variously and quoted so frequently elsewhere in this volume and in all the critical literature that here they only need be summarized.[20] They are especially

---

20. In addition to the introduction and other essays in this volume, see the introductions to Fitzgerald, *Stories of F. Scott Fitzgerald;* F. Scott Fitzgerald, *Afternoon of an Author: A Selection of Uncollected Stories and Essays;* Fitzgerald, *Pat Hobby;* Fitzgerald, *Basil and Josephine;* Fitzgerald and Fitzgerald, *Bits of Paradise;* Bruccoli, ed., *Price Was High;* Bryer, ed., *Short Stories of F. Scott Fitzgerald;* Bruccoli, ed., *Short Stories.* Kuehl, ed., *Apprentice Fiction,* is devoted to the themes that appear in all of Fitzgerald's fictions, long or short, and does not discuss Fitzgerald's attitudes toward writing short fiction. Four book-length

applicable to the short stories, and most especially to the late writings among which the Pat Hobby stories take their place.

Legacy One: Fitzgerald had contempt for his short stories—they were "trash," a "poor old debauched form" he had "grown to hate"; writing stories only for the money, he was an "old whore" who got "$4000 a screw . . . because she's mastered the forty positions," as he told Hemingway; he stripped the stories of good prose that he then used for his novels, which he considered the true art form and his real forte; he wrote stories in haste, his repetitive activity and formulaic product both lubricated by drink. All of this was true of some of the stories.

Legacy Two: No matter how cheap the story or its purpose, Fitzgerald brought to it, at a very high price of talent, the extra touch of his commitment and intelligence; he always tried for "something new . . . in substance," as he wrote to his agent, Harold Ober; he took pride in many of his stories and, knowing that they were too good for the mass-circulation outlets that rejected some of the best of them, he wrote them anyhow and sold them for small payment to appreciative magazines; he revised and rerevised even the least of his stories, protesting angrily that you can't write a saleable story—at least not for George Horace Lorimer's *Saturday Evening Post*—on the bottle; he was a veteran who took a true professional's pride in his professionalism. All of this legacy was true, too, and more true than the first.

Some of the Pat Hobby stories belong more to the truth of one legacy, some belong more to the other. Most of them, in very uneven proportion of mix, belong to both, and in this too they are paradigmatic. In his mood swings, all his professional life Fitzgerald further dichotomized art and trash into failure and success, another double complex that has had its effect on all commentators. Essentially, he saw two groups of values and

---

studies of Fitzgerald's short fiction touch on the topic throughout: John A. Higgins's *F. Scott Fitzgerald: A Study of the Stories*, a helpful series of story-by-story statements about the Pat Hobby episodes; Alice Hall Petry, *Fitzgerald's Craft of Short Fiction: The Collected Stories—1920–1935*, a bright study that discusses the four volumes of short stories published during Fitzgerald's lifetime and therefore does not include the Pat Hobby stories; John Kuehl's very useful and informative *Fitzgerald: Study of the Short Fiction;* and Bryant Mangum's thoughtful *Fortune Yet*. Most essays on the short stories also repeat self-evaluative quotations from Fitzgerald.

identities. One: commercial success, pandering, trash, the short story, and, most of all, Hollywood bed down together in the exciting palace of contemporary glitz, fame, and quick disintegration. Two: commercial failure, integrity, art, and the novel wander hand in hand in the desert of neglect toward an Elysian oasis of immortal reputation. And, in fact, the statistics generated by Fitzgerald's sales and income over the years support his sense of things, statistics supplied and discussed enough by several scholars that, like Fitzgerald's self-assessments, they need not be repeated and developed here.[21] It is sufficient to assert that like his legacies of self-evaluation, each of his categories of success and failure was more applicable to some of his writings than to others. Some of his fictions *are* trashy. Some are immortal. There are trashy moments and there are fine touches in almost everything he wrote. It's a matter of preponderance.

Preponderantly (despite the fact that it is supposed to be fun to kick scholar-critics), scholar-critics—as distinct from reviewers through the 1940s—generously have sought the fine touches. Consequently, the academic critical commentary on Fitzgerald's short fiction, especially the lesser-known variety, tends to be based on benevolence and appreciation resulting in the assertion that the stories deserve more and better attention than they have received.[22] But the impulse involves more than generosity of critical spirit. It involves tidying up in the house of literary history. All scholars, teachers, editors, and readers who are entranced by the glowing achievement of Fitzgerald's lovely masterpieces wish to

21. A study of the categories at work throughout Fitzgerald's short fiction, Kuehl's *Fitzgerald: Study of the Short Fiction* offers a handy summary overview of the facts and figures of Fitzgerald's productivity and of his financial success and failure (3–8 and passim). See also Bryer's introduction to *Short Stories of F. Scott Fitzgerald*, xi–xiv and passim; and Bruccoli's introduction to *Price Was High* (passim). There are also materials on the topic in the various biographies and in specialized periodical studies, especially the *Fitzgerald/Hemingway Annual*. The most productive suppliers of the facts and figures are Bruccoli and Bryer, who have made references readily available for Fitzgerald studies in specialized bibliographies.

22. Bryer's introduction to *Short Stories of F. Scott Fitzgerald* is an angry and eloquent demand on behalf of Fitzgerald's poor ghost. And one of the few essays devoted entirely to the Pat Hobby stories asserts that Fitzgerald's "sardonic picture of a worn-out screen writer deserves to be better known" (John O. Rees, "Fitzgerald's Pat Hobby Stories," 553). The essay is a sane summary and appreciation of the stories.

solidify Fitzgerald's immortality once and for all and tie up the loose ends. But this just proclivity of scholarship can sometimes lead to an over-redress of balances, an impulse that becomes most noticeable in attempts to justify some of Fitzgerald's early stories that were mostly tinsel, such as "The Offshore Pirate" (1920), and to claim for the Pat Hobby stories (which by and large but not unexceptionably are far superior to Fitzgerald's early fluff) the major coherence of an extended work of fiction.

The deep itch in literary commentators to complete unfinished business by making another Fitzgerald volume, of which *The Pat Hobby Stories* is symptomatic, is one more of Fitzgerald's peculiar legacies. He left a codicil in literary history that what is arguably his richest book, *Tender Is the Night,* be reissued in a new form that revises the shape from a beginning in media res to a straight chronological development of narrative. He left it as a book waiting to be done.[23] But he died too soon and in an impotent relationship with publishers. Furthermore, he left the tantalizingly unfinished chunk of what now can be only the eternal promise of a magnificent novel in the fragment of *The Last Tycoon,* another book waiting to be done. Moreover, in groups of short fictions such as the Pat Hobby stories and the Basil and Josephine stories, he left obvious and tempting material for volumes waiting to be compiled to supplement the four collections of short stories issued in his lifetime. Consequently, makers of posthumous Fitzgerald volumes are psychologically canted to see them as important literary stocktaking, a compensation for neglect and fate, a tying together and summing up that Fitzgerald should have and would have done but was never able to do. Thus, when Malcolm Cowley wrote one of the best summations of the author ever written, his lovely introduction to the 1951 edition of *The Stories of F. Scott Fitzgerald,* lifting the Fitzgerald revival into orbit, the very title suggested a completion. The words *"A Selection"* were reserved for the subtitle, and in his final paragraph Cowley as much as stated that the volume was a summing up. The stories "speak

23. In 1951, Malcolm Cowley prepared a revised version, which generally became available in *Three Novels of F. Scott Fitzgerald.* However, a fully corrected "received" edition of the revised version is yet to be published.

for the author; and taken together they form a sort of journal of his whole career." Then, in 1957, when Arthur Mizener fashioned a volume of Fitzgerald's uncollected stories and essays in *Afternoon of an Author,* he offered the collection as a partial summation because at that time he thought it "probable that a representative selection of the forty-nine stories Fitzgerald wrote between his last collection of stories in 1935 and his death in 1940 will never be made into a book."[24]

When Gingrich published *The Pat Hobby Stories,* he wrote that the "book's seventeen stories, comprising [*sic*] the entire Pat Hobby sequence, bridge the last major gap in the collected writings of F. Scott Fitzgerald," and, "with this volume, . . . the Fitzgerald cast of characters is at last complete." However, in 1965 a last "last major gap in the collected writings of F. Scott Fitzgerald" was filled by John Kuehl, followed by the filling of a last, last "last major gap" by Kuehl and Jackson R. Bryer in 1973. A year later this last, last last was followed by a last, last, last last by Matthew Bruccoli and Scottie Fitzgerald Smith, in which Smith announced that "this is the last book which will ever be published devoted to previously uncollected writings of my parents." Thereupon, Bruccoli almost immediately published a last, last, last, last last, whose subtitle was *The Last Uncollected Stories of F. Scott Fitzgerald.* In his introduction, Bruccoli accounts for the accumulation of volumes, in which (at last) all but eight of Fitzgerald's 164 published stories appear. Those eight "remain uncollected because Scottie Fitzgerald Smith feels that they are so far below her father's standards that they should be left in oblivion."[25]

Clearly, there are lasts and lasts. In 1982, in his introduction to *The Short Stories of F. Scott Fitzgerald,* Bryer noted that "F. Scott Fitzgerald wrote 178 short stories; 146 of them were published during his lifetime; 18 have been published since his death [accounting for Bruccoli's figure of 164 published stories]; 14 remain unpublished."[26] Bryer's figures suggest that there are still six to go beyond the eight that Mrs. Smith felt "should be left in oblivion." Fitzgerald's daughter is dead, and those

---

24. Fitzgerald, *Stories of F. Scott Fitzgerald,* xxv; Fitzgerald, *Afternoon of an Author,* 7.
25. Gingrich, "Introduction," ix, xxiii; Kuehl, ed., *Apprentice Fiction;* Fitzgerald, *Basil and Josephine;* Fitzgerald and Fitzgerald, *Bits of Paradise,* 1; Bruccoli, ed., *Price Was High,* xi–xii.
26. Bryer, ed., *Short Stories of F. Scott Fitzgerald,* xi.

remaining fourteen still generate an urge toward the last, last, last, last, last, last, posthumous tidying up and putting in place.

The implications herein for final summations were in part realized by yet another selection when, in 1989, Bruccoli published *The Short Stories of F. Scott Fitzgerald*, whose title, so very much like Cowley's, suggests a final totality. The volume comes full circle in intent to what Cowley began in 1951: the overall summary representation of the best of Fitzgerald's short fiction. Cowley had included two Pat Hobby stories, Bruccoli but one. The production of finalizations and summary overviews indicates that despite Mizener's plaint about the collection of Fitzgerald's last forty-nine short stories, and despite Smith's reservations about eight of her father's stories, one need only hang on long enough before there are the full volumes of *The Complete Stories of F. Scott Fitzgerald*. A remaining question about future volumes of selections is how many Pat Hobby stories each will include.

The placement of the Pat Hobby stories in these legacies of editorial housekeeping and Fitzgerald's shifting, revisions, and evaluations can be approached within the context of the evolution of recognition of the stories. That context and the legacies are the explanatory framework for the reason that the Pat Hobby stories have been written about so sparsely. Some of them are first-rate, but, though good, many are less than distinguished; the "neglect" of commentators has been a reflection of the inexorable judgment of time; though there is something to say about any of them and much to say about some of them, there is the richness of the literary masterpiece in none of them. That context and the legacies are also the explanatory framework for the reason that we come back to them now. As truly good professional writing, the best of them offer model examples of the stylistic modulation in Fitzgerald's prose; as such, they can accommodate more attention than they have received.

Poor Pat, the hack, the rat, one wants to say. What the stories lack in richness and complexity makes it easy to sum up the red-eyed has-been. But poor Fitzgerald, the overburdened genius, both hack and stunning writer—that is another story and one not easy to sum up. Whatever one wants to say on the one hand requires an immediate "BUT" and a complicating opposite on the other. So, too, one wants to say that the Pat Hobby stories are undeveloped BUT that they have force; that many are ephemera BUT some of them most surely will last; that they are not short prose fiction masterpieces BUT that several of them are beautifully wrought successes. If collectively they fall short of greatness, they are the shortfalls of a writer of greatness, and that makes all the difference. The real Pat Hobby might be two-dimensional, but he sticks in the mind. He remains as a bleak yet comic vision of what all of America's most notable Hollywood fiction has conjured up, a specter of the possibility of soulless national culture and identity-destroying vulgarity that the most eminent American literature has brooded upon from the beginning. The balding, pathetic, funny, awful, little gray rat with a "purr" of alcohol on his breath will be around. Although only a few scraps of attention have been thrown to him, he won't go away.

BIBLIOGRAPHY

Alcott, Louisa May. *Behind a Mask: The Unknown Thrillers of Louisa May Alcott.* Ed. Madeleine B. Stern. New York: William Morrow, 1975.

———. *Little Women.* 1868–1869. Reprint, New York: Collier Books, 1962.

Alderman, Taylor. "*The Great Gatsby* and *Hopalong Cassidy.*" *Fitzgerald/Hemingway Annual* 7 (1975): 83–87.

Aldrich, Nelson W., Jr. *Tommy Hitchcock: An American Hero.* New York: Fleet Street, 1984.

Allen, Joan M. *Candles and Carnival Lights: The Catholic Sensibility of F. Scott Fitzgerald.* New York: New York University Press, 1978.

Anderson, Hilton. "*Daisy Miller* and 'The Hotel Child': A Jamesian Influence on F. Scott Fitzgerald." *Studies in American Fiction* 17 (1989): 213–18.

Baker, Carlos, ed. *Ernest Hemingway: Selected Letters—1917–1961.* New York: Charles Scribner's Sons, 1981.

Banfield, Ann. *Unspeakable Sentences: Narration and Representation in the Language of Fiction.* Boston: Routledge and Kegan Paul, 1982.

Bodeen, DeWitt. "F. Scott Fitzgerald and Films." *Films in Review* 28 (1977): 285–94.

Bruccoli, Matthew J. *The Composition of "Tender Is the Night": A Study of the Manuscripts.* Pittsburgh: University of Pittsburgh Press, 1963.

———. *F. Scott Fitzgerald: A Descriptive Bibliography.* Pittsburgh: University of Pittsburgh Press, 1972.

———. *F. Scott Fitzgerald: A Descriptive Bibliography.* Rev. ed. Pittsburgh: University of Pittsburgh Press, 1987.

———. *Fitzgerald and Hemingway: A Dangerous Friendship.* New York: Carroll and Graf, 1994.

———. "On F. Scott Fitzgerald and 'Bernice Bobs Her Hair.'" In *The American Short Story,* ed. Calvin Skaggs, 219–22. Vol. 1. New York: Laurel Books, 1977.

———. *Some Sort of Epic Grandeur: The Life of F. Scott Fitzgerald.* New York: Harcourt Brace Jovanovich, 1981.

———. *Supplement to "F. Scott Fitzgerald: A Descriptive Bibliography."* Pittsburgh: University of Pittsburgh Press, 1980.

———, ed., with the assistance of Jennifer McCabe Atkinson. *As Ever, Scott Fitz—: Letters between F. Scott Fitzgerald and His Literary Agent, Harold Ober—1919–1940.* Philadelphia: J. B. Lippincott, 1972.

———, ed. *F. Scott Fitzgerald: Manuscripts, Vol. VI, Part 3.* New York: Garland, 1991.

———, ed. *The Notebooks of F. Scott Fitzgerald.* New York: Harcourt Brace Jovanovich/Bruccoli Clark, 1978.

———, ed. *The Price Was High: The Last Uncollected Stories of F. Scott Fitzgerald.* New York: Harcourt Brace Jovanovich, 1979.

———, ed. *Selected Letters of John O'Hara.* New York: Random House, 1978.

———, ed. *The Short Stories of F. Scott Fitzgerald: A New Collection.* New York: Charles Scribner's Sons, 1989.

———, and Jackson R. Bryer, eds. *F. Scott Fitzgerald in His Own Time: A Miscellany.* Kent, Ohio: Kent State University Press, 1971.

———, and Margaret M. Duggan, eds., with the assistance of Susan Walker. *Correspondence of F. Scott Fitzgerald.* New York: Random House, 1980.

Bryer, Jackson R. *The Critical Reputation of F. Scott Fitzgerald: A Bibliographical Study—Supplement One through 1981.* Hamden, Conn.: Archon Books, 1984.

———. "The Short Stories of F. Scott Fitzgerald: A Checklist of Criticism." In *The Short Stories of F. Scott Fitzgerald: New Approaches in Criticism,* ed. Jackson R. Bryer, 303–77. Madison: University of Wisconsin Press, 1982.

———, ed. *F. Scott Fitzgerald: The Critical Reception.* New York: Burt Franklin, 1978.

————, ed. *The Short Stories of F. Scott Fitzgerald: New Approaches in Criticism.* Madison: University of Wisconsin Press, 1982.

Buell, Lawrence. "The Significance of Fantasy in Fitzgerald's Fiction." In *The Short Stories of F. Scott Fitzgerald: New Approaches in Criticism,* ed. Jackson R. Bryer, 23–38. Madison: University of Wisconsin Press, 1982.

Butterfield, Herbie. "'All Very Rich and Sad': A Decade of Fitzgerald Short Stories." In *Scott Fitzgerald: The Promises of Life,* ed. A. Robert Lee, 94–112. London: Vision Press; New York: St. Martin's Press, 1989.

Callaghan, Morley. *That Summer in Paris.* New York: Cowan, 1963.

Costa, P., and D. Caldi, eds. *F. S. Fitzgerald e E. Hemingway: Selected Short Stories.* Turin, Italy: Petrini, 1973.

Cross, K. G. W. *F. Scott Fitzgerald.* New York: Grove Press, 1964.

Dardis, Tom. *Some Time in the Sun: The Hollywood Years of F. Scott Fitzgerald, William Faulkner, Nathanael West, Aldous Huxley, and James Agee.* New York: Charles Scribner's Sons, 1976.

de Lancre, Pierre. *Tableau de l'inconstance des mauvais anges et demons.* Ed. Nicole Jacques-Chaquin. 1613. Reprint, Paris: Éditions Aubier Montaigne, 1982.

Donaldson, Scott. *Fool for Love: F. Scott Fitzgerald.* New York: Congdon and Weed, 1983.

————. "Money and Marriage in Fitzgerald's Stories." In *The Short Stories of F. Scott Fitzgerald: New Approaches in Criticism,* ed. Jackson R. Bryer, 75–88. Madison: University of Wisconsin Press, 1982.

————. "Scott Fitzgerald's Romance with the South." *Southern Literary Journal* 5 (1973): 3–17.

Dos Passos, John. *Manhattan Transfer.* 1925. Reprint, Boston: Houghton Mifflin, 1963.

Drake, Constance. "Josephine and Emotional Bankruptcy." *Fitzgerald/ Hemingway Annual* 1 (1969): 5–13.

Eble, Kenneth. *F. Scott Fitzgerald.* 1963. Rev. ed. Boston: Twayne, 1977.

————. "Touches of Disaster: Alcoholism and Mental Illness in Fitzgerald's Short Stories." In *The Short Stories of F. Scott Fitzgerald: New Approaches in Criticism,* ed. Jackson R. Bryer, 39–52. Madison: University of Wisconsin Press, 1982.

Edwards, Owen Dudley. "The Lost Teigueen: F. Scott Fitzgerald's Ethics and Ethnicity." In *Scott Fitzgerald: The Promises of Life,* ed. A. Robert

Lee, 181–214. London: Vision Press; New York: St. Martin's Press, 1989.

Eliot, T. S. *After Strange Gods.* London: Faber and Faber, 1934.

―――. *Selected Poems.* New York: Harcourt, Brace, 1930.

Ewen, David. *American Composers: A Biographical Dictionary.* New York: G. P. Putnam's, 1982.

Fetterley, Judith. *The Resisting Reader: A Feminist Approach to American Fiction.* Bloomington: Indiana University Press, 1978.

Fitzgerald, F. Scott. *Afternoon of an Author: A Selection of Uncollected Stories and Essays.* New York: Charles Scribner's Sons, 1957.

―――. *The Basil and Josephine Stories.* Ed. Jackson R. Bryer and John Kuehl. 1971. Reprint, New York: Popular Library, 1976.

―――. *The Beautiful and Damned.* 1922. Reprint, New York: Charles Scribner's Sons, 1950.

―――. "Bernice Bobs Her Hair" and Other Stories. Vol. 4 of *The Stories of F. Scott Fitzgerald.* Harmondsworth, England: Penguin, 1968.

―――. *The Bodley Head Scott Fitzgerald.* Vol. 4. London: Bodley Head, 1961.

―――. *The Bodley Head Scott Fitzgerald.* Vol. 5. London: Bodley Head, 1963.

―――. *The Bodley Head Scott Fitzgerald.* Vol. 6. London: Bodley Head, 1963.

―――. "The Count of Darkness." *Redbook* 65 (June 1935): 20–23, 68, 70, 72.

―――. "The Diamond as Big as the Ritz" and Other Stories. Vol. 1 of *The Stories of F. Scott Fitzgerald.* Harmondsworth, England: Penguin, 1967.

―――. "The Education of Dorothy Richardson." *Fitzgerald/Hemingway Annual* 11 (1979): 227–28.

―――. *F. Scott Fitzgerald's Ledger: A Facsimile.* Washington, D.C.: NCR/ Microcard Editions, 1972.

―――. *The Fitzgerald Reader.* Ed. Arthur Mizener. New York: Charles Scribner's Sons, 1963.

―――. *Flappers and Philosophers.* New York: Charles Scribner's Sons, 1920.

―――. *Flappers and Philosophers.* 1920. Reprint, New York: Charles Scribner's Sons, 1959.

———. "Gods of Darkness." *Redbook* 78 (November 1941): 30–33, 88–91.

———. *The Great Gatsby.* Ed. Matthew J. Bruccoli. Cambridge: Cambridge University Press, 1991.

———. "In the Darkest Hour." *Redbook* 63 (October 1934): 15–19, 94–98.

———. *John Jackson's Arcady.* Arranged by Lilian Holmes Strack. Boston: Walter H. Baker, 1928.

———. "The Kingdom in the Dark." *Redbook* 65 (August 1935): 58–62, 64, 66–68.

———. *The Pat Hobby Stories.* New York: Charles Scribner's Sons, 1962.

———. *The Pat Hobby Stories.* Vol. 3 of *The Stories of F. Scott Fitzgerald.* Harmondsworth, England: Penguin, 1967.

———. *Six Tales of the Jazz Age and Other Stories.* New York: Charles Scribner's Sons, 1960.

———. *The Stories of F. Scott Fitzgerald: A Selection of 28 Stories.* New York: Charles Scribner's Sons, 1951.

———. *Tales of the Jazz Age.* New York: Charles Scribner's Sons, 1922.

———. *Taps at Reveille.* New York: Charles Scribner's Sons, 1935.

———. *Tender Is the Night.* 1934. Reprint, New York: Charles Scribner's Sons, 1960.

———. *Tender Is the Night.* With the author's final revisions. New York: Charles Scribner's Sons, 1951.

———. *This Side of Paradise.* New York: Charles Scribner's Sons, 1920.

———. *Three Novels of F. Scott Fitzgerald.* New York: Charles Scribner's Sons, 1953.

———, and Zelda Fitzgerald. *Bits of Paradise: 21 Uncollected Stories by F. Scott and Zelda Fitzgerald.* Selected by Matthew J. Bruccoli with the assistance of Scottie Fitzgerald Smith. New York: Charles Scribner's Sons, 1973.

Fowler, Roger. *Linguistics and the Novel.* London: Methuen, 1977.

Friedman, Melvin J. " 'The Swimmers': Paris and Virginia Reconciled." In *The Short Stories of F. Scott Fitzgerald: New Approaches in Criticism,* ed. Jackson R. Bryer, 251–60. Madison: University of Wisconsin Press, 1982.

Fryer, Sarah Beebe. *Fitzgerald's New Women: Harbingers of Change.* Ann Arbor, Mich.: UMI Research Press, 1988.

Gidley, Mark. "Notes on F. Scott Fitzgerald and the Passing of the Great Race." *Journal of American Studies* 7 (1973): 171–81.

Gilmore, Thomas B. *Equivocal Spirits: Alcoholism and Drinking in 20th-Century Literature.* Chapel Hill: University of North Carolina Press, 1987.

Gingrich, Arnold. "Introduction." In *The Pat Hobby Stories,* by F. Scott Fitzgerald, ix–xxiii. New York: Charles Scribner's Sons, 1962.

Gold, Michael. *Jews without Money.* 1930. Reprint, New York: Carroll and Graf, 1990.

Goldhurst, William. "An Answer to Barry Edward Gross." *Fitzgerald Newsletter* 21 (summer 1963): 125–26.

———. *F. Scott Fitzgerald and His Contemporaries.* Cleveland: World, 1963.

———. "Literary Anti-Semitism of the 20s." *American Jewish Congress Bi-Weekly* 24 (December 1962): 10–12.

Goodwin, Donald W. "The Alcoholism of F. Scott Fitzgerald." *Journal of the American Medical Association* 212 (April 6, 1970): 86–90.

Graham, Sheilah. *College of One.* New York: Viking Press, 1967.

Greene, David Mason. *Greene's Biographical Encyclopedia of Composers.* Garden City, N.Y.: Doubleday, 1985.

Gross, Barry Edward. "Fitzgerald's Anti-Semitism—A Reply to William Goldhurst." *Fitzgerald Newsletter* 21 (spring 1963): 118–19.

Harding, Brian. " 'Made for—or against—the Trade': The Radicalism of Fitzgerald's *Saturday Evening Post* Love Stories." In *Scott Fitzgerald: The Promises of Life,* ed. A. Robert Lee, 113–30. London: Vision Press; New York: St. Martin's Press, 1989.

Hemingway, Ernest. *A Moveable Feast.* New York: Charles Scribner's Sons, 1964.

———. *The Short Stories of Ernest Hemingway.* New York: Charles Scribner's Sons, 1938.

———. *The Sun Also Rises.* 1926. Reprint, New York: Charles Scribner's Sons, 1954.

Higgins, John A. *F. Scott Fitzgerald: A Study of the Stories.* Jamaica, N.Y.: St. John's University Press, 1971.

Higham, John. *Send These to Me.* New York: Atheneum, 1975.

Hindus, Milton. *F. Scott Fitzgerald: An Introduction and Interpretation.* New York: Holt, Rinehart and Winston, 1968.

————. "F. Scott Fitzgerald and Literary Anti-Semitism." *Commentary* 3 (1947): 508–16.

Holman, C. Hugh. "Fitzgerald's Changes on the Southern Belle: The Tarleton Trilogy." In *The Short Stories of F. Scott Fitzgerald: New Approaches in Criticism*, ed. Jackson R. Bryer, 53–64. Madison: University of Wisconsin Press, 1982.

Howe, Irving. "History and the Novel." *New Republic* (September 1, 1990): 29–34.

Howells, W. D. *April Hopes.* 1888. Reprint, Bloomington: Indiana University Press, 1974.

Irwin, Julie M. "F. Scott Fitzgerald's Little Drinking Problem." *American Scholar* 56 (1987): 415–27.

Jackson, Charles. *The Lost Weekend.* New York: Farrar and Rinehart, 1944.

James, Henry. *Novels 1881–1886.* New York: Library of America, 1985.

Jones, Daryl E. "Fitzgerald and Pulp Fiction: From Diamond Dick to Gatsby." *Fitzgerald/Hemingway Annual* 10 (1978): 137–39.

Katterjohn, William. "An Interview with Theodora Gager, Fitzgerald's Private Nurse." *Fitzgerald/Hemingway Annual* 6 (1974): 75–85.

Kopf, Josephine Z. "Meyer Wolfsheim and Robert Cohn: A Study of a Jewish Type and Stereotype." *Tradition: A Journal of Orthodox Jewish Thought* 10 (1969): 93–104.

Kreuter, Kent, and Gretchen Kreuter. "The Moralism of the Later Fitzgerald." *Modern Fiction Studies* 7 (1961): 71–81.

Kuehl, John. *F. Scott Fitzgerald: A Study of the Short Fiction.* Boston: Twayne, 1991.

————, ed. *The Apprentice Fiction of F. Scott Fitzgerald: 1909–1917.* New Brunswick, N.J.: Rutgers University Press, 1965.

————, and Jackson R. Bryer, eds. *Dear Scott/Dear Max: The Fitzgerald–Perkins Correspondence.* New York: Charles Scribner's Sons, 1971.

Lalli, Biancamaria Tedeschini, ed. *Francis Scott Fitzgerald: Selected Stories.* Milan, Italy: U. Mursia, 1970.

Latham, Aaron. *Crazy Sundays: F. Scott Fitzgerald in Hollywood.* New York: Viking Press, 1971.

Lehan, Richard D. "F. Scott Fitzgerald and Romantic Destiny." *Twentieth Century Literature* 26 (1980): 137–56.

————. *F. Scott Fitzgerald and the Craft of Fiction*. Carbondale: Southern Illinois University Press, 1966.

————. *"The Great Gatsby": The Limits of Wonder*. Boston: Twayne, 1990.

————. "The Romantic Self and the Uses of Place in the Stories of F. Scott Fitzgerald." In *The Short Stories of F. Scott Fitzgerald: New Approaches in Criticism*, ed. Jackson R. Bryer, 3–21. Madison: University of Wisconsin Press, 1982.

Le Vot, André. *F. Scott Fitzgerald: A Biography*. Trans. William Byron. Garden City, N.Y.: Doubleday, 1983.

Lewis, Janet. "Fitzgerald's 'Philippe, Count of Darkness.'" *Fitzgerald/ Hemingway Annual* 7 (1975): 7–32.

Lewis, R. W. B., and Nancy Lewis, eds. *The Letters of Edith Wharton*. New York: Charles Scribner's Sons, 1988.

Malin, Irving. "'Absolution': Absolving Lies." In *The Short Stories of F. Scott Fitzgerald: New Approaches in Criticism*, ed. Jackson R. Bryer, 209–16. Madison: University of Wisconsin Press, 1982.

Mancini, Joseph, Jr. "To Be Both Light and Dark: The Jungian Process of Individuation in Fitzgerald's Basil Duke Lee Stories." In *The Short Stories of F. Scott Fitzgerald: New Approaches in Criticism*, ed. Jackson R. Bryer, 89–110. Madison: University of Wisconsin Press, 1982.

Mangum, Bryant. *A Fortune Yet: Money in the Art of F. Scott Fitzgerald's Short Stories*. New York: Garland, 1991.

Margolies, Alan. "'Particular Rhythms' and Other Influences: Hemingway and *Tender Is the Night*." In *Hemingway in Italy and Other Essays*, ed. Robert W. Lewis Jr., 69–75. New York: Praeger, 1990.

Martin, Robert A. "Hollywood in Fitzgerald: After Paradise." In *The Short Stories of F. Scott Fitzgerald: New Approaches in Criticism*, ed. Jackson R. Bryer, 127–48. Madison: University of Wisconsin Press, 1982.

McInerney, Jay. "Fitzgerald Revisited." *New York Review of Books* (August 15, 1991): 23–28.

McKay, Mary A. "Fitzgerald's Women: Beyond Winter Dreams." In *American Novelists Revisited: Essays in Feminist Criticism*, ed. Fritz Fleischmann, 311–24. Boston: G. K. Hall, 1982.

Mellow, James R. *Invented Lives: F. Scott and Zelda Fitzgerald*. Boston: Houghton Mifflin, 1984.

Milford, Nancy. *Zelda: A Biography*. New York: Harper and Row, 1970.

Mizener, Arthur. *The Far Side of Paradise: A Biography of F. Scott Fitzgerald.* 1951. Reprint, New York: Vintage Books, 1959.

Monteiro, George. "Fitzgerald vs. Fitzgerald: 'An Alcoholic Case.'" *Literature and Medicine* 6 (1987): 110–16.

Morrell, David. *The Fifth Profession.* New York: Warner Books, 1990.

Morsberger, Robert E. "The Romantic Ancestry of *The Great Gatsby.*" *Fitzgerald/Hemingway Annual* 5 (1973): 119–30.

Murray, Margaret. *The Witch Cult in Western Europe.* Oxford, England: Oxford University Press, 1921.

Perosa, Sergio. *The Art of F. Scott Fitzgerald.* Trans. Charles Metz and Sergio Perosa. Ann Arbor: University of Michigan Press, 1965.

Petry, Alice Hall. *Fitzgerald's Craft of Short Fiction: The Collected Stories— 1920–1935.* Ann Arbor, Mich.: UMI Research Press, 1989.

Phillips, Gene D., S.J. *Fiction, Film, and F. Scott Fitzgerald.* Chicago: Loyola University Press, 1986.

Piper, Henry Dan. *F. Scott Fitzgerald: A Critical Portrait.* New York: Holt, Rinehart and Winston, 1965.

Prenshaw, Peggy Whitman. "Southern Ladies and the Southern Literary Renaissance." In *The Female Tradition in Southern Literature,* ed. Carol S. Manning, 73–88. Urbana: University of Illinois Press, 1993.

Prigozy, Ruth. "'Dalyrimple Goes Wrong.'" In *Instructor's Manual for "Short Stories: A Critical Anthology,"* by Ensaf Thune and Ruth Prigozy, 1–55. New York: Macmillan, 1973.

———. "F. Scott Fitzgerald." In *Dictionary of Literary Biography.* Vol. 86 of *American Short Story Writers, 1910–1945,* ed. Bobby Ellen Kimbel, 99–123. Columbia, S.C.: Bruccoli/Clark, 1989.

———. "Fitzgerald's Short Stories and the Depression: An Artistic Crisis." In *The Short Stories of F. Scott Fitzgerald: New Approaches in Criticism,* ed. Jackson R. Bryer, 111–26. Madison: University of Wisconsin Press, 1982.

Rascoe, Burton, and Groff Conklin, eds. *"The Smart Set" Anthology.* New York: Reynal and Hitchcock, 1934.

Reed, John Shelton. *Southern Folk, Plain and Fancy: Native White Social Types.* Athens: University of Georgia Press, 1986.

Rees, John O. "Fitzgerald's Pat Hobby Stories." *Colorado Quarterly* 23 (1975): 553–62.

Ring, Frances Knoll. *Against the Current: As I Remember F. Scott Fitzgerald*. Berkeley, Calif.: Creative Arts, 1985.

Rogers, Robert. *The Double in Literature*. Detroit: Wayne State University Press, 1970.

Roulston, Robert. "Whistling 'Dixie' in Encino: 'The Last Tycoon' and F. Scott Fitzgerald's Two Souths." In *Modern Critical Views: F. Scott Fitzgerald*, ed. Harold Bloom, 157–65. New York: Chelsea House, 1985.

Scharnhorst, Gary. " 'Scribbling Upward': Fitzgerald's Debt of Honor to Horatio Alger, Jr." *Fitzgerald/Hemingway Annual* 10 (1978): 161–69.

Skipp, Francis E., ed. *The Complete Short Stories of Thomas Wolfe*. New York: Charles Scribner's Sons, 1987.

Sklar, Robert. *F. Scott Fitzgerald: The Last Laocoön*. New York: Oxford University Press, 1967.

Slater, Peter. "Ethnicity in *The Great Gatsby*," *Twentieth Century Literature* 19 (1973), 53–62.

Snyder, Mark. "Self-Fulfilling Stereotypes." In *Racism and Sexism*, ed. Paula S. Rothenberg, 263–69. New York: St. Martin's Press, 1988.

Spacks, Patricia Meyer. *The Female Imagination*. New York: Alfred A. Knopf, 1975.

Stallman, Robert W. "Gatsby and the Hole in Time." *Modern Fiction Studies* 1 (1955): 2–16.

Steiner, George. *The Death of Tragedy*. New York: Oxford University Press, 1961.

Sweeney, Patricia. *Women in Southern Literature: An Index*. Westport, Conn.: Greenwood Press, 1986.

Tageman, Robert. "The Songs of Theodore Chanler." *Modern Music* 22 (1945): 227–33.

Thompson, Francis. *Complete Poems of Francis Thompson*. New York: Modern Library, [1913?].

Thune, Ensaf, and Ruth Prigozy. *Instructor's Manual for "Short Stories: A Critical Anthology."* New York: Macmillan, 1973.

———, eds. *Short Stories: A Critical Anthology*. New York: Macmillan, 1973.

Turnbull, Andrew. *Scott Fitzgerald*. New York: Charles Scribner's Sons, 1962.

———, ed. *The Letters of F. Scott Fitzgerald.* New York: Charles Scribner's Sons, 1963.

Tuttleton, James W. *The Novel of Manners in America.* 1972. Reprint, New York: W. W. Norton, 1974.

Varet-Ali, Elizabeth M. "The Unfortunate Fate of Seventeen Fitzgerald 'Originals': Toward a Reading of *The Pat Hobby Stories* 'On Their Own Merits Completely.' " *Journal of the Short Story in English* 14 (spring 1990): 87–110.

von Eschenbach, Wolfram. *Parzival.* Trans. Helen M. Mustard and Charles E. Passage. New York: Vintage, 1961.

Way, Brian. *F. Scott Fitzgerald and the Art of Social Fiction.* London: Edward Arnold, 1980.

Wells, Walter. *Tycoons and Locusts: A Regional Look at Hollywood Fiction of the 1930s.* Carbondale: Southern Illinois University Press, 1973.

West, James L. W., III. "Fitzgerald and *Esquire.*" In *The Short Stories of F. Scott Fitzgerald: New Approaches in Criticism,* ed. Jackson R. Bryer, 149–66. Madison: University of Wisconsin Press, 1982.

———. *The Making of "This Side of Paradise."* Philadelphia: University of Pennsylvania Press, 1983.

Wharton, Edith. *The House of Mirth.* 1905. Reprint, New York: Signet, 1964.

White, Ray Lewis. "The Pat Hobby Stories: A File of Reviews." *Fitzgerald/Hemingway Annual* 11 (1979): 177–80.

Wilson, Charles Reagan, and William Ferris, eds. *Encyclopedia of Southern Culture.* Chapel Hill: University of North Carolina Press, 1989.

Wilson, Edmund. *The Shores of Light: A Literary Chronicle of the Twenties and Thirties.* 1952. Reprint, Boston: Northeastern University Press, 1985.

———, ed. *The Crack-Up.* New York: New Directions, 1945.

NOTES ON THE CONTRIBUTORS

Susan F. Beegel is visiting Assistant Professor of English at the University of Idaho and editor of *The Hemingway Review*. She is author of *Hemingway's Craft of Omission: Four Manuscript Examples* and editor of *Hemingway's Neglected Short Fiction: New Perspectives*.

Jackson R. Bryer is Professor of English at the University of Maryland. He is cofounder and president of the F. Scott Fitzgerald Society and author of *The Critical Reputation of F. Scott Fitzgerald*, editor of *F. Scott Fitzgerald: The Critical Reception* and *The Short Stories of F. Scott Fitzgerald: New Approaches in Criticism*, and coeditor of *F. Scott Fitzgerald in His Own Time: A Miscellany, Dear Scott/Dear Max: The Fitzgerald–Perkins Correspondence*, and *The Basil and Josephine Stories*.

Heidi Kunz Bullock is Adjunct Assistant Professor of English at Randolph-Macon Woman's College. She has presented papers on Fitzgerald at the Fitzgerald/Hemingway International Conference and at meetings of the Northeast Modern Language Association, the Midwest Modern Language Association, and the Southern American Studies Association.

Alan Cheuse is Professor of English at George Mason University. He is author of the novels *The Grandmothers' Club* and *The Light Possessed*, of the short story collections *Candace and Other Stories* and *The Tennessee Waltz*, and of the memoir *Fall out of Heaven*. Since 1983 he has been the regular book reviewer on National Public Radio's *All Things Considered*, and for the past five years he has been the producer and host of National Public Radio's *The Sound of Writing.*

Scott Donaldson retired in 1992 as Cooley Professor of English at the College of William and Mary. He is author of *Poet in America: Winfield Townley Scott, By Force of Will: The Life and Art of Ernest Hemingway, Fool for Love: F. Scott Fitzgerald, John Cheever: A Biography,* and *Archibald MacLeish: An American Life.* He is editor of *Critical Essays on F. Scott Fitzgerald's "The Great Gatsby," Conversations with John Cheever, New Essays on "A Farewell to Arms,"* and *The Cambridge Companion to Hemingway.*

Victor A. Doyno is Professor of English and American Literature at the State University of New York at Buffalo and author of *Writing "Huck Finn": Mark Twain's Creative Process.* He is currently working on the newly discovered manuscript of Huckleberry Finn.

Eric Fretz is Assistant Professor of English at Loras College. He has presented papers at the Popular Culture Association Conference and at the Midwest Modern Language Association convention and has published an essay in the *Nathaniel Hawthorne Review.*

Edward Gillin is Associate Professor of English at the State University College of New York at Geneseo. His essays have appeared in the *O'Casey Annual, Colby Library Quarterly, Modern Language Studies, Mid-Hudson Language Studies,* and the *Thomas Wolfe Review.* He has presented papers at meetings of the Northeast Modern Language Association, the College English Association of Ohio, and the Mid-Hudson Modern Language Association.

Bruce L. Grenberg retired in 1995 as Associate Professor of English at the University of British Columbia. He is author of *Some Other World to Find: Quest and Negation in the Works of Herman Melville* and of essays in the *Chaucer Review, Modern Fiction Studies,* and the *Fitzgerald/Hemingway Annual.*

Barry Gross is Professor of English and Director of Jewish Studies at Michigan State University. His essays on Fitzgerald have appeared in the *Fitzgerald Newsletter; University Review; Bucknell Review; Papers of the Michigan Academy of Science, Arts, and Letters; Studies in the Novel; Centennial Review; Arizona Quarterly; Western American Literature;* and *Midamerica.* He is currently working on a book about American culture and literature of the 1950s.

Peter L. Hays is Professor of English at the University of California, Davis. He is author of *The Limping Hero in Literature, Ernest Hemingway,* and *A Concordance to Hemingway's "In Our Time."*

John Kuehl recently retired as Professor of English at New York University. He is author of *John Hawkes and the Craft of Conflict, Alternate Worlds: A Study of Postmodern Antirealistic American Fiction,* and *F. Scott Fitzgerald: A Study of the Short Fiction.* He is editor of *The Apprentice Fiction of F. Scott Fitzgerald: 1909–1917* and *Write and Rewrite: A Study of the Creative Process* and coeditor of *Dear Scott/Dear Max: The Fitzgerald–Perkins Correspondence, The Basil and Josephine Stories, In Recognition of William Gaddis.*

William H. Loos is Curator of the Rare Book Room of the Buffalo and Erie County Public Library in Buffalo, New York. In 1988 he began to speak on the history of his library's greatest treasure, the only known surviving portion of the manuscript of Twain's *Adventures of Huckleberry Finn.* Following the discovery in 1991 of the long-lost first half of the manuscript and its return to the Buffalo and Erie County Public Library, he has given talks at the Lilly Library, the Mark Twain House, and at the Center for Mark Twain Studies.

Bryant Mangum is Professor of English at Virginia Commonwealth University and author of *A Fortune Yet: Money in the Art of F. Scott Fitzgerald's Short Stories.* His essays have appeared in the *Fitzgerald/Hemingway Annual, Exercise Exchange, American Literary Realism, American Notes and Queries, Notes on Contemporary Literature,* and the *Lost Generation Journal.* He is presently at work on a reader's guide to Fitzgerald's short stories.

Alan Margolies is Professor of English at John Jay College of Criminal Justice, CUNY, editor of *F. Scott Fitzgerald's St. Paul Plays: 1911–1914,* and associate editor of *F. Scott Fitzgerald: Manuscripts*. His essays on Fitzgerald have appeared in the *Fitzgerald/Hemingway Annual, Princeton University Library Chronicle, Papers of the Bibliographical Society of America, CUNY English Forum, Journal of Modern Literature*, and *Resources for American Literary Study*. He is the cofounder and vice president of the F. Scott Fitzgerald Society.

James J. Martine is Professor of English at Saint Bonaventure University. He is author of *Fred Lewis Pattee and American Literature* and *"The Crucible": Politics, Property, and Pretense* and editor of *Critical Essays on Arthur Miller* and *Critical Essays on Eugene O'Neill*. Currently, he contributes the chapter titled "Drama" to *American Literary Scholarship: An Annual*.

Robert Merrill is Foundation Professor of English and Chair of the department at the University of Nevada, Reno. He is author of *Norman Mailer, Joseph Heller, Norman Mailer Revisited*, and editor of *Critical Essays on Kurt Vonnegut*. His essays have appeared in *American Literature, Modern Fiction Studies, Studies in American Fiction, Critique, Modern Philology*, and *Texas Studies in Literature and Language*.

George Monteiro is Professor of English and Professor of Portuguese and Brazilian Studies at Brown University. He is author of *Henry James and John Hay: The Record of a Friendship* and *Robert Frost and the New England Renaissance* and coauthor of *The Experienced Emblem: A Study of the Poetry of Emily Dickinson* and *A Guide to the "Atlantic Monthly"'s Contributors' Club*. He is editor of *The Correspondence of Henry James and Henry Adams* and *Critical Essays on Ernest Hemingway's "A Farewell to Arms"* and coeditor of *The John Hay–Howells Letters: The Correspondence of John Milton Hay and William Dean Howells*.

James Nagel is J. O. Eidson Distinguished Professor of American Literature at the University of Georgia and founder of *Studies in American Fiction*, which he edited for twenty years. He is author of *Stephen Crane and Literary Impressionism* and coauthor of *Sarah Orne Jewett: A Reference Guide*. He is editor of *Critical Essays on "Catch-22," American Fiction: Historical and Critical Essays, Critical Essays on Hamlin Garland*,

Critical Essays on Joseph Heller, and *Ernest Hemingway: The Writer in Context* and coeditor of *American Literature: The New England Heritage* and *Hemingway in Love and War: The Lost Diary of Agnes von Kurowsky.*

Alice Hall Petry is Professor of English and Chair of the department at Southern Illinois University at Edwardsville. She is author of *A Genius In His Way: The Art of Cable's "Old Creole Days," Fitzgerald's Craft of Short Fiction: The Collected Stories—1920–1935,* and *Understanding Anne Tyler* and editor of *Critical Essays on Anne Tyler.*

Gerald Pike is Professor of English at Santa Barbara City College. He has published an essay on Fitzgerald's "Winter Dreams" in *Studies in Short Fiction* and is currently working on a book-length study of Fitzgerald's short stories.

Ruth Prigozy is Professor of English at Hostra University. She is coeditor of *Short Stories: A Critical Anthology* and editor of the Enriched Classics edition of Fitzgerald's *This Side of Paradise.* Her essays and reviews on Fitzgerald have appeared in *Commonweal, New York Times Book Review, Fitzgerald/Hemingway Annual, Twentieth Century Literature, Prospects,* and *Dictionary of Literary Biography.* She is cofounder and executive director of the F. Scott Fitzgerald Society.

Robert Roulston retired in 1992 as Professor of English at Murray State University. He is author of *James Norman Hall* and coauthor of *The Winding Road to West Egg: The Artistic Development of F. Scott Fitzgerald.* He has contributed essays on Fitzgerald to the *Fitzgerald/Hemingway Annual, Literature and Psychology, South Atlantic Quarterly, Arizona Quarterly, Southern Quarterly, Journal of Narrative Technique, Journal of Popular Culture,* and *Modern Fiction Studies.*

Milton R. Stern retired in 1991 as Professor of English at the University of Connecticut. He is author of *The Fine Hammered Steel of Herman Melville, The Golden Moment: The Novels of F. Scott Fitzgerald, Contexts for Hawthorne,* and *"Tender Is the Night": The Broken Universe* and editor of *Critical Essays on F. Scott Fitzgerald's "Tender Is the Night."*

Arthur Waldhorn retired in 1975 as Professor of English at City College of New York. He is author of *Concise Dictionary of Americanisms* and *A Reader's Guide to Ernest Hemingway,* coauthor of *From Homer to Joyce,* editor of *Ernest Hemingway: A Collection of Criticism,* and coeditor of *American Literature: Readings and Critiques, Good Reading,* and *The Rite of Becoming.*

James L. W. West III is Distinguished Professor of English and Director of the Center for the History of the Book at Pennsylvania State University. He is author of *The Making of "This Side of Paradise,"* and of *American Authors and the Literary Marketplace since 1900.* He has compiled descriptive bibliographies of William Styron and Reynolds Price and has edited scholarly texts of Dreiser's *Sister Carrie* and *Jennie Gerhardt.* He has held fellowships from the Guggenheim Foundation, the National Humanities Center, and the National Endowment for the Humanities. West is general editor of the *Cambridge Edition of the Works of F. Scott Fitzgerald* and is completing a biography of William Styron.

Index

All titles of short stories, novels, and essays are by Fitzgerald unless otherwise indicated.

"Absolution," 2, 25
"Adjuster, The," 3
Afternoon of an Author, 118, 119, 308, 336
"Alcoholic Case, An": publishing history of, 244–45; critical commentary previously published on, 244–46; alcoholism in, 244–52; circumstances of composition of, 246–47; narrative of, 247–48; denial and dependency of alcoholic in, 248–49; nurse's perceptions in, 249–52, 250*n*, 251*n*
Alcoholism: of Fitzgerald, 139, 150, 155–56, 163, 167, 244, 245–47, 246*n*; water as surrogate for alcohol in "The Swimmers," 151–52, 155–57; in *Tender Is the Night,* 152, 156, 249; in "The Camel's Back," 156, 244; in Wolfe's "The House of the Far and Lost," 235–36; in "Her Last Case," 236; in "Crazy Sunday," 244; in "A New Leaf," 244, 245; in "An Alcoholic Case," 244–52; in "The Lost Decade," 255–58
Alcott, Bronson, 73
Alcott, Louisa May, 59*n,* 60–73. *See also* Barnard, A. M.
Alger, Horatio, 161, 282
Allen, Joan M., 38

All the Sad Young Men, 157*n,* 308
Anderson, Hilton, 189
Anderson, Sherwood, 272, 320
Anti-Semitism, 190–92
April Hopes (Howells), 242, 242*n*
"At Your Age," 154, 178
Austen, Jane, 61*n*

"Babes in the Woods," 107
"Babylon Revisited": critical commentary on, 2; success of, 2, 25, 36, 87, 106, 161; melancholy in, 77, 81; irony in, 119; money in, 153*n;* compared with "Two Wrongs," 168; as *Tender Is the Night* cluster story, 180–81, 226; compared with "One Trip Abroad," 183, 185, 188; style of, 218
Banfield, Ann, 13
Barnard, A. M., 72–73. *See also* Alcott, Louisa May
Barron, Father Joseph, 48
"Basil and Cleopatra," 265, 266, 266*n,* 268, 283–84
Basil and Josephine Stories, The: publication of, 2; Basil stories, 130, 272–84, 290; publication history of, 265–66; Fitzgerald's assessment of, 266; critical commentary previously published on, 266–71; themes of, 267, 270; autobiographical nature of, 271; importance of, 271–72; Josephine stories, 284–90

Petry, Alice Hall: publications of, 2; as Fitzgerald scholar, 4; on "The Lost Decade," 6, 253–62; on "Dalyrimple Goes Wrong," 25, 29, 34; on "Benediction," 38–42; on "The Camel's Back," 51–52; on "Bernice Bobs Her Hair," 59, 59*n;* on "The Bowl," 107; on "Outside the Cabinet-Maker's," 118–19; on "The Last of the Belles," 131, 136; on "Two Wrongs," 165, 172; on "Her Last Case," 232; on the Basil and Josephine stories, 270, 280, 290; biographical information on, 355

Philippe or Count of Darkness stories: publication history of, 291, 291*n;* Fitzgerald's ideas of extending, 291–92, 292*n;* Fitzgerald's assessment of, 292; weaknesses of, 292–97; dialogue in, 293–94; historical blunders in, 294–95; Philippe as democrat in, 295–96; integration of early details with later plot lines, 296–97; Philippe as wise fool in, 297–98; Philippe's egalitarian treatment of women in, 298–304; witch cult in, 300–302, 301*n,* 302*n,* 304; Catholicism in, 301–2

Pike, Gerald, 4, 6, 9–23, 355

Pinky, 81

Piper, Henry Dan, 37, 51, 59, 105, 118, 120, 121, 153*n,* 208

Porter, Geneva Thompson, 145–47

Price Was High, The, 2, 74, 105, 106, 207, 232

Pride and Prejudice (Austen), 61*n*

Prigozy, Ruth, 4, 5, 26, 33, 131, 206–18, 355

"Pusher-in-the-Face, The," 158

Pygmalion (Shaw), 89–90

"Rags Martin-Jones and the Pr-nce of W-les," 3

Random House, 90–91

Rawlings, Marjorie Kinnan, 247

Redbook, 291, 291*n,* 292

Rees, John O., 310

"Rich Boy, The," 2, 6, 97, 99, 103, 106, 108–9, 112

Ring, Frances Kroll, 303

Rogers, Robert, 184

Romantic Egoist, The, 9, 26

"Room with the Green Blinds, The," 95

"Rough Crossing, The": publication history of, 138; autobiographical nature of, 138, 140, 143–47, 150; circumstances of composition of, 138, 154; critical commentary previously published on, 138, 181; structural conflicts in, 139; as *Tender Is the Night* cluster story, 140, 152*n,* 167, 175, 226; storm at sea in, 140–41, 183; anthropological and folkloric approaches to, 140–42; character names in, 142–43; "new critical" examination of motifs and image patterns in, 142–44; betrayal or infidelity motif in, 143–49; genetic criticism of artistic and thematic achievement of, 149–50; water or liquid imagery in, 149–50

Roulston, Robert, 4, 6, 132, 151–64, 355

"Rubber Check, The": circumstances of composition of, 206–7; Fitzgerald's assessment of, 207; publication history of, 207; critical commentary previously published on, 207–9; autobiographical nature of, 208, 209; themes of, 209, 217; imagery in, 210; plot summary of, 210; name of hero in, 210–11; circular pattern of, 210–11, 217; clothing of hero in, 211–12; hero's character in, 211–12, 216, 217–18; snobbery in, 213–14; female love interest in, 214–16; romantic love in, 214–16; and the depression, 216–17; style of, 217, 218

Runyon, Damon, 320

Sabatini, Raffael, 162

Saturday Evening Post, 3, 26, 50, 58, 59, 59–60*n,* 72, 74, 81, 83, 85, 89, 90, 95, 105–8, 130, 138, 157, 157*n,* 161, 165, 169, 175, 189, 203, 207, 219, 232, 239*n,* 242, 257, 265, 291, 333

Save Me the Waltz (Z. Fitzgerald), 207, 219, 227

Sayre, Zelda. *See* Fitzgerald, Zelda